# Remaking Canadian Social Policy

# Remaking Canadian Social Policy
## Social Security in the Late 1990s

edited by

# Jane Pulkingham and Gordon Ternowetsky

We are grateful to the Employability and Social Partnerships Program
(formerly National Welfare Grants) Human Resources Development Canada
(Project #4572-10-90-001)
for the financial and program support it provided for this publication.

(The views expressed in this publication do not necessarily represent
those of the Employability and Social Partnerships Program.)

# Fernwood Publishing
## Halifax

Editing: Donna Davis
Design and production: Beverley Rach
Cover illustration: Canadian Union of Public Employees (CUPE)
Printed and bound in Canada by: Hignell Printing Limited

A publication of:
Fernwood Publishing
Box 9409, Station A
Halifax, Nova Scotia
B3K 5S3

Fernwood Publishing Company Limited gratefully acknowledges the financial support of The Ministry of Canadian Heritage and the Canada/Nova Scotia Cooperation Agreement on Cultural Development.


**Canadian Cataloguing in Publication Data**
Main entry under title:
Remaking Canadian social policy

Includes bibliographical references.
ISBN 1-895686-59-8

1. Canada -- Social policy. 2. Social security -- Canada.
I. Pulkingham, Jane. II. Ternowetsky, Gordon.

HN107.R45 1996   361.6'1'0971   C95-950329-3

# CONTENTS

# ACKNOWLEDGMENTS

As these acknowledgments are being written, the future of Canada's social programs remains uncertain. The scrapping of the Canada Assistance Plan (CAP) will have a profound influence on national standards, on the provinces' and territories' ability to deliver social programs and on the security of the Canadian people. We know that in the place of the CAP, 1996 will usher in the era of the block funded Canada Health and Social Transfer (CHST). This reduced transfer is taking place in a period of persistent, mass unemployment and underemployment, escalating demand for welfare assistance and demographic shifts in the aging of the population. All of these factors are responsible for the growing demand for government assistance. Unemployment and underemployment, in particular, are major forces that propel people to the doors of social service agencies as they turn to public and private organizations for support and help. This will be exacerbated by the reform of U.I. While we can expect the demand for government intervention to grow, the CHST will diminish the resources available to the provinces and territories as they work out ways to respond to growing levels of need. In the end, it is the ordinary people across this nation that will be most affected as the state continues to downsize its commitments and responsibilities for their collective well-being.

There are other casualties. We have just been notified that, as a part of the restructuring of Human Resources and Development Canada, National Welfare Grants (NWG) is gone. National Welfare Grants has an important tradition and history in promoting community based research, education and social policy initiatives in Canada. It was a small but major federal body concerned with issues of social welfare and policies that affect the well-being of Canadians in the different regions and communities across this nation. NWG funded a range of national workshops, conferences and publications on Canadian social welfare. Indeed, we are grateful to NWG for supporting both the Seventh Conference on Canadian Social Welfare Policy and this book *Remaking Canadian Social Policy: Staking Claims and Forging Change*. In particular we want to thank Sandra Chatterton, Evariste Thériault and David Thornton formerly from National Welfare Grants. While NWG is gone, we are hopeful that we will be able to work with these individuals in the future, under the auspices of another federal body that is devoted to promoting community based research and developments in Canadian social policy.

A number of other key people were involved in different stages in the planning of the Seventh Conference on Canadian Social Welfare Policy that gave rise to this book. The steering committee consisted of Sandra Chatterton (National Welfare Grants), Drew Johnson who organized the Fifth Conference at Bishop's University, and Leslie Bella and Penny Rowe, the co-organizers of the Sixth Conference held at Memorial University in St. John's, Newfoundland. These individuals shared their experiences and expertise and helped a great deal in the initial planning stages of this conference.

The Seventh Conference on Canadian Social Welfare Policy was held in Vancouver from June 25th to 28th, 1995. In addition to ourselves, the organizing committee consisted of Michael Goldberg of the Social Planning and Research Council of British Columbia (SPARC of BC); Andrew Armitage, Social Work at the University of Victoria; Roop Seebaran and

Frank Tester, Social Work at the University of British Columbia; Stuart Alcock of the British Columbia Association of Social Workers; and Dan Smith of United Native Nations. The planning for this conference was greatly facilitated by the administrative and organizational work of Lisa Griffith and Loralee Delbrouck. The conference would not have been the same without the guidance of Lorelee. She has the unique ability to manage a raft of details in a manner that relaxed both the conference participants and all of the members of the organizing committee. We are particularly grateful to Michael Goldberg. He guided the development of this conference in a very skillful and participatory way and in the process we gained a great deal of respect for his integrity and leadership.

Two people helped us with the preparation of the manuscript: Christina Moretti, an M.A. student in sociology and anthropology at Simon Fraser University; and Jackie Stokes, an M.S.W. student at the University of Northern British Columbia. Both were very efficient and helpful. We also want to thank Vicki McKendrick, the Social Work secretary at UNBC and Pam Fairweather the Research secretary for the Child Welfare Research Centre. Throughout the course of editing this book, they assisted us with many details such as typing letters and sending faxes to the contributors. We also want to thank Professor Glen Schmidt for his comments on earlier versions of some of the papers included in this volume.

During July, August and September, we put in a number of long days and hours in order to get the manuscript to the publisher by mid-September. We felt that the currency of the debates examined in *Remaking Canadian Social Policy* required that this information be published as soon as possible. To this end we owe a great deal to all of the contributors. They responded quickly to our requests for further information or changes to their papers. We would also like to thank the folks at Fernwood Publishing—Errol Sharpe, Donna Davis, Beverley Rach, Brenda Conroy, Lindsay Sharpe and Chauna James.

We especially want to thank our families who helped us see this project to the end. First, Carroll Ternowetsky and Edward Kruk, our spouses. As always they were both most supportive and patient in helping us complete this manuscript within the deadline we had set for ourselves. There are also our respective children. Through the writing of this piece Alex and Joe Ternowetsky became increasingly interested in this work as they began to appreciate the way Canadian social policy affected them personally. Finally, through July to September, while we worked on the manuscript, we were always accompanied by Liam Andrew who was born to Jane and Edward on October 1, 1995. We welcome Liam to this world. The social policy changes discussed in this book will have a direct bearing on the kind of society in which our children will grow up. It is our hope that it will contribute to a future that is more caring, kinder and responsive to the collective needs of those who live in this country.

*Jane Pulkingham*
*Gordon Ternowetsky*
September, 1995

# About The Contributors

**Michael Bach** is a senior researcher with the Roeher Institute and assistant professor (part-time), Faculty of Environmental Studies, York University. He has acted as principal researcher on a number of the Institute's studies in the areas of service provision, individualized funding, deinstitutionalization and service brokerage for persons with disability. He has participated in training and social development projects for the Institute of Canada, the Caribbean and Latin America.

**Ken Battle** is president of the Caledon Institute of Social Policy. He was the former Director of the National Council of Welfare.

**Martha Friendly** is the coordinator of the Child Care Resource and Research Unit, University of Toronto, and adjunct professor at the Centre for Urban and Community Studies. She recently completed *Child Care Policy in Canada: Putting the Pieces Together* (Addison-Wesley Canada, 1994). Martha works with the National Action Committee on the Status of Women on child care and is a member of the council of the Ontario Coalition for Better Child Care.

**Gloria Geller** has been the director of the Social Administration Research Unit (SARU) since January, 1991. She is an associate professor in the Faculty of Social Work. She has been teaching and researching as an activist in feminist studies for over twenty years.

**Jonathan S. Greene** is a Masters student in political science at Wilfrid Laurier University. His publications include *From Parent to Child: A Comparison of the Ideological Bases of the Canadian CCF/NDP and British Labour Party*. He was the co-organizer of the conference on "The Future of Higher Education in Canada" held at the University of Manitoba.

**Melanie Hess** has a MSW from the University of British Columbia, specializing in social policy. She worked on the Ontario Social Assistance Review Committee's report *Transitions*, and served as senior researcher and director of programs at the Canadian Council on Social Development. Now working as a consultant, her publications include *The Canadian Fact Book on Income Security Programs* and *Children, Schools and Poverty*.

**Therese Jennissen** teaches social administration and policy at the School of Social Work, Carleton University in Ottawa. She has a Ph.D. from McGill University, and has been a researcher for the Library of Parliament and for the Royal Commission on New Reproductive Technologies.

**Jan Joel** has been the research co-ordinator at SARU since December 1990. She has been active in the women's movement and involved in international solidarity work for the last fifteen years. Her current focus is on the necessity of creating "economic literacy" as a foundation for social policy analysis and advocacy.

**William Low** is a lecturer in the economics programme at UNCB with special reference to economics and social policy. Previously, he worked for the Ministry of Social Services in

Victoria and the Welfare State Programme at the London School of Economics. The author, his wife and toddler, three dogs and two horses live in Prince George.

**Joan McFarland** is a feminist economist who has been working on social policy issues and the role that neoclassical economists have been playing in designing social reforms. She teaches economics and gender studies at St. Thomas University in Fredericton.

**Robert Mullaly** writes in the area of social policy and radical social work theory. His recent works have focused on the restructuring of the Canadian welfare state along lines of class, gender and race. He teaches in the Department of Social Work at St. Thomas University in Fredericton.

**Mab Oloman** recently joined Westcoast Child Care Resource Centre in Vancouver as the resource and information coordinator. Previously she worked as manager of program development at the Child Care Branch, Ministry of Women's Equality (British Columbia) where initially she was researcher for the Task Force on Child Care. Mab has been an active advocate for the development and support of child care services for the past twelve years.

**Jane Pulkingham** is an assistant professor of sociology in the Department of Sociology and Anthropology, and director of the Social Policy Issues Post-Baccalaureate Diploma Programme in the Faculty of Arts, Simon Fraser University. Her teaching and research interests are in the area of feminist political economy of the welfare state, gender and social policy, employment and income security policy and family law (economics of divorce and child custody determination).

**Diana Ralph** is a community organizer and social activist, particularly around anti-poverty issues and opposing the corporate agenda. She is an associate professor of social work, Carleton University.

**Graham Riches** is currently a professor of social work at UNBC. He was previously professor and head of the Department of Social Work at James Cook University of North Queensland, Australia. He is a founder and former co-editor of the Canadian Review of Social Policy. Publications include Food Banks and the Welfare Crisis (CCSD: 1986) and Unemployment and Welfare: Social Policy and the Work of Social Work (Co-edited with Gordon Ternowetsky, Garamond: 1990).

**Marcia Rioux** is the executive director of the Roeher Institute and teaches social policy in the Faculty of Environmental Studies at York University. Her previous experience includes a range of research, policy analysis and policy development initiatives, including work done as director of research at the Canadian Advisory Council on the Status of Women and as policy analyst and senior researcher for the Law Reform Commission of Canada. She has published and presented extensively in Canada and around the world.

**Grant Schellenberg** is a research associate in the Centre for International Statistics at the Canadian Council on Social Development. He has recently completed a book entitled *The Road to Retirement: Demographic and Economic Changes in the 90s* and has also published several articles on small business and non-standard employment. He holds an undergraduate degree in sociology from the University of British Columbia and a master's degree from Carleton University, where he is currently completing his doctorate.

**Richard Shillington** has a Ph.D. in statistics and conducts quantitative research in the fields of economic and social policy. He has worked for social policy research organizations and various provincial and federal departments and commissions. In particular, he was director of data analysis for the Ontario government's Fair Tax Commission.

**Susan Silver** is an assistant professor in the School of Social Work at Ryerson Polytechnic University. Her research interests include health policy, comparative social policy, the role of values in political debates and the social costs of economic restructuring.

**Jim Stanford** is an economist with the Canadian Auto Workers union, the largest private-sector trade union in Canada. He is completing his Ph.D. in economics from the New School for Social Research in New York, and holds an M.Phil. in economics from Cambridge University, U.K., and a B.A. (Hons.) in economics from the University of Calgary. His work has been published in the *Annals of the American Academy of Social and Political Science*, the *Hofstra Labor Law Review*, *Perspectives* (Journal of the Canadian Council on Social Development), and by the Canadian Centre for Policy Alternatives.

**Gordon Ternowetsky** is a professor of social work at the University of Northern British Columbia. His research and teaching interests are in the area of unemployment, poverty, social policy and social work practice. He is the founding editor of Australian Canadian Studies: An Interdisciplinary Review and a former editor of The Canadian Review of Social Policy. He is the coordinator of the Child Welfare Research Centre at the University of Northern British Columbia.

**Sherri Torjman** is vice president of the Caledon Institute of Social Policy. She also writes the Welfare Series of reports for the National Council of Welfare. She lectured in social policy at the McGill University School of Social Work in the Fall 1994 term.

**Yves Vaillancourt** is a professor in the Département de Travail social at the Université du Québec at Montreal. He has written extensively on social issues and his recent publications include *La réforme Axworthy et le Québec* and *Québec and the Federal Government: the Struggle over Opting Out*.

**Leah F. Vosko** is pursuing her doctorate in women's studies at York University. She received her M.A. from Simon Fraser University where she produced a thesis entitled "Shrink, Cut...Dye? NAFTA and Women's Work in the Canadian Clothing Industry." Apart from her academic pursuits, she is a member of the NAC Social Policy Working Group and Women to Women Global Strategies, an international organization that educates women on economic issues.

**John Wiseman** has written extensively on Australian social policy and labour market issues and is currently head of the Department of Social Work, Royal Melbourne Institute of Technology, Melbourne, Australia.

## PART 1

# INTRODUCTION:
# REMAKING SOCIAL PROGRAMS IN CANADA

# CHAPTER 1

# THE CHANGING LANDSCAPE OF SOCIAL POLICY AND THE CANADIAN WELFARE STATE

*Jane Pulkingham and Gordon Ternowetsky*

## INTRODUCTION

The mid-1990s represent landmark years for Canadian social policy and changes in this nation's welfare state. Starting with the Speech from the Throne in early 1994, the Chrétien Liberals gave notice that Canada's social programs would be altered (House of Commons 1994a). In the view of the new government, these programs no longer met the needs of Canadians in ways that reflected the social, economic, technological and fiscal realities of the 1990s. On January 31st 1994, the Minister of Human Resources Development Canada, Lloyd Axworthy, announced the social security review (SSR) and invited Canadians to consult, give their input and provide ideas for government as it charted a new course for social programs in the late 1990s and beyond (House of Commons 1994b).

In October 1994, Axworthy released the discussion paper, *Agenda: Jobs and Growth. Improving Social Security in Canada* (HRDC 1994). This offered Canadians a glimpse of the direction and type of reforms the government was planning in the core areas of "working, learning and security." Some of the major objectives of the proposed reforms were: to help Canadians "get and keep jobs" by emphasizing training that would equip workers with the skills needed "to succeed in today's job market"; to target income support and "tackle child poverty"; and to restructure programs that are in line "with current . . . fiscal realities" (HRDC 1994: 10, 28). Child care initiatives and new schemes for funding post-secondary education were also put forward for consideration. The discussion paper stimulated a good deal of national attention and called for further public consultation. The SSR process was, however, slowed down by the Québec election in the fall of 1994. Later it came to a halt as "reforms were put on hold until after the Minister of Finance (Paul Martin) brought down his budget" for 1995-96 (Morton 1995: 6; Manning 1995).

The agenda for social security reform was clarified in Martin's budget of February 26, 1995 (Department of Finance 1995a). This document signaled a fundamental shift or "historic retreat" (Greenspon 1995) for the federal government in its role in Canada's social programs. It announced the April 1996 termination of the Canada Assistance Plan (CAP) that was based on a federal and provincial "cost shared" approach to the funding of social programs. This would be replaced by the "block funded" Canada Social Transfer (later renamed the Canada Health and Social Transfer, the CHST). Currently health and post-secondary education are the only areas supported through the Established Program Financing (EPF) method of block funding. Starting in 1996, CAP programs will be added and the CHST will result in a single block fund for federal transfers to the provinces for health, post-secondary education, social assistance and welfare services.

Alongside these changes to social assistance, Canada's system of unemployment insurance was earmarked as a prime example of a program that "lagged behind the pace of economic change" (HRDC 1994: 8). The budget outlined $700 million in savings in the administration of U.I. It also announced the Human Resources Investment Fund, a new program designed to advance "active" forms of income support that foster employability through training, instead of relying on "passive" measures that it claimed did little to help recipients become self-reliant (Department of Finance 1995a: 10). The budget was silent on child poverty, child care and changes in the funding of post-secondary education.

As this chapter is being written, the scope of the U.I. reforms are still being worked out. What appears to be unfolding is more emphasis on training (a noble objective when jobs are available), a program that requires longer periods of work to qualify for U.I., lower benefits for "frequent users," and a reduction in maximum U.I. coverage from fifty to forty weeks (Greenspon and Delacourt 1995: A1, A6). The main impact of changes in eligibility and coverage will further accent the uncertainty and insecurity of Canadian workers. According to the National Anti-Poverty Organization (NAPO) the implementation of these proposals would mean that more than 60 percent of the unemployed will no longer qualify for U.I. benefits, resulting in a situation reminiscent of the 1930s when most workers had little protection from unemployment (NAPO 1995b: 1).

Canadians are now witnessing the undoing of a welfare state that, in spite of its shortcomings, was geared to providing, as a right, income assistance to those in need. What the future holds awaits to be seen and is a central issue addressed in this book *Remaking Canadian Social Policy: Social Security in the late 1990s*. It does seem clear, however, that the restructuring of U.I. and the demise of CAP will weaken the security of Canadian people and lead to a patchwork of diverse provincial programs akin to those that existed in the 1950s and earlier periods.

How did we get here? What forces propelled us back to a welfare state that is reminiscent of the 1950s, and what evidence is there that these changes in fact mirror the views of the different constituents that participated in the SSR? This introduction to *Remaking Canadian Social Policy* addresses these questions. It begins by considering some of the salient problems inherited by the Chrétien government when it assumed office in October 1993. These had an impact on what the Liberals defined as key issues and problems as it began to reshape social policies for the late 1990s. This section also suggests that the new government's solution and explanation of these problems represented a continuation of the neoconservative, promarket policies pursued by the Mulroney Conservatives during the 1980s.

Some argue (Battle and Torjman 1996) that the Finance Department under Paul Martin captured the initiative of the social security review and that the February 1995 budget presented the "real" social security review. This assertion has considerable credence. A second concern of this introductory chapter is to assess this position by reviewing selected implications of this budget, particularly the CHST, for the future of social policy in Canada. What does a shift from the "cost shared" approach of CAP to the "block funded" CHST mean for social security in Canada?

A third purpose is to survey briefly the structure and phases of the social security review. This includes an examination of the objectives of the Seventh Conference on Canadian Social Welfare Policy from which the contents of this book are taken. The Axworthy challenge for Canadians to consult and participate in the rebuilding of Canadian social programs was a central purpose of this conference.

The social security review asked Canadians to consult and provide their views on the direction for Canadian social programs. As witnessed in the report of the House of Commons "all parliamentary" Standing Committee on Human Resources Development (House of

Commons 1995: 2, 5) a large number engaged in this process. In two rounds of consultations there were some 1400 submissions, town hall meetings organized and sponsored by 200 members of parliament and 25,000 responses to the *Have Your Say* workbook distributed by the Department of Human Resources Development. Taken together these views, rather than the budget, would constitute the "real" social security review. Whether these opinions are reflected in the policies charted by the Liberals is, however, questionable. For example, the CHST, the blueprint of future Canadian social policy, departs considerably from the oft repeated public support for CAP and for "a continuing federal government leadership role in CAP to maintain national standards" (House of Commons 1995: 51). A final purpose of this chapter is to consider some of the different views and voices that may be either forgotten or more or less silenced in the government's agenda for social policy. In doing so we review contributions to this book. This discussion introduces the perspectives of different sectors and summarizes some of the problematic areas in the directions for social policy change that have so far emerged from the social security review.

## THE SOCIAL AND ECONOMIC CONTEXT OF SOCIAL POLICY IN THE 1990s

This section considers some of the economic, employment and fiscal constraints inherited by the Liberals in 1993. It looks at how these may have influenced both the decision to establish the social security review and some of the key issues the government chose to focus on in the review process. It examines the Liberal's response to these problems and demonstrates that the steps to economic recovery it fashioned represent an extension of neoconservative, promarket policies pursed a decade earlier. In fact many of the promarket policies eagerly pursued by the Conservatives, and now the Liberals, show how both have embraced the market proposals put forth ten years ago by the *Macdonald Royal Commission on Economic Union and Development Prospects for Canada* (Minister of Supply and Services 1985).[1]

Economic growth in Canada was beginning to recover as the Liberals assumed office in 1993. Gross Domestic Product (GDP) was up by 2.3 percent and by the end of 1994 this rate accelerated and surpassed 4 percent. Over 400,000 jobs had been created, manufacturing output was up, Canada witnessed a trade surplus, and business confidence, as measured by investments, was at its highest level since 1979 (Department of Finance 1995a). Still all was not well. Despite solid economic growth, the Liberals had inherited the legacies of high unemployment, underemployment and poverty that proved difficult to dislodge even in the best of economic times. Indeed a number of supplementary papers published for the SSR[2] document trends that seemed to be immutable. These impacted on both the demand for government assistance and the government's ability to meet these demands. These trends include the persistence of unemployment and underemployment in both good and bad economic times; the creation of non-standard, poor paying jobs; the growth of poverty; and the increased reliance on social assistance.[3]

More than 1.6 million Canadians were officially unemployed at the start of the Liberals term in office. Unemployment levels had been creeping up and, since the 1950s, had jumped from average rates of less than 5 percent to over 10 percent by the 1990s. These levels of joblessness stemmed from the growth of "chronic" unemployment where the demand for labour continues to fall short of the number of workers seeking jobs (Sherraden 1985). In introducing the social security reform (House of Commons 1994b), the minister also noted the rise in the duration of joblessness. In the 1990s over 30 percent of the unemployed were without jobs for six months or longer compared to 14 percent in 1976. The average length of unemployment exceeded 25 weeks, almost double the average 13.9 weeks in 1976. Older workers (those over 45 years of age) were, on average, without jobs for 32 weeks while youth found it difficult to even find a job. These labour market realities were major factors precipitating the review of social programs. It was the view of the government that program reforms were needed to "restore employment as a central focus of government policy" (House of Commons 1994b: 1).

The expansion of "non-standard" and low wage work also placed a strain on Canada's systems of social security. Since the 1980s the jobs that have grown the fastest are part-time and in the service sector. Women also accounted for more than 80 percent of all employment growth between 1975 and 1989, a trend that continued into the 1990s. This demographic shift in the gender composition of the new workforce has several implications for policy. First, it generates greater demand for the provision of child care spaces (HRDC 1994: 54). Second, jobs that are part-time, in the service sector and filled by women, are generally lower paying, less stable and have few of the occupational benefits associated with good jobs. These jobs tend to impoverish women and reinforce their dependency on the state and/or male partners (Pulkingham 1995). Finally, these jobs provide a smaller and more unreliable source of tax revenue for governments. Both the growth in joblessness and poor paying employment reinforce the economic vulnerability of the employed as well as the unemployed.

The stagnation of income since the mid-1970s is one indicator of this mounting economic vulnerability. This trend has not been halted by the growing number of dual-earner families and the increase in part-time work that some turn to in order to "make ends meet" (Department of Finance 1994a: 27). Other indicators of economic vulnerability are the decline in middle incomes and the growth of income inequality (Picot, Myles and Wannell 1990).

The high incidence of poverty and the increasing numbers relying on social assistance also point to the spreading levels of insecurity faced by Canadians when the Liberals took office. Some 4.7 million Canadians or 17.4 percent of the population were considered to be in poverty. Of these poor, more than 1.4 million were children, saddling Canada with a child poverty rate of 20.8 percent (National Council of Welfare (NCW) 1995: 8). In a background paper asking *Why Social Security Reform*, Axworthy also noted that, in March 1993, some 3 million Canadians were dependent on social assistance. This included 1.1 million children (House of Commons 1994c).

### MANAGING DEMAND: DEFICIT CONTROL, ECONOMIC GROWTH AND JOB CREATION
One of the major issues facing the new Liberal government was how to manage this growing need for government assistance. This was particularly acute because at the other end of this demand spectrum were budgetary constraints deemed to be important by the government. On assuming office, the deficit for March 1, 1994 was $45 billion while the accumulated debt stood at $508.2 billion (Department of Finance 1994a: 1). Service charges on this debt exceeded $40 billion for 1994-95 (Department of Finance 1994a: 71).

While in opposition the Liberals designed an expansionary infrastructure improvement program geared to create jobs and help offset unemployment, underemployment and poverty. The objectives of the infrastructure program were based on Keynesian solutions that favoured state intervention to stimulate employment, consumption and economic growth. In this framework the state assumed a pivotal role to ensure job creation and strong levels of economic activity. Although the infrastructure program was initiated, once in office the policies turned to by the Liberals paralleled those used by the Conservatives a decade earlier. Like the Conservatives before them, they asserted the primacy of the private sector as the engine of economic growth and job creation. Once profits are secure and predictable, the private sector will invest, jobs will be created, resulting in increased consumer demand that will translate into further investments and jobs. To "liberate" this market potential required action on several fronts: deficit and debt control; spending restraint; less government; the privatization of public companies; and the remaking of social programs that tend to exacerbate deficits, produce labour market disincentives and, in today's global market, impair Canada's international competitiveness (Johnson, McBride, Smith 1994: 4; Ternowetsky 1994: 103). All of these concerns are interrelated but deficit and debt control were "key" matters and point to the similar approaches of the neoconservatives in 1980s, and the neoliberals of the 1990s (Department of Finance 1994a: 71; Department of Finance 1984: 2).[4] The following examples illustrate this.

On coming into office in 1984 the new Conservative government tabled its course of action in the document *A New Direction for Canada: An Agenda for Economic Renewal* (Department of Finance 1984). The prescriptions in this document centred first on deficit reduction as a necessary step for restoring economic growth and job creation. Witness Mr. Wilson (Department of Finance 1984: 13, 15, 21), the Minister of Finance at that time.

> The magnitude of the debt problem, if not managed prudently, will clearly have increasing adverse impacts on investor confidence. This would deny Canada the investment, both foreign and domestic, it requires to generate growth and jobs.

In an effort to cut the deficit "public spending in general and social expenditures in particular were singled out for reduction" (Mishra 1990: 70). It was in this period that "social policy by stealth" was invented to control spending. Previously federal benefits were indexed to keep up with costs and inflation. The Conservatives "siphoned billions" from social programs by de-indexing benefits to less than the growth of inflation. Following the recommendations of the Forget (1986) Commission of Inquiry on Unemployment Insurance, benefit entitlements, periods of qualification and levels of support were also reduced for most workers. However, expenditures on social programs still rose as the demand for assistance continued to grow because the economy did not create enough good paying jobs (Battle 1993: 1, 3). Mishra (1990: 71) also suggests that costs rose because the Conservatives retreated from their assault on the deficit. Mullaly (1993: 21) argues that this explanation has little validity. He notes that in the years 1989 to 1990 the Conservatives ended the government's contribution to U.I. The Conservatives also brought an end to "universality" by "clawing back" family allowance and OAS payments from middle income Canadians. They managed to dismantle key components of Canada's welfare state, universality and the public funding of U.I.

In 1995 we are again subject to explanations that present the deficit and the debt as major impediments to economic growth, private sector investment and the creation of jobs. The key to creating jobs hinges on restoring Canada's fiscal health.

> Deficit reduction and debt control are essential parts of a strategy to create jobs through economic growth. Failure to reduce the deficit and control the debt will

prejudice growth and job creation in both the short and long terms. Success will strengthen the prospects for jobs through growth. (Department of Finance 1994b: vi)

In an effort to lower the deficit, the Liberals have continued to cut spending by allowing benefit levels and social program spending to drop through de-indexation. They also have initiated a range of direct cutbacks to squeeze government expenditures. The 1995 budget (Department of Finance 1995: 29) put forward spending reductions of $25.3 billion over a three year time frame. More than $4 billion of this is scheduled to come from social programs generally and 66 percent from Human Resources and Development, the department that administers and funds programs for those in greatest economic need. The introduction of the CHST, however, changes the structure of social program financing in Canada. The CHST does more than signal a further retrenchment or a "marginal slowdown in spending and programs" (Courchene 1987: 4). It reformulates federal and provincial powers and responsibilities and has the potential to "demolish" what we now accept as a legitimate welfare role for governments. This is discussed in more detail in the upcoming "Martin Budget and Social Programs" section.

The impetus to changing Canada's social programs by reducing the "interventionist" role of government is linked to global pressures and the increasing constraints on the ability of nation states to chart their own social policies. According to Clark (1995: 82) the size of Canada's debt prompted Moody's to review Canada's credit rating and the *Wall Street Journal* to relegate Canada to the "third world." What this means is that global financiers will not allow the Chrétien government to proceed with its social policy reforms independently of how these are viewed by the international financial community. In addition to this fiscal pressure, Clark (1995) and others (Kerans 1994: 123-124; Watkins 1992: 86-88; McBride and Shields 1993: 135-139) note that globalization and the emergence of free trade blocks force nations to "harmonize" their social programs and wages to facilitate "level playing fields" with their trading partners. For Canada in relation to the U.S. and Mexico there is pressure to bring our programs into line with the lower welfare standards and wages in the U.S. and Mexico. Harmonization for Canada involves moving from "higher to lower common standards" by sharply reducing social spending (Clark 1995: 82-83).

But where do these policies of spending reductions on social programs, deficit and debt control, and the assumption that a strong and growing economy will create jobs, leave us? Do they provide credible solutions to the issues of unemployment, poverty and the demand for government assistance that now plague Canada's economy? In terms of the deficit, government action has often been one-sided, emphasizing program spending and ignoring relative declines in revenue. A recent study by Statistics Canada (Mimoto and Cross 1991) shows that from 1975 to 1991 only 6 percent of the federal debt could be attributed to social spending. In contrast, 50 percent was an outcome of declining revenue resulting from tax expenditures and corporate tax breaks. As in the past, public officials are reticent about removing tax breaks to the private sector. Martin argues, for example, that taxes on business have been increasing and offer little scope for additional revenue. He concludes that "spending restraint, and not tax increases, must bear the brunt of fiscal adjustment" (Department of Finance 1994a: 86). However, if business, particularly the large corporate sector, is under such a heavy tax burden, why is it that many profitable firms pay no taxes at all? Something is amiss in this explanation when one considers that between 1980 to 1987 and 1990, more than $140 billion in profits of Canadian firms were not taxed (Ternowetsky 1994: 106). To its credit, the Standing Committee on Human Resources recognized this bias and omission and placed tax expenditures back on the agenda for social security reform.

In terms of growth and job creation, the following suggests that this relationship be treated with caution. First, consider the outcome of economic growth from the middle to late 1980s, the longest period of uninterrupted and sustained growth in the post-war period in Canada. Huge profits were made, the private sector boomed (Eadie 1989: B1-B2), and between 1983 and 1989 some 1.3 million new jobs were created (Statistics Canada 1994: 83, 71-529; Wong 1987: 92). But in these good times, Canada was drifting into a society of growing economic inequality and income polarization. In this setting of apparent prosperity one of the fastest growth areas was the foodbank industry (Oderkirk 1992; Riches 1986).

The prime reason for the expansion of poverty in the midst of affluence is a lack of decent paying, decent quality jobs. Unemployment remained historically high and did not fall back to its pre- 1981-82 recession levels (Economic Council of Canada 1989: 33). The period was also marked by the increased labour force participation of women, whose wages at that time were around two thirds of those earned by men, and a growth in contingent, non-standard, low paying jobs that afforded few, if any, benefits. Mass unemployment and the growing size of the marginal labour force kept up the demand and pressure for government assistance. It is precisely these kinds of jobs that are again on the rise in the current liberal era of economic recovery. In a table summarizing general trends and major employment shifts the Department of Finance (1994a: 24) notes that service industries, which pay on average lower wages and offer insecure, part-time employment, continue to represent the fastest areas of employment growth.

A second issue is NAIRU, the non-accelerating inflation rate of unemployment. When unemployment falls below certain levels, inflation is pushed up. The Liberals refer to this non-accelerating rate as the "core rate" and peg it at "at least 8 percent" (Department of Finance 1994a: 20). This implies that 8 percent unemployment is now the "benchmark for full employment." Recent 1994 labour force data indicate that this measure of full employment accepts 1,186,000 unemployed people as an admissible standard (Statistics Canada 1994, 71-001: Table 1: 2). Canada may have never fully pursued the Keynesian policy of full-employment. Yet, to treat 8 percent unemployment as full employment suggests that government policy accepts mass unemployment as inevitable and "unavoidable in market economies" (Mishra 1990: 71, 22). What this means, however, is that the structure of opportunity has collapsed for a million plus workers in Canada. Gone is even the pretense of interventionist measures that set "full employment" as a policy priority.[5]

Another factor casting doubt on the economic growth–jobs scenario is that Canada's largest and most profitable firms, those that have the capacity to provide stable and secure employment, are in a period of jobless or "jobloss" growth (HRDC 1994: 16). Downsizing labour requirements is one form of restructuring that took hold in Canada in the 1980s, but remains to be fully recognized or dealt with in government policy. What this restructuring means is that expanding profits and business commitments are being managed by a smaller and shrinking workforce. This retrenchment of workers not only increases the demand for government assistance in the form of U.I. or social assistance, but it further restricts government's capacity to respond. Fewer workers mean fewer paycheques, lower consumption, and less income and consumption tax for governments to fund programs. The majority of all new employment is taking place in small firms (those with less than five employees). These are the firms that have fewer assets and less resources to continue employing Canadian workers during downturns in the business cycle.

Other factors will continue to increase the demand for government intervention in both good and bad economic times. One is the aging of the population. This issue is left out of the current SSR, but a review of income support programs for seniors was announced in the 1995 budget (Department of Finance 1995a: 20). The other is the need for child care to accommodate the growing number of women entering the paid labour force. While this is mentioned in the Axworthy discussion paper (HRDC 1994: 53), like child poverty, child care issues are left out of the budget and appear to be stalled or left to the discretion of provinces as they work out the implications of the CHST on spending choices.

Commenting on the impact of the neoconservative policies brought in to solve the economic crises of the 1980s, Mel Watkins (1992: 11) argues that the "single contribution . . . of these solutions has been to worsen the crises and add to our discontents." Is this what the future holds? Little seems to have changed in the mid-1990s. Unemployment and underemployment persist, poverty and economic dependency have increased and the federal government, in the name of fiscal responsibility, deficit control and a market led recovery, is fading "from the scene as a provider and guardian of state welfare" (Ternowetsky 1994: 101). In place of our current welfare state we are asked to consider a new generation of programs. The central focus of these is to upgrade the skills of the unemployed, support the most vulnerable (through increased selectivity), become more affordable in the context of current fiscal realities, and overcome the disincentives of the current system that "seems designed to keep people dependent" (HRDC 1994: 22). More to the point, we are in the throes of demolishing what may be left of the Keynesian welfare state (KWS) in Canada. Although simple defense of the KWS is not the answer (some dismantling and rebuilding is required), neither is the answer to be found in attacking the levels of public provision for collective well-being, which are no longer deemed "affordable" or fiscally responsible. The proposed changes to U.I. confirm that even programs based on client contributions cannot escape "the stigma of dependency" traditionally associated with welfare and public assistance (Pulkingham 1995). The sacredness of universal programs has long disappeared. Canadian social programs are being reshaped to fit a market driven, global model of competition where norms of social protection are harmonized downwards to match the lowest standard in a trading block.

At the start of this chapter we asked, "How did we get here? What forces propelled us back to a welfare state that is reminiscent of the 1950s?" Part of the answer lies in a market where mass unemployment and labour market marginality are the norm. This excludes people from full participation in society and creates levels of demand for assistance that governments argue are unsustainable, exacerbating the crises of deficits, debts, economic decline, unemployment and poverty. The other part of the answer lies in how Canadian governments have chosen to respond. Since the early 1980s Canada's welfare state has been squeezed, downsized, restructured and dismantled. Now in the 1990s, social security programs are being redesigned to foster "employability . . . as though there are actual jobs waiting for all those being trained, retrained, motivated, supplied with life skills and stripped of disincentives" (Kerans 1994: 119). The post-war balance between labour and capital is changing as governments wind down their social policy commitments to people. The security, protection and power people struggled to win are increasingly undermined by new market forces and policies geared to deficit reduction and social spending restraint. A minimalist role for government and a leaner, residual model of welfare protection has resurfaced. As argued below the retreat of the Canadian welfare state will continue. The CHST, which permits the federal government to regain control over its fiscal outlays, also provides an opportunity for it to redefine and reduce its role and responsibility for the collective well-being of those who live and work in this country.

## THE MARTIN BUDGET AND SOCIAL POLICY

Two sets of interrelated questions are explored in this section. First, did the 1995 budget derail the social security review by changing the parameters and choices available in the review of social programs? Second, what impact will the changes to social programs presented in the budget have on the security of Canadian people? Has the protection for the people in this country been strengthened or undermined by the social policy initiatives in this budget? What do the changes announced in the budget mean for the future of Canada's welfare state and the well-being of its citizens?

The initial question is addressed by considering some of the financial outcomes of the budget and then the impact of the new Canada Health and Social Transfer (CHST) on the SSR. Currently federal transfers to the provinces and territories are made through equalization[6] payments, Established Program Financing (EPF) and the Canada Assistance Plan (CAP). The latter two methods are used for funding social programs. EPF is a "block fund" composed of cash transfers and tax points to support health and post-secondary education (PSE) programs in the provinces and territories.[7] The PSE transfers are without conditions while health funding requires that the delivery of health services meet the five conditions of the Canadian Health Act (1984): universality, comprehensiveness, accessibility, portability and public administration (Torjman 1993).

CAP on the other hand is a "50-50 cost shared" program where Ottawa pays half the cost of provincial social assistance and welfare services. To receive these cost shared dollars the territorial and provincial social welfare programs are required to establish a "needs test," set up an appeals procedure "for people to challenge the decision of welfare officials," and ensure that residency is not a requirement for the receipt of social assistance (NCW 1994: 11). In addition, clients are entitled to an income that takes into account budgetary requirements and they cannot be forced to work for welfare (NAPO 1995a). For the fiscal years 1995-96 Ottawa expects to transfer $29.7 billion to the provinces and territories through EPF and CAP. This amount is comparable to dollars transferred in 1994-95 and fulfills a 1994 (Hansard 1994) budget promise to establish two years of financial predictability for the provinces.[8]

Beginning in April 1996, the new CHST combines CAP and EPF funding into a single block fund for health, education, welfare and social services. In the announcement of the CHST, Martin (Department of Finance 1995a: 18) noted that receipt of transfers are still contingent upon the provinces and territories complying with national standards. The five conditions of the Canada Health Act and the provision of social assistance without a residency requirement must be maintained.

Does this new CHST affect the SSR by changing the boundaries of the review? An affirmative answer seems appropriate. First, from a budgetary perspective the new CHST, when compared with current transfer levels, offers less revenue to the provinces and territories. The CAP/EPF transfer for 1995-96 is $29.7 billion. According to the government's calculation, under the CHST this is reduced to $26.9 billion in 1996-97 (a 9.4 percent decline) and $25.1 billion in 1997-98 (a further 6.7 percent drop) (Department of Finance 1995a: 19, 1995b: Table 2). Second, collapsing CAP into a "reduced" block fund changes the very nature of funding social programs. Previously the territories and provinces had to comply with CAP requirements. While the budget suggests this will continue (Department of Finance 1995a: 18, 1995b), it will be difficult to monitor. The CHST is a "single consolidated block transfer" and does not specify if funds are to be used for health, education, welfare or social services. None of the transfer is "legally designated for any of the four areas" (NCW 1995: 11). Not only is there less money, but there is no compulsion to spend CHST dollars on social assistance and welfare services.

Block funding arrangements create other difficulties for enforcing national standards. These transfers come in two forms, tax points and cash. Tax points "are the income tax power the federal government gave up to the provinces when it introduced the EPF in 1977, and which still counts as part of the social transfer" (Battle and Torjman 1996: 60). The overall value of the tax point portion of the block fund transfer has been increasing and now accounts for 79 percent of federal transfers to the provinces (Department of Finance 1994a: 18). To calculate the EPF dollar obligation, the difference between the "total EPF commitment" and the value of the tax point assignment equals the size of the cash transfer (NCW 1995: 9). The cash component of these block transfers is declining. Some predict this will drop to zero by 2009-10, although the introduction of the CHST will likely extend this final date (Battle and Torjman 1993: 5; Vaillancourt 1996; Greene 1996: Table 1). The main implication is that, as the cash component of this transfer erodes, so will Ottawa's power to ensure national standards.[9]

The CHST covers more programs with less money and no legal designation that these funds be spent on health, post-secondary education, social assistance or welfare services. It is up to the discretion of the provinces where these funds will be distributed. It is likely that the choices made by each province and territory will differ, reflecting the sum of the financial, social, economic and political constraints each confronts. The net result will be programs and procedures that vary from province to province.

In response to the earlier questions, "How did we get here?" and "What forces propelled us back to a welfare state that is reminiscent of the 1950s?," it is clear that the provisions of the CHST are partially responsible. Once again a comment by the National Council of Welfare is instructive. It concludes that the CHST is a "giant step backward" reminiscent of earlier periods with a patchwork of "hit and miss" provincial programs and the "end of any semblance of national standards" (NCW 1995: 1, 2). Indeed, under the guise of fiscal prudence and deficit control, this budget introduced by Paul Martin has captured the initiative of the social security review. It left us with the CHST that fundamentally changes the relations between the provinces and Ottawa in terms of social programs. Without the opportunity to increase their allotted funds, the provinces and territories will map out programs, policies and procedures that reflect their own needs and concerns. The CHST leaves the provinces with a diminished financial capacity and little impetus to consider the delivery of its social programs within the context of national standards. It leaves Canadians with a federal government that, in the name of debt management and greater fiscal control over its own spending, has chosen to discard CAP and the power to influence national standards. The devolution of social program powers to the provinces raises questions about the relevance of a national social security review. If the social security review was not derailed by the budget, it is clear that its focus has been fundamentally altered.

This leads to the second set of questions concerning the impact of the budget on the security of Canadians. A first point to note is that with the CHST several rights guaranteed by CAP are lost. Gone is the right to assistance when in need, the right to an income that considers budgetary requirements, the right not to have to work for welfare, and the right to an appeal (NAPO 1995a). Coupled with reduced funding and the questionable enforceability of the standards that do remain, it is clear that basic levels of protection for people in this country have weakened. The next recession will demonstrate this. In the past, when rising unemployment pushed up the demand for assistance and provincial expenditures on welfare, half of these costs were recouped from Ottawa. The fixed fund approach of the CHST eliminates this. Increased provincial caseloads and costs for welfare will be borne by the provinces. These will have no bearing on Ottawa as its "costs will no longer be driven" by provincial expenditures (Department of Finance 1995b: np). The range of choices for provinces are limited by shrinking funds and those most likely to feel the brunt of these restrictions are the poor, the powerless and those most dependent upon social programs.

## THE SOCIAL SECURITY REVIEW AND THE SEVENTH CONFERENCE ON CANADIAN SOCIAL WELFARE POLICY: *REMAKING CANADIAN SOCIAL POLICY: STAKING CLAIMS AND FORGING CHANGE*

A description of the different phases and documents presented during the social security review are detailed in Therese Jennissen's (1996a) outline of the chronology of the federal social security review included in this volume (Chapter 2). The purpose of the discussion in this section is as follows: to briefly summarize the stages, structure and process of the SSR; to describe some of the responses (both positive and negative) to the review; and to discuss the linkages between the planning and objectives of the Seventh Conference on Canadian Social Welfare Policy and Axworthy's request for public participation and input to into the review process. This leads to the final section of this chapter which reviews the outline of this book, and the views, ideas and opinions regarding the developments and changes emanating from the social security review.

The review of social programs announced by Axworthy on January 31, 1994 was entitled *Creating Opportunity . . . Through Social Security Reform* (House of Commons 1994b). People were invited to consult, identify the issues facing Canadians and offer clear options for change. A key initiative of the review process was the formation of a Standing Committee on Human Resource Development to oversee the reform and to report to Parliament. Two stages for the review were established. Stage 1 (February to April 1994) was designed to give people, groups and organizations an opportunity to present their views on social program reform. Stage 2 (April to October 1994) involved setting an "action plan" that would provide a framework for legislation planned for the fall of 1994 or early 1995.

Parliamentary approval for the Standing Committee was received on February 8, leaving "six weeks" for it to complete Stage 1 and submit an interim report to Parliament by March 25, 1994 (Leblanc 1994: 1). While hurried and compressed, these initial consultations were later described as "a national brainstorming session" that demonstrated to the Standing Committee the importance Canadians attached to their social programs. They were viewed as a "defining quality of our nationhood" (House of Commons 1995: 2, 4). Stage 2, scheduled for completion in October 1994, was extended to February 6, 1995, the date the Standing Committee submitted its final report entitled *Security, Opportunity and Fairness: Canadians renewing their social programs*. This extension accommodated the need for more time to consult and gauge responses to the discussion paper, *Agenda: Jobs Growth* and the eight supplementary papers Human Resources prepared to inform the review process. The interim and final reports of the Standing Committee detail the scope of the consultation and briefings and are not repeated here. However, it is important to note that, in the view of the committee, this work constituted one of the most thorough and comprehensive Parliamentary reviews ever undertaken on Canadian social programs (House of Commons 1995: 4).

The social security review was greeted with both optimism and reservation by the Canadian public. There was widespread recognition that social programs needed reform. Provincial welfare rates were deemed inadequate, and in relation to Canada's low income cut-offs (LICOS), dependence on social assistance reinforced the impoverishment of the welfare poor (NCW 1990). Welfare regulations also make it difficult for people to move from welfare into the workforce. This "welfare wall" (Torjman and Battle 1993; Kerans 1994) resulted from the loss of "income in-kind" benefits, high "tax back rates on earned income" and the payment of direct taxes. There is little incentive for welfare clients to return to the workforce as they can end up with less income and security than they get while on public assistance.

There were also reservations about the SSR. As soon as it was announced, questions about the process and purpose of the review arose. One issue was the time frame that offered only six weeks for Stage 1 involving input, consultation and briefings with Canadians, as well as an interim report. During some of the consultation meetings, individuals and groups were excluded from participating because of the tight time frame. A second problem was the purpose of the review. Would this be a valid exercise to reform a system that was unable to provide adequate support for ever increasing numbers? Or, was this another deficit reduction exercise? Would its main focus be on cutbacks and spending restraint in an effort to restructure social programs and make them more "affordable"?

There were mixed messages on this front. In introducing the social security review, Axworthy (House of Commons 1994b: 2) assured Canadians that the object was not to "slash and trash" ... in order to "cut costs." However, eight months later in the discussion paper (HRDC 1994: 23), he linked social security reform directly to fiscal realities and deficit control. There would be "no new money . . . for social programs" and expenditure levels for CAP, education and health would be capped at their 1993-94 levels. Second, during the SSR the Department of Finance, in its documents, *A New Framework for Economic Policy* (Department of Finance 1994a) and *Creating a Healthy Fiscal Climate* (Department of Finance 1994b), put social programs into the context of the deficit, debt control and affordability. Indeed it was this emphasis on spending restraint and deficits that linked this review to those that took place in the 1980s under the governance of Brian Mulroney. There was concern that the current SSR, like those initiated in the 1980s, might represent another chapter in the devolution of state responsibility for the collective well-being of the citizens of Canada.

The validity of this concern was acknowledged by the Standing Committee. In its report it recognized the importance of deficits and debt control but, persuaded by public opinion, admitted that the framework of the SSR was too limited. The SSR and the Department of Finance included only direct spending on social programs in its estimates of program costs and means of reducing expenditures. The Standing Committee broadened the focus to include tax expenditures or the spending side of taxation. Tax expenditures, like direct spending, reduce government revenue but tend to benefit the well-off. The addition of tax expenditures into the review is an important step forward. This inclusion has been advanced for years by the social policy community.

## OTHER VOICES: DIFFERENT VIEWS ON SOCIAL SECURITY REFORM

A central objective of the Seventh Conference on Social Welfare Policy was to provide an alternative venue to the "official" consultation process of the social security review while taking seriously the Axworthy challenge to participate in the rebuilding of Canadian social programs. The major work on developing the conference themes and objectives began in April and May 1994, near the start of the second phase of the social security review. The work on the organization and clarification of the conference objectives continued through to the spring of 1995. During this time frame there was the fall release of the Axworthy discussion paper (HRDC 1994) and the February 1995 budget. From the start, a goal set by the Conference Planning Committee was to use this venue to provide input into the SSR. We wanted to ensure the constituencies we represented (academe, the public sector, First Nations, social workers, community groups and the voluntary sector) had a forum for engaging in the debate on Canadian social programs. It was recognized that Canadian social programs were under considerable pressure and that the outcome of the Axworthy review would result in important changes to the Canadian welfare state. We also acknowledged that in the history of Canadian social programs this was a strategic moment and that the post-review era would likely result in programs quite different from those in place today—thus the title of the conference, *Remaking Canadian Social Policy*, and the subtitle, *Staking Claims and Forging Change*. This reflected the view that programs would be changing, and that the conference would take up the Axworthy challenge by providing a forum for diverse populations to stake their claims in terms of the type of welfare state they wish to see unfold.

The initial advertisement and call for papers for the conference took the standpoint that the status quo for Canadian social programs was no longer viable.

> The current process of remaking social policy in Canada is critical in setting the social policy stage for the twenty-first century. Given the interplay of global, federal, provincial and local pressures, the present social policy "round" may radically alter Canada's welfare state.

In the Call for Papers we asked people to consider the following questions.

- What social policy options best respond to the current and future social policy needs of diverse groups in Canada?
- What collaborative and advocacy efforts are important in addressing social, economic, racial and cultural inequalities, for example, issues relating to gender, First Nations peoples, ethnicity, sexual orientation, disability and poverty?

The organization of the presentations emphasized discussion and participation. The aim of these were: to provide an update of the changes that have taken place in Canadian social programs; to consider alternative ways of dealing with inequalities that have persisted in spite of our social programs; and to work collaboratively so in the end we would have our say in the remaking of Canadian social policy. The chapters that follow, in Parts 2 through 6, represent a selection of the many voices represented at the conference in the debate about social security reform in Canada.

In Part 2, *Canadian Social Policy at the Crossroads*, two common themes emerge. First, although social policy reform is ostensibly within the purview of Human Resources Development Canada, the Ministry of Finance, through successive budgets and tax policy, is an equal if not more powerful player in the social policy arena. Notably, however, while the Liberal federal government has sought public input with respect to HRDC deliberations, policies pursued by the Ministry of Finance remain closed to public scrutiny. One outcome is that social policy reform typically proceeds through a process of "stealth." This issue reappears in contributions to Parts 5 and 6 as well. Second, the SSR, and more specifically, the 1995 federal budget (primarily through the CHST), places Canadian federalism at a critical juncture. With this budget, the federal government appears poised to strip itself of fiscal power and moral authority in relation to Canada's social programs. By relinquishing its fiscal levers, will the federal government have any relevance as far as social policy is concerned? What are the implications for national standards?[10]

Arguing that the *real* social security review has been accomplished through the 1995 federal budget, Ken Battle and Sherri Torjman (Chapter 4) suggest that the potential erosion of federal spending power through the CHST could result in "constitutional reform *de facto—* by stealth." In this regard, the Liberals are not simply continuing the Tory tradition of social program change through "social policy by stealth"(of which they had been critical while in opposition), rather they are escalating this process, moving beyond "tinkering" to undertake a more fundamental transformation of the role of the federal and provincial governments. The loss of CAP, in particular, is argued to represent a significant retreat in the federal government's commitment to social programs and its role in encouraging and assisting provinces to provide counter-cyclical protection, previously an important economic policy objective.

The SSR is not about what the Liberals originally purported it would be (the agenda was usurped by the budget, and it is focused on dismantling rather than rebuilding). But they suggest that there is a silver lining in an otherwise disappointing and misleading process: the SSR has resulted in a large number of well thought out options that have received public attention and could form the basis of future social program reform. To this end, Battle and Torjman outline briefly some of the reforms they would like this review to accomplish. These include: "returning" U.I. to its "original purpose"—providing insurance against the risk of short-term and occasional unemployment (a proposal that appears to be very similar to the one the government will likely introduce in the autumn of 1995); as part of the reform of U.I., creating a new national employment assistance program for those who are not eligible for U.I., including those who under the current system are "employable welfare recipients"; and creating an integrated child benefit or income-tested program of family benefits for all low income families regardless of the source and mix of income. The latter two proposals would take a significant proportion of welfare recipients off provincial income assistance programs, moving them onto national programs, thus transforming provincial welfare into a program of "true" last resort.

Assessing the prospects for national standards under the proposed CHST, Susan Silver

(Chapter 5) examines earlier experiences with block funding under EPF for medicare. As with the current debate about the introduction of the CHST, the introduction of EPF raised concerns about its potential "balkanizing" effect on the Canadian health care system and the likely erosion of national program conditions. At the time, EPF arrangements represented the single largest transfer of revenues and power from the federal to the provincial governments in Canadian history. Apart from the original (five) national standards (universal coverage, accessibility, portability, comprehensiveness and public administration) there were no other conditions attached to the block grant. Then, as now, the retreat of the federal government was justified on the grounds that the closed-ended nature of the new financial arrangements were necessary in order to establish funding predictability. With block funding the provinces were solely responsible for any cost increases that exceeded the annual growth in the GNP. Importantly, however, provinces were free to allocate their funds in accordance with their own priorities in order to achieve cost savings. It was also (incorrectly) assumed that once a national program was "established," the federal government could assume a more limited role without it being jeopardized.

As time would tell, however, without a federal role in operationalizing the program principles and linking an enforceable penalty to the EPF block fund, "established" programs, even ones that enjoyed an unprecedented level of public support, were vulnerable. Equal access to medicare was threatened on a number of fronts, and the ensuing policy debate culminated in the introduction of the Canada Health Act (CHA) (1984) which represented a battle fought in the name of universality. In this instance universal health care was interpreted as free access to those services that are publicly insured. To ensure compliance with this principle, an enforceable financial penalty was introduced with the CHA. According to Silver, while EPF weakened medicare, the CHA demonstrated that this program could be strengthened. However, the "teeth" in the CHA rested on the existence of a significant federal "cash" transfer under the EPF block funding formula, a condition that will likely disappear under the CHST. This does not augur well for medicare as the new debate concerning "access in medicare," in other words, which services should be publicly insured and which should be "delisted," attests.[11]

Yves Vaillancourt (Chapter 6) indicates that Canada is at a crossroads in more ways than one. Not only has the SSR come at a time when Québec will be holding a referendum on sovereignty, the federal retreat from the domain of social policy implied by the CHST raises many questions about what the future will hold for existing social programs. In terms of the Québec question, Vaillancourt argues that the federal political system in Canada has to be renewed in order to provide more powers and fiscal revenues either to all provinces (symmetrical decentralized federalism) or to Québec alone (asymmetrical decentralized federalism). Thus, in contrast to Battle and Torjman's paper in this volume, Vaillancourt suggests that the Human Resources Investment Fund (HRIF) represents an *increase* in the federal governments direct intervention in program responsibilities and financial commitments. From the perspective of a Québec sovereignist, the proposed role of the HRIF in training and other programs to help the unemployed, combat child poverty, eliminate illiteracy, support day care services and income supplementation, is seen as an incursion into existing and/or potential programs of provincial jurisdiction. Also, contrary to many social policy analysts, Vaillancourt emphasizes that the elimination of two program envelopes (CAP and EPF) into one (the CHST) will actually lengthen the lifetime of federal cash transfers to provinces. He argues that as long as there is any federal cash contribution, the federal government is in a position to enforce national standards. Vaillancourt also reminds readers of the history to the provincial acquisition of fiscal powers (tax points, as opposed to cash transfers) from the federal government, in order to demonstrate that the magnitude of cuts imposed through the CHST are substantially larger than the federal government forecasts in its 1995 budget.

In terms of social policy reform, Vaillancourt challenges those involved in the debate on remaking social policy to reject both the position of the old-style progressives and the neoliberals and instead to opt for a "new progressive paradigm." According to Vaillancourt, the post-war model is defunct. In order to successfully counter the neoliberals, a new social development model is required. Rather than idealizing post-war social policy programs associated with the Keynesian fordist welfare state, what is required is a new model that stresses the importance of self-determination, citizen participation, decentralization, local (community) economic development, and an expanded and more innovative role for the voluntary sector. Specifically, Vaillancourt argues for the concept of "communautarisation," a shift of resources to the community. Thus decentralization should be a "principled" shift to less costly community based institutions, rather than a simple downloading and downsizing of financial obligations.

In the seventh and final chapter in this section, Shillington explores the many fallacies associated with the Canadian tax system and its role as a social policy instrument. The misconceptions include that Canada is a high tax country, Canadians are over-taxed and the tax system is progressive. Shillington challenges all of these assumptions, pointing to the composition of taxes, specifically Canada's reliance on income taxes and tax expenditures, in perpetuating these myths. For example, preferential treatment of wealth (Canada is one of only three Organization for Economic and Co-operative Development (OECD) countries that do not have a wealth transfer or estate/inheritance tax) is why Canada relies more heavily on income taxes and why middle income Canadians feel "overtaxed." Tax incidence analysis demonstrates that the rate of taxation is flat, between 30 percent and 35 percent across the entire income range, further underlining the misconception that high income Canadians pay proportionally more in taxes than middle and lower income people. In fact, beyond the $40,000 income level, the tax system is not really progressive at all: the empirical marginal tax rate is 35 percent for incomes ranging between $35,000 and $150,000.

Though not coined this way, Shillington's analysis of the tax system and social policy reform, points to another dimension of the system of "social policy by stealth." Although the SSR does not include a review of tax expenditures, he argues that this not only limits the scope of the review but "more importantly biases the analysis by excluding types of social spending which differentially benefit higher income Canadians." Tax expenditures, or government revenue foregone, not only undermine the progressivity of the tax system and benefit disproportionately higher income Canadians, they are very difficult to control and are largely unaccountable as a method of spending. Further, despite rhetoric to the contrary, direct social spending (on those programs slated for review) is already highly targeted to low income earners. On the other hand, tax expenditures are poorly targeted to those in need, but are not part of the review. He suggests that it is ironic indeed that the SSR disregards these expenditures as they represent a major source of social spending. According to Shillington, however, the prospects for changing this situation are not good. The lethargy in relation to establishing greater accountability regarding tax expenditures is politically motivated. While reducing direct spending wins governments kudos in the opinion polls and financial markets, a reduction in tax expenditures increases government revenue. This is seen as increasing the size of government, a politically inexpedient move when the motto "small is beautiful" prevails.

In Part 3, *Social Security Reform, Globalization and Labour Market Restructuring*, the authors consider the dynamics and effects of employment restructuring and of national policies pursued to facilitate this restructuring with a view to enhancing the international competitiveness of Canada's economy. This typically involves policies designed to reduce costs through labour shedding, wage reductions, deregulating labour markets, and scaling back income support programs.

In the first chapter (Chapter 8) in this section, John Wiseman emphasizes the need to situate debates about globalization in the experience of particular nation states, arguing against an overly generalized understanding of this process. He therefore compares Canadian and Australian experiences. Although there are a number of important differences and many similarities between the two countries, the most important similarity is that they share a common vulnerability to international economic transformations given that both can be characterized as semi-peripheral economies, resource dependent, with high levels of foreign ownership. Thus, globalization does "matter," and has a number of consequences for their sovereignty and relative autonomy. Wiseman suggests that there have been three "ideal type" political responses to globalization, characterized as "champions," "competitors" and "challengers." For the most part, Australian and Canadian government responses fall into the second category, accepting the inevitability of globalization but focusing on maximizing the competitiveness of national and regional economies. Consequently, both countries have focused on labour market rigidities, in particular unemployment, as a central concern.

In Australia, this led to an inquiry into employment options and the publication of *Working Nation,* (commonly referred to as the White Paper on Employment/Unemployment) in May 1994. In Canada, the impact of the internationalization of the economy (through free trade agreements with the United States and, more recently, Mexico) appears to be more severe. Wiseman indicates that the full significance of these agreements is their role as a "surrogate constitution or 'corporate bill of rights' protecting the unrestricted and unregulated mobility of capital." It was only with the election of the Chrétien Liberals in 1993, however, that the welfare state came under full scale attack, reflected in part by the process and implications of the 1994 Canadian social security review. Thus, Wiseman analyses Australia's White Paper on Unemployment and the SSR which are said to bear a number of "startling resemblances."

Wiseman concludes his chapter by considering the "challengers," the third ideal type political response to globalization. He argues that more consideration should be given to alternative responses to the politics of globalization. These include: internationalist strategies focusing on the creation of alternative political, financial and legal global institutions which can form a democratic counterweight to the power of transnational capital; the creation of multilateral and bilateral social charters specifying minimum standards of living and standards of social service provision; and the creation of the conditions for an "upward" rather than "downward" harmonization in which wages and working conditions are raised toward the living standards of workers in more prosperous economies, rather than in the opposite direction.

The backdrop to the SSR is government preoccupation and dissatisfaction with sluggish labour market adaptation to the changes that have swept the Canadian and global economies. Noting this, Jim Stanford (Chapter 9) explores some of the theoretical and empirical dimensions of flexibility-enhancing labour market and social policy proposals. Arguing that Canada's labour market has actually become hyper-flexible (reflected in increasing employment volatility, weakening job tenure security and the expansion of non-standard work arrangements), Stanford points out that the rate of total job turnover in Canada (jobs created and destroyed as a share of total employment) was among the highest of all industrialized economies during the last recession. In addition, fully one-half of the new jobs created in Canada during the 1980s were non-standard (i.e., part-time, part-year or multiple job holding). At the same time, a polarization of the labour market between those who cannot find enough hours of work and those who are working too many (reflected in an increase in overtime hours worked by full-time employees) has developed. Contrary to popular belief, not only is Canada's labour market more flexible than that of the U.S., but this pattern is intensifying.

In light of these trends, Stanford underlines the significance of the focus in the current social policy reform exercise on scaling back U.I. and other "passive" income support programs. As he points out, these programs are under threat because they have been instrumental in assisting Canadian labour in retaining bargaining power, despite the integration of Canada into a global economy. Scaling back income support programs, and other labour market deregulation initiatives, is part of a broader strategy to harmonize Canada's labour market outcomes with those of its trading partners. Intended to enhance the international competitiveness of Canada's economy on a low wage basis, the reforms aim to deliberately increase the economic insecurity facing Canadian workers, in order to moderate their wage demands and discipline their behaviour in the workplace. Rather than an increase in real flexibility or a reduction in unemployment, however, these pressures will be reflected in a marked decline in the wages of *employed* persons. Stanford concludes by arguing that even with the current system of U.I., Canadian workers are not very secure. Therefore, a more effective set of income security policies is required to address the poor level of labour market demand. Government must proactively focus on job creation initiatives, in addition to providing decent income security for intervening periods of unemployment.

In the tenth and last chapter of this section, Grant Schellenberg examines the effect of employment restructuring on retirement and labour force exit. A number of important trends are noted: unemployment rates among older workers are at their highest point since the Second World War; over the same time period, the exit of workers from the labour force at younger ages is a striking economic trend; and in the 1990s, for the first time, an increase in labour force exit now appears to be occurring among men in the forty-five to fifty-four year old range. Given that the range of socio-economic inequality in Canadian society is reflected in patterns of labour force exit, for some, early retirement is a welcome and secure prospect. For others, however, retirement is simply a disguised form of joblessness. Many recent labour force leavers are displaced workers, and among those aged fifty-five to sixty-four years, approximately one-quarter left their last job because of lay-off or job loss. One result of these changes is that unemployment has become a pathway leading from the labour market into "retirement."

These trends, eroding the economic security that older workers derive from the labour market, will place greater pressure on public income security programs precisely at a time when the latter are being scaled back. Schellenberg considers the implications of this for the reform of the Canada/Québec Pension Plans (C/QPP), and other income security programs for the elderly (e.g., Old Age Security (OAS), the Guaranteed Income Supplement (GIS), and the Spouse's Allowance (SPA)) which will soon top the federal government's social policy review agenda. A number of proposals are evaluated. These include proposals to raise or lower the age of public pension eligibility, and whether the OAS, GIS and SPA should be rolled together into a single income-tested benefit designed to assist low and moderate income Canadians aged sixty and over (a "super-GIS"). Given that the retirement transition is being transformed along a number of dimensions, Schellenberg argues that it is necessary to rethink our traditional views of retirement as a clearly demarcated and discrete event. Instead, he explores the idea of "partial retirement": rather than an abrupt end to paid employment, retirement could be reshaped to allow a gradual or partial withdrawal from paid employment.

The concept of workfare is becoming increasingly popular in Canada. And with the advent of the CHST (specifically the demise of the CAP), the door is opened for further moves in this direction. In Part 4, *Workfare, Training, Education and Social Security Reform*, the first three contributors consider the dynamics behind the introduction and reinforcement of the use of work incentives and workfare programs. Graham Riches (Chapter 11) argues that, given that Canada is not alone in responding to issues of high unemployment, labour market restructuring and social security reform in response to global economic pressures, the opportunity to learn from overseas experience should not be lost. Like Wiseman, he also looks to Australia, seeking to draw lessons for the Canadian welfare reform agenda by examining the proposals for labour market and social security reform, with particular reference to unemployment, announced in the Australian government's White Paper *Working Nation*.

Riches asks the question why, despite the many similarities between the welfare reform agendas of both countries, the possibility for progressive reform seems more likely in Australia than in Canada today. In both countries, deficit reduction, economic growth, international competitiveness and private sector job creation are the backdrop against which work incentives and workfare are being re-introduced and reinforced. The difference is that welfare reform Down Under has been introduced by an avowedly Labour government, one which is seeking political rejuvenation after a decade of pursuing an agenda entirely driven by the pressure toward global structural adjustment. In addition, reforms in Australia are about recasting its sense of national identity. Importantly, the response to managing long-term structural unemployment is very different. Riches therefore suggests that Canada could learn a few lessons from Australia. First, there are a number of commitments and policy proposals which, with qualification, merit consideration. Second, in Australia the debate about citizenship, full employment and an alternative economic agenda appears to have greater public legitimacy.

The key elements of the Australian reform package which merit further debate are the focus on chronic and structural unemployment and the idea of guaranteed work and training through the "Job Compact" (e.g., the guarantee of a job for six to twelve months). He argues that although it is informed by the workfare principle, the commitment to a real job for up to twelve months is a significant opportunity for those out of work. This policy demonstrates that the Commonwealth government is willing to invest the necessary public funds to create jobs either directly or through the private sector, and recognition of the fact that no amount of labour market and social security reform will work if jobs are not created. Even so, despite the Australian government's concern not to leave the jobless behind, the White Paper, like its Canadian counterpart, contains no specific commitment to full employment (instead there is a target unemployment rate of 5 percent by the year 2000). Riches concludes by arguing that what is absent, but needed, in both countries is not simply a full employment strategy, but one where work, remuneration and the distribution of work are redefined.

In Chapter 12, William Low considers two voluntary programs (the Enhanced Earnings Exemption program and the Self-Sufficiency Project) in British Columbia that target single parents with incentives to move off welfare and into work in order to demonstrate the pointlessness of compulsory workfare. Compulsory workfare assumes that welfare recipients do not want to work. The evidence from these two voluntary programs suggests otherwise. However, although there is no question that single parents respond to financial (and restrictive) incentives, there is little evidence that long-term "independence" from welfare, the goal of these programs, results.

Low argues that both programs are likely to fall far short of their ultimate goal because they assume an unrestricted "job ladder" in which low paid, part-time work leads to well paid full-time work. Projects such as these ignore elements of the transition from welfare to work which go beyond individual choice: the nature of the job market and the "social infrastructure" needed to support families. It is assumed that there is ample opportunity for upward mobility, but many social assistance recipients are in "casual jobs" which may or may not lead to "bad jobs," but rarely lead to "good jobs." Using the analogy of the game "Snakes and Ladders," he argues that workfare is likely to increase the "snakes" that the working poor encounter in the labour market without increasing the number of "ladders."

"NB Works" is another program designed to promote independence or "self-sufficiency" among social assistance recipients. In Chapter 13, Joan McFarland and Bob Mullaly describe this national demonstration project mounted in New Brunswick, a province that has one of the highest unemployment, but lowest welfare rates, in the country. This project is intended to help participants achieve skills/education, obtain work experience so that they can "achieve permanent labour force attachment," change their attitude towards social assistance (i.e., change their work ethic) and save social assistance dollars. Emphasizing the distinction between voluntary and mandatory workfare, they examine work incentive strategies along three continuums: voluntary/compulsory, rights/obligations and passive/active. NB Works is officially voluntary, active (by providing work and training) and based on the concept of opportunity rather than rights or obligations.

Reaching a conclusion similar to that drawn by Low, they argue that in a high unemployment, low wage economy, programs like NB Works cannot succeed. Not only are there too few jobs to go around but, if a job is found, parents (especially those with more than one child) cannot survive on the minimum wages they typically obtain. What these programs amount to is a "shuffling" of jobs, in which one set of unemployed take jobs away from another, rather than job creation. In their view, "the reality of NB Works is just as much about ideology, saving money and appearing to be doing something about cleaning up the welfare mess as it is about providing opportunities to welfare recipients." Their concern is that, while NB Works is not a yet a mandatory program, it would not take much to make it so. This fear is heightened by the introduction of the CHST and the orientation of the New Brunswick government which suggest a stronger likelihood of the implementation of mandatory workfare programs in the future.

Whereas the first three chapters in this section focus on the issue of training, work and unemployment, the last chapter (14) by Jonathan Greene considers the issue of post-secondary education and employment. It is projected that, in the future, one-half of all new jobs will require a post-secondary degree. Thus the proposed reform of funding for post-secondary education entailed in the SSR and the 1995 budget have far-reaching implications for the accessibility of university education and consequently, the distribution of employment opportunities. Greene argues that underlying the various options for reform is a fundamental change in thinking regarding post-secondary education: this entails a rejection of the commitment to collective provision of educational opportunity on the premise that the individual is the main beneficiary who should therefore assume more responsibility.

Implementation of the CHST is especially bad news for "have not" provinces, where the effect of reduced federal funding is disproportionate. Reduced funding to provinces dashes any hopes of maintaining comparable standards across the provinces regarding quality and tuition fee levels. This has heretofore enabled greater parity in access to post-secondary education for those with low incomes. Despite the fact that disparities in access to post-secondary education remain, increasing tuition fees (an inevitable consequence of any of the options considered) would undo the little progress achieved in the past few decades and, furthermore, would do nothing to change the disparities that currently exist.

In Part 5, *Women and the Social Security Review*, the contributors examine the SSR in terms of its potential impact on women and the programs and services upon which they most rely. Although the official documents and process of the SSR failed to consider (or take seriously the issue of) the gender effects of the proposed reforms, the contributors underscore the differential impact they will have on women in the areas of employment development services, unemployment/employment insurance, child care, learning and the CAP/CHST.

In Chapter 15, Therese Jennissen argues that the federal government has undermined its commitment to advancing women's equality by ignoring gender differences in the way it structured the framework for the debates over the future of social security. In choosing to focus on non-gendered categories (e.g., "the family," "the household," "the labour force," "children living in poverty," "youth" and "unemployed and underemployed adults"), the government does not acknowledge the unique status of women within these categories. Five social policy areas in the SSR are deemed to be of particular relevance for women in general and to specific groups of marginalized women, including women with disabilities, Aboriginal women, older women and impoverished women. These are employment development services, unemployment/employment insurance, child care, learning and the CAP/CHST.

Jennissen argues that the failure to incorporate a gender analysis is all the more disturbing given the fact that this issue was repeatedly raised as a central concern by women's organizations, anti-poverty groups and some labour unions. Although the final report of the Standing Committee of Human Resources Development noted the importance of gender sensitivity in policy discussions, it is not incorporated into any analysis. Once again, the work of analyzing social policy from a gender-sensitive framework is left to women and women's organizations. But now, this is occurring at a time when groups that have traditionally provided research and advocacy functions on women's issues have had their funding eliminated or have been disbanded entirely. Jennissen concludes by arguing that what is required is the creation of standard, gender-sensitive methodologies for policy analysis and development (following the example of organizations such as the International Labour Organisation), and greater active participation of women in the process of policy-making.

One of the central preoccupations of the SSR is reform of U.I. In Chapter 16, Leah Vosko examines the implications for women of proposed changes to U.I. She argues that U.I. reforms today are not only rooted in, but are fortifying, post-war distinctions between *regular* and *irregular* workers. Embedded in the various options for U.I. reform are specific recommendations regarding experience-ratings, life-long employment measures and how to distinguish frequent claimants (i.e., *irregular* workers) from occasional claimants (i.e., *regular* workers). Although women have become full social citizens of Canada's liberal welfare state, a growing number of Canadian women are becoming *irregular* workers (for example, in 1993, 60 percent of new jobs created were non-standard—temporary, part-time, part-year or contingent work—the majority of which went to women). Through this process and U.I. reforms, women are being transformed into *new* involuntary social exiles in the sense that the basis of their status as exiles has changed from one of "natural" or "innate" exclusion (predicated on their role as mothers/housewives), which prevailed in the earlier part of the post Second World War period, to exclusion based on their status as workers.

Vosko points out the irony of the image of the *regular* worker underpinning U.I. reform today: reinforcement of this image occurs precisely at a time when its elusiveness is intensifying. U.I. reforms actively construct an image of the "ideal" worker, unattainable for most women workers, implying that full-time continuous employment is readily available. Irregular work, then, is construed as an activity engaged in by choice rather than by necessity. Yet the reality is that employment restructuring, reflected in the collapse of the opportunity structure for full-time work, makes *irregular* work increasingly the only "choice."

In the 1993 federal election campaign, the Liberals and the New Democrats identified the importance of child care in supporting both parental employment and job creation: this was the first time an election campaign placed child care within an economic context. The Liberals election document, the Red Book, also pledged *new*, cumulative expenditures for child care. As Friendly and Oloman (Chapter 17) point out, the SSR discussion paper, *Agenda: Jobs and Growth*, was also a federal "first" in identifying child care as central to working/employment, learning and security. It appeared, then, that the SSR would reinforce the importance of, and commitment to, child care that emerged during this election campaign. Optimism among the child care lobby was buoyed.

The legacy of the Mulroney era, particularly since 1988, had worsened considerably the child care situation in much of Canada. The child care lobby was hopeful that, through the SSR, a national child care policy would transpire. But their optimism was short-lived. The ensuing budget made no mention of child care. More importantly, it is argued that implementation of the CHST through this budget will not only entrench child care as a purely regional program but also it will erode the fragile network of services that evolved throughout the 1980s and 1990s. If provinces are forced to impose deep cuts to the more established programs, such as welfare, post-secondary education and health, child care, which is not well established and where wide provincial variations prevail, will likely be demoted further on the list of provincial priorities. Friendly and Oloman conclude by proposing alternative ways child care might be placed back on the agenda, and funds allocated toward it. They also suggest that, in order to ensure a secure a place on the social policy agenda for child care, it should be treated as an issue of children's well-being and development, rather than as an issue pertaining to welfare, women, parental employability or business expenses.

In Part 6, *Citizenship, Advocacy and Social Security Reform*, the contributors reflect on the achievements and limitations of the welfare state in Canada in the post-Second World War period focusing on the role played by "popular sector" groups (e.g., labour, women's groups and the disabled). In the face of global economic pressures, old strategies no longer work and new ones must be forged. This is deemed to be particularly important in order to safeguard against the attack on newly formed and emerging equality rights, especially the principle of equality of condition or outcome (substantive equality), which are, arguably, the most important achievements of the welfare state in this period.

What are the prospects for achieving greater social justice in the face of global economic and political pressures dictating national social policy agendas? This is the question posed by Diana Ralph (Chapter 18) as she assesses popular sector struggles in the past twenty years and proposes strategies which could be more effective now and for the long haul. Ralph argues that, until the mid-1970s, the Canadian working class was more organized and in a relatively stronger position in relation to the state than was the business class. Despite the fact that the KWS represented a concession to business interests, welfare state gains in this period also represented "real victories for the mass of Canadian people." But in 1976, with the formation of the Business Council on National Issues (BCNI), the tables were reversed. Canadian business interests became organized, capturing the strategic initiative in the area of social policy. The goal of the BCNI (the "shadow government") is to bring structural adjustment to Canada, removing the buffer that social programs provide in order to lower wage demands. To this end, the North American Free Trade Agreement (NAFTA) was necessary to consolidate gains achieved by the BCNI.

Now capital, rather than workers, is driving revolutions. NAFTA, transnational corporations (TNCS), speculative currency manipulations and corporate pull-outs have undermined the ability of politicians to represent citizens. Therefore, she argues, we cannot expect governments to fix things. However, even though the ground rules have changed, popular sector groups and labour are still trying to operate under the old rules. This places them in a reactive and defensive position. The SSR is presented as a classic example of this, where business has refined the tactic of turning the popular sector's tendency to respond reactively against itself. In the SSR, the government/business set the terms of the debate, forcing people to react to this rather than set their own agenda. Ralph argues, however, that an "effective people's strategy" must be devised, one that targets corporations (e.g., banks and TNCS) which are the real cause of our problems. Corporations are vulnerable to consumer and labour actions and must be targeted. Concluding with a number of concrete suggestions as to where to go from here, Ralph stresses, among other things, the importance of rebuilding a membership base, including the unemployed; forging solidarity linkages with resistance movements in Central and South America; and severing dependence on government funding ("aid") to facilitate solidarity with Third World countries ("mutual solidarity").

In Chapter 19, Gloria Geller and Jan Joel also reflect on the implications of globalization for popular sector groups (women's groups being in the forefront) who are struggling to be heard. They argue that the domestic political process is becoming increasingly irrelevant to the "national interest," which itself is defined by the interests of international finance capital. No longer are governments responsible to the electorate, but to "international money lenders and the bond raters." While the KWS was about socializing the costs of reproduction (in part to stem the upward pressure on wages, especially for the low paid), today the demise of the welfare state is about reprivatizing the costs of reproduction. In an era of global capital, the costs of reproducing labour are easily avoided, therefore capital is less dependent on the state for this function. Women and children are especially threatened by this because increasing responsibilities fall to the "family" and the "community."

Geller and Joel argue, however, that fundamentally, the attack on the welfare state is not so much an attack on women *per se*, but an attack on the principle of "equality," specifically "equality of condition." This latter principle is one which women have been instrumental in advocating. As such, and despite appearances to the contrary, (e.g., the current obsession with the deficit, flexibility and competitiveness, etc.) the attack on the welfare state is driven by politics, not economics. But the language of economic imperatives serves particular political interests in delegitimizing alternative political, cultural and moral claims. In light of this, they ask, how do popular sector groups reclaim alternative political agendas?

They argue that the opportunity exists for popular sector groups to create a new, more inclusive concept of citizenship, one which challenges the privileging of "economic man" as the model individual market-citizen. This new concept should be formed within a vision of collective action and participation (e.g., an alternative economic framework through community economic development (CED)). Pointing to women's CED as a possible model, they suggest that this small scale, community based approach has the potential to translate to a wider scale. This is important because while working at the grassroots level is critical, it is insufficient. Given the overriding legitimacy accorded fiscal constraints in informing social policy reform, popular sector groups will have to work at a number of levels simultaneously—locally, provincially and internationally.

Many argue that Canada's welfare state never developed beyond its Poor Law roots, remaining residualist even in the period of KWS expansion. In this context, do the current reforms mean anything? Are they of any consequence? Raising these questions, Michael Bach and Marcia Rioux (Chapter 20) argue that the current reforms will have a significant and detrimental effect. By examining the impact of the CHST on persons with disabilities, they maintain that the current reforms underline the extent to which the welfare state in the post-war period had moved beyond simple residualist functions to incorporate a framework of human rights. This framework challenged the worthy/unworthy poor distinction that underpins the residualist/Poor Law-inspired welfare state. While the worthy/unworthy poor distinction is typically analyzed from the perspective of those considered to be "unworthy," the assumption being that this designation is the most injurious, Bach and Rioux critique the distinction from the perspective of those typically deemed to be "worthy"—the disabled. With respect to the disabled, the KWS was never "residualist" (though it was, perhaps, minimalist). Rather, the cost of being designated the "worthy poor" was exclusion, socially, politically and economically. Welfare for the disabled entailed enforced dependency, denial of basic citizenship rights and no self-determinacy.

But in the 1960s, this exclusion began to be challenged. In response, a new foundation of rights was forged. This entailed international and national human rights legislation establishing constitutional equality rights. Key elements of this new framework are principles of self-determination (enabling a commitment to respect differences), democratization (participation in decision-making, greater representation and voice) and equality (substantive versus formal). Implementation of the CHST and ending of conditionality places these newly found and emerging rights under threat. The federal government played a key role in facilitating the social and economic inclusion of disabled persons. Bach and Rioux express particular concern about the devolution of responsibilities to lower levels of government (regionalization and decentralization). They argue that, as decisions take place at more localized levels, the levers of accountability become more dispersed and difficult to lobby, threatening greater democratization.

The concluding chapter and section of the book (Part 7) suggests that the social security review and the agenda for change has been one-sided in a number of key ways. The focus on social spending and its impact on the deficit is very restricted. The area of foregone revenue resulting from tax expenditures in the corporate and personal tax systems is virtually ignored. In addition, much of the rationale behind the SSR was driven by fiscal and market imperatives, while the importance of protecting people in need seems to have been forgotten. It is our intent that the issues addressed throughout this book will help raise corners of the debate that have been either overlooked or inadequately addressed in the social security review. In our view, the social security changes that are required can best be determined and shaped by the needs of people and communities. For this to happen their voices have to be heard and brought to the forefront of the review of Canada's social programs.

## NOTES

1. In a recent review of a decade of "Macdonaldism" Andrew Coyne (1995: D3) notes that major recommendations such as privatization of Crown corporations, transport and communication deregulation, support for free trade, the elimination of the national energy policy and the deregulation of foreign takeovers of Canadian firms now have "bipartisan support" from Conservatives and Liberals alike. Coyne also suggests that even "the general direction of federal social policy has been clearly in line with the commission's desire for greater simplicity, closer targeting of those in need and restoration of work incentives."

2. A list of these supplementary papers appears in the reference section of Therese Jennissen's paper included in this volume.

3. The trends examined in this discussion are taken mainly from *A New Framework for Economic Policy* (Department of Finance 1994a), *Creating A Healthy Fiscal Climate* (Department of Finance 1994b), *Improving Social Security in Canada* (HRDC 1994), *Creating Opportunity . . . Through Social Security Reform* (House of Commons 1994b), and a number of the supplementary papers published for the social security review.

4. The concepts of "neoconservatism" and "neoliberalism" are used interchangeably as their economic prescriptions for economic growth, debt control, productivity and free trade, as noted in this paragraph, are essentially the same (see Coyne 1995: D3).

5. The new HRIF will offer greater scope for training which in itself is positive if there are enough jobs around to be found. The problem is that the demand for labour is increasingly falling far below the number of workers seeking employment. There are not enough jobs to parcel out, no matter what the level of training and skills of unemployed workers. This emphasis on training and updating the skills of the unemployed, while they are sound objectives, has the potential to individualize what is essentially a structural problem. People remain unemployed because there are not enough jobs.

6. Equalization payments started in 1957. These are calculated from a formula based on thirty-three separate revenue sources. This formula compares the ability of provinces to raise money according to the average standard of five provinces: British Columbia, Saskatchewan, Manitoba, Ontario and Quebec. Only provinces falling below the average standard for a particular year receive equalization payments (Taylor 1995: A19). These funds are geared to benefit lower income provinces and from 1995-96 to 1996-97 are scheduled to grow from $8.5 billion to $9.3 billion (Department of

Finance 1995a: 33). Equalization payments are not included in this discussion as they are separate from federal transfers that are earmarked specifically for social programs.

7. For further details of EPF funding and the changes that have been introduced to save federal expenditures, see Table 1, "Summary of federal-provincial programs and initiatives for post-secondary education," in Jonathan Sydney Greene's paper included in this volume.

8. In the 1990 Conservative federal budget a "cap on CAP" was introduced. This changed the cost sharing formula for the three wealthiest provinces, British Columbia, Ontario and Alberta. The cap meant that Ottawa would not cover CAP costs for welfare and social services that exceed a 5 percent increase a year in these provinces.

9. There is some debate and disagreement concerning this interpretation (see Yves Vaillancourt's paper in this volume).

10. As the recent premiers' conference (August 1995) underscores, provincial leaders are already challenging the federal government's role in enforcing national standards. In a communique released at the conclusion of this conference, they declared it "unacceptable," on the one hand, for the federal government to impose national standards on provinces, and on the other, to cut funding to provinces (Mark Kennedy, *Ottawa Citizen*, reported in the *Vancouver Sun*. "Budget ended federal role in social policy" August 28, 1995: A3).

11. That federal fiscal clout is the only thing standing in the way of provinces allowing extra-billing and charges (e.g., Alberta's private clinic facility fees) was driven home in the summer of 1995 when Diane Marleau, the federal Health Minister, agreed to discuss with her provincial counterparts how medicare should be defined (i.e., which services should be publicly insured and which should not). Also, at the premier's meeting (August 1995), consensus appears to have been reached that medicare be confined to "basic" health services to be outlined in a list (Mark Kennedy, *Ottawa Citizen*, reported in the *Vancouver Sun*. "Budget ended federal role in social policy" August 28, 1995: A3).

## REFERENCES

Battle, Ken. 1993. "The Squeeze on Social Spending." *Caledon Commentary* Ottawa: Caledon Institute of Social Policy. (June): 1-3.

——— and Sherri Torjman. 1996. "Desperately Seeking Substance: A Commentary on the Social Security Review." In J. Pulkingham and G. Ternowetsky (eds.), *Remaking Canadian Social Policy: Staking Claims and Forging Change*. Halifax: Fernwood.

———. 1993. "Federal Social Programs: Setting the Record Straight." *Caledon Commentary* Ottawa: Caledon Institute of Social Policy.

Clarke, Tony. 1995. "Harmonizing Canada's Social Policies—Through Fortress America." *Canadian Review of Social Policy/Revue canadienne de politique sociale* 35 (Spring): 82-83.

Courchene, Thomas J. 1987. *Social Policy in the 1990s: Agenda for Reform*. Scarborough: Prentice-Hall.

Coyne, Andrew. 1995. "NAFTA Blueprint: A Decade of Macdonaldism." *Globe and Mail* September 9: D3.

Department of Finance. 1995a. *Budget Speech*. Ottawa: Minister of Supply and Services.

———. 1995b. *Budget 1995*. Ottawa: Minister of Supply and Services.

———. 1994a. *Agenda: Jobs and Growth. A New Framework for Economic Policy*. Ottawa: Department of Finance.

———. 1994b. *Agenda: Jobs and Growth. Creating a Healthy Fiscal Climate: The Economic and Fiscal Update*. Ottawa: Department of Finance.

———. 1985. *Account of the Cost of Selective Tax Measures*. Ottawa: Minister of Supply and Services.

———. 1984. *A New Direction for Canada: An Agenda for Economic Renewal*. Ottawa: Department of Finance.

Eadie, A. 1989. "Corporate Profits up 59% in '88." *Globe and Mail* February 20: B1-B2.

Economic Council of Canada. 1989. *Legacies: Twenty Sixth Annual Review*. Ottawa: Minister of Supply and Services.

Forget, C. et al. 1986. *Commission of Inquiry on Unemployment Insurance*. Ottawa: Minister of Supply and Services.

Greene, Jonathan Sydney. 1996. "Hedging Your Debts: An Analysis of the Federal Government Proposals on Higher Education in Canada." In J. Pulkingham and G. Ternowetsky (eds.), *Remaking Canadian Social Policy: Staking Claims and Forging Change*. Halifax: Fernwood Publishing.

Greenspon, Edward. 1995. "Social Cuts Deep; Old-age Review Next." *Globe and Mail* February 28: A1, A8.

———— and Susan Delacourt. 1995. "Liberals Lay Groundwork for U.I. Overhaul." *Globe and Mail* August 10: A1, A6.

Hansard. 1994. *The Budget*. Commons Debates. February 22: 1708-16.

House of Commons. 1995. *Security, Opportunities and Fairness: Canadians Renewing Their Social Programs*. Ottawa: Queen's Printer.

————. 1994a. "Speech from the Throne." Ottawa. January 18.

————. 1994b. "Creating Opportunity . . . Through Social Security Reform." Ottawa. January 31.

————. 1994c. "Why Social Security Reform?: Backgrounder #1. Notes for an Address. Ottawa. January 31.

Human Resources Development Canada. 1994. *Agenda: Jobs and Growth. Improving Social Security in Canada. A Discussion Paper*. Ottawa: Minister of Supply and Services.

Jennissen, Therese. 1996a. "Chronology of the Federal Social Security Review: Process and Related Events (December 1993—June 1995)." In J. Pulkingham and G. Ternowetsky (eds.), *Remaking Canadian Social Policy: Staking Claims and Forging Change*. Halifax: Fernwood.

————. 1996b. "The Federal Social Security Review: A Gender-Sensitive Perspective." In J. Pulkingham and G. Ternowetsky (eds.), *Remaking Canadian Social Policy: Staking Claims and Forging Change*. Halifax: Fernwood.

Johnson, Andrew F., Stephen McBride and Patrick Smith. 1994. *Continuities and Discontinuities: The Political Economy of Social Welfare and Labour Market Policy in Canada*. Toronto: University of Toronto Press.

Kennedy, Mark. 1995. "Budget Ended Federal Role in Social Policy." *Vancouver Sun* August 28: A3.

Kerans, Patrick. 1994. "Universality, Full Employment and Well-Being. The Future of the Canadian Welfare State." *Canadian Review of Social Policy/Revue canadienne de politique sociale*. 34 (Winter): 119-35.

Leblanc, Francis. 1994. "Concerns and Priorities Regarding the Modernization and Restructuring of Canada's Social Security System." *Interim Report of The Standing Committee on Human Resources Development*. Ottawa: Queen's Printer.

Manning, Lorelee. 1995. "The Future of Social Security." *N.E.T.W.O.R.K. of Saskatchewan Women* 9 (3): 20-22.

McBride, Stephen and John Shields. 1993. *Dismantling a Nation: Canada and the New World Order*. Halifax: Fernwood.

McQuaig, Linda. 1992. *The Quick and the Dead*. Toronto: Penguin Books.

Minister of Supply and Services. 1985. *Macdonald Royal Commission on Economic Union and Development Prospects for Canada*. Ottawa: Minister of Supply and Services.

Mimoto, H. and P. Cross. 1991. "The Growth of the Federal Debt." *Canadian Economic Observer* 3 (June): 10-17.

Mishra, Ramesh. 1990. *The Welfare State in Capitalist Society: Policies of Retrenchment and Maintenance in Europe, North America and Australia*. Toronto: University of Toronto Press.

Morton, Bonnie. 1995. "Development or Reform ????" *N.E.T.W.O.R.K. of Saskatchewan Women* 9 (3): 5-8.

Mullaly, Robert. 1993. *Structural Social Work: Ideology, Theory, and Practice*. Toronto: McClelland and Stewart.

National Council of Welfare (NCW). 1995. *The 1995 Budget and Block Funding*. Ottawa: Minister of Supply and Services.

———. 1994. *A Blueprint for Social Security Reform*. Ottawa: Minister of Supply and Services.

———. 1990. *Welfare Incomes 1989*. Ottawa: Minister of Supply and Services.

National Anti-Poverty Organization (NAPO). 1995a. *What Bill C-76 Means for Social Assistance*. March: 1-2.

———. 1995b. "U.I. Cuts Could Return Us to the '30s." *The Long Haul* 2, (5): 1-12.

Oderkirk, Jillian. 1992. "Food Banks." *Canadian Social Trends* 4 (Spring): 6-14.

Picot, G., J. Myles and T. Wannell. 1990. "Good Jobs, Bad Jobs and The Declining Middle: 1967-1986. Statistics Canada Analytical Studies Branch, Research Paper Series.

Pulkingham, Jane. 1995. "Remaking the Social Divisions of Welfare: Gender, 'Dependency' and Social Security Reform." Paper presented at the 30th Annual Meeting of the Canadian Sociology and Anthropology Association, University of Québec at Montreal, June 7: 1-17.

Riches, G. 1986. *Food Banks and the Welfare Crisis*. Ottawa: Canadian Council on Social Development.

Sherraden, M. 1985. "Chronic Unemployment in the United States: Implications for Social Work." Paper Presented at the Unemployment and Its Implications for Social Work Conference. Stockholm, Sweden.

Statistics Canada. 1994. *Historical Labour Force Statistics*. Catalogue No. 71-201 Ottawa: Statistics Canada.

Taylor, Alastair M. 1995. "Quebec and the Equalization Program." *Globe and Mail* July 13: A19.

Ternowetsky, Gordon. 1994. "Hunger in Regina: Where Do We Go From Here?" *Canadian Review of Social Policy/Revue canadienne de politique sociale* 34 (Winter): 100-10.

Torjman, Sherri.1993. "The Health and Welfare of Social Programs. *Caledon Commentary* Ottawa: Caledon Institute of Social Policy. (July): 1-3.

——— and Ken Battle. 1993. "Breaking Down the Welfare Wall." *Caledon Commentary* Ottawa: Caledon Institute of Social Policy. (June): 1-3.

Vaillancourt, Yves. 1996. "Remaking Canadian Social Policy: A Québec Viewpoint." In J. Pulkingham and G. Ternowetsky (eds.), *Remaking Canadian Social Policy: Staking Claims and Forging Change*. Halifax: Fernwood Publishing.

Watkins, Mel. 1992. *Madness and Ruin: Politics and the Economy in the Neo-Conservative Age*. Toronto: Between the Lines.

Wong, F. 1987. "A Review of Employment and Earnings Data, 1983-1986." *The Labour Force* Catalogue No. 70-001. Ottawa: Statistics Canada. (August): 87-113.

# CHAPTER 2

# THE FEDERAL SOCIAL SECURITY REVIEW, PROCESS AND RELATED EVENTS (DECEMBER 1993-JUNE 1995): A CHRONOLOGY

*Therese Jennissen*

**1993**

December 8-9    "Canadian Paper on New Orientations for Social Policy"—presented by the Minister of Health and Welfare, Benoît Bouchard, at the meeting of the Employment, Labour and Social Affairs Committee at the Ministerial Level on social policy, OECD. This paper formed the basis of the "phantom white paper" of the former federal Conservative government, and bears a striking resemblance to the framework of the current Liberal social security review.

**1994**

January 18    In the Speech from the Throne, the Governor General announced that a review of social security was on the government's agenda for the coming year.

January 31    Human Resources Development Canada Minister Lloyd Axworthy made a motion (seconded by Finance Minister Paul Martin) "That the Standing Committee on Human Resources Development Canada be directed to consult broadly, to analyze and to make recommendations regarding the modernization and restructuring of Canada's social security system, with particular reference to the needs of families with children, youth and working age adults . . . . " The Standing Committee consisted of representatives from the Liberal, Bloc Québecois and Reform parties. The chair of the committee was Francis LeBlanc; Francine Lalonde and Maria Minna were vice-chairs.

February 8    Social security review was referred to the Standing Committee of Human Resources Development Canada.

February 17    A Ministerial Task Force was assembled to advise Minister Axworthy personally on social reform. Team members included: Ken Battle, John Fryer, Patrick Johnston, Arthur Kroeger, Aldéa Landry, Judith Maxwell, Lorna Marsden, Alice Nakamura, John Daniel O'Leary, Guylaine Saucier, Brian Steck, Joseph Stern, Michel Vennat, David Zussman.

February    *A Study on the Modernization and Restructuring of Canada's Social Security System: A Focus Paper* was made available to members of the public who wanted to appear before the Standing Committee on Human Resources Development Canada (HRDC).

February 21-25    Public hearings were held before the Standing Committee on HRDC.

March 7-11    Public hearings were held before the Standing Committee on HRDC.

| | |
|---|---|
| March 9 | Last day for written submissions to the Standing Committee on HRDC; over 200 submissions were received. |
| March 25 | Interim Report of the Standing Committee on HRDC (*Concerns and Priorities Regarding the Modernization and Restructuring of Canada's Social Security System*) was tabled in Parliament. |
| May/94-Jan./95 | Second round of public hearings before the Standing Committee on HRDC. |
| October | *Have your say. . . in changing Canada's social programs: information and questions on social security;* this was a workbook (produced by HRDC) aimed at getting input from the public. |
| October | Department of Finance produced an update on the state of economy in Canada and the state of government finances in the document *Creating a Healthy Fiscal Climate.* |
| October 5 | *Improving Social Security in Canada: A Discussion Paper* (produced by HRDC) was tabled in the House of Commons. This becomes the main discussion paper of the SSR. It has variously been called the Green Paper, the discussion paper, the discussion document. |
| October 17 | Finance Minister Paul Martin tabled a document, *A New Framework for Economic Policy*, proposing a framework for economic growth. |
| Oct. 17- Dec. 5 | Standing Committee on Finance held pre-budget consultations with the public. Chaired by Jim Peterson. |
| Oct./94-Dec./95 | The federal government released eight supplementary papers providing more information for the debates on the SSR. The papers included: *Persons with Disabilities: A Supplementary Paper*—October 1994 *From Unemployment Insurance to Employment Insurance: A Supplementary Paper*—October 1994 *Income Security for Children: A Supplementary Paper*—October 1994 *Child Care and Development: A Supplementary Paper*—October 1994 *Reforming the Canada Assistance Plan: A Supplementary Paper*—December 1994 *Employment Development Services: A Supplementary Paper*—December 1994 *The Context of Reform: A Supplementary Paper*—December 1994 *Federal Support to Post-Secondary Education: A Supplementary Paper*—January 1995 |
| December 5 | Members of the Standing Committee on HRDC met with the National Consultation of Women's Groups organized by the National Action Committee on the Status of Women and attended by over eighty women's groups. |
| December 5 | 10th Report of the Standing Committee on Finance reported to the House of Commons—*Confronting Canada's Deficit Crisis: Building Our Next Budget through Consultation.* |

**1995**

| | |
|---|---|
| February 6 | Final Report of the Standing Committee on Human Resources Development was tabled in the House of Commons. The paper is called *Security,* |

|  | *Opportunities and Fairness: Canadians renewing their social programs.* |
|---|---|
| February 27 | The budget speech was read in the House of Commons. |
| March 20 | First reading of Bill C-76—An Act to Implement Certain Provisions of the Budget tabled in Parliament on February 27, 1995 (short title is the Budget Implementation Act, 1995). |
| March 30, 31, April, 3, 6, 26. | Bill C-76 debated at second reading. |
| April 26 | Bill C-76 referred to Standing Committee on Finance. |
| April - May | Witnesses appeared before the Standing Committee on Finance. |
| May 19 | Standing Committee on Finance tabled Report with amendments. |
| May 31 | Bill C-76 debated at report stage. |
| June 5 | Bill C-76 passed at report stage. |
| June 6 | Bill C-76 passed at third reading and sent to the Senate. |
| June 7 | Bill C-76 received first reading in the Senate. |
| June 14 | Bill C-76 received second reading and sent to Senate Committee on National Finance. |
| June 15 | Senate Committee on National Finance reported on Bill C-76 without amendments. |
| June 21 | Bill C-76 passed through third reading in the Senate. |
| June 22 | Bill C-76 received Royal Assent and was made law. |

# CHAPTER 3

# MAJOR DIRECTIONS AND PROPOSALS FOR REFORM FROM THE FEDERAL GOVERNMENT: A LISTING

*Melanie Hess*

The following is a condensed summary of key directions, proposals, options and ideas for the reform of federal social programs as put forward in the federal government's *Agenda: Jobs and Growth. Improving Social Security in Canada: A Discussion Paper* (the "Green Paper") (HRDC 1994a) and its various supplementary papers; the Report of the Standing Committee on Human Resources Development, *Security, Opportunities and Fairness: Canadians renewing their social programs* (the "LeBlanc Report") (House of Commons 1995); and the *Report of the Advisory Group on Working Time and the Distribution of Work* (HRDC 1994b).

## EMPLOYMENT DEVELOPMENT SERVICES (EDS)

### KEY DIRECTIONS, PROPOSALS, OPTIONS AND IDEAS FOR REFORM

Examples of services under EDS include the following: assessment, counselling, literacy programs, institutional and workplace training, job finding assistance, community development, wage subsidies and earning supplements.

"[R]enewed and strengthened set of employment development services capable of providing more highly structured and predictable assistance to the unemployed." [Green Paper]

Build a new model of employment development services based on "greater coordination of the activities of all partners within a flexible, locally-managed, community-based structure." [Green Paper]

Enhanced needs assessment and counselling to help tailor various employment development services to individual needs. [Green Paper]

Better labour market information—e.g., "electronic hiring hall," a computerized database that specifies employer job requirements and employee skills and credentials. Ottawa, in cooperation with provinces and other partners, should invest in better labour market information networks (e.g., information kiosks). [Green Paper, LeBlanc Report]

Enhance basic skills development by making training more accessible: use new technologies; offer basic skills training in the workplace, public housing, youth shelters, churches, community centres and other accessible community locations; recognize prior learning for transferability between literacy and training programs; and develop quality standards. [Green Paper]

More experimentation with varied training formats that include classroom and on-the-job training, computer-based and distance learning, and dual apprenticeships that combine classroom with workplace training. [Green Paper]

Greater role for the private sector, volunteer groups and labour in identifying and designing local training needs and the delivery of training services. [Green Paper, LeBlanc Report]

Government incentives to employers (especially small- and medium-sized businesses) to provide workplace training through tax credits, wage subsidies, direct cash assistance, paid educational leave, individual training accounts and work sharing arrangements. [Green Paper]

Governments should provide start-up funding to sector councils (representing employers and employees within an industry). The role of these councils is to: identify current and future training needs in their industry; establish occupational or skills standards; and develop industry-wide training programs (e.g., in cooperation with local colleges and universities). [Green Paper]

Ottawa should give provinces a larger role to include the following: strategic planning of federal employment programs and services; managing the purchase of institutional training; and taking the lead role in planning and establishing a network of "single window" offices to provide various federal and provincial social programs. [Green Paper, LeBlanc Report]

The federal government should continue to work with provinces and sector councils to ensure nationally recognized and portable training credentials. [LeBlanc Report]

To build a knowledge base through experiments and evaluations of new and different programs. [Green Paper]

Establish direct employment measures to (re)integrate people into labour force through earnings supplementation, self-employment assistance and community employment combining work with training. [Green Paper]

Management of employment development services that focus on results rather than by the book. [Green Paper]

Improve access to employment development services for persons with disabilities. This includes the following: update of the Vocational Rehabilitation of Disabled Persons Act to directly link it to employment development services; foster partnerships among employers, the disabled community and provinces to remove barriers and provide accessible workplaces, create flexible working conditions; develop appropriate training and proactive management policies for the disabled, as well as women, Aboriginal Canadians, minorities and welfare recipients. [LeBlanc Report, Green Paper]

## UNEMPLOYMENT INSURANCE
*KEY DIRECTIONS, PROPOSALS, OPTIONS AND IDEAS FOR REFORM*

*Direction A*: A new Employment Insurance program based on a two-tiered structure—"basic insurance" for occasional claimants, "adjustment insurance" for frequent claimants. [Green Paper]

Occasional claimants would get "basic insurance," which would operate along the lines of the present U.I. program regarding eligibility requirements and the level, duration and range of benefits. Basic insurance would continue to provide sickness, parental, maternity and adoption benefits. Depending on their particular needs and the resources available, basic insurance recipients would have access to individually tailored employment development services.

Frequent claimants, those with three or more claims in five years, would get "adjustment insurance" which would provide lower income benefits than basic insurance (possibly income-tested on an individual or family income basis), possibly for a longer duration. Adjustment insurance claimants would have expanded access to employment development services. Eligibility for income assistance could be made conditional on a claimant's willingness to participate in employment development programs or perform community service work.

*Direction B*: Maintain U.I. but further tighten the eligibility requirements and benefit duration which were initiated under the Conservatives and extended the Liberals' 1994 budget. [Green Paper]

Increase entrance requirements, linking benefits more closely to a claimant's length of work. This includes the following suggestions: raise the current twelve to twenty weeks requirement to fourteen to twenty weeks; drop the variable entrance requirement based on regional unemployment rates and replace this with a uniform minimum number of weeks worked; base eligibility on an employee's work history over two years, rather than the present one year, or some combination thereof (e.g., twenty-six weeks over two years); require new entrants to labour force to build up eligibility for U.I. over a longer period than the standard minimum qualifying period.

Reduce the level of benefits. Some options include: reducing earnings replacement from the present dual rate structure of 60 percent for low wage claimants with dependents/55 percent for the rest to a new dual rate of 55/50 percent; introduce a graduated benefit rate which decreases with each subsequent claim.

Reduce duration of benefits. This could include reducing or abolishing current features where claimants in higher unemployment regions get benefits for a longer time and shortening the current fifty weeks maximum duration of benefits.

Note that the LeBlanc Report, while generally supporting a reduction in U.I. benefits and/ or increase in eligibility requirements, argued that income support under U.I. should be available "through the entire working year, particularly for those seasonally unemployed."

*Direction C*: To consider, over longer term, the creation of a "working lifetime" U.I. in which entitlement would be based on the worker's lifelong labour market attachment. Workers would accumulate benefit entitlements throughout their working life and later use these "banked" credits for a longer or richer claim period or to finance retraining and skills upgrading. [LeBlanc Report]

## OTHER PROPOSALS

Expand U.I. coverage to nonstandard work. Provide full U.I. coverage (whether present system, Direction A, B C or any other model) to part-time, temporary, self-employed and multiple job holders who presently get reduced or no coverage. [Green Paper, LeBlanc Report]

Switch from basing benefits upon claimant's most recent weeks of work (which penalizes them if they accept work that lasts only a few days or that involves shorter days near the end of season), to their best paid weeks of work, and allow workers to combine days or hours into their week of work totals. [LeBlanc Report]

## FINANCING U.I. AND EMPLOYMENT DEVELOPMENT SERVICES

### KEY DIRECTIONS, PROPOSALS, OPTIONS AND IDEAS FOR REFORM

Adjust premiums during recessions in order to avoid substantial premium hikes during recessions (when payouts rise). Allow the U.I. fund to accumulate a substantial surplus during periods of economic growth that could provide a cushion when a recession hits. This would help to maintain premiums at a lower and relatively steady rate. [Green Paper, LeBlanc Report]

Require employers to pay U.I. premiums on their total payroll rather than the present relatively narrow base of insurable earnings. Premium rates for employers could fall. This would eliminate incentives for employers to create part-time jobs under fifteen hours a week to avoid paying U.I. premiums. It would also lessen the incentive for employers to pay overtime rather than create new jobs. [Green Paper]

Consider adjusting the balance in U.I. premiums paid by employees and employers (the latter currently pay 1.4 times as much as employees). [Green Paper]

Introduce an "experience rating" by levying higher premiums for frequent-claim employers or industries, and perhaps reducing premiums for employers which support training to certified standards. [Green Paper]

Pay for enhanced employment development services with savings from reformed U.I. How much of the U.I. savings should go to this purpose and how much to lowering U.I. premiums is still unanswered. [Green Paper, LeBlanc Report]. The LeBlanc Report opposed any further reduction in the premium rate, arguing that all savings from U.I. reform must be channeled into employment development services.

Pay for enhanced employment development services through savings from administrative simplifications gained through technological improvements. [Green Paper]

## WORKING TIME AND FLEXIBLE WORK ARRANGEMENTS

### KEY DIRECTIONS, PROPOSALS, OPTIONS AND IDEAS FOR REFORM

The federal government is assessing its own employment practices to provide greater opportunities for flexible work arrangements. [Green Paper]

The federal government will support the development and exchange of information on flexible work time and make it available to employers and unions across Canada. [Green Paper]

The federal government should provide for more flexible work arrangements and the redistribution of work in the public service to help workers balance family responsibilities and paid work, stimulate employment and set an example for the provinces and private sector employers. [LeBlanc Report]

The federal government should develop initiatives to measure unpaid work and estimate its economic value. [LeBlanc Report]

### ADVISORY GROUP ON WORKING TIME AND THE DISTRIBUTION OF WORK'S RECOMMENDATIONS

Employers, unions and employees should place greater emphasis on working-time issues and their implications in collective bargaining and workplace decision-making.

The Minister of Human Resources Development should begin a national dialogue on the report, and provincial ministers of labour should participate and/or conduct their own consultations.

*Work-time alternatives and innovations*: Governments, as largest employers, and their collective bargaining agents should support alternative and innovative workplace practices to reduce, reorganize and redistribute work time in the public service. Federal and provincial labour ministers should give priority to work-time issues and examine their own policies that would support new arrangements in the public and private sectors with the potential for creating additional jobs.

*Standard work week*: The legislated standard work week should be no longer than forty hours per week in any jurisdiction. Governments should periodically review the legislated standard work week to ensure that the standard changes with the normal full-time work week in their jurisdictions.

*Overtime*: Employees should have the right to refuse overtime work after the legislated standard work week of forty hours. This right should be incorporated into employment standards legislation. Employers and employees should use time off in lieu of overtime pay after the standard work week.

*Annual hours and time off in lieu of overtime*: The maximum amount of overtime in excess of regular working hours for which compensation can be paid should be set at one hundred hours annually. Overtime in excess of the one hundred hours should be compensated only on the basis of time-off in lieu of overtime, at the overtime rate. The hours of work coverage under employment standards legislation should be broadened to include salaried employees and other full-time workers who may now be excluded. Similar annual limits on overtime and the requirement for time-off in lieu of overtime pay beyond one hundred hours would apply to this group.

*The contingent workforce*: Employment standards must be vigorously enforced, especially for part-time workers and those outside the normal workplace. Non-standard workers require special attention to ensure they are: fully covered and protected under legislation; have access to collective bargaining rights; and receive at least the minimum hourly wage and other workplace benefits. A registry for all jurisdictions needs to be created to cover employees who work at home (employers would have to provide information on hours of work and pay, and the registry should include a mechanism for employees to sign up and verify the accuracy of the information about their hours of work and pay).

*Regular part-time workers*: Employers should be required to provide prorated benefits to regularly employed part-time employees.

*Retirement*: Phased-in retirement, under which older employees are encouraged to work reduced regular hours or take leaves of absence as a transition to retirement, should be more broadly used. Governments, employers, unions and employees should ensure that phased-in retirement does not substantially reduce future pension benefits.

*Family leave*: Employment standards in all jurisdictions should provide a right to take an unpaid leave of absence from work after the birth or adoption of a child at least equal to the period of entitlement to unemployment insurance maternity and parental benefits—fifteen weeks maternity benefits and ten weeks of parental benefits payable to the mother or father. Serious consideration should be given to adopting Québec's standard of thirty-four weeks of leave. Canadians should be entitled to five days of unpaid family leave (for the care and health of immediate family members) per year, the current standard in Québec.

*Education and training*: Through the joint agreement of employers, employees and unions, paid education and training leave plans should be used more frequently. A basic entitlement to unpaid education and training should be entrenched in federal and provincial standards to expand opportunities for learning. Access to this entitlement should be linked to length of service with an employer, and the federal government should support greater use of education leave by considering changes to the tax system, such as income averaging.

*Unemployment Insurance Work Sharing Program*: This program should continue to reduce short-term layoffs. However, the applications process should be reviewed to ensure that it is more accessible, particularly to small business.

*Post-report processes*: The responsibilities of existing organizations should be expanded to promote and report on work-time redistribution and flexible work arrangements over the long term. The Canadian Labour Market and Productivity Centre should focus on ongoing consultations between business and labour, while the Bureau of Labour Information should disseminate information on changing work-time practices.

*Information needs*: Statistics Canada should monitor trends in the changing workplace by conducting periodic surveys of work-time preferences and practices of employers and employees. Statistics Canada should monitor and provide more data on the non-standard work force.

## CHILD BENEFITS
*KEY DIRECTIONS, PROPOSALS, OPTIONS AND IDEAS FOR REFORM*
Strengthen the federal Child Tax Benefit through better targeting of the current benefit to low income families. Some funding could also be reallocated from federal CAP spending to the increased benefit, with the aim of providing low income families with $1000 to $1500 extra per child annually. To ensure that families on welfare also fully benefit from this reform, provincial social assistance benefits made on behalf of children could be integrated with an enhanced Child Tax Benefit. [Green Paper]

*ENHANCED AND RE-TARGETED CHILD TAX BENEFIT*
*[SUPPLEMENTARY PAPER ON INCOME SECURITY FOR CHILDREN]*
*Approach 1A*: Use federal CAP funding to create a new child benefit of up to $2500 for the first child, $2000 for the second child and $1500 for the third and each subsequent child. Maximum benefits would be payable to families with incomes up to $15,000. This option would provide increased benefits to 1.3 million families with children—those with incomes below $25,000. The average increase would be $1370 a year. Some families with incomes between $25,000 and $45,000 would receive a slight increase in benefits, though for most there would be no change. Most families with incomes over $45,000 would get reduced benefits. This option would cost the federal government $1 billion, in addition to the $5.1 billion currently spent on the Child Tax Benefit. The cost would be covered by a reallocation from another federal program, such as federal CAP funding.

*Approach 1B*: This option would provide greater support for modest and middle income families. It could provide $2500 for the first child in a family, $2000 for the second child and $1500 for the third and each subsequent child. Under this option, many more families would receive increased benefits—2.4 million families would receive an average increase in benefits of $950 per year and somewhat fewer would see their benefits reduced. The major trade-off in this approach is a higher net program cost of $2 billion.

*Approach 1C*: Families with net income of less than $18,250 would receive maximum benefits, but benefit levels would be lower than in the other two approaches: $2000 for the first child; $1500 for the second; and $1300 for the third and subsequent children. This design would be of greatest benefit to low income families—1.4 million would receive increased benefits—but the average increase in benefits ($610 per year) would be less than in Approach

1A. The net cost would be $800 million, so it would not be necessary to reallocate as much from higher income recipients of the Child Tax Benefit.

*Approach 1D*: No reallocation from CAP or other federal programs would occur. Rather, this design would involve relatively severe reductions in the Child Tax Benefit for modest and middle income families (2.2 million or close to 70 percent). A program that is cost neutral and provides the same benefit increases for low income families as in Approaches 1A and 1B would require that benefits be reduced more rapidly than at present on incomes exceeding $25,921.

## INTEGRATED FEDERAL-PROVINCIAL BENEFIT (REMOVE CHILDREN FROM WELFARE)
Federal Child Tax Benefit spending and federal and provincial welfare spending on behalf of children could be combined to create a new benefit for children of all low income families, regardless of the family's source of income (e.g., whether from welfare, U.I., employment or some combination thereof). The federal and provincial governments would reallocate funds from current expenditures and decide which level of government—including the possibility of joint government participation—would deliver the program. [Green Paper and Supplementary Paper on Income Security for Children]

The federal government should make the integrated federal–provincial benefit available to mothers as soon as a qualified physician certifies a pregnancy. [LeBlanc Report]

## ENHANCED WORKING INCOME SUPPLEMENT [GREEN PAPER, SUPPLEMENTARY PAPER ON INCOME SECURITY FOR CHILDREN, LEBLANC REPORT]
In order to increase the benefit of work over welfare, funds from the Child Tax Benefit currently paid to high income families could be reallocated to double the Working Income Supplement for low income families from the present maximum of $500 to a maximum of $1000 per family. The supplement would continue to be paid when annual family earnings reach $3750. For every dollar of earnings over this amount, a family would receive 16 cents in benefits until the maximum benefit of $1000 was reached at earnings of $10,000. The maximum benefit would be payable on earnings between $10,000 and $20,921. On net family income exceeding $20,921, the supplement would be reduced by 20 cents on the dollar until it disappeared at $25,921.

Enhancing the Working Income Supplement could be a first step towards an integrated and expanded child benefit, with the longer-term goal of an integrated federal-provincial benefit, or it could be done on its own. Funding for an enhanced Work Income Supplement could come from another source, in which case no families would experience reductions in their Child Tax Benefit.

## CHILD CARE AND DEVELOPMENT
### KEY DIRECTIONS, PROPOSALS, OPTIONS AND IDEAS FOR REFORM
*Accountability:* To ensure that further investments in child care and development are efficient and effective in creating systems which operate in the best interests of children and their

parents. [Supplementary Paper on Child Care and Development]

*Provincial and Territorial participation*: The federal government must determine the interest of provinces and territories in participating in a shared investment to strengthen Canada's child care system. [Supplementary Paper on Child Care and Development]

Ottawa and the provinces should discuss a more coordinated approach to child care. [LeBlanc Report]

*Quality*: The federal government must determine its role in efforts to improve the quality of child care services. There are a number of possibilities for federal leadership and collaboration with the provinces and territories:

1. continued federal investment in research and development;
2. sharing the funding of measures to improve quality, for example, by improving the training of child care providers through wage enhancement tied to training;
3. direct new growth to the non-profit, rather than the for-profit child care sector, as research points to non-profit operation as a significant predictor of quality child care;
4. take interim measures to improve the quality of existing for-profit child care operations, for example, through increased accountability and/or community management structures; and
5. redesign dependent care allowances to meet child development objectives as well as employment objectives. This option would involve developing a means of directing the allowances to licensed child care. [Supplementary Paper on Child Care and Development]

The quality and integration of child care delivery should be considered at the same time as governments plan increases in the number of available spaces. [LeBlanc Report]

Governments should discuss establishing standards appropriate to high quality child care that are attuned to early childhood development needs. [LeBlanc Report]

*Affordability:* The federal government should discuss, with the provinces and territories, whether to provide improved subsidies for existing spaces and whether this should be a priority use of investments in child care. [Supplementary Paper on Child Care and Development]

The federal government should discuss, with the provinces and territories, ways of expanding the number and/or amount of subsidies, or implementing sliding fee scales based on ability to pay, so that more families can afford quality child care. [Supplementary Paper on Child Care and Development]

Federal-provincial discussions should also include different ways of financing child care to make provincial and territorial systems more affordable. [Supplementary Paper on Child Care and Development]

The federal government will be considering the effectiveness of all its child care investments—including the Child Care Expense Deduction (e.g., whether it should continue as a tax measure or be redesigned)—to ensure that they meet their objectives and benefit families and children. [Supplementary Paper on Child Care and Development]

*Availability:* The federal government should discuss with the provinces, territories and the public whether the first priority should be to establish new child care spaces or to stabilize existing underfunded spaces. [Supplementary Paper on Child Care and Development]

The federal government must determine what priorities should guide the development of additional child care services, e.g., more flexible child care options for parents working non-standard hours; new spaces for traditionally underserved groups, such as rural families, infants and children with disabilities; or incentives to employers to create additional work-related child care programs. [Supplementary Paper on Child Care and Development]

*Aboriginal child care:* The federal government must determine, in consultation with Aboriginal leadership and communities, the types of child care services that should be created for aboriginal children, both on and off reserve. Access to these services needs to be improved, particularly in northern Aboriginal communities. [Supplementary Paper on Child Care and Development]

Aboriginal child care services must be harmonized with Aboriginal Head Start programs, both on and off reserve. [Supplementary Paper on Child Care and Development]

The federal government must collaborate with provincial and territorial governments to ensure comparable standards of care within Aboriginal communities, while respecting Aboriginal control over services and their need for appropriate, culturally-sensitive services. [Supplementary Paper on Child Care and Development]

A portion of federally provided child care financing should be designated to provide Aboriginal child care services. [LeBlanc Report]

*Children with disabilities*: A portion of federal child care financing should be allocated for the needs of children with disabilities to ensure full participation in the community. [LeBlanc Report]

*Child development:* Governments must determine how best to promote child development for all families. The federal government is prepared to discuss with the provinces and territories the possibility of including child development and family resource programs within the new child care initiative and allocating a portion of new funds for this purpose. This is in addition to amounts already spent on child development through other programs. [Supplementary Paper on Child Care and Development]

Where provincial governments agree, child care programs could be linked to preventive, community based child development and family support programs. [Green Paper]
*Child care workers*: In governmental discussions, the work of child care workers should be properly valued and their access to educational opportunities in early childhood development should be improved. [LeBlanc Report]

## Child Support
*Key Directions, Proposals, Options and Ideas for Reform*
Governments should review the experience of jurisdictions outside Canada that have been testing systems that provide an assured minimum level of child support for custodial parents. [Green Paper and Supplementary Paper on Income Security for Children]

## Canada Assistance Plan (cap)
*Key Directions, Proposals, Options and Ideas for Reform*
The federal government should initiate talks with the provinces and territories about changing cap to a block funded program with more flexible provisions to encourage preventive social programs. [LeBlanc Report]

Governments should make reducing child poverty a fundamental goal in these discussions. [LeBlanc Report]

Governments should address the issue of general principles, such as portability, and specific standards for programs like child care. [LeBlanc Report]

*Interim steps towards cap reform:* The federal government could change cap provisions to encourage provincial innovations to better meet the needs of families with children and reduce work disincentives—e.g., relax cap earnings exemptions guidelines for social assistance recipients to facilitate self-sufficiency and ease up on the Work Activity Guidelines to alleviate the administrative burden on the provinces and territories. [Green Paper and Supplementary Paper on Reforming the Canada Assistance Plan]

The federal and provincial governments should work together to reduce administrative overhead—e.g., by streamlining needs tests, developing "single window" offices for all social security programs, making greater use of technology and greater information sharing among agencies and governments. [Green Paper]

### Longer-term Steps Towards cap Reform
*First approach*: Replace cap cost-sharing with a block fund for welfare and social services. The federal government would transfer an annual amount of money to the provinces which would then design their welfare systems based on their own priorities and needs. The scope of the block could include the current range of cap's welfare and social services and new provincial/territorial initiatives intended to increase employment and reduce child poverty. [Green Paper and Supplementary Paper on Reforming the Canada Assistance Plan]

*Second approach*: Fundamentally restructure the federal government's role in Canada's social safety net by re-channeling some or all federal transfers under CAP into programs that provide more direct support to individuals—e.g., expand child care, a new child benefit, an enhanced working income supplement, improved access to disability-related supports and services, and continued federal support for social services through a conditional block fund. [Green Paper and Supplementary Paper on Reforming the Canada Assistance Plan]

Social services: Under the second approach to CAP reform (re-channeling federal CAP transfers into programs that provide more direct support to individuals), funding must be protected for a wide range of vital social services, including services for seniors and health-related spending. Federal CAP money could be transferred to the provinces and territories through a social services block fund or through some other more specific initiative that helps fund the provision of these benefits. Provinces and territories would decide how best to allocate funding through a block fund, if such an approach to vital social services were to be pursued. [Green Paper and Supplementary Paper Reforming on the Canada Assistance Plan]

## PERSONS WITH DISABILITIES
### *KEY DIRECTIONS, PROPOSALS, OPTIONS AND IDEAS FOR REFORM*
Under the second approach to CAP reform (re-channeling federal CAP transfers into programs that provide more direct support to individuals), provincial and territorial programs with federal funding support could provide persons with disabilities the means of acquiring disability-related supports without having to be on social assistance. This would serve as an incentive to enter the labour market rather than depend on welfare as the only way of obtaining these supports. [Supplementary Paper on Reforming the Canada Assistance Plan]

The federal government should develop initiatives that promote independent living, including the Independent Living Resource Centres operating across Canada. [LeBlanc Report]

Governments should reconcile the definitions and eligibility criteria of their programs in consultation with persons with disabilities. To the fullest extent possible, definitions and criteria of private insurance plans should also be harmonized. [LeBlanc Report]

The social security system should be realigned to reflect the goals of independent living and improved access to the economic and social mainstream for persons with disabilities. [Green Paper and LeBlanc Report]

Separate access to disability-related supports and services from eligibility for income assistance, as Québec has done. In Québec, regardless of status (age, sex, disability or income), health care, rehabilitation services, technical aids and social services are provided by the provincial health and social services department on the basis of need for service. Appropriate authorities are responsible for other disability-related accommodations, such as house adaptations. [Green Paper and Supplementary Paper on Persons With Disabilities]

Improve the portability of disability-related supports and services as people move from one setting to another (e.g., home to school, work to play, from one geographic location to another). [Green Paper and Supplementary Paper on Persons with Disabilities]

Support for community integration must become a part of overall social policies and programs. Approaches include community based programs for institutional care, research and development into applying new technologies and experimenting with innovative models of independent living and working. [Green Paper]

All persons with disabilities should have reasonable, appropriate and timely access to disability-related supports and services [Supplementary Paper on Persons with Disabilities]. However, current financial realities would have to be constrained within existing funding parameters.

To the extent possible, persons with disabilities should be provided with the funding to purchase and manage their individual supports and services. [Supplementary Paper on Persons with Disabilities]

Tailor services to meet individual needs. [Supplementary Paper on Persons with Disabilities]

## EMPLOYMENT DEVELOPMENT SERVICES FOR PEOPLE WITH DISABILITIES
Federal and provincial discussions should examine ways to make employment development services more available as well as dealing more effectively with the particular barriers persons with disabilities face—e.g., creating partnerships among employers, the disabled community and the provinces to remove barriers and provide accessible workplaces, flexible working conditions, appropriate training and proactive disability management policies. [Green Paper]

Discussions should consider updating the approach to vocational rehabilitation—e.g., disability management is a workplace based reintegration program that helps employees who become disabled return to work. This program can save financial and human resources. [Green Paper and Supplementary Paper on Persons with Disabilities]

The federal government should discuss with the provinces updating the Vocational Rehabilitation of Disabled Persons Act—e.g., VRDP could be connected directly to employment development services as a link to mainstream training and employment opportunities. [Green Paper and Supplementary Paper on Persons with Disabilities]. A guide for these discussions might be the updated standards concerning vocational rehabilitation and employment of the International Labour Organisation:

1. apply job-preparedness measures available to the general population equally to people with disabilities;
2. expand and create employment opportunities by providing financial incentives to employers; and
3. focus on employment in addition to providing vocational rehabilitation.

Build the principles of access and accommodation into the design of training and employment development services as an integral part of an overall approach to more active job-preparedness measures for all Canadians. [Supplementary Paper on Persons with Disabilities]

## LEARNING AND TRAINING FOR PEOPLE WITH DISABILITIES

Replace segregated training programs with mainstream education and training, with adaptations wherever necessary. [Supplementary Paper on Persons with Disabilities]

Assure that adequate supports and accommodations are available and portable from one stage of the educational system to another. [Supplementary Paper on Persons with Disabilities]

Specific needs of people with disabilities could be recognized and accommodated in delivering training. These include flexible policies that would extend course completion dates and flexible work arrangements, or an extension of the age limit for youth programs which would make it easier for students with disabilities to successfully complete their training. [Supplementary Paper on Persons with Disabilities]

Improved access to work experiences, such as co-op and apprenticeships, and more flexible on-the-job training arrangements in the regular work environment so that students with disabilities can acquire skills and give prospective employers an opportunity to consider their potential as employees. [Supplementary Paper on Persons with Disabilities]

Build components such as acquiring basic skills and/or a gradual familiarization with the world of work into mainstream programs. [Supplementary Paper on Persons with Disabilities]

## EMPLOYMENT FOR PEOPLE WITH DISABILITIES

Build upon approaches already tried (e.g., address systemic discrimination in advertising jobs, recruitment, hiring and promotion). [Supplementary Paper on Persons with Disabilities]

Provide accommodations such as restructuring of work, part-time work, reassignment of duties and training. [Supplementary Paper on Persons with Disabilities]

Arrange for on-the-job supports for individuals—e.g., sign interpreters, attendant care, day care services. [Supplementary Paper on Persons with Disabilities]

Assist job applicants and employees with disabilities to articulate their needs for accommodations. [Supplementary Paper on Persons with Disabilities]

Establish jointly funded programs by employers and governments which include on-the-job training and supported employment. [Supplementary Paper on Persons with Disabilities]

Implement effective policies that encourage and enable employers to retain their disabled employees. [Supplementary Paper on Persons with Disabilities]

## Administrative Reforms

Encourage flexibility and linkages among programs to reduce administrative red tape. [Supplementary Paper on Persons with Disabilities]

Encourage linkages at the program development and delivery level among various federal programs to give persons with disabilities easier access to all the tools Human Resources Development Canada has available. [Supplementary Paper on Persons with Disabilities]

Efforts can promote successful models of disability management with public and private sector employers. [Supplementary Paper on Persons with Disabilities]

Explore ways to use vehicles, such as the current federal cost sharing instruments, to support provincial programs that assist persons with disabilities to live more independently and to participate in mainstream activities, including training and employment. [Supplementary Paper on Persons with Disabilities]

Focus on delivering programs in a timely and coordinated way and on disseminating comprehensive information to Canadians about the various HRDC programs that support opportunities for persons with disabilities. [Supplementary Paper on Persons with Disabilities]

## Learning

### Key Directions, Proposals, Options and Ideas for Reform

*Literacy*: The federal government should continue its commitment to recognize the right to literacy training based on principles such as accessibility of programs, learner-centred programming, recognition of prior learning for transferability between levels of programs and quality standards that are also applicable to learning in general. [LeBlanc Report]

*Post-secondary education*: Maintain the current EPF post-secondary funding arrangements, allowing the cash portion of the transfer to decline gradually, disappearing in about a decade [Green Paper] *or* shift federal spending from support to institutions via provinces towards an expanded and permanent system of aid to individuals based on loans and grants to replace declining cash transfers through an income-contingent repayment loan (ICR) plan. [Green Paper]

*A possible ICR outline*: Federal funding would be used to guarantee loans to individuals. Access to loans would not depend on proving need. Provinces could opt out and run their own similar schemes as Québec now does with the existing student loans program. Loans would be in addition to the $1 billion in loans and grants provided through existing programs. ICR loans would be repayable only after the borrower had left college or university and entered the work force. At that point, the borrower's repayment schedule would be adjusted to match his or her ability to repay, depending on income. A student's income after leaving school would determine the rate of repayment. Borrowers who earn less would bear a smaller annual repayment load. ICR loans could be tied to the income tax system so that repayments could be deducted from every pay cheque. [Green Paper]

Increased flexibility in RRSPs could be used to encourage personal savings for lifelong learning, along the lines of the First-Time Homebuyer's Plan, and would further expand the resource base for learning. People could use these sources to help pay for tuition or living expenses while attending a certified education or training program. [Green Paper]

Existing loan support under the Canada Students Loan Program could continue to be available up to current levels. This would complement provincial grants and loans. The ICR approach could then be applied to future tuition increases and to expanding access to learners not now eligible for help through existing programs. [Green Paper]

Existing loan programs could be integrated with an ICR program. [Green Paper]

ICR loan principle should be endorsed as part of a comprehensive approach to improved student assistance. Concrete proposals for an ICR loan scheme should be developed in consultation with all stakeholders, including provinces, post-secondary institutions and students. [LeBlanc Report]

The shift of cash transfers for post-secondary education into the ICR loan program should be phased in gradually to allow post-secondary institutions time to adjust to the change. [LeBlanc Report]

Various institutional and administrative arrangements could be envisioned for the operation of an expanded loans program: government guarantees of private lending by financial institutions; federal direct lending or, if provinces prefer, provincial direct lending; or setting up an arm's-length crown agency, possibly jointly, with interested provinces. The arrangement with the lowest overhead consistent with sound stewardship would be best suited to expanding student access to post-secondary education. [Green Paper]

Within an enriched student aid system, measures should be implemented that would ensure access to learning opportunities for Canadians. These measures should include grants for low income students, interest subsidization where necessary to avoid excessive debt, universal access to ICR loans and enhanced tax measures to assist learners. [LeBlanc Report]

The federal government, both in the review of its support for post-secondary education within social security reform and in its science and technology review, should consider measures to ensure continued support for university research. [LeBlanc Report]

A national conference on post-secondary education should be convened. [LeBlanc Report]

*School-to-work transition:* The federal government would like to work with the provinces and the private sector to see what else might be done (in addition to what Ottawa is already doing through Youth Service Canada and the Youth Internship Program) within available resources. The aim is to close the large gap in moving from school to work. [Green Paper]

*Portable learning:* A learning passport would, in one place, document an individual's learning experiences as well as any academic and vocational credentials and would be recognized across Canada by employers and learning institutions. This arrangement would require provincial agreement. [Green Paper]

The federal government should work with the provinces, employers, unions and voluntary groups to develop a Canada-wide system of "credit recognition" to help immigrants find and keep meaningful employment, commensurate with their skills and knowledge. [Green Paper]

*Learning and new technology:* The federal government must ensure that the "information highway" can be used to expand access to learning opportunities across Canada and to prepare learners for a knowledge-based economy. The federal government proposes to examine, with the provinces, learning institutions and the private sector, the role technology can play in learning and to facilitate initiatives and partnerships. [Green Paper]

*International educational opportunities:* To foster more Canadian exposure to international education in today's global economy, and to increase student exchanges with Canada's competitors and trading partners, we need to rapidly expand our learning connections to international educational institutions. These networks, such as the European Erasmus Program linking colleges, universities and research institutes across the continent, would facilitate exchanges of students, faculty and information. [Green Paper]

## TAX EXPENDITURES

### KEY DIRECTIONS, PROPOSALS, OPTIONS AND IDEAS FOR REFORM

Tax expenditures should receive careful attention from government through an open process (e.g., by appropriate Standing Committee of Parliament). [LeBlanc Report]

All federal tax expenditures should be embedded in an annual review of estimates by Parliament in order to strengthen financial management by government and improve Parliamentary control of public finances. [LeBlanc Report]

Social tax expenditures should be evaluated using guidelines (including the criterion of equity) similar to those applied to direct program spending. [LeBlanc Report]

## REFERENCES

House of Commons. 1995. *Security, Opportunities and Fairness: Canadians Renewing Their Social Programs.* Ottawa: Queen's Printer.
———. 1994a. *Agenda: Jobs and Growth. Improving Social Security in Canada. A Discussion Paper.* Ottawa: Minister of Supply and Services.
———. 1994b. *Advisory Group on Working Time and the Distribution of Work. 1994 Report.* Ottawa: Minister of Supply and Services.
Human Resources and Development Canada. 1994. *Persons with Disabilities: A Supplementary Paper.* Ottawa: Minister of Supply and Services.
———. 1994. *From Unemployment Insurance to Employment Insurance: A Supplementary Paper.* Ottawa: Minister of Supply and Services.

————. 1994. *Income Security for Children: A Supplementary Paper.* Ottawa: Minister of Supply and Services.

————. 1994. *Employment Development Services: A Supplementary Paper.* Ottawa: Minister of Supply and Services.

————. 1994. *Reforming the Canada Assistance Plan: A Supplementary Paper.* Ottawa: Minister of Supply and Services.

————. 1994. *Child Care and Development: A Supplementary Paper.* Ottawa: Minister of Supply and Services.

————. 1994. *The Context of Reform: A Supplementary Paper.* Ottawa: Minister of Supply and Services.

————. 1994. *Guaranteed Annual Income: A Supplementary Paper.* Ottawa: Minister of Supply and Services.

————. 1994. *Federal Support to Post-Secondary Education: A Supplementary Paper.* Ottawa: Minister of Supply and Services.

## PART 2

# CANADIAN SOCIAL POLICY AT THE CROSSROADS: THE SOCIAL SECURITY REVIEW

# CHAPTER 4

# DESPERATELY SEEKING SUBSTANCE:
# A COMMENTARY ON THE SOCIAL SECURITY REVIEW

*Ken Battle and Sherri Torjman*


## INTRODUCTION

The landscape of Canadian social policy is littered with the skeletons of proposals for reform. The current conventional wisdom in government policy-making circles that the social programs built in the 1950s and 1960s are no longer relevant to the rapidly changing demands and resources of the 1990s is myopic and ahistorical: throughout the history of our welfare state, there have been periodic complaints about its inadequacies and suggestions as to how to fix it. The lament "our social programs aren't up to the challenge of today's realities" is anything but new.

Perhaps there is a form of the business cycle to the process of social reform in this country. Proposals come and proposals go; task forces meet and task forces report; governments consult and governments ignore. Meanwhile, Canada's social security system trundles along, dispensing increasing billions of dollars in cheques and services, despite the best efforts of governments in recent years to tame the beast and rein it in. The thorny problems that social policy is supposed to tackle, and the endlessly documented failings of social programs, persist.

This is not to say, however, that Canadian social policy is static—far from it federal and, to a significant extent, provincial social programs have been undergoing substantial and far-reaching changes over the past decade. "Transformation" is not too strong a word to characterize the series of social policy changes initiated by the Wilson Conservatives and (it would appear so far) continued by the Martin Liberals. But the real impetus for change is not coming from social policy departments or social advocates; nor are they the agents of reform. The Department of Finance—and the world of finance—rule social policy in the 1990s.

There is nothing novel about the assertion that the Department of Finance plays a key role in Canadian social policy; always has it been thus and it would be strange if it were otherwise. But Finance does not *share* power over social policy with Health and Welfare and its reincarnation as Human Resources Development Canada: Finance *is* the power in social policy.

This is by no means a recent development. The Minister of Finance and his officials assumed the dominant power over federal social policy twenty years ago when they nixed Health and Welfare Minister Marc Lalonde's core proposal of the federal-provincial social security review to expand Canada's welfare state by adding an income supplementation program for the working poor. Ever since, Finance Ministers and their departments have held the trump cards in the game of social policy, even when Health and Welfare Ministers and their officials have tried to act as if they were still important players. The long hand and firm grip of Finance were evident in the 1977 shift from cost sharing to block funding of insured health care under Established Programs Financing (EPF) in order to curb rising and unpredictable federal transfers to the provinces; during the not-so-great pension debate of the early 1980s, scotching proposals to expand the Canada Pension Plan and extend the Spouse's

Allowance to all low income Canadians aged sixty to sixty-four; and in ignoring periodic but futile calls from social policy groups, progressive tax reformers and the Auditor General to put tax expenditures on the same examination table as direct social programs.

The transformation of Canadian social policy that was launched by the Mulroney government was led by Finance Minister Michael Wilson—the father of the new social policy—and finessed by a small group of clever and capable officials. These changes have been amply chronicled by social policy experts, but are still poorly understood by, the public and media. Largely by means of "social policy by stealth" (engineering cutbacks through partial rather than full indexation of benefits and entitlements), the Tories imposed a host of changes—small, medium and large—on federal social programs and the tax system (Battle 1990).

Their major initiatives include: the abolition of universal family allowances and old age pensions and their replacement with income-tested benefits (the Child Tax Benefit and the "clawed back" Old Age Security); the removal of inflation protection from child benefits and the personal income tax system; the conversion of personal income tax exemptions and deductions to non-refundable credits; increases to the child care expense deduction and refundable child tax credit; improvements to the Canada Pension Plan, Spouse's Allowance and tax assistance for (taxpaying) persons with disabilities; the creation of a flawed (because it is only partially indexed) GST credit; cuts to social housing; belt-tightening of unemployment insurance and withdrawal of federal funding from the program; and cuts to federal transfer payments to all the provinces for health and post-secondary education and to Ontario, Alberta and British Columbia for cost shared welfare and social services. Not all of these changes were "bad"—depending on your point of view, of course—and not all involved expenditure cuts. However, social advocates generally opposed Tory social policy which was motivated as much by deficit reduction obsession as anti-welfare state ideology.

The Liberals came to office vowing not to pursue the politics and policy of stealth. To prove the point they launched a highly public and visible social security review (SSR) under the leadership of Lloyd Axworthy, Minister of Human Resources Development Canada. This paper argues that, at least to date, the Minister and Department of Finance have continued to dominate the social policy scene; have significantly furthered the transformation of social policy begun by the Tories, moving far beyond the scope of the formal SSR; and have left fully intact the machinery of stealth constructed under the Conservatives.

However, while many social advocates and the media were quick to write their obituaries on the Axworthy review—the always authoritative national newspaper of the rest of Canada, the *Globe and Mail*, peevishly said of Axworthy that "he came, he saw, he floundered" (May 17, 1995: A20)—the SSR did achieve one of its primary objectives: to put forward for public consideration a number of proposals for reform. While the main impetus for and substance of *action* on social policy change thus far have emanated from Finance, nonetheless the Axworthy exercise and the cross-Canada consultations and report of the Standing Committee on Human Resources Development (House of Commons 1995) did air and debate numerous options for reform. It is easy and tempting to dismiss the SSR as a failure or farce, but the social policy community should not simply dismiss or give up on the ideas that have been put forward; some of them may get their day, someday, for better or worse.

## Proposals: The Social Security Review

It is not our intention here to discuss or assess the many proposals for reform presented during the ssr—an important task that has been done elsewhere.[1] We simply want to remind readers that the ssr sparked a flood of ideas, arguments, concerns and proposals on a wide range of social policy issues.

The federal discussion paper, *Agenda Jobs and Growth. Improving Social Security in Canada* (HRDC 1994a), along with its nine more detailed supplementary papers—on the context for reform, employment development services, unemployment insurance (U.I.), the Canada Assistance Plan, child benefits and child support, child care and child development, guaranteed annual income, persons with disabilities, federal support for post-secondary education—drew upon a large volume of work over the years from various sources as well as analysis done by Human Resources Development Canada staff. Lloyd Axworthy established a task force composed of experts from outside government to advise him in the preparation of the discussion paper, as well the Advisory Group on Working Time and the Distribution of Work and the Working Group on Seasonal Work and Unemployment; the latter two wrote their own reports. The Standing Committee on Human Resources Development, chaired by Francis LeBlanc, issued two reports, travelled the land to hear many witnesses and received submissions from a large number of individuals and organizations— over 200 briefs in its initial phase of consultation in February and March of 1994, and 637 witnesses and more than 1200 briefs in its second phase in the fall of 1994 and winter of 1995. Over 200 members of Parliament organized or sponsored town hall meetings, and community groups throughout Canada held meetings and conferences before and after the release of the discussion paper. Some social policy groups issued their own recommendations for reform. An astonishing 25,000 Canadians mailed in the federal workbook, *Have Your Say*, giving their reactions to reform options in the discussion paper.

The major ideas, suggestions and options for social policy reform put forward in the discussion paper (HRDC 1994a), the 1995 Report of the Standing Committee on Human Resources Development (House of Commons 1995) and the Advisory Group on Working Time and the Distribution of Work (HRDC 1994c) are summarized in the third section of the introductory chapter of this book entitled *Remaking Canadian Social Policy*. The proposals range from the vague and general to the concrete and specific. Whatever one thinks of the merit of the various ideas, one has to admit that the ssr did manage to dig up a considerable number and variety of substantive proposals for reform. Some of these ideas, if properly linked together, could lay the foundation for a stronger and more effective social policy for Canada in the twenty-first century.

## Proposals: The Caledon Institute

The ssr announced by the Minister of Human Resources Development Canada in January 1994 was billed as a comprehensive overhaul of Canada's social security system. We welcomed the announcement of the ssr, seeing it as a once-in-a-generation opportunity to introduce badly needed improvements to social programs and having called for just such a public review during the 1993 federal election campaign (Caledon Institute 1993).

Our perspective on social policy reform is strongly influenced by our work in the area of social spending. Our initial analysis of social expenditure trends, patterns and factors in Canada was presented in a report entitled *Opening the Books on Social Spending* (Battle and

Torjman 1993c). A more recent version of this numbers was published in the latest annual report of the auditor general (Auditor General of Canada 1994: 6-14). Social spending represents a large and growing share of government expenditure; total social expenditure has risen significantly over both the long run and short term and shows no indications of abating in the future. The forces driving rising social spending are deeply rooted in profound developments in the economy and society, including population aging, the restructuring of the labour market, the rising labour force participation of women and marriage breakdown, to name some of the key factors. We have made it clear in all our work that the renewal of social programs requires more cost-effective administration and delivery as well as redesign of the programs. We also agree that the deficit and debt pose a threat to Canada's economic well-being as well as our ability to sustain social programs.

Despite the serious constraints and pressures on spending, we believe that it is possible to build a stronger and more progressive social security system that is both effective and fiscally sustainable. It is this context that shaped our proposals for the ssr. Briefly, we would: replace the Canada Assistance Plan with new programs providing comprehensive services for children and supports for persons with disabilities; return U.I. to its original purpose of insurance against short-term and occasional unemployment; create a new program of income support and employment development services for employable welfare recipients and unemployed workers not eligible for the smaller U.I. program; radically reform child benefits; and, as a result of our various reforms, largely dismantle provincial welfare systems (Caledon Institute 1995c).

The Caledon proposals would return U.I. to its original purpose of social insurance for people who are unemployed on a short-term and occasional basis. This change would make the program smaller than it is now, since it would remove the *de facto* income supplementation role that U.I. has grown to play for Canadians and communities who rely upon it as a regular part of their income. Regionally extended and fishermen's benefits would be replaced by some form of income supplementation outside of U.I. However, benefits for illness, temporary disability and maternity/parental leave would remain. Moreover, eligibility would be extended to workers in the non-standard jobs that are a fast growing part of the labour market, including part-time workers and people who hold down several part-time jobs.

Key to our reform of U.I. would be the creation of a new employment assistance program that would be open not only to workers who do not qualify for the new U.I. program or exhaust their U.I. benefits, but also to employable welfare recipients who constitute close to one-half the welfare caseload (hrdc 1994a: 20). This program would provide a range of employment development services as well as income-tested financial assistance. An employment assistance program that removed employable people from social assistance would be an important step in the dismantling of provincial welfare—which would become a truly last resort form of assistance in the event of emergencies or when all other sources of support had been tapped.

The centerpiece of our package of reforms is an integrated child benefit that would combine federal expenditures on the Child Tax Benefit with the funds that Ottawa and the provinces spend on children through their welfare systems (Battle and Muszynski 1995). The essence of the proposal is to redirect the social assistance payments made on behalf of children and the Child Tax Benefit to a separate, income-tested program outside the welfare system that would serve all low income families with children, whatever their sources and mix of income.[2] An integrated child benefit would remove a major barrier that discourages some families from moving off social assistance into the labour force—the fact that welfare benefits take children into account, whereas wages do not. An integrated child benefit would provide an incentive for parents to remain in the workforce because they would receive a significant supplement to their income. This proposal would substantially increase child benefits for working poor families and reduce the depth and extent of child poverty.

Another important component of the package for social security reform is new legislation to forge and sustain the links among child care, child development and child welfare. Child care is generally regarded as a service for working parents; its potential impact upon child development is rarely recognized. Moreover, child care can provide preventive services that may reduce the need for child welfare services down the road. Comprehensive services for children could be financed partly by redirecting funds now spent on child-related services under the Canada Assistance Plan (CAP).

We also proposed that various sources of funds which support a range of programs for persons with disabilities be consolidated into a block fund for personal supports. "Personal supports" refer to disability-related goods and services including technical aids, equipment, and homemaker and attendant services. Persons with disabilities and the elderly require personal supports to participate in the labour market and to live independently in the community.

We recognized that governments might well not buy our notion of dismantling CAP and replacing it with separate programs of children's services, supports for persons with disabilities, child benefits and employment assistance, so we made a "second best" proposal to convert CAP to a block fund with conditions. The latter would ensure that federal dollars are spent for their intended purposes.

Our proposed reforms would improve not only the individual parts of the social security system, but would work together to dismantle Canada's archaic and outmoded welfare and U.I. systems, fight child poverty and encourage the development of stronger preventive social services.

This package of reforms comprised the framework within which we analyzed the 1995 federal budget. We found the budget to be profoundly deficient when assessed against the screen of comprehensive reform that is required to build a better social security system. The budget did a lot of the dismantling which we had, in fact, strongly recommended. However, it did none of the associated rebuilding that must accompany the "profound demolition" now under way (Wolfson 1987).

## ACTIONS: THE MINISTER OF FINANCE'S SOCIAL POLICY REFORMS

Lloyd Axworthy is not the first social policy minister to have his review eclipsed by the Finance Minister: witness the defeat of Marc Lalonde's income supplementation proposal by then Minister of Finance John Turner in 1975. Ten years later, the same fate befell Jake Epp's consultation paper on child and elderly benefits, which argued for maintaining universal family allowances and against imposing a clawback on Old Age Security; by the time Finance Minister Michael Wilson was through, universal child and elderly benefits had gone the way of the dodo bird. Fast forward another decade and the same game is in the process of being played out. Social policy ministers propose; finance ministers act.

Anyone who thought that the Prime Minister would allow Lloyd Axworthy and Paul Martin to ride off in different directions does not understand Chrétien's style of leadership.

It was clear from the outset that Lloyd Axworthy's social security review not only would have to live under the Finance Minister's anti-deficit roof, but also would have to contribute substantially to the cause through sizable cuts to social programs. Paul Martin's first (1994) budget announced the biggest cut to unemployment insurance—$5.5 billion between 1994-95 and 1996-97—since Bryce Mackasey enlarged the system in 1971, thereby reinforcing the belt-tightening changes made by the Tories in the 1980s. The 1994 budget also stated that federal social transfers to the provinces for welfare, social services and post-secondary education would have to yield savings of a minimum of $466 million in 1995-96 and $1.5 billion in 1996-97.

The speculation leading up to the 1995 budget further weakened Axworthy's image, and the budget itself lived up to the leaks. The Finance Minister announced a new Canada Health and Social Transfer (CHST) that would replace federal cost sharing of provincial welfare and social services (under CAP) and transfers to the provinces for health and post-secondary education (under EPF).

The 1995 budget also announced that the federal government was contemplating major changes to elderly benefits. The Canada Health and Social Transfer will have serious implications for the health care system. Thus Paul Martin's changes to social policy are extending beyond the scope of the social security review to include old age pensions and medicare.

The 1995 budget will have an enormous impact on social programs over the years because of the massive withdrawal of federal dollars. Equally importantly, the budget represents a withdrawal of federal presence in social programs and in human services more generally. Indeed, its potential erosion of the federal spending power could result in constitutional reform *de facto*—by stealth (Battle 1995a).

## CANADA HEALTH AND SOCIAL TRANSFER

In appearances before the Finance Committee and Social Policy Subcommittee of the Liberal Caucus, we characterized the Canada Health and Social Transfer as the worst social policy move in a generation. Our primary concern relates to the implications of integrating the Canada Assistance Plan into a block fund with few or no conditions other than residence prohibitions. Our fear also arises from the integration of CAP with transfers for health and post-secondary education into a new mega-block Canada Health and Social Transfer (CHST). The funds that had originally been designated for welfare and social services likely will get lost in the mix; they never will have the importance or support accorded to services intended for the general population (Battle and Torjman 1995: 10).

Already the poor cousin of social policy, welfare and social services will rank consistently at the end of the priority list as provincial health, post-secondary education and welfare ministries compete for declining federal funds. Some people would argue that this is how it should be, that programs which do not have high Gallup approval do not deserve public funding. This is a dangerous presumption. It means that programs for people who are poor or vulnerable no longer will be deemed worthy of public support. Those who do not require income assistance will not want to fund it for those who do. Canadians who are well off will buy their own social services as they do now—nannies for their children, counselling in the event of marital or family problems and private caregivers for elderly parents. The "haves" will not want to purchase these services on behalf of the "have nots."

Block funding is much more palatable to provinces than cost shared arrangements which "tie their hands." However, there is a problem with untied money. The dollars intended for human services could be used, at the end of the day, for whatever purposes the provinces desire. If the funds go out with no stipulations attached to their use, these monies are no different than equalization payments which compensate for fiscal imbalances and effectively are used for any public programs and services the provinces decide. There must be some way of ensuring that transfers intended for services to people are not transferred to some other purpose (Torjman and Battle 1995a: 7).

Another important aspect of CAP is that it provides matching funds to provinces. By virtue of the fact that costs are shared with Ottawa, provinces must make the initial contribution to welfare and social services. While this may be difficult for most "have-not" provinces, at least the arrangement requires some degree of provincial commitment. It is questionable whether this commitment will be maintained in poorer provinces in the absence of a financial partner, especially during recessions. Certainly the loss of 50-cent dollars (provided through CAP)will make it all that much harder for provinces to sustain—let alone strengthen—their social programs, even during favourable economic times.

The loss of CAP also means the loss of built-in countercyclical protection, which has been an important economic policy objective of the federal government. When provincial costs rise in the face of higher welfare caseloads that result from recession, federal costs increase as well. This makes sense in that welfare caseloads and costs are linked directly to economic performance; they go up with high unemployment because they are intended to act as safety nets in the event of high joblessness. The federal contribution under CAP helped provinces respond to the economic troughs which forced their costs to rise. In the next recession, provinces will have to cope with the pressures of rising caseloads entirely on their own; there will be no federal offset to compensate the higher costs. Ontario provides a case study of what happens when Ottawa no longer shares half the cost of welfare. By its account, Ontario lost $7.7 billion from 1990-91 through 1994-95 as a result of the "cap on CAP" which took effect in 1990 and which limited federal cost sharing increases to five percent a year (Battle and Torjman 1995: 8).

The 1995 budget indicates that Ottawa will negotiate with the provinces regarding the principles and objectives for the new CHST. We are not optimistic about the possibility of enforceable standards necessary to turn principles and objectives into reality, primarily because the dwindling dollars render almost academic the ability of the federal government to impose conditions on how the provinces spend the money (Torjman and Battle 1995a, 1995b). While CAP sets out few conditions for the receipt of federal funds, the conditions in place are nonetheless very important. The budget did announce that residence requirements would be prohibited; this will prevent the creation of interprovincial barriers for people. But the other two crucial conditions now ensured by CAP—with respect to need and appeals—are likely to be lost (Torjman 1994a: 100).

In the area of need, CAP ensures that Canadians who lack financial resources can qualify for assistance regardless of the cause of that need. The loss of CAP invariably means the loss of that protection. Provinces will be free to provide financial assistance to whichever "deserving" applicants they so choose. This change will turn back the social policy clock and constitutes one of the potentially worst mistakes in the history of our social security system.

Moreover, there will be no guarantee of a safety net in Canada. If provinces are no longer required to provide financial assistance on the basis of need, they can introduce any form of income support they like. While welfare systems are nothing to be proud of, at least they exist. Saying farewell to welfare as we know it would not be so bad if there were something more adequate to take its place. But the budget offered not the slightest offset—such as a small enhancement to the Child Tax Benefit—that would improve even marginally the financial security of most Canadians. The substantial cuts to U.I. most certainly will make the unemployed worse off and will once again dump many would-be beneficiaries onto provincial welfare rolls. The simple presence of a safety net has become all the more important, especially in the face of a turbulent and insecure labour market that is unlikely to stabilize for some time, if ever.

Our fears about the ramifications of the CHST are not theoretical: Witness the anti-welfare actions of the Alberta government over the past few years and the recent election of a provincial Conservative government in Ontario that campaigned on a platform of cutting welfare and requiring work-for-welfare.

In the area of appeals, CAP requires provinces to have an appeal system in place to allow welfare recipients to question decisions made with respect to their cases. The protection of this right is by no means a certainty with the loss of CAP. Appeal systems are important for welfare, in particular, because its highly complex, discretionary nature leaves the door wide open to administrative error and inconsistent treatment.

## MEDICARE

Our second major concern is the uncertain future of medicare. The need to reduce health care spending—at least to move away from costly treatment-oriented health care—is indisputable and long recognized. Medicare costs are high; the system is skewed toward expensive acute care treatment and population aging is another growing pressure. Countless reports and provincial commissions over the years have reached that conclusion. They have recommended more prevention and health promotion as well as a wider range of community supports in the form of homemaker care and attendant care to ease the pressure on costly medical and hospital care. But financial support for these home based services will be cut as CAP is replaced by the Canada Health and Social Transfer. It will be increasingly difficult to support community based programs that ease the burden on expensive treatment, both at the front end through preventive programs and at the post-care end to relieve the pressure on the acute care system.

The other crucial factor is that health care services actually have a relatively small impact on health status. Evidence from a wide range of disciplines, including public health and mental health, has found that the primary determinants of health are socioeconomic factors, in the form of adequate income, shelter and social supports (Premier's Council 1991).

But the more effective and efficient use of money is just one side of the story. The only way that Ottawa can enforce the conditions of the Canada Health Act—which guarantee the presence of a universally accessible, comprehensive health system—is by withholding dollars for non-compliance with the act. This leverage disappears as the dollars disappear. Despite the fact that the Finance Minister publicly swore his allegiance to the Canada Health Act, there is no protection for medicare without federal dollars. The dollars provide the enforcement clout. The declining cash transfers—both the direct withdrawal of funds and the partial indexation of the funding formula—spell the end of medicare (Battle and Torjman 1995: 9).

This is not a new problem; the Tories began bleeding federal transfers for health care by partially indexing EPF in 1986—and more stringently in 1989. But the Liberal budget does not redress the problem of declining cash transfers; it perpetuates it. Assuming that the CHST is only partially indexed using the established GNP-less-three-percentage point formula and also adjusted for changes in provincial population, we estimate that federal cash transfers will disappear by 2009-10 (see Figure 1). The federal cash transfer will end two years sooner in 2007-08 if the CHST does not adjust for population growth. If the federal government were simply to freeze its entitlement at the starting level of $26.9 billion and provide no annual adjustment, then the end to cash transfers will come in 2005-06. Whether the entitlement is frozen or partially indexed, and whatever assumptions we use, the inevitable result is a gradual decline and eventual disappearance of federal cash transfers to the provinces under the CHST. Only by replacing the partially-indexed, tax-point-cum-cash transfer formula with a fully-indexed, cash-only transfer will federal payments to the provinces be preserved (Battle and Torjman 1995: 7-8).

It is also possible that non-compliance with the conditions of the Canada Health Act will begin to show well before the precise termination date of the cash transfers. As the cash declines, the federal contribution will become increasingly irrelevant. Some provinces may even decide to forego the federal dollars altogether if they can more than offset the loss by imposing user fees and/or de-listing insured services.

Figure 1
**Total Federal Cash Transfers to Provinces for Welfare, Social Services, Health and Post-Secondary Education**

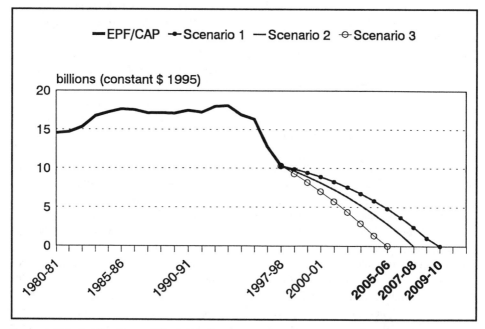

Source: Caledon Institute of Social Policy

## Unemployment Insurance

Unemployment insurance was tightened up in the first Liberal budget. An increase in the qualifying period, a reduction in the duration of benefits and a cut in the level of benefits for all but low income recipients with dependents will yield $5.5 billion in savings between 1994-95 and 1996-97. The 1995 budget dictated fiscal parameters for additional changes to U.I. that will be announced in legislation planned for this fall. U.I. expenditures are to drop by at least 10 percent—about $700 million—as a result of both the reforms to the program as well as a forecast drop in the jobless rate.

One option for reforming U.I. discussed by the federal cabinet was leaked to the *Globe and Mail* (Greenspon 1995). In some important respects, the approach looks very much like the changes already announced in the 1994 budget. It would increase the qualifying period (either by raising the number of weeks that must be worked or shifting to an hourly rather than weekly accounting basis); reduce the maximum duration of benefits; and possibly soften the blow of these changes by raising the earnings-replacement rate for low income recipients with dependents. Other possible changes include hitting frequent users by means of a sliding scale earnings-replacement rate (i.e., one that declines with frequency of claims); calculating benefits over a fixed period (whether or not the person worked); and imposing a longer qualifying period for new labour market entrants. (Note that most of these changes are mentioned in the table of proposals presented in Part 1 of this volume.) A key decision will be how much of the projected $700 million savings will be redirected to employment development services (e.g., retraining and wage supplements) and how much passed along to employees and employers in the form of lower premiums. The former is essential if the federal government is to grapple with the underlying problem that has skewed this program—the chronic use of U.I. associated with seasonal and regional unemployment. Employment-related services are not the whole answer to this difficult problem, but they are an important part of the answer.

## Human Resources

The 1995 budget announced a Human Resources Investment Fund (HRIF) to "help the unemployed find and keep jobs, combat child poverty and provide assistance to those most in need" (Department of Finance 1995: 110). But announcements of new "funds" usually come with dollars attached; this fund likely will come with dollars detached. In fact, employment services will lose $200 million in the first year alone (HRDC 1995: 2-11).

It is possible that the new fund may simply provide a vehicle for combining the developmental uses of unemployment insurance (funded by employer and employee premiums) and employment services (funded through general tax revenues) and then shrinking the funds for employment services. This tactic could spell the end to the government's contribution; employers and employees could pick up the full tab for employability training. So the "fund" may simply act a cover for cuts.

Another possibility is that Ottawa will use the fund—which likely will be financed primarily through U.I. premiums—to pay for the Working Income Supplement of the Child Tax Benefit. This would be one way of cutting back on government spending and using employer and employee dollars to attain the government's stated goal of "combating child poverty." Because there is no new money going into these areas, it is difficult to imagine that the "fund" will serve any purpose other than to find creative ways to finance existing programs.

The Human Resources Investment Fund may also be used to house the dollars that had been set aside for child care, conspicuous in this year's budget by its absence. The Red Book committed the government to expand existing child care in Canada by 50,000 new quality child care spaces in each year that follows a year of three percent economic growth, up to a total of 150,000 spaces. The 1994 budget had designated $120 million and $240 million for child care for 1995-96 and 1996-97, respectively.

If child care gets any funding at all, it will not be in the manner envisaged in the Red Book or in the context of building an infrastructure of service for all Canadians. Rather it likely will simply be an adjunct to a given individual's employability enhancement program. This move toward an employability service is positive in that it will help parents enter or re-enter the labour market; it is negative from the perspective of child development programs for all children. Perhaps the government plans to invest in a better child care system in the future. But such an announcement at this time would not have been well received in the board room of Moody's.

## CHILD POVERTY

The 1995 budget announced no changes to the Child Tax Benefit. This omission likely would have gone unnoticed had not the government itself focused so much attention on child benefits during the SSR. Minister Axworthy's discussion paper on social security reform and a supplementary paper on child benefits proposed a set of possible enhancements to the Child Tax Benefit (HRDC 1994c: 10-14). These were costed options with associated impact assessments—more than a mere musing on how "nice" it would be to do something about child poverty. The only action on this front that the government likely will take during the present mandate—if any—is a modest increase to the Working Income Supplement of the Child Tax Benefit.

It is unfortunate that the serious problem of child poverty went completely unaddressed in light of the most recent poverty data. Child poverty has grown steadily since 1989, reaching 1,447,000 or 21.3 percent of all children under 18 at last count (1993), despite the all-party House of Commons resolution in that year to move toward the eradication of poverty by 2000.[3] Child poverty poses grave risks to both physical and mental health (Canadian Institute of Child Health 1994: 113-29) and puts children at an early and lifelong disadvantage in the educational systems.[4] The cycle of poverty continues.

One could argue that the silence on child poverty had nothing to do with the need for a bad news budget. There is simply no money for any additional expenditure. Caledon and other social policy groups have long argued that there are funds that could be freed up for this purpose, if the government chose to capture some of the many billions that it spends on tax breaks for high income Canadians and profitable corporations. The Finance Minister had given some preliminary signals that he had his eye on this area. Yet the budget is notable for its non-action on tax expenditures. Tax loopholes, such as meals and entertainment allowances, could be closed. Badly-needed revenues could be raised by taxing lottery winnings, inheritances and wealth, and by reducing the generous help-the-affluent tax breaks for dividend income and tax assistance for retirement savings, among others. The surtax on high incomes could be increased.

We are not advocating the wholesale elimination of tax breaks. That would be too blunt a measure and an act of political hara-kiri for any government that tried it. Tax expenditures were introduced over the years to achieve certain purposes and some of the latter may still be worthwhile. However, there is a need to reassess the rationale of every single tax break to determine its continued relevance and to examine its distributional impact. The budget made only passing reference to the fact that tax expenditures will be subject to further study; it probably couldn't do any more given the widespread perception that Canadians will not put up with further tax increases.

## Pensions

Battle (1993) proposed in 1993 that Old Age Security, the Guaranteed Income Supplement, the Spouse's Allowance, and the pension and age credits be replaced by a single income-tested benefit geared to poor and middle income seniors to create, in effect, a super-GIS or guaranteed annual income for seniors.

Although Canada's retirement income system is far from perfect, it has made considerable progress against poverty in old age and improved the retirement income prospects of most Canadians. While we want to improve the system further, we are worried about its ability to maintain the current level of income security for future lower income pensioners. The aging of the population, coupled with the growth of low wage jobs and insecure employment and the high rate of marriage breakdown, will add up to a large increase in the number of low income pensioners in the decades to come. There is simply no way to sustain the current system, given the demographic and cost pressures. The number of old age pensioners has grown steadily over the years to reach 3.4 million in 1995 or 12 percent of the population. Demographic projections put the number of elderly Canadians at more than 8 million or one in four Canadians by the year 2035. Old Age Security payouts will grow from $16 billion in 1995 to an estimated $39 billion (in inflation adjusted 1995 dollars) by 2035 under the present system.

The 1995 budget announced that the government is considering applying a family income test to Old Age Security, while maintaining the income-tested Guaranteed Income Supplement and full indexation of all benefits. We see this as a positive and necessary move toward the income-tested system of elderly benefits that we proposed in 1993, though the new scheme must provide a fully indexed threshold and should replace the age credit and pension income credits. We believe that tax deductions for contributions to Registered Pension Plan (RPP) and Registered Retirement Savings Plans (RRSPS) should be reduced as well.

In the fall of 1995 Ottawa and the provinces will conduct their regular five-year review of the contribution rate schedule for future Canada Pension Plan (CPP) contributions. We favour an acceleration of contribution rate increases and an expansion of the CPP's earnings-replacement capacity; we oppose income-testing of benefits or raising the eligibility age to sixty-seven. The latter moves in the opposite direction of the preferences and behaviour of most Canadians, who want to retire sooner than later. It would hurt low wage workers, who would have to work longer at what are typically physically taxing jobs, and would have dire consequences for older workers who experience higher than average rates of unemployment. Moreover, it is possible that unemployed workers will not have a welfare system to which to turn in future, thanks to the new CHST.

## MORE FLEXIBILITY

These are unquestionably difficult political times and Ottawa is seeking ways of "renewing" itself and its relationship with the provinces—especially in light of the Québec referendum which threatens to break up the country. The Canada Health and Social Transfer has high symbolic value in that it represents a move by the federal government to retreat from provincial territory. And if provinces continue to invest in income programs and social services, the flexibility they gain from the arrangement can greatly improve the quality and responsiveness of certain social programs. It can enhance their capacity to test new approaches to social problems.

In theory, the CHST will allow provinces to be innovative and flexible. In practice, however, the availability of funds likely will determine how "innovation" and "flexibility" are defined. Unless the federal government changes its mind and decides to maintain a cash transfer to the provinces, all the talk about national standards, flexibility and innovation will turn out to be just that—talk.

## THE MACHINERY OF STEALTH STILL HUMS ALONG

It comes as no surprise that the Department of Finance under Paul Martin has left intact the machinery of stealth it built for Michael Wilson. Stealth pays handsomely in terms of tax increases and benefit cuts, with no political price attached.

The personal income tax system is still partially indexed; the result is a hidden, automatic federal and provincial income tax increase and a taxpaying threshold that falls further and further below the poverty line each year. The refundable GST credit is partially indexed; the result is a hidden, automatic hike in the GST paid by poor Canadians each year. The Child Tax Benefit is partially indexed; the result is a hidden, automatic cut in the value of benefits and a declining number of families that qualify for maximum benefits with every passing year. The income threshold for the clawback on Old Age Security is partially indexed; the result is a hidden, automatic cut to benefits for upper income seniors and a steady lowering of the threshold each year.

## CONCLUSION

The social security review opened a window of opportunity for comprehensive reform. That window was soon slammed shut by the Department of Finance and, more specifically, by the 1994 and 1995 Liberal budgets. Nonetheless, the review succeeded in putting forward a wide range of options, many of which would improve dramatically the quality and delivery of social programs and the overall well-being of Canadians. In lamenting the unfortunate process of recent events, a major challenge will be to keep alive the considerable substance that emerged as part of the social security review.

## NOTES

1.   See, for example: Caledon Institute of Social Policy. 1995b. *Critical Commentaries on the Social Security Review*. Ottawa, January. This is a collection of responses by forty-two social policy experts to the federal government's paper, *Improving Social Security in Canada*.
2.   This is the model often referred to as "taking children off welfare" outlined by Ontario in its 1993 report *Turning Point* with its proposal for an Ontario Child Income Plan to replace the child benefit portion of social assistance.

3.  The child poverty rate rose from 15.4 percent in 1980 to 20.6 percent in 1984 as a result of the lingering effects of the 1981-82 recession. It declined somewhat in the economic recovery to 14.8 percent in 1989 and then increased again because of the recent recession to reach 21.3 percent in 1993 (1.4 million children live in poverty). The percentage of children in female-headed single-parent families has risen and fallen since 1980 but is always high and reached a whopping 64.5 percent in 1993 (Caledon Institute of Social Policy 1995a).

4.  Children from poor families are twice as likely as children from non-poor families to suffer death in the first year, death from accidents and physical disabilities. Poor kids experience a higher incidence of health problems including bronchitis, asthma, digestive disorders, anemia, sight disorders, mental disorders, diabetes and heart disease. There is a strong and consistent relationship between low family income and psychiatric disorder, poor school performance and social impairment. Children from poor families have higher than average rates of school drop-out (Canadian Institute of Child Health 1994).

## REFERENCES

Auditor General of Canada. 1994. *Report of the Auditor General of Canada to the House of Commons*. Ottawa: Minister of Supply and Services Canada.

Battle, Ken. 1995a. *Constitutional Reform by Stealth*. Ottawa: Caledon Institute of Social Policy, May.

———. 1995b. *Government Fights Growing Gap Between Rich and Poor*. Ottawa: Caledon Institute of Social Policy, February.

———. 1993. *Thinking the Unthinkable: A Targetted, Not Universal, Old Age Pension*. Ottawa: Caledon Institute of Social Policy, October.

———. 1990. "Social Policy by Stealth." *Policy Options* 11 (2): 17-29. Published under the pseudonym Grattan Gray.

——— and Leon Muszynski. 1995. *One Way to Fight Child Poverty*. Ottawa: Caledon Institute of Social Policy, February.

Battle, Ken and Sherri Torjman. 1995. *How Finance Re-formed Social Policy*. Ottawa: Caledon Institute of Social Policy, May.

———. 1993a. *Federal Social Programs: Setting the Record Straight*. Ottawa: Caledon Institute of Social Policy, Spring.

———. 1993b. *Federal Social Policy Agenda*. Ottawa: Caledon Institute of Social Policy, May.

———. 1993c. *Opening the Books on Social Spending*. Ottawa: Caledon Institute of Social Policy, May.

———. 1992. *Child Benefit Primer: A Response to the Government Proposal*. Ottawa: Caledon Institute of Social Policy, May.

Betcherman, Gordon, Katherine McMullen, Norm Leckie and Christina Caron. 1994. *The Canadian Workplace in Transition*. Kingston: Industrial Relations Centre Press, Queen's University.

Caledon Institute of Social Policy. 1995a. *Child Poverty Trends*. Prepared for the Colloquium on Child Poverty. Ottawa: Caledon Institute of Social Policy. January 26.

———. 1995b. *Critical Commentaries on the Social Security Review*. Ottawa: Caledon Institute of Social Policy. January.

———. 1995c. *The Comprehensive Reform of Social Programs*. Brief to the Standing Committee on Human Resources Development. Ottawa: Caledon Institute of Social Policy. February.

———. 1993. *Federal Social Policy Agenda*. Ottawa: Caledon Institute of Social Policy. September.

Canadian Institute of Child Health. 1994. *The Health of Canada's Children: A CICH Profile*. second editon. Ottawa.

Department of Finance. 1995. *Budget Plan*. Tabled in the House of Commons by the Honourable Paul Martin. Ottawa: Department of Finance.

——— 1994. *A New Framework for Economic Policy*. Ottawa: Department of Finance. October 2.

Economic Council of Canada. 1991. *Good Jobs, Bad Jobs: Employment in the Service Industry*. Ottawa: Supply and Services Canada.

Globe and Mail. 1995. "As Mr. Axworthy Fades Away." May 17: A20.

Greenspon, Edward. 1995a. "New U.I. Plan Would Cut Benefits." *Globe and Mail*. June 10: A1.

House of Commons. 1995. *Security, Opportunity and Fairness: Canadians Renewing Their Social Programs*. Report of the Standing Committee on Human Resources Development. Ottawa: House of Commons.

Human Resources Development Canada (HRDC). 1995. *1995-96 Estimates. Part III: Expenditure Plan*. Ottawa: Minister of Supply and Services Canada.

———— 1994a. *Agenda: Jobs and Growth. Improving Social Security in Canada: A Discussion Paper*. Ottawa: Minister of Supply and Services.

————. 1994b. *Reforming the Canada Assistance Plan: A Supplementary Paper*. Ottawa: Minister of Human Resources Development.

————. 1994c. *Report of the Advisory Group on Working Time and the Distribution of Work*. Ottawa: Minister of Supply and Services.

Myles, John. 1994. *Old Wine in New Bottles: Privatizing Old Age Pensions*. With Reply by Ken Battle. Ottawa: Caledon Institute of Social Policy.

National Council of Welfare. 1991. *Funding Health and Higher Education: Danger Looming*. Ottawa: Minister of Supply and Services.

————. 1987. *Welfare in Canada: The Tangled Safety Net*. Ottawa: Minister of Supply and Services Canada.

————. 1982. *Medicare: The Public Good and Private Practice*. Ottawa: Minister of Supply and Services Canada.

Ontario. 1993. *Turning Point: New Support Programs for People with Low Incomes*. Toronto: Ministry of Community and Social Services.

Premier's Council on Health Strategy. 1991. *Nurturing Health: A Framework on the Determinants of Health*. Toronto: Government of Ontario. March.

Torjman, Sherri. 1995. *The Let-Them-Eat-Cake Law*. Ottawa: Caledon Institute of Social Policy, May.

————. 1994a. "Is CAP in Need of Assistance?" In K. Banting and K. Battle (eds.), *A New Vision for Social Canada? Perspectives on the Federal Discussion Paper on Social Security Reform*. Kingston: School of Policy Studies and Caledon Institute of Social Policy, 99-113.

————. 1994b. *Social Programs: Tail or Dog?* Ottawa: Caledon Institute of Social Policy, February.

Torjman, Sherri and Ken Battle. 1995a. *Can We Have National Standards?* Ottawa: Caledon Institute of Social Policy, June.

————. 1995b. *The Dangers of Block Funding*. Ottawa: Caledon Institute of Social Policy, February.

Wolfson, Michael. 1987. "The Arithmetic of Income Security Reform." In S. Seward and M. Iacobacci (eds.), *Approaches to Income Security Reform*. Halifax: Institute for Research on Public Policy.

# CHAPTER 5

# THE STRUGGLE FOR NATIONAL STANDARDS: LESSONS FROM THE FEDERAL ROLE IN HEALTH CARE

*Susan Silver*

## INTRODUCTION

The February 1995 federal budget constitutes a defining moment in Canadian social policy. Given that a nation's budget is the economic expression of collective values and shared commitments, this budget represents the symbolic and substantive retreat of the federal government's commitment to social programs. The reconceptualized role of the federal government is one in which "smaller" government is equated with "smarter" government (Department of Finance 1995a: 6). With the new budget, program spending as a ratio of Gross Domestic Product (GDP), will be reduced to 1950-51 levels (Department of Finance 1995b: 5). In addition to this financial withdrawal, the new budget proposes a restructuring of the policy instruments available to the federal government purportedly to insure that enforceable national standards exist. The proposed Canada Health and Social Transfer (CHST) introduced in the 1995 budget represents a critical juncture in Canadian federalism, one which will result in profound changes in the manner in which Canadians access health care, post-secondary education and social assistance programs. Clearly the intent of the budget is debt management through deficit control. However, a government that limits its capacity to do "harm" by lowering deficit spending also reduces its capacity for benevolence.

The normative shifts represented in this budget have sparked a national debate about the degree to which we can sustain equitable social programs within the newly defined legislative framework. A number of key issues resonate in the current debate. How established are the "established" programs? Is there a need for enforceable national standards or can national standards be formulated by consensus and voluntarily adhered to, as suggested in the budget speech?

This paper addresses these concerns. Using a normative approach to policy analysis, the case for national standards will be mounted on the premise that there are contending perspectives and interpretations of the fundamental principles or values that govern social programs. A normative analysis attempts to expose and clarify the values that influence policy debates and policy outcomes (Titmuss 1974).

In order to assess the prospects for national standards under the proposed CHST, earlier experiences with block funding under Established Programs Financing (EPF) for the Canada Health Act (CHA 1984) will be examined. The CHA represents a battle fought in the name of universality. The various dimensions of universal health care were aggressively argued during the political debate surrounding this legislation. This policy debate was explicitly about values, and how these values would be operationalized as program conditions. This paper will show there are contending interpretations of "equity," even when a program enjoys a resounding level of public support and commitment to the principle of equity. With the CHA, the federal government legislated a particular vision of "universality," grounded in a limited conception of equity. The federal government unilaterally redefined "equity" in relation to financial barriers to access. While other dimensions of "equity" were invoked by various stakeholders, the defining issue specifically pertained to the various types of direct charges. Universal health care would be synonymous with "free" access to those services that are publicly insured. An enforceable financial penalty for non-compliance was introduced with the CHA. This penalty was premised on the existence of a significant federal "cash" transfer under the EPF block funding formula.

With all its limitations, the success of medicare, our most egalitarian achievement, could not have been sustained without the federal role in operationalizing the program principles and linking an enforceable penalty to the EPF block. As the analysis will demonstrate, the only "national" aspects of our health care system are those in which the federal government has asserted a substantive role.

From a normative perspective, national standards provide the interpretive framework in which the fundamental principles informing our social programs can be shared uniformly by all Canadians. The federal role in achieving and sustaining national standards is pivotal. This paper argues that the prospects for national standards under the proposed CHST are not encouraging.

## THE 1995 FEDERAL BUDGET:
### DEVOLUTION OF FINANCIAL AND SUBSTANTIVE RESPONSIBILITY

It is initially important to summarize the 1995 federal budget in terms of the declining financial and substantive role of the federal government. The new budget introduces a $29 billion deficit reduction package of which $7 billion will be siphoned off through the new CHST. The CHST will replace the Canada Assistance Plan (CAP) and EPF for health and post-secondary education. Therefore, funding for major social programs will be consolidated into a single block transfer to begin in 1996-97. The CHST does not repeal the CHA.

The elimination of $7 billion from these programs represents a decrease of 24 percent by 1997-98. It is interesting to note that the federal transfer under CAP is $7.9 billion for 1995-96 and $6.2 billion for post-secondary education under EPF (Department of Finance 1995c: 51). The reduced amount is strikingly similar to the size of the federal contribution for one of these key programs, signifying the severity of the proposed spending cuts.

In addition to declining federal contributions, the CHST will retain the mix of cash and tax points allocated through EPF. Due to the partial deindexation of the funding formula, the cash portion of the CHST will disappear soon after the year 2000. Social policy analysts strongly contend that the disappearance of the cash portion of the transfer will eliminate the ability of the federal government to enforce the CHA and any further conditions which may accompany the CHST.

It seems evident that the current CHST goes beyond being a simple change in the funding formula. It is a clear indication of political intent, explicitly for social assistance and implicitly for medicare. By allowing the levers of enforcement to wither away, the federal government is retreating from its traditional commitment to these social programs. The difficult allocative decisions will now rest completely with the provinces. Given the economic imperative that is framing the current political climate, this new found provincial power could result in profound changes within all three programs incorporated in the CHST. The "popular" programs such as medicare and post-secondary education may see shifts towards privatization while social assistance, the "unpopular" program, could become more exclusionary and conditional.

This budget comes after almost a decade of declining federal contributions with each round of cutbacks being imposed unilaterally. Declining federal contributions under EPF began as early as 1982 and continued with the Conservative budget in 1986 and the partial deindexation of EPF transfer payments. These actions suggested that provinces could expect no predictability in federal transfers and would have to live year to year with the prospect of further federal cutbacks (Milne 1986).

Federal cutbacks continued in the 1989 budget with further deindexation and, by the 1990-91 budget, the transfer payments were frozen through 1994-95. The cutbacks for 1994-95 represent a revenue loss of $5.9 billion in EPF transfers for health and post-secondary education (Carter 1994). These dramatic reductions have significantly contributed to rising provincial deficits with the future of these programs becoming increasingly more uncertain.

With the transfer of responsibility to the provinces, the key issue that emerges relates to the structure of these programs under relatively exclusive provincial auspices. To address this issue, the principles informing medicare and our early experiences with block funding under EPF will be examined.

## MEDICARE UNDER EPF

Canada's national health care system, known as medicare, is by far our most collective achievement. Medicare eliminated both private insurance plans for the affluent and means-tests for the poor, establishing a right to all health care services that are publicly insured. The public model eliminates the freedom of patients to purchase additional insured services and the freedom of physicians to provide insured services on a private basis. Medicare escaped the residual thrusts (Taylor 1978), characteristic of other social welfare measures, by adopting a one-tiered publicly financed model of health insurance for all Canadians, rich and poor alike.

Medicare originated with two pieces of legislation: the Hospital Insurance and Diagnostic Services Act of 1957, insuring hospital services; and the *Medical Care Act* of 1966, insuring doctors' services. Five federal-provincial cost sharing conditions were imposed:

1. Universal coverage: every provincial resident must be covered under uniform terms and conditions;
2. Accessibility: services should be provided in a manner that does not impede or preclude, whether by fees or other means, reasonable access to insured services;
3. Portability: requires that all Canadians can receive health care services across Canada;
4. Comprehensiveness: all approved hospital services and physician services are to be covered;
5. Public administration: each provincial plan must be publicly administered on a non-profit basis without the involvement of the private sector.

It is important to note that our national program has always been limited to medically necessary physician and hospital services. The five program conditions attached to federal funding only apply to these "insured" services. We have always maintained a category of "non-insured" services, "add-ons" delivered at the discretion of the provinces and not nationally insured. Within this category, there is a distinction between extended health care services recognized within the EPF funding formula and all other remaining health care services. Extended health care services are not considered "insured services" and federal contributions towards these are unconditional with the only obligations placed on provinces being disclosure and federal recognition. Other uninsured services are further designated by a complete lack of federal involvement and can include a wide range of services such as preventive dental programs, prescription drug plans, services of chiropractors, naturopaths, optometrists, podiatrists, physiotherapists, air ambulance services to remote northern communities, and prosthetic and orthodontic devices and services. The degree of provincial variation in terms of availability and conditions for access are substantial and one need only examine any of the annual federal reports on the CHA to understand the full extent of this variation. Many of these "non-insured" services are delivered on a categorical basis and either age or income-tested. The standard of universal coverage on "uniform terms and conditions" has never applied to these non-insured services.

By the end of 1971, every province had taken advantage of the federal cost sharing incentive and approximately 100 percent coverage was attained in Canada. The national plan was achieved through interlocking ten provincial plans, all of which share certain common features. Canadians are free to choose their own physician and hospital. There is no limit on the benefits payable as long as medical need is determined. There are no limits on the number of days of hospital care or the number of visits to physicians. With respect to the scope of coverage, benefits are intended to be virtually complete. There is no distinction between basic and non-basic services. Instead all medically necessary physician and hospital services are covered by all provincial plans. From the onset, physician and hospital services have been the defining national aspects of our health care system.

By 1974, medicare had successfully replaced income based access with needs based access resulting in the close alignment of consumption patterns with health care risks (Manga 1987). The association between income and health care utilization was inversed, with the lowest income groups consuming more than double the health care services of the higher groups (National Council of Welfare 1982: 23).

What is uniquely Canadian is the degree of collective responsibility and equity evident in the one-tiered nature of medicare. We do not limit "guaranteed access," nor do we impose conditions or "stream" patients into different public plans, as do several of the European health care systems. With medicare (insured "medically necessary" physician and hospital services) any explicit status or class based care was eliminated.

With the achievement of equal access, the politics of medicare moved on to the issue of cost control, supported by the growing awareness that health care costs could be controlled without endangering the public's level of health. The influential Lalonde (1974) report questioned the assumptions built into the insurance approach, that doctors and hospitals equalled health. Lalonde concluded that, based on the data gathered under universal health insurance, increased expenditures on curative services would yield fewer returns than expenditures in areas that influenced health such as human biology, environment and lifestyle factors. This report proposed a new role for the federal government, one which called into question the cost sharing arrangement between the two levels of government.

With cost sharing, approximately half of all the costs of insured services were met by the federal government, whereas the full costs of providing uninsured services were borne by the provinces. There were no incentives for provincial governments to economize. This had an inflationary impact given that the insured services tended to emphasize highly technological and curative medical care to the detriment of preventive and less costly forms of care. Prior to 1977, a provincial government was often faced with the choice of whether to establish extended care programs and pay the full costs or use the cost shared acute care beds to achieve the same purpose. Faced with this cost sharing incentive, provincial governments tended to choose the higher cost alternative (Van Loon 1978: 458).

In addition to the problem of economics, the cost shared arrangements were also viewed as producing serious constitutional problems. The provinces objected to the inflexibility of the arrangements, arguing that the ability to plan and deliver other social programs was hampered by the incentive structure of cost sharing (Weller and Manga 1983: 231). The provinces maintained this represented an unwarranted intrusion in an area of provincial jurisdiction. These debates set the stage for a fundamental restructuring of the financial underpinnings of Canada's national health insurance system.

## Established Programs Financing

The federal government formally began the process of renegotiating the cost shared arrangements for medicare in 1971. The negotiations lasted for six years and culminated in the passage of the Federal-Provincial Fiscal Arrangements and Established Programs Financing Act (EPF) in 1977 for a five year period. The transfer for post-secondary education was also incorporated in EPF with approximately 32 percent of the transfer intended for education and the remaining 68 percent going to health. However there was not a formal distinction in the original block transfer for each program.[1]

The negotiations were "lengthy, often bitter and always complex" (Taylor 1987: 424). Provincial governments feared that the proposed arrangements would lead to lower levels of federal funding. To meet the projected increases in program costs, the provinces of Ontario, Québec and Alberta urged that half the grant be paid in cash and the other should take the form of transferred tax points. The poorer provinces, with their small revenue base, regarded tax points as an unsatisfactory alternative and feared that the federal government, having brought them into these costly programs, would now abandon them. Saskatchewan was opposed on the grounds that the reduced federal role would erode the national standards.

A compromise was reached and a complex funding formula was implemented. The new arrangement included a cash portion equalling about one quarter of the costs, conditional upon the provinces continuing to meet the national standards and the federal government transferring to the provinces 13.5 percentage points of personal and one point of corporate income tax. A new grant of $20 per capita was included to assist provinces in providing the less expensive "extended health services" such as nursing homes, home care and ambulatory services (Van Loon 1978: 462).

## National Standards Under EPF

The EPF arrangements represented the "most massive transfer of revenues (and therefore the substance of power) from the federal to the provincial governments in Canadian history" (Taylor 1987: 435). Other than the original national standards, there were no other conditions attached to the block grant. The substantive, if not funding, retreat of the federal government was justified on the grounds that, once a national program was "established," the federal government could safely assume a more limited role (Gray 1991). EPF essentially returned full responsibility for health policy determination to the provinces. From the federal perspective, the closed-ended nature of the new arrangements provided the financial predictability they had desired. With block funding, the provinces were solely responsible for any cost increases that exceeded the annual increases in the GNP. Provinces were free to allocate their funds in accordance with their own priorities to achieve cost savings.

The most feared impacts of EPF was its "balkanizing" effect on the Canadian health care system and that the national program conditions would be eroded. According to Monique Bégin's (1988: 66) review of the events associated with EPF, a clear link was not established between the five program conditions and EPF.

> ... [I]n the event of non-compliance with one of the five conditions ... the penalty provided for in the 1977 Agreement was ... practically unenforceable. If there was an infraction, the federal minister's only recourse was to hold back the entire monthly payment. [Yet] the "army" of federal civil servants in charge of auditing provincial bills and repaying half had been dismantled. The "army" had been reduced to twelve people! All of a sudden the Regulations of the 1957 and 1967 laws were no longer in effect.

By the early 1980s there was clear evidence that, while the previous cost sharing arrangement tended to harmonize certain features of the national health care system, the shift to a disentangled block ushered in an environment that could promote a significant degree of provincial variation.

Bearing in mind the fact that the five program conditions attached to federal funding apply to "insured" (medically necessary) physician and hospital services only, under EPF further provincial variation was facilitated within the area of direct charges. Direct charges, whether through physician extra-billing or hospital user fees, reflected the privatization thrusts of right-leaning physicians and provincial governments. The potential of these direct charges to erode the egalitarian nature of medicare provided the impetus for the CHA. Before moving on to the policy debate surrounding the CHA and the dimensions of "equity" that emerged, the use of direct charges prior to the CHA will be briefly reviewed.

## DIRECT CHARGES AND EXTRA-BILLING BY PHYSICIANS

One of the most distinguishing features of Canada's national insurance plan is that from the onset it included all physicians. However, each province allowed an escape hatch for physicians not willing practice within the plan (Taylor 1978). Physicians dissatisfied with the schedule of fees paid by the provincial insurance plans have been able to charge patients an amount in excess of the approved rate. Patients are required to pay this extra fee on their own. This practice is commonly known as extra-billing, though terms such as "balanced billing" and "patient participation" are also used.

The mechanisms of extra-billing are further complicated by whether or not physicians are required to "opt-out" of provincial plans if they wish to charge patients this additional fee. Physicians who have chosen to opt-out of their provincial plans have continued to bill their patients directly, while opted-in physicians bill the provincial plans directly. Most provincial medical associations discouraged extra-billing of the elderly, those on social assistance or those claiming financial hardship. However, the final decision rested with each physician.[2]

With respect to extra-billing, the key factor distinguishing the various provincial plans is whether the patient of an opted-out physician can submit a claim to the provincial plan and be reimbursed up to the fee schedule rate. Four different types of extra-billing models emerged, with the Alberta model being the most physician-friendly and the Québec model being most restrictive. Québec physicians who wish to extra-bill must opt out of the plan completely and their patients are not eligible for any provincial reimbursement.[3]

According to the 1984-85 annual report of the CHA, the year in which the CHA was passed, extra-billing occurred in the following five provinces: New Brunswick, Manitoba, Saskatchewan, Alberta and Ontario (National Health and Welfare 1986: 21). The total amount of extra-billing in 1984-85 was $50,429,000, representing approximately 1 percent of the total cash transfer to the provinces and less than 10 percent of all physician charges. Although the aggregate magnitude of extra-billing was not extensive, the National Council of Welfare (1982) documented the distributive ramifications and concluded that extra-billing was more prevalent in certain medical specialties and in various communities.

## Hospital User Fees

Hospital user fees represented a further direct charge in which a number of provinces required patients to pay an authorized charge for certain insured hospital services. These charges ranged from a daily rate in general hospitals of $7.50 in British Columbia to $3.00 in Newfoundland. In Alberta a $5.00 admission charge was imposed when a patient entered hospital and British Columbia also had a charge for each visit to the emergency department. There were no hospital user fees in the Yukon, Northwest Territories, Saskatchewan, Nova Scotia and Prince Edward Island (National Council of Welfare 1982: 28). According to the 1984-85 annual report of the CHA, the total amount of hospital user fees was $35,532,000, representing 0.69 percent of the cash transfer (National Health and Welfare 1986: 21).

Prior to EPF, federal auditors would deduct the amount of user fees a province had charged from the federal contribution to that province. Under EPF, the federal audits ended and provinces could no longer be penalized in this manner (Bégin 1988). The unilateral actions of the federal government in decreasing its funding commitment under EPF provided the more conservative provinces with a handy rationale for offsetting this shortfall through collecting and increasing hospital user fees.[4]

During the early 1980s, the policies of the federal Liberals clearly signalled a commitment to reducing the deficit through spending restraints and an overriding concern for inflation. Social policy initiatives were profoundly affected by the recession and reflected the broader concerns with efficiency and affordability. A key anti-inflationary strategy used by the Trudeau Liberals included general wage and price control legislation. This legislation, introduced in the 1982 budget, limited federal public sector pay increases to "6" percent in 1983-84 and "5" percent in 1984-85. This "6 and 5" package also limited the indexation of a number of income security programs such as family allowances and old age security. By 1983, EPF was subjected to this anti-inflationary strategy, translating into a $1.9 billion loss spread over five years (Bégin 1988: 83). The reductions to EPF were depicted as part of the overall anti-inflationary package and not as anti-education or anti-health. Anti-inflationary approaches were "portrayed as the high road to responsible social policy" (Doern and Aucoin

1983: 32). It was in this economic context favoring "social policy without big dollars" (Doern and Aucoin 1983: 34) that the legislative framework for the CHA emerged.

## THE CANADA HEALTH ACT (1984)

Monique Bégin, federal Minister of Health, formally opened the campaign for the CHA in 1982, armed with the recommendations of two public inquiries, the Health Services Review of 1980 (Hall 1980) and the Parliamentary Task Force on Fiscal Federalism in 1981 (House of Commons 1981). Each of these inquiries conducted extensive public hearings in which the importance of the federal role in maintaining national programs was affirmed. Specifically addressing the issue of extra-billing, the Commissioner of the Health Services Review, Mr. Justice Emmet Hall (1980: 2) states that

> . . . if extra-billing is permitted as a right and practiced by physicians in their sole discretion, it will, over the years destroy the program, creating in that downward path the two-tier system incompatible with the societal level which Canadians have attained.

The Task Force on Fiscal Federalism (House of Commons 1981: 115) concluded that, despite the constitutional division of powers,

> . . . there is an overriding national interest in the operation of health insurance plans and in the effectiveness of health care delivery and that the appropriate role for the federal government, in consultation with provincial governments, is the formulation, monitoring and enforcement of conditions on federal financial support of provincial programs.

These recommendations, coming from an all-party committee of Parliament, paved the way for the CHA and the elimination of direct charges.

The campaign for the CHA, as chronicled by Bégin, the national Minister of Health and the architect of the CHA, documents a bitter and acrimonious struggle, both within Cabinet and with provincial health ministers. Repeated voluntary attempts at initially controlling direct charges and eventually eliminating them were unsuccessful, with provincial acts of defiance continually escalating. A turning point came in March 1983 when the Alberta government announced that health premiums would be raised by 47 percent and a $20-a-day hospital user fee would be established (Bégin 1988). In July 1983, Bégin issued a position paper, *Preserving Universal Medicare* (National Health and Welfare 1983), in which the proposed CHA was announced. Specifically addressing the issue of direct charges, this document stated that

> Medicare is being eroded by the spread of direct charges in the form of user charges and extra-billing. Existing legislation is not adequate to deal with the problem because it does not clearly tell provinces, health care providers and the public that direct charges for health services will not be supported. It is time for a new Canada Health Act. (33)

On December 12, 1983, the proposed CHA was introduced in the House as Bill C-3, and received all-party approval upon first reading. The purpose of the CHA was to consolidate the Hospital Insurance and Diagnostic Services Act of 1957 and the Medical Care Act of 1966 and to define more precisely the terms and conditions upon which federal payments would continue to be made. The new Act (1985) reaffirmed the five program conditions that had been previously included in the Medical Care Act of 1967. The most controversial aspect of the Act pertained to Section 12(1) in which the conditions relating to the criterion of accessibility were specifically operationalized. This section stated that

> . . . insured health services [must be provided] on uniform terms and conditions and on a basis that does not impede or preclude, either directly or indirectly whether by charges made to insured persons or otherwise the reasonable access to those services by insured persons.

Further, it stipulated that for every dollar of extra-billing or hospital user fees, the federal government will withhold one dollar from its cash contribution. Provinces would be able to recover this money, without interest, if they banned these practices by April 1, 1987.

## The Debate on the Canada Health Act[5]

Bill C-3 was subsequently referred to the House of Commons Standing Committee on Health, Welfare and Social Affairs. The House committee, headed by David Weatherhead, began consideration of Bill C-3 on Tuesday January 31, 1984. From February 7 to February 23 the committee heard testimony from witnesses representing fifty interest groups.

The concept of "universality" was at the foreground of the debate on the CHA. The CHA represents the first major reaffirmation and redefinition of universality since the original inception of Canada's national health care system. With the CHA, the federal government unilaterally redefined "universality" within the Canadian health care system solely in relation to the elimination of extra-billing and hospital user fees. These extra charges were considered a barrier to "reasonable access" and threatened a necessary condition of universal health care.

In contrast to the EPF which demonstrated that an "established" program such as medicare could be weakened, the CHA demonstrated the same program could be modified and, in this situation, strengthened. Canada's national health insurance system was once again "open" for debate and renegotiation, constituting a crucial moment in Canadian health policy. Expectations were heightened within various sectors while extreme concern was voiced by many. New losers would be the physicians and the provincial governments. These two interest groups, striving to at least maintain the status quo, revived a number of previously settled normative concerns, adamantly maintaining that direct charges do not undermine the universal nature of medicare. Other groups, such as public interest organizations and nurses associations, welcomed the new conditions and used their submissions to move the health policy debate forward by focusing on future-oriented organizational and delivery structures.

## The Use of Equity in the Submissions

The debate on the CHA was highly normative. Values were used extensively by all participants to justify their position. The value of equity was consistently and extensively invoked by all groups. The general conception of equity as "fairness" was developed in relation to various dimensions of equal access in health care and reflected the limited nature of our national health care system. Three types of equity of access were identified: equity of access *to* medicare, equity of access *in* medicare and equity of access to *health.* Arguments within each of these dimensions focused on different barriers to access, suggesting different interpretations of the program conditions.

The first dimension, equity of access *to* medicare, would require that all publicly insured services be available to all Canadians on equal terms and conditions. This is a relative conception of equity in that everyone should have equal access to what is publicly available (Daniels 1985). Although every submission invoked a concern with this dimension of "equity," there was not a consensus on what constituted significant barriers to access. Groups named direct charges or the limited availability of insured services as barriers, but no group highlighted both types of barriers in their submissions.

Nursing organizations and public interest groups primarily maintained that the greatest threat to accessing medicare was the existence of direct charges. These groups maintained that, with direct charges, financial criteria would once again determine who gains entry to medicare services. While these participants did not deny the lack of sufficient funding, they did not premise their argument on funding grounds.

The majority of physicians, groups and the provincial governments were in support of direct charges and thus interpreted the problem of accessibility from an availability perspective. The typical argument that evolved from this concern with availability was that services were not distributed in accordance with need, but instead, there were geographic inequities between provinces as well as within provinces. Geographic inequities in the level of services were attributed to the lack of sufficient "federal" and "private" funds.

These two barriers that framed the dimension of access to medicare appear as conceptual "trade-offs" in this context and were suggestive of the groups overall position on the CHA. Those groups supporting the CHA argued that direct charges threaten accessibility. Groups that opposed the CHA maintained that insufficient federal funds threatened accessibility and that direct charges were a necessary source for generating additional revenues. Groups that supported direct charges adamantly maintained that these charges would not erode and were, in fact, consistent with the universal nature of medicare.

The second dimension of equity, access *in* medicare, specifically addresses the question of which services should be publicly insured and thus available on equal terms and conditions. In this conception, equity requires that individuals with different health needs have an equally effective chance of meeting their specific needs. This dimension reflects substantive concerns (Daniels 1985) with the comprehensiveness of medicare and could require the expansion or contraction of existing services. Again, two key barriers were invoked within this dimension and were directly derived from the first dimension of equity. Those groups opposing direct charges went on to address the issue of comprehensiveness, arguing that medicare emphasized physician and hospital services to the exclusion of preventive and community based alternatives. This argument represents a recognition of the distinction between "insured" and "non-insured" services and the unaccountability associated with non-insured services. These groups were proposing that the bundle of insured services be increased so that all health services would be subjected to the five program conditions.

Provincial governments opposing the CHA continued to mount a funding argument, maintaining that the "add-on" services, because of the lack of federal cost sharing, were funded by hospital user fees and health care premiums. Consequently, these forms of direct charges actually increased accessibility to non-insured services. Physician groups did not address this dimension of equity.

The third dimension of equity, access to *health*, expands the parameters of the equity debate to the non-medical determinants of health. This dimension was only invoked by the public interest groups. The inequities in the broader economic and social structure of Canadian society are identified as barriers to achieving healthy outcomes. In this structural dimension, states of poverty and unemployment were identified as major barriers to health, reaffirming the federal role in improving and equalizing the life chances of Canadians. With this third level of equity, Canadians are reminded of the limits of an egalitarian subset of services within an otherwise inegalitarian social structure.

## ACHIEVEMENTS OF THE CHA

The CHA was unanimously passed in 1984 with all provincial governments passing enabling legislation within the three year time limit. With the CHA, an equity framework was reaffirmed in which "equity of access" was defined solely in terms of the elimination of direct charges for insured services. Although this interpretation is limited, it has successfully harnessed efforts at privatizing costs. Provincial governments have been forced to look within the system and contain costs through enhancing efficiency. Provincial strategies have included the move to global budgets for hospitals, capping physicians' fees, reducing enrolments to medical schools, closing hospitals and encouraging community based alternatives. While some of these "cutbacks" have been painful and may have negatively impacted on other barriers and dimensions of equity, direct charges for insured services have been successfully eliminated.

Our experiences with the CHA would indicate that certain types of national standards can and do generate compliance. Effective national standards are: specific, incorporating the principle as well as the means; enforceable, incorporating an appropriate penalty that is suited to the violation; and financially packaged, offering either additional funds or threatening to decrease funds.

## THE IMPORTANCE OF NATIONAL STANDARDS AND THE CURRENT CONTEXT

The national elements of our health care system are those in which the federal government has assumed a substantive responsibility. These universal aspects of medicare continue to represent a defining aspect of our nationhood, clearly distinguishing us from our southern neighbour. Medicare represents a degree of egalitarianism unrivaled by any other national public program. With medicare, we entrenched the right of access through curtailing otherwise legitimate economic freedoms, resulting in a unique relationship between the individual and the state in Canadian society.

The striking similarity across provincial plans in terms of the bundle of "insured services" under medicare is a testimony to the importance of enforceable conditions attached to federal funds. The proverbial "stick" of the CHA has been effective as long as the federal government has the political will and financial means to enforce it.

The federal financial and substantive retreat under the CHST ushers in yet another new phase of provincial sovereignty in medicare. All political parties, at both the federal and provincial levels, are acutely aware of the public support for medicare. The "Canada Social

Transfer" was renamed to include "Health" in the title shortly after Prime Minister Jean Chrétien told Canadians that medicare should be a no frills, just-the-basics type of health care system.[6] In the recent Ontario provincial election, the new Progressive Conservative Premier, Mike Harris, while campaigning on a "right wing" platform of workfare, tax cuts, "boot camps" for young offenders and controlled access to abortion, has nevertheless vowed to maintain and even strengthen medicare.

However, a new and perhaps decisive battle over universality is again occurring primarily between Ottawa and Alberta. While the earlier battle pertained to the first dimension of equity (access *to* medicare), the new battle is being fought within the second dimension (access *in* medicare) in terms of which services will be considered "insured services." The new route to privatizing costs is through "delisting services," thus shrinking the bundle of publicly insured services. The current federal Health Minister, Diane Marleau, has declined to specify which specific services are to be insured. However, Ottawa continues to denounce Alberta's experimentation with private eye-care clinics maintaining that they contravene the accessibility conditions of the CHA. Prime Minister Jean Chrétien and his Health Minister adamantly maintain that Ottawa remains committed to medicare and will continue to enforce the CHA.

However, with the projected elimination of the cash portion of the CHST and the corresponding devolution of power, the federal government will no longer be able to enforce the conditions of the CHA. The CHST goes well beyond the disentangled nature of the early EPF, with program conditions no longer linked to any specific federal funds. As earlier experiences have indicated, provincial variations will undoubtedly continue to increase, fuelled by the privatizing efforts of "right-leaning" provincial governments operating within a deficit reduction mode. Under the CHST, the one-tiered medicare system covering insured services will eventually transform into a two-tiered system, incorporating both a public tier and a private tier and will shrink the range of insured services. With the return to financially determined access, the uniquely collective and inclusionary properties of medicare will erode. A restructured medicare will further contribute to the polarizing thrusts of the current Canadian political and economic context.

The professed commitment of Ottawa to medicare needs to be substantiated in a meaningful manner. An enforceable reaffirmation of the CHA seems necessary in the current political climate. The New Democratic Party government of British Columbia has recently announced that it plans to amend and rename its Medical and Health Care Services Act to the Medicare Protection Act in recognition of the precarious nature of the program (McInnes 1995: A1). The new amendments would reinforce the public aspects of the program, eliminating some of the incentives that now exist for operating private clinics. Other provinces have not as yet responded in a similar manner and may be waiting for a resolution between Ottawa and Alberta before preceding with their own approaches.

With the CHST, the success of the twenty-five year battle for national standards in medicare dissipates. The CHA has been a successful policy instrument. If Ottawa is indeed committed to medicare a significant cash portion of the CHST should be maintained to allow for the continued enforcement of the CHA.[7] This would afford Canadians with some modicum of security, preserving national standards for a least one of the programs incorporated in the CHST. Protecting the egalitarian vision in medicare will continue to remind Canadians of our political propensity for collectivism and humanitarianism. A question that remains to be answered, however, is what will happen to the status of other programs if national standards for medicare are incorporated into the CHST? Will this result in funding cutbacks to these programs?

In conclusion, the federal government continues to maintain a pivotal role in national programs. Through earlier acts of commission the federal government facilitated the emergence of a national health insurance program, framed by a unique interpretation of "equity." The current acts of omission indicate the federal government's capacity to dismantle the national health insurance program. Consequently the current national standard of "equity" will be replaced by a national standard of "inequity" with the implementation of the proposed Canada Health and Social Transfer.

## NOTES

1. In 1984, Bill C-12 required that the EPF transfer be separated, indicating the amount designated for health and post-secondary education.
2. It is important to recognize that not all opted-out physicians charge their patients above the provincial fee schedule. A study of opted-out physicians in Ontario found that there are physicians who are ideologically opposed to being reimbursed by the provincial governments. These physicians contend that billing patients directly is essential to demonstrating that their relationship is exclusively with the patient (Wolfson and Tuohy 1980). This study also found that these physicians earned less than those who were opted-in.
3. For a detailed account of the various models of extra-billing and the differential impact, please refer to National Council of Welfare 1982.
4. One additional type of direct charge involves the collection of health premiums to help finance the province's health costs. Health premiums are collected in the following three provinces: Ontario, Alberta and British Columbia.
5. The analysis of the debate on the Canada Health Act is derived from the author's doctoral dissertation, *Universal Health Care: The Canadian Definition*; Bryn Mawr College, 1993. This study incorporated a qualitative analysis of the written submissions presented to the House of Commons Standing Committee on Health, Welfare and Social Affairs in relation to Bill C-3, the Canada Health Act, in 1984. Other central values such as "responsibility," "efficiency" and "rights" were examined in the dissertation. This research was supported by a National Welfare Fellowship from the Department of National Health and Welfare.
6. Mr. Chrétien stated this in an interview on the CBC Radio's *Morningside*, Wednesday, March 1, 1995.
7. Health Minister Diane Marleau has recently indicated, after meeting with provincial ministers of health, that she would like to maintain a designated cash portion of the CHST, similar to what the provinces now receive under EPF. No firm guarantee can be made until Finance Minister Paul Martin is able to reach an agreement with his provincial counterparts (Thanh Ha 1995: A4).

## REFERENCES

Bégin, Monique. 1988. *Medicare: Canada's Right to Health*. Ottawa: Optimum Publishing International.

Canada. House of Commons. 1984. *Canada Health Act*. Ottawa: Queen's Printers.

Carter, George, E. 1994. "Federal Restraints on the Growth of Transfer Payments to the Provinces Since 1986-87: An Assessment." *Canadian Tax Journal* 42 (6): 1504-32.

Daniels, Norman. 1985. *Just Health Care*. Cambridge: Cambridge University Press.

Department of Finance. 1995a. *Budget Speech*. Ottawa: Minister of Supply and Services.

———. 1995b. *Budget in Brief*. Ottawa: Minister of Supply and Services

————. 1995c. *Budget Plan*. Ottawa: Minister of Supply and Services.

Doern, G. Bruce and Peter Aucoin. 1983. *Canadian Public Policy*. Toronto: Methuen.

Gray, Gwendolyn. 1991. *Federalism and Health Policy: The Development of Health Systems in Canada and Australia*. Toronto: University of Toronto Press.

Hall, Emmett M. 1980. *Canada's National-Provincial Health Insurance Program for the 1980s: A Commitment for Renewal*. Ottawa: Department of National Health and Welfare.

House of Commons. 1981. *Fiscal Federalism in Canada. Report of the Parliamentary Task Force on Federal Provincial Fiscal Arrangements*. Ottawa: Minister of Supply and Services.

Lalonde, Marc. 1974. *A New Perspective on the Health of Canadians*. Ottawa: Department of National Health and Welfare.

Manga, Pran. 1987. "Equality of Access and Inequality in Health Status: Policy Implications of a Paradox." In P. Coburn et al. (eds.), *Health and Canadian Society*. Markham: Fitzhenry and Whiteside.

McInnes, Craig. 1995. "B.C. won't outlaw private health care." *Globe and Mail* June 30: A1.

Milne, David. 1986. *Tug of War: Ottawa and the Provinces Under Trudeau and Mulroney*. Toronto: James Lorimer.

National Council of Welfare. 1982. *Medicare: The Public Good and Private Practice*. Ottawa: Minister of Supply and Services.

National Health and Welfare. 1983. *Preserving Universal Medicare*. Ottawa: Minister of Supply and Services.

————. 1986. *1984-85 Canada Health Act Annual Report*. Ottawa: Minister of Supply and Services.

Taylor, Malcolm. 1987. "The Canadian Health Care System After Medicare." In D. Coburn (ed.), *Health and Canadian Society*. Second Edition. Markham: Fitzhenry and Whiteside.

————. 1978. *Health Insurance and Canadian Public Policy: The Seven Decisions that Created the Canadian Health Insurance System*. Montreal: McGill-Queen's University Press.

Thanh Ha, Tu. 1995. "Marleau Tries to Ease Worries About Medicare." *Globe and Mail* July 5: A4.

Titmuss, Richard. 1974. *Social Policy*. London: Allen and Unwin.

Van Loon, Richard, J. 1978. "From Shared Cost to Block Funding and Beyond: The Politics of Health Insurance in Canada." *Journal of Health Politics, Policy and Law* 2 (Winter): 454-78.

Weller, Geoffery and Pran Manga. 1983. "The Development of Health Policy in Canada." In Michael Atkinson and Marsha Chandler (eds.), *The Politics of Canadian Public Policy*. Toronto: University of Toronto Press.

Wolfson, A.D. and C. Tuohy. 1980. *Opting Out of Medicare: Private Medical Markets in Ontario*. Toronto: Ontario Economic Council.

# CHAPTER 6

# REMAKING CANADIAN SOCIAL POLICY: A QUÉBEC VIEWPOINT

*Yves Vaillancourt*

## INTRODUCTION

The issue of "remaking Canadian social policy" in the 1990s, as in the 1940s, is a twofold reform process. Because the Canadian political system is a federal rather than a unitarian system, the remaking of Canadian social policy is, at once, a federal-provincial process and a social policy process (Vaillancourt 1991, 1994a; Duperré 1987, 1990, 1992). After the failure of the Meech Lake and Charlottetown Accords, and on the eve of a referendum on Québec sovereignty, this distinction is particularly important in Québec.

With regard to the federal-provincial dimension and more specifically to the Québec/Canada issue, there are four possible positions. The first is to treat the Canadian political system as a unitarian system. The second assumes that the current Canadian federal system is viable. The third recognizes that the federal political system in Canada has to be renewed in order to provide more powers and fiscal revenues either to all provinces (symmetrical decentralized federalism) or to Québec alone (asymmetrical decentralized federalism). The fourth position is to take for granted that Québec should separate, in one way or another, from Canada. My position here is the fourth one, although I could accept asymmetrical federalism that gives Québec special status in a renewed federalism.

With regard to the social policy dimension, those involved in the debate on remaking social policy in Québec, as well as in Canada and other countries, are faced with three scenarios. The first, adopted by the old-style progressives, is to accept and continue to advance the basic principles of the post-war social policy paradigm. The second is the approach underlying the Axworthy and Martin reforms. It consists of remaking social policy within a neoliberal framework. A third scenario is a "new progressive paradigm" that demarcates itself from both the neoliberal framework and the old post-war welfare state model. This is the perspective I favour. It means that I do not accept the Axworthy reforms or the "Campaign to Save Our Social Programs" launched by the Council of Canadians (Vaillancourt 1994b).

It is clear from the above that the analysis in this paper is influenced by a dual perspective. First, there is the perspective of a nationalist Québécois that favours more sovereignty for Québec in the 1995 referendum. Second, there is the viewpoint of a progressive social policy researcher that acknowledges the crisis of the welfare state and prefers to work towards a new paradigm of social and economic development.

The preparation of this paper was made possible with the support of a research grant from the Québec Department of Health and Social Services for the project "Politiques sociales/Québec-Canada 1995," and with the contribution of Luc Thériault PhD, a research assistant on this project. I wish to acknowledge the help of Francine Lalonde, member of Parliament for Mercier, for providing me with documentation on the Axworthy reforms and the Martin budgets. I wish also to thank the editors of this book for their helpful suggestions.

This paper is structured around two parts. First, paying attention to federal/provincial and Canada/Québec issues, it critically assesses some main components of the Axworthy/Martin reforms. Second, it addresses the task of rethinking and remaking social policy within a new progressive paradigm. In particular the issue of establishing a new partnership between the public and voluntary sectors is considered. The second part of the paper concludes by briefly considering the current restructuring of health and social services in Québec. It suggests that this process illustrates the forging of new partnerships that are essential to the development of "a new progressive paradigm."

## CRITIQUE OF THE AXWORTHY/MARTIN REFORM OF SOCIAL PROGRAMS

The current federal social policy initiatives have two major objectives. On the one hand, in the area of indirect intervention, the federal government through the Canada Health and Social Transfer (CHST) is cutting back on the funding of provincial social programs, arguably without abandoning its control of national standards. On the other hand, in the area of direct intervention, the government's new Human Resources Investment Fund (HRIF) opens the door for greater federal intervention. The reduced block funding component of the CHST suggests that the federal government is short of money. Paradoxically, the new initiatives planned for the HRIF indicates that there are funds for programs of direct intervention.

### FEDERAL OFFLOADING: THE CANADA HEALTH AND SOCIAL TRANSFER

The proposals and the actions of the federal government with regard to the CHST are better understood when it is recognized that in these domains of social policy, the federal government intervenes indirectly rather than directly. Historically, through the Canada Assistance Plan (CAP) and the Established Program Financing (EPF) federal action is indirect in the areas of social assistance and social services, post-secondary education and health. In the Canadian Constitution these fields of social action are exclusively under the jurisdiction of the provinces. To act in these areas, the federal government, through its spending power, uses "conditional grants" and therefore assumes a financial role in cost sharing the expenses of provincial social programs. Since it shares the cost of provincial programs, the federal government is in a position to set national standards or conditions the provinces must meet in order to receive federal funds.

To fully appreciate the meaning of the fusion of CAP and EPF in the CHST presupposes an understanding of the initial differences between these two transfer programs. CAP, created in 1966, is a classical cost shared program. The federal government, through signed agreements with the provinces, is bound to pay provincial claims for cost sharable services if the provincial claims meet the requirements of the CAP Act. CAP stipulates that the federal government pays 50 percent of the cost of provincial expenses in the areas of social assistance and welfare services. Here federal transfers are "open ended." They are bound by provincial costs as long as these are sharable according to the guidelines of CAP. For example, in the 1981-82 and 1990-91 recessions, when expenditures on social assistance increased by 25 percent to 30 percent, the federal government was obliged to pay for half of these increases (Duperré 1987; Courchene 1994: 117-21).

EPF, created in 1977, is a "block funding" method. Here there is a net separation between federal payments and provincial expenses. The dollar value of federal transfers paid to the provinces is calculated by a formula based on demographic and economic indicators. This formula is defined in a federal act and is amendable unilaterally by the federal government (Duperré 1987; Courchene 1994: 108-17). When it was introduced in 1977, some provinces (including Québec) believed that block funding was more flexible (i.e., less conditional) at the constitutional level and financially more stable because of the 1977 formula. Some government leaders treated EPF like an unconditional grant but this was not justified. From 1982 on, it was clear the federal government was able, without negotiating with the provinces, to change the EPF formula. This had the effect of lowering transfers to some provinces. In the health sector, for example, the federal financial contribution represented 48 percent of Québec's health expenses in 1975-76 but only 34 percent in 1994-95 (MSSS 1995b: 3-8 and Table 3 in the Appendix). In 1984, with the debate around the five conditions of the Canada Health Act, it became clear that EPF is a conditional grant. To obtain these transfers, provinces had to comply with the Canada Health Act conditions: universality; portability; accessibility; comprehensiveness; and public administration.

In addition to the distinction between cost sharing and block funding, attention must be given to the historical and political meaning of the distinction between the fiscal component (mainly personal income tax points) and the cash or financial component of federal transfers. Québec has special status with regard to the issue of fiscal points. Indeed, although all provinces have 13.5 tax points (of personal income tax) on EPF, Québec has an additional 8.5 tax points related to the "Québec Tax Abatement" (Duperré 1992: 19; Courchene 1994: 114). With regards to CAP, Québec is the only province that has special status with 5 fiscal points (of personal income tax). This special status originated with the Established Programs (Interim Arrangements) Act of 1964. This agreement is not known by many social policy commentators in Canada or even in Québec. One outcome is that there are misleading analyses on the tax points issue, suggesting that it started in the 1970s with EPF.[1] My hypothesis is that the tax point factor and Québec's special status regarding tax points are not unconnected with the advent of the CHST.[2]

Two other points must be kept in mind. First, with the unilateral reduction of federal cash transfers since 1982, the annual value of the financial component of the EPF transfers has decreased. Second, because of its special status with EPF (and CAP), the Québec EPF cash component is smaller (about 34 percent in 1994-95) than the average percentage for all provinces combined (approximately 51 percent in 1994-95) (Department of Finance 1995b; MSSS 1995b; Courchene 1994: 112). The Caledon Institute of Social Policy predicted that "federal cash transfers to all the provinces and territories will disappear by around 2009-10" (Battle and Torjman 1993: 5). The Gérard D. Lévesque budget speeches of the late 1980s put forward two dates for the end of cash transfers to Québec, 2002-03 (Lévesque 1987: see Appendix E, 7) or 1997-98 (Lévesque 1991: see Appendix E).

## THE SIZE OF THE CHST CUTS

The exact size of the cuts imposed through CHST in April 1996 and April 1997 have been underestimated by many people, starting with the federal Minister of Finance. Regarding the magnitude of the cuts, Paul Martin (Department of Finance 1995a: 19) put forward some questionable figures in his budget speech.

As we have said, no changes in major transfers are being made for next year—1995-

96—even though we are taking substantial action that year to reduce our own spending.

For the following year, the new Canada Social Transfer will be $26.9 billion—cash and tax points combined. This will be about $2.5 billion less than the projected transfer would be under the present system.

This means that the total of all major federal transfers to the provinces in 1996-97 will be 4.4 per cent lower than they are today. That compares favourably with the reduction in spending in our own backyard—that is, everything except transfers to the provinces—which will be down 7.3 per cent by that same year.

If the Minister was correct in predicting a reduction of 4.4 percent, he would be on solid ground to invite the provinces to reduce their own social program expenses and demonstrate more "flexibility." However, to obtain this 4.4 percent figure Martin makes two questionable calculations: he includes *equalization payments* with EPF and CAP under the CHST; and he treats tax points in the same manner as cash transfers.

Recent analyses of the impact of the CHST cuts in April 1996 and 1997 noted Martin's questionable inclusion of equalization payments (Battle and Torjman 1995: 12-13; National Council of Welfare 1995). It is customary to deal separately with equalization payments and social transfer payments. Equalization payments represent an interregional redistribution instrument rather than a social policy instrument. When these are excluded, both the Caledon Institute and the National Council of Welfare offer estimates of the size of the cuts that more than double the 4.4 percent figure in Martin's budget. The Caledon Institute suggests 8.5 percent while the National Council of Welfare calculates a 9.4 percent reduction in transfers.[3] However, the parallel treatment of tax and cash transfers is missed.[4]

It is important to point to the error these two groups make in their treatment of tax points. For example, as the following quote suggests, Caledon (Battle and Torjman 1995: 13-14) appears to accept the federal government's treatment of tax points transferred to the provinces as though they are a *federal social transfer*.

> The new Canada Social Transfer will arrive with deeper cuts than proposed in last year's Budget. When it is put in place in 1996-97, the CST [or CHST since Bill C-76] will pay the provinces $26.9 billion—$2.5 billion less than the $29.4 billion that would have been spent under the present system (CAP and EPF). In its second year, 1997-98, the CST will transfer $25.1 billion—$4.5 billion less than the $29.6 billion they would have received from the old system. These reductions amount to 8.5 percent for 1996-97 and 15.2 percent for 1997-98. These figures are for total entitlements: the Canada Social Transfer will continue the current approach whereby Ottawa divides its social transfer (provincial 'entitlement') into two parts—cash transfers and 'tax points' (i.e., the income tax power that the federal government gave up to the provinces when it introduced EPF back in 1977 and which it still counts as part of its social transfers to the provinces).

This treatment of the fiscal component of federal social transfers is one with which I strongly disagree. As noted above, the federal government, in 1977, did indeed give some tax points to all provinces. This was a delicate political move of damage control to defuse opposition to Québec's *de facto* special status created in 1965 when, through a struggle led by the Lesage government, Québec obtained 20 tax points from Ottawa (Vaillancourt 1993b). It is important to understand that, from Québec's perspective, these tax points belong to Québec as it has collected its own personal income tax revenue since the 1950s, which increased in 1965 with the opting out interim arrangements. These tax points are not a gift given in 1977 by the federal government. They represent the result of a political struggle on the part of Québec to have the fiscal means to master its own jurisdictional responsibilities in the areas of social policy, education and training.

The action of the federal government, in the last thirty years, has weakened the political meaning of fiscal points and created collective amnesia about the origin of tax points in Canada and Québec. To deal accurately with the fiscal points issue connected to EPF, CAP and the CHST, the fiscal components of federal transfers need to be seen for what they are: as provincial revenue, not federal revenue transferred from Ottawa to the provinces. It is not easy for analysts from other provinces to grasp this reality because, with the exception of Québec, other provincial governments do not collect tax revenues connected with tax points. On the contrary, the federal government first collects these taxes and then transfers them back to the provinces as "provincial fiscal revenue." In Québec, however, we clearly distinguish federal from provincial personal income tax. In other words, the tax points obtained in the 1960s and the 1970s are not "rented" from the federal government. Tax points were obtained through a political struggle and cannot be taken away without another political battle. In Ottawa this reality is well understood.

This position is shared by the Departments of Finance and Health and Social Services in the current PQ government (Campeau 1995; MSSS 1995b) and by the Finance Department in the former Liberal government led by Robert Bourassa (Lévesque 1991: see Appendix E). This is also clearly understood in Tom Courchene's (1994: 114, 115, 116) analysis of *Social Canada in the Millennium*.

> Since the tax transfer is incorporated in the provincial taxes, they become provincial own-source revenues. Thus, it is not obvious that much, other than confusion, is achieved by referring to the tax-point transfer under EPF as federal transfers. What these tax point transfers are really used for in the context of EPF is essentially to determine how much in the way of cash transfers to the various provinces is needed to bring each province up to the EPF ceiling.
>
> . . . To this point, there is no real or financial transfer from Ottawa to the provinces. All of this is notional. Therefore, all that is truly transferred under EPF is the cash component. . . .
>
> . . . EPF is not a $20.8 billion transfer, as might be assumed. . . . Rather, it is a $9.6 billion transfer (the cash component), with potentially an extra billion or so for the Québec abatement.

These affirmations were made before the last Martin budget for 1992-93 EPF and CAP figures. To calculate the real impact of the 1996-97 and 1997-98 cuts imposed by the CHST one must focus only on the cash component of these transfers. This is done in Table 1 which shows that the percentage of cuts is 20.2 percent from 1995-96 to 1996-97 or 35 percent from 1996-97 to 1997-98.[5] This means that the magnitude of fiscal constraint imposed on the provinces on the first of April 1996 and 1997 will be much greater than is suggested by either the Martin budget, the Caledon Institute or the National Council of Welfare.

Assuming cuts are proportional in the Martin budget (Department of Finance 1995a: 19), Québec will absorb about 27 percent of the cuts in 1996-97 as it now receives around 27 percent of the total EPF and CAP cash transfers.[6] This would mean about $750 million less (in cash transfers) in 1996-97 than in 1995-96. The Québec share of the CHST reduction in 1997-98 cannot be as easily established. This is because the formula for calculating cash transfers will be defined later through consultations between the Minister of Human Resources Development Canada and the provinces and territories (Department of Finance 1995a: 18). In the meantime a *per capita* formula is being given serious consideration. If such a formula is used, Québec will receive about $1.75 billion less in social transfer payments in 1997-98 than in 1995-96.[7]

As noted by social policy analysts, the most serious impact resulting from the shift to the block funding formula of the CHST will occur in the next economic recession (National Council of Welfare 1995). The recession will push up the number of users and the costs of provincial social assistance but this will no longer influence the level of income transferred to the provinces from Ottawa.

Finally, the funding formula for the CHST after 1998-99 is still undecided. Given the size of the cuts to come in April 1996 and 1997, what guarantee do we have that the same kind of unilateral cutting process will not take place in the future (Greenspon 1995)? What kind of budget planning will the provinces be able to perform in such a context? This is an important concern and was raised in the last Campeau budget (1995: see Appendix E, 16) in Québec.

Table 1
**Federal Social Transfers to the Provinces** (in millions of dollars)

|  | 1994–95 | 1995–96 | 1996–97 | 1997–98 |
|---|---|---|---|---|
| EPF | 21,476 | 21,734 | — | — |
| CAP | 7,952 | 7,952 | — | — |
| CHST (CAP +EPF) | 29,428 | 29,686 | 26,900 | 25,100 |
| –Value of Fiscal Points | 11,729 | 12,572 | 13,248 | 13,968 |
| = Financial (cash) Transfers | 17,699 | 17,114 | 13,652 | 11,132 |
| **Percentage of cuts** |  |  | -20.0% | -18.5% |
| **Percentage of cuts from 1995–1996 to 1997–1998** |  |  |  | -35.0% |

Source: Department of Finance 1995b: 51.
Note: Calculations by Yves Vaillancourt.

## The Consequences of the chst Cuts

Several consequences are apparent. First, in dismantling the CAP and establishing the CHST, the Liberal government found a way to escape an obligation to repair some of the financial damage inflicted on Ontario, British Columbia and Alberta since the 1990 cap on CAP. Second, by collapsing the EPF and CAP transfers (fiscal and cash) into a single envelope, the federal government will lengthen the apparent lifetime of EPF *cash* transfers. Recall that in this fiscal year (1995-96), the $8 billion CAP envelope is smaller than the $21.7 billion EPF envelope. However, the *cash* component represents 85 percent of the CAP envelope and less than 50 percent of the EPF envelope in all provinces. The figure is less than 34 percent in Québec. With one comprehensive envelope instead of two, the federal government is adding a few extra years before these diminishing cash transfers go down to zero.

A final consequence is that, while reducing its financial contributions to the provinces, the federal government will still be able to insist on national standards as long as it continues to make cash transfers. In Canada some social policy groups and experts think differently. It is suggested that a reduction of cash transfers will result in the immediate elimination of national standards (Battle and Torjman 1995; Torjman and Battle 1995a, 1995b; National Council of Welfare 1995; Canadian Council on Social Development 1995; Banting and Battle 1994). A careful examination of Bill C-76 (Canada 1995) as well as the government's own response to these concerns does not support this conclusion. Witness Lloyd Axworthy's (1995) answer to Maude Barlow:

> Maude Barlow has it wrong ... in her attack on the recently announced Canadian Health and Social Transfer, she has it completely backwards by claiming that this will mean that the federal government won't be able to enforce its national standards.
>
> On the contrary, the CHST means that by consolidating the cash transfers from the existing EPF (Established Program Financing) and CAP (Canada Assistance Plan), the federal government will be in a position to ensure maintenance of the five principles of the Canada Health Act and the residency requirements for social assistance recipients. If there had not been this consolidation, then what Ms. Barlow claims could have occurred in that the individual cash transfer under the existing program would have ratcheted downward as the revenue to the provinces increased.
>
> ... The new CHST program presents an opportunity for the federal and provincial governments to sit down over the coming year to work on new principles, to look at how we can co-operate on developing coherent approaches to such present-day issues as family and child poverty. There can be the evolution of a new social policy framework, based on mutual consent that will serve future needs.

My point here is that the federal government will be in a position to impose national standards as long as there are cash social transfers. Of course, the cutbacks to cash transfers mean that national standards will disappear sooner than would have been the case without these cutbacks. However, with the decision (through the CHST) to create one unique social transfer envelope instead of maintaining the former two separate envelopes, the federal government has found a subtle way to keep the power to impose national standards for about five extra years. In other words, let us assume that the same size of cutbacks would have been introduced in two separate envelopes (i.e., EPF and CAP), the EPF cash payments to Québec would have ended in 1996-97 and the federal government would have found itself in a weak political position to impose national standards in the health domain.

## THE NEW HUMAN RESOURCES INVESTMENT FUND (HRIF)

Paradoxically, while trimming its financial obligations to the provinces in indirect intervention, the federal government is increasing its responsibilities and financial commitments in some areas of social policy and training in which it intervenes directly. Here the Axworthy reforms are not dead. To understand federal initiatives in this area, it is helpful to examine what was said about the new Human Resource Investment Fund in the last Martin budget (Department of Finance 1995a, 1995b).

At the beginning of the 1990s, the $5.5 billion cumulative deficit of the U.I. program was used to dramatize the financial problems of the federal government. As a result of the cutbacks introduced to U.I. in the 1994 Martin budget (Department of Finance 1994a, 1994b; Bloc Québécois 1995), in addition to those announced in the 1995 budget, the U.I. program has generated a surplus. The figures provided in Table 2 show the size of this surplus and suggest it will continue in future years.

Table 2

**Surplus in Unemployment Insurance 1993 to 1996** (in millions of dollars)

|  | 1993–94 | 1994–95 | 1995–96 | 1996–97 | Total 1993–96 |
|---|---|---|---|---|---|
| U.I. premiums | 18,200 | 18,900 | 19,700 | 18,500 | 75,300 |
| –U.I. benefits | 17,600 | 15,300 | 14,300 | 13,700 | 60,900 |
| –Admin. costs | 1,000 | 1,000 | 1,000 | 1,000 | 4,000 |
| =Surplus | (–400) | 2,600 | 4,400 | 3,800 | 10,400 |

Source: Department of Finance 1995b: 81 and 85.
Note:   Administrative costs are estimates.

Based on figures given in the last Martin budget, the U.I. program will generate a surplus of more than $10 billion between 1993-94 and 1996-97. This means that the cumulative U.I. deficit of more the $5.5 billion in the early nineties will be replaced by a surplus of more than $4 billion in 1996-97.

According to Martin (Department of Finance 1995b: 110) a part of this surplus will be used to fund the new HRIF.

> Current programs financed through the Consolidated Revenue Fund will be combined into a unified Human Resources Investment Fund which will focus on actively helping unemployed people find and keep jobs, combating child poverty, and providing assistance to those who need help most. In addition as stated in last October's discussion paper, *Improving Social Security in Canada*, consideration

will be given to more flexible use of unemployment insurance funds in order to provide more effective employment assistance to Canadians.

The consolidation of programs and services will result in savings of $600 million in 1995-96 and $1.1 billion in 1996-97 and each year thereafter. This will be achieved primarily by reducing the current Canadian Jobs Strategy, spending less than originally planned under the Strategic Initiatives program, and freezing maximum transfers to provinces under the Vocational Rehabilitation for Disabled Persons program at the 1994-95 level, as well as streamlining departmental operations including the consolidation of some offices and the closure of others.

As we see, the Martin budget is explicit in some respects but ambiguous in others concerning what will constitute the funding for the HRIF. The budget speech says explicitly that parts of the U.I. surplus will be transferred to the HRIF. It says less explicitly that part of the money saved through the "consolidation of programs and services" in the Department of Human Resources Development (i.e., $600,000 million in 1995-96 and $1.1 billion in 1996-97) could be moved to the HRIF. It does not say that the $2 billion, taken from U.I. revenues year after year, to finance employment and training services, will be moved under the umbrella of the HRIF. Obviously, the funding of the new HRIF will not be organized through new or additional funds, but through the reallocation of funds siphoned from existing sources.

The restructuring of programs and services, along with the reallocation of a significant portion of the savings generated by U.I. reform, is intended to ensure the most effective and efficient use of available resources to support better employment opportunities and prospects for Canadians.

The political future of Lloyd Axworthy in the Chrétien government is connected with the HRIF. What will be the use of an HRIF exclusively controlled by Ottawa? Even though the 1995 budget is silent on this matter, there is some evidence that the federal government is planning to use the HRIF as a means to maintain and develop a variety of options in the social policy arena. It will use the HRIF to intervene in training and different programs to help the unemployed. It also intends to use the HRIF for "combating child poverty, and providing assistance to those who need help most," and for initiatives "to support better employment opportunities and prospects for Canadians" (Department of Finance 1995b: 110). The Minister of Finance also recognizes that the federal government will be able to use the HRIF to act in the fields of literacy, day care services and income supplement programs (Department of Finance 1995b: 110). Hence the HRIF will be a major instrument for developing programs in the fields of jurisdiction that Québec considers as its own or wants to recover. It also appears that Mr. Axworthy is at liberty to define the structure and terms of reference of the HRIF.

> The Minister of Human Resources Development will be developing program parameters over the coming months and announcing the details of the new Human Resources Investment Fund in the fall as part of Social Security Reform (Department of Finance 1995b: 111).

These plans are far from reassuring for Québec. This brand of federalism creates a constant problem centering around a lack of harmonization and integration for Québec social policies. This is the case with training. It is also the case in U.I. and the province's welfare programs as people are constantly shuffled between the two.

## TOWARDS A NEW SOCIAL POLICY PARADIGM

### A CHALLENGE FOR PROGRESSIVES: GOING BEYOND THE DEFENSIVE

To respond more effectively to the social policy proposals of the neoliberals the progressive social policy community needs to do more than react negatively. We will have to do more than say "no" to free trade, privatization, decentralization and workfare. We will need to do more than talk nostalgically about the post-war welfare state and programs like the CAP.[8]

To be socially and politically productive, it is important to put forward a progressive alternative. It needs to be acknowledged that the post-war model of social development and social policy is now behind us. To weaken the neoliberal agenda requires counter-proposals within the framework of a new model of social development. It is necessary to rebuild confidence in our capacity to influence history and to make a creative contribution to a *new social welfare paradigm*. The challenge is similar to the one facing our progressive ancestors who, in the 1930s and 1940s, developed fordist and keynesian models of economic and social development that influenced Canada and other countries.

I would like to illustrate this new theoretical and political approach with the following examples: the Roeher Institute's (1993: 25) publication *Social Well-Being: A Paradigm for Reform* contains a chapter entitled "The Limitations of the Post-War Framework in Achieving Well-Being."[9] This chapter focuses on the lack of self-determination and participation for citizens in the post-war welfare state.

> Welfare state arrangements [of the Post-War framework] have also been criticized because they have undermined other aspects of people's well-being: their self-determination and participation in decisions affecting their lives. The bureaucratic and hierarchical organization of welfare state programs—in health care, income support and social services—has failed to effectively address the diverse needs, interests and identities of the individuals and groups the programs serve. Nor have these structures enabled consumers of various welfare state services to participate in the decisions affecting how their needs will be met. (18)

The Roeher Institute's discussion of the limitations of post-war social policy is often omitted in today's progressive social policy literature. Indeed this literature often appears to defend the status quo against neoliberal attacks. In doing so, progressives are often led to idealize post-war social policy programs and services. This tendency weakens their own arguments and proposals.

By contrast *Critical Choices, Turbulent Times* (Pollak et al. 1994) is a more ambiguous example, reflecting ambivalence between the old and the new progressive paradigms. Some parts, mainly the section on "First Nations Social Policy," are creative and innovative (67-79). The principles of decentralization, self-determination, local economic development and "community-controlled social services" are presented in a creative and genuine manner. In other parts, a more defensive and orthodox tone emerges. This is evident in the sections on "decentralization: dumping or community control" and the discussion on the public, voluntary and private sector involvement in the delivery of human services (55-57). While there are elements of a progressive paradigm of the 1970s, social progress remains essentially associated with the development of a strong, centralized and idealized conception of the public sector. The private sector is linked with the evils of human services privatization. The voluntary sector, on the other hand, is well defined.[10] However, the role it could play in the future is not dealt with in a constructive and strategic manner. Instead it is represented as a pool of resources unable to defend its own identity within the neoliberal environment of restructuring. There is room for a more a creative way of looking at the voluntary or "third sector" in the new progressive paradigm. In this regard, the contributions of some European and Québec researchers working in the framework of "regulation theory" are instructive.[11]

## THE THIRD SECTOR: CONCEPT AND THE LITERATURE

This section focuses on the linkages between the voluntary, public and private sectors. In the field of social and health services the new paradigm favours a sharing of responsibilities between these sectors. Drawing from my recent work (Vaillancourt 1993b, 1994b, 1994c), I distinguish between privatization and "communautarisation" and put forward some theoretical and political considerations for a new partnership between the state and the third sector. The development of this new paradigm is still in its early stages and other issues like the future of work and employment, income security and fiscal reform need to be better integrated into this framework.

I used the concept of "third sector" for the first time in 1993 in a preliminary report on the privatization of social services (Vaillancourt et al. 1993). This was influenced by the work of an economist from the French Regulation School, Alain Lipietz (1989). There is indeed a rich literature on the "third sector" in both Europe and the United States. In France, Jacques Delors (1994: 54, 63-67) recalled how he used this concept in the mid-1970s.[12] In the U.S. it is often called the "non-profit sector." In Europe it is also designated in different ways, depending on the country. In the U.K., for example, most authors refer to the "voluntary sector" while in France, Belgium and Italy it is also referred to as the "mouvement associatif et coopératif." This tradition of research and practice on the "third sector" is clearly traced by Defourny and Monzon Campos (1992), Perri 6 (1995), Perri 6 and Vidal (1994) and Smith, Rochester and Hedley (1995). This literature is not well known in Canada or Québec. It is, however, most relevant to the rethinking of the post-welfare state model as it develops the linkages and interfaces between the voluntary sector and the welfare state literature (Room and Perri 6 1994: 46-48). The work by Jeremy Kendall and Martin Knapp (1995) in England also illustrates this approach. They define the third sector as follows:

> . . . first these organizations are formal (not only informal); second, they are independent of governments and of private enterprizes; third, they are self-governing . . . a voluntary organization should be constitutionally or institutionally independent of government and self-governing, that is with its own internal decision-making structures and not controlled by a private (for-profit) firm or by government. (86)

Fourth, these organizations are "not profit-distributing and primarily non-business" (Kendall and Knapp 1995: 87). Fifth, they are committed to voluntarism. This last criterion is explained in this way (Kendall and Knapp 1995: 88):

To be regarded as part of the voluntary sector, the structural operational definition requires that an organization benefits to a meaningful degree from philanthropy or voluntary citizen involvement. Even if 100 per cent of an organization's income came from government or from fees paid by clients, there might still be voluntarism in the form of gifts in kind or of time from volunteers, either in the labour force or on the management committee.

Of course this "structural operational definition" of the third sector requires a more detailed explanation and can be challenged in many ways (Perri 6 1995: 132-33). Still it provides a good reference point for developing more concrete proposals for the role of the third sector in a new model of social development.

## THE VISION OF A NEW PARTNERSHIP BETWEEN THE THIRD SECTOR AND THE PUBLIC SECTOR IN THE AREA OF HUMAN SERVICES

When discussing the scenario of a new partnership between the public sector and the third sector in the area of human services, it is useful to keep in mind three functions of the state or local authorities. Local authorities have the following responsibilities: (1) to provide or enable human services; (2) to fund (or not to fund) these services; and (3) to monitor (or not to monitor) services in this area. These distinctions are clarified in recent literature from Britain on "community care" (Hoyes and Means 1993; Le Grand and Barlett 1993; Lewis 1994; Means and Smith 1994; Smith, Rochester and Hedley 1995: Jamieson 1991). Since the beginning of the 1990s, the local authorities in health, social services and housing have been legislated to play less of a "provider" role and more of an "enabler" role while still maintaining responsibilities for funding and monitoring. The implications for Québec (and perhaps other regions of Canada) is that this helps us to consider different functions local state authorities can play to meet new social needs within their communities. Is it really necessary for the public sector to continue to deliver services as it has in the past? Could this be done by others as long as the state monitors these functions?[13]

What does this mean in light of the objections about privatization and the dismantling of public services? First, privatization means a transfer of responsibility (for provision and/or funding and/or monitoring) from the public to the private, for-profit sector. To counter this model of privatization which is proposed by neoliberal forces, progressives can offer alternative approaches of "communautarisation" where the third sector develops new partnerships with the public service in some areas of human services delivery.[14] This requires a strengthening and consolidation of the third sector (Pestoff 1994; Ranci 1994; Stryjan 1994). It also implies the following: more stable financial and political support from public authorities; more legitimacy for the third sector within civil society; an institutionalized contract for ten to twenty years between components of the third sector and the state; and a clearer definition of what the sharing of responsibilities between the public, private and third sector means.[15] On the labour front this should support the creation of decent jobs. Too often jobs in the third sector are non-standard forms of labour that exacerbate the vulnerability of workers in this sector.

Second, we are heading "towards a post-fordist welfare state" (Burrows and Loader 1994), an era in which the state will play a less important role in the provision of services. One outcome could be a continuation of the kind of dismantling pursued by neoliberals now. State activities could continue to be moved to the market and the voluntary sector in ways that threaten the future of jobs and human services. Part of the neoliberal agenda is to use the third sector as a mechanism for contracting cheap labour and services. The challenge for progressives is to preempt this by articulating a more equitable and symmetrical partnership between the third sector and the state.

Third, what is at stake here is the shifting of human and fiscal resources from the "heavier" and more costly institutions in the health and social policy domains to the "lighter" and less costly community based institutions. The new paradigm requires that this is a principled shift to community care, not a downloading and downsizing of financial support. In Québec this implies more, not less, resources in the hands of the community based organizations (Favreau and Hurtubise 1993; Vaillancourt 1994c). It means greater availability of services for the elderly, people with learning and physical disabilities and the mentally challenged.

Finally, we have to consider the linkages between the process of deinstitutionalization and those of privatization and/or "communautarisation." They overlap as deinstitutionalization, like privatization, lowers the demand for public resources. However, this can be described more positively as a shift of resources to the community or "communautarisation." For example, the deinstitutionalization process for people with learning disabilities has meant some degree of replacement of public resources (i.e., public buildings, public employees and public budgets) by private (for-profit) or community (non-profit) resources.[16] People with learning disabilities are now living in smaller and less expensive sheltered residences or at home with the availability of different kinds of community support. It is clear that for many this type of privatization and/or "communautarisation" has positively affected their well-being.

## "Communautarisation" and the Debate About Health and Social Service Reform in Québec

The new Conseil de la santé et du bien-être (1995a, 1995b)[17] put forward public statements that are relevant to the discussion about the role of the third sector and communautarisation. The council argues that with a price tag of $13 billion, which represents 10 percent of GNP, the Québec system of health and social services is not under-funded. Based on research on the costs of health services in Canada and other countries the council suggests there is enough money.[18] However, it also argues that this money should be allocated differently: less money should be allocated to the drug industry, doctors and acute care beds, and more should be directed to the Centres Locaux de Services Communautaires (CLSCs—local centres for community services), community groups and domiciliary home care services.

This statement came in the midst of the current Rochon health and social services reform in Québec. Rochon has outlined two objectives: to work toward a genuine transformation of health and social services; and to apply cutbacks representing $547 million in the 1995-96 fiscal year and $400 million in 1996-97. The Rochon reforms have stimulated a heated debate in Québec. Some trade unionists and hospital managers are demanding a moratorium on these reforms. From their vantage point the Rochon reforms are not well planned. The underlying objective is to save money without paying sufficient attention to the quality of services and job security.

Others (myself among them) support the Rochon reforms. These represent a coherent effort in line with the Côté reforms which started under the Bourassa and Johnson governments (MSSS 1990, 1994, 1995a; Québec 1991, 1992; Régie régionale de la santé et des services sociaux de Montréal Centre 1995; Régie régionale de la santé et des services sociaux de l'Estrie 1994). The Rochon reforms are a transition from institutional to community care. Potentially these are important components of the new paradigm I have put forward in the second part of this paper. As such they merit careful evaluation.

## CONCLUSION

In the first section of the paper in which I critique the Axworthy-Martin reforms, I argue that in spite of appearances these reforms do not mean (at least for the coming five years) that a real decentralization process will take place in favour of the provinces. On the contrary, the creation of the CHST and HRIF (the two main components of the Axworthy-Martin reforms) lead us to the opposite conclusion. With regard to the CHST, which is a tool to intervene *indirectly* to regulate some provincial social programs, the federal government is retreating financially by unilaterally imposing cutbacks of $7 billion in cash social transfers over two years. However, it is not retreating on the political front because it will stay in a position to control national standards as long as it continues to provide cash transfer payments to the provinces. Instead of negotiating a genuine mechanism for provincial opting out of EPF and CAP arrangements at this time, which Québec has sought for thirty years, the federal government is imposing on the provinces a phase-out period of a few years. It is using this phase-out period to limit the fiscal capacity of provinces regarding social policy and is limiting their fiscal capacity more severely than it is its own. With regard to the HRIF, which is a tool for *direct* federal intervention, the federal government seems to be less interested in decentralizing than in reallocating money saved through cutbacks to U.I. Therefore, a comprehensive analysis of the two sets of maneuvers (the CHST and HRIF) raises the question as to whether the federal government is using the coming four or five years to transfer a maximum of financial resources from the CHST towards the HRIF, using the struggle against the deficit to hide and legitimize this internal transfer.

In the second part of the paper, I argue that the best way to counter the influence of the neoliberal agenda for remaking social policy is to put forward a new progressive social policy paradigm. To explain more concretely some features of this new paradigm, I examine the scenario of a new partnership between the state and the "third" or "nonprofit" sector of the economy. I suggest that the Rochon reforms in the area of health and social services were closer to a new progressive paradigm than to the neoliberal one. In contrast, the Axworthy-Martin reforms are closer to the neoliberal than the new progressive paradigm because they rely more on the private market or the for-profit sector than on the third sector. It is in this context that the coming referendum will have a decisive influence on social policy possibilities in the coming years for Québec. The referendum will be decisive because the majority of "progressive" social movements and forces in Québec that favour reforms along the lines of the "new progressive paradigm" also support Québec sovereignty. Therefore, if the "Yes" side loses the referendum, these influences will be weakened politically. On the other hand, if the "Yes" side wins, there is no guarantee that the progressive paradigm outlined above will prevail. However, at least there would be a potential opportunity for working toward remaking social policy in a progressive manner.

## Notes

1.  See for example the National Council of Welfare (1995) or Battle and Torjman (1995: 14).

2.  The history of the special fiscal status of Québec with regard to federal transfers in social programs can be summed up as follows. In the mid-1960s, the Québec Lesage government made a political breakthrough in its struggle for Québec to opt out of social, health and employment training. For a while the Pearson government in Ottawa accepted Québec's demands. It also offered interim arrangements to all provinces but only Québec accepted this. Québec was allowed to opt out of Hospital Insurance (in exchange for 14 tax points) and some social assistance programs (and received 4 tax points). These arrangements were for a five year *interim* (until 1970) to let the programs become *established*, that is until more was known about the cost and number of users. The transition from interim to permanent opting out was to take place in 1970. In 1970 opting out was to be completed and the volume of tax points received from Ottawa was to be harmonized with the real costs of the programs during the interim period. But in 1970 the federal government refused to provide Québec with a permanent arrangement and found various ways to continue the interim agreement. This was the situation until the EPF arrangements of 1977, through which it applied the "federal opting out" strategy articulated many years earlier. This meant that all of the provinces were given 13.5 fiscal points (on personal income tax) plus 1 point on corporate tax. The end result was that Québec's special status was substantially reduced, although Québec kept 8.5 additional tax points on EPF (for post-secondary education) and 5 tax points on CAP which the other provinces were not offered. From 1977 to 1995, the 1977 arrangements were maintained and this explains why Québec still possesses 16.5 additional tax points on personal income taxes.

3.  The difference between the Caledon and National Council of Welfare percentages occurs as Caledon takes as a departure point the 1994-95 EPF and CAP figures while the Council uses 1995-96 information.

4.  However, in another paper Sherri Torjman and Ken Battle (1995b: 7) seem to acknowledge that tax points are no longer federal money. "The fiction that Ottawa 'transfers' part of the CHST in the form of tax points—i.e., taxing power transferred many years ago to the provinces—should be dropped."

5.  Using the same method of calculation, Edward Greenspon (1995) of the *Globe and Mail* discussed cash transfer reductions of almost 40 percent in three years, from 1994-95 to 1997-98.

6.  This figure is the global result of the share of Québec on CAP (almost 33 percent) and EPF (just under 25 percent) in 1995-96.

7.  Campeau's last budget calculated that Québec would receive $1.88 billion less from the CHST in 1997-98 than it would from CAP and EPF in 1995-96 (Campeau 1995: Appendix E, 9). It is predicted that the trend in cash reductions would mean the end of cash transfers from the CHST for Québec by 1999-2000 (Campeau 1995: Appendix E, 9).

8.  CAP with its very selective philosophy (proper in the case of welfare programs but not in the case of social services) has been a hindrance for provinces like Québec, Manitoba, British Columbia and Saskatchewan that wanted, under progressive governments, to develop more universal social services (Vaillancourt 1992).

9.  A paper published by SPARC of BC (1993) is very similar to the Roeher publication. SPARC's paper is entitled *Well-Being: A Conceptual Framework and Three Literature Reviews*.

10.  The voluntary sector is defined as follows: "The voluntary sector includes non-profit organizations and charities, such as community-based agencies, advocacy groups, churches and food banks. This sector relies on government funds, private fund-raising and often a combination of the two. The term 'voluntary' sector is deceptive because it implies the work is done by volunteers. In fact, most non-profit societies in the social services field are managed and run by paid staff, although some also rely on volunteers" (Pollak et al. 1994: 55).

11.  I mention among others Lipietz 1989; Taylor and Hoggett 1994; Bélanger and Lévesque 1991, 1992; Lévesque and Malo 1992; Bélanger, Boucher and Lévesque 1994; Vaillancourt 1993b,

1994c. Out of regulation theory other authors have added important ideas for health policies (Renaud 1994), home care (Laville 1992) or popular sovereignty (Centre Saint-Pierre 1995) for the new progressive paradigm.

12. Talking about the third sector, Jacques Delors, the former president of the European Union, mentions that he used this concept unsuccessfully for the first time in the 1970s. He thinks it could be used more productively in the coming years. "C'est pourquoi je continue de penser qu'un troisième secteur fortement structuré donnerait un autre visage à notre système économique et à notre société" (Delors 1994: 65).

13. Ironically, with regard to the organization of health and social services, Québec is closer to the British model than any other Canadian province. Indeed, in Québec, the role of the public sector in the provision of services is more public than in provinces like Ontario and Manitoba.

14. I was less aware of the importance of this distinction between privatization and "communautarisation" in my research on privatization of the social services in the 1980s (Vaillancourt et al. 1988).

15. In Québec, according to some researchers, this type of "institutionalized contract" between the state and community organizations has started to emerge in the areas of health and social services over the last five years (see Panet-Raymond 1994; Gagné and Dorvil 1994; Caillouette 1994; Vaillancourt 1994c; Bélanger and Lévesque 1992; Bélanger, Boucher and Lévesque 1994).

16. The deinstitutionalization of peoples with intellectual disabilities must be distinguished from the deinstitutionalization of peoples with mental problems. Indeed, in the mental health domain, the deinstitutionalization process has not been completed and is much more controversial.

17. This council was created by the Québec government in the fall of 1993. It is composed of twenty-three members and chaired by Norbert Rodrique. An English edition of these papers will be available by the fall of 1995.

18. For example, the Québec Health and Welfare Council says: "Le Québec canalise vers les services de santé une part plus élevée de sa richesse que la moyenne des provinces canadiennes. En 1991, les dépenses pour les services de santé représentaient 9,9% du PIB au Québec, la moyenne canadienne s'établissant à 9,8%. Quant au Canada, il se classait bon deuxième, juste après les États-Unis (13,4%). Il était suivi de la France (9,1%), de la Finlande (8,9%), de la Suède et de l'Australie (8,6%) et de l'Allemagne (8,5%). À titre illustratif, pour rejoindre la France au troisième rang mondial, le Québec aurait du soustraire 1,3 milliard de dollars à ses dépenses de services de santé, en 1991." (Conseil de la santé et du bien-etre 1995a: 5).

## REFERENCES

Axworthy, Lloyd. 1995. "Barlow Has it Backwards" [An Answer to Maude Barlow]. *Globe and Mail* April 17: A16.

———. 1994. *La sécurité sociale dans le Canada de demain. Document de travail*. Hull: Centre des renseignements du gouvernement fédéral, octobre.

Banting, Keith and Ken Battle (eds.). 1994. *A New Social Vision for Canada? Perspectives on the Federal Discussion Paper on Social Security Reform*. Kingston: School of Policy Studies and Caledon Institute of Social Policy.

———. 1995. *How Finance Re-formed Social Policy*. Ottawa: The Caledon Institute of Social Policy, March.

Battle, Ken and Sherri Torjman. 1993. *Federal Social Programs: Setting the Record Straight*. Ottawa: Caledon Institute of Social Policy, Spring.

———. 1992. "Le mouvement populaire et communautaire: de la revendication au partenariat (1963-1992)." In Gérard Daigle and Guy Rocher (eds.), *Le Québec en jeu*. Montréal: PUM.

Bélanger, Paul R. and Benoît Lévesque. 1991. "La 'théorie' de la régulation, du rapport salarial au rapport de consommation. Un point de vue sociologique." *Cahiers de recherche sociologique* (hiver) 17: 17-51.

Bélanger, Paul R., Jacques Boucher and Benoît Lévesque. 1994. "L'économie solidaire au Québec: la question du modèle de développement." In Jean-Louis Laville (ed.), *L'économie solidaire. Une perspective internationale*. Paris: Desclée de Brouwer.

Bloc Québécois. 1995. "Pour faire face aux défis du XXIᵉ siècle: une réforme différente et mieux adaptée." Rapport minoritaire du Bloc Québécois, dans Comité permanent du développement des ressources humaines, *Équité, sécurité et perspectives d'avenir: Les Canadiens, maîtres d'œuvre du renouveau social*. Rapport du Comité permanent du développement des ressources humaines. Ottawa: Chambres des communes, 6 février.

Burrows, Roger and Brian Loader (eds.). 1994. *Towards a Post-Fordist Welfare State?* London and New York: Routledge.

Caillouette, Jacques. 1994. "L'État partenaire du communautaire: vers un nouveau modéle de développement." *Nouvelles pratiques sociales* 7 (1): 161-75.

Campeau, Jean. 1995. *Budget 1995-1996. Discours sur le budget et renseignements supplémentaires.* Québec: Gouvernement du Québec, 9 mai.

Canada. 1995. *Projet de loi C-76. Loi portant exécution de certaines dispositions du budget déposé au Parlement le 27 février*. Ottawa: 20 mars.

Canadian Council on Social Development. 1995. *Social Policy Beyond the Budget*. Ottawa: CCSD, April.

Centre d'animation St-Pierre Inc. 1995. *Redonner leur souveraineté aux pauvres et aux exclus*. Mémoire présenté devant la Commission de Montréal sur l'avenir du Québec, 28 février.

Conseil de la santé et du bien-être. 1995a. *Un juste prix pour les services de santé. Avis au ministre de la Santé et des Services sociaux*. Québec: Gouvernement du Québec.

———. 1995b. *Un juste prix pour les services de santé. Rapport du groupe de travail formé par le Conseil de la santé et du bien-être*. Québec: Gouvernement du Québec, le 17 mai.

Courchene, Thomas C. 1994. *Social Canada in the Millennium. Reform Imperatives and Restructuring Principles*. Toronto: C.D. Howe Institute.

Defourny, Jacques and José L. Monzon Campos (eds.). 1992. *Économie sociale (entre économie capitaliste et économie publique)/The Third Sector (Cooperative, Mutual and Nonprofit Organizations)*. Bruxelles: Centre international de recherches et d'information sur l'économie publique, sociale et coopérative, De Boeck Université.

Delors, Jacques. 1994. *L'unité d'un homme. Entretiens avec Dominique Wolton*. Paris: Éditions Odile Jacob.

Department of Finance. 1995a. *Budget Speech*. Ottawa: Department of Finance, February 27.

——— . 1995b. *Budget Plan*. Ottawa: Department of Finance, February 27.

——— . 1994a. *Discours du budget*. Ottawa: Ministère des Finances, le 22 février.

——— . 1994b. *Le plan budgétaire*. Ottawa: Ministère des Finances, février.

Duperré, Thomas. 1992. "Twists and Turns in Federal-Provincial Arrangements for Social Policy." In Terrance Hunsley (ed.), *The Social Contract in Canada's Future*. Kingston: Queen's University, School of Policy Studies. Social Policy Series, No. 1, 17-28.

———. 1990. "La nouvelle problématique du financement fédéral-provincial des programmes sociaux." *Canadian Review of Social Policy/Revue canadienne de politique sociale* 25: 59-62.

———. 1987. *La perspective fédérale-provinciale, Québec. Les publications du Québec*. Annexe no 32 au Rapport de la Commission Rochon. Québec: Les Publications du Québec.

Favreau, Louis and Yves Hurtubise. 1993. *CLSC et communautés locales: les contributions de l'organisation communautaire*. Québec: Les Presses de l'Université du Québec.

Gagné, Jean and Henri Dorvil. 1994. "Le défi du partenariat: le cas des ressources communautaires dans le secteur de la santé mentale." *Nouvelles pratiques sociales* 7 (1): 63-78.

Greenspon, Edward. 1995. "Ottawa Trying to Heal Health-care Strife." *Globe and Mail* April 13: A1 & A6.

Hoyes, Lesley and Robin Means. 1993. "Quasi-Markets and the Reform of Community Care." In Julian Le Grand and Will Bartlett (eds.), *Quasi-Markets and Social Policy*. London: Macmillan.

Jamieson, Anne. 1991. "Community Care for Older People." In Graham Room (ed.), *Towards a*

*European Welfare State?* Bristol: SAUS Publications.

Kendall, Jeremy and Martin Knapp. 1995. "A Loose and Baggy Monster: Boundaries, Definitions and Typologies." In Justin Davis Smith, Colin Rochester and Rodney Hedley (eds.), *An Introduction to the Voluntary Sector.* London and New York: Routledge.

Laville, Jean-Louis. 1992. *Les services de proximité en Europe.* Paris: Syros Alternatives.

Le Grand, Julian and Will Bartlett (eds.). 1993. *Quasi-Markets and Social Policy.* London: Macmillan.

Lévesque, Benoît and Marie-Claire Malo. 1992. "L'économie sociale au Québec: une réalité méconnue, une réalité économique importante." In Jacques Defourny, and José L. Monzon Campos (eds.), *Économie sociale (entre économie capitaliste et économie publique)/The Third Sector (Cooperative, Mutual and Nonprofit Organizations).* Bruxelles: Centre international de recherches et d'information sur l'économie publique, sociale et coopérative,De Boeck Université.

Lévesque, Gérard D. 1991. *Discours sur le budget et renseignements supplémentaires.* Appendix E: "Les transferts fédéraux aux provinces: le point de vue du Québec." Québec: Ministère des Finances.

———. 1987. *Budget 1991-1992. Discours sur le budget et renseignements supplémentaires.* Québec: Les Publications du Québec.

Lewis, Jane. 1994. "Developing the Mixed Economy of Care: Emerging Issues for Voluntary Organisations." *Journal of Social Policy* 22(2): 173-92.

Lipietz, Alain. 1989. *Choisir l'audace. Une alternative pour le XXIe siècle.* Paris: Éditions La Découverte.

Means, Robin and Randall Smith (eds.). 1994. *Community Care. Policy and Practice.* London: Macmillan.

Ministère de la Santé et des Services sociaux (MSSS). 1995a. *Transformer le système de santé et de services sociaux et décentraliser ses pouvoirs de décision. Plan stratégique triennal 1995/1998.* Québec: Ministère de la Santé et des Services sociaux, janvier.

———. 1995b. *Les dépenses de santé du Québec et le financement des programmes établis.* Québec: MSSS, avril.

———. 1994. *Les services à domicile de première ligne. Cadre de référence.* Québec: Gouvernement du Québec, MSSS, mai.

———. 1990. *Une réforme axée sur le citoyen.* Québec: Gouvernement du Québec.

National Council of Welfare. 1995. *The 1995 Budget and Block Funding. Report of the National Council of Welfare.* Ottawa: Minister of Supply and Services.

Panet-Raymond, Jean. 1994. "Les nouveaux rapports entre l'État et les organismes communautaires à l'ombre de la Loi 120." *Nouvelles pratiques sociales* 7 (1): 79-93.

Perri 6. 1995. "The Voluntary and Non-Profit Sectors in Continental Europe." In Justin Davis Smith, Collin Rochester and Rodney Hedley (eds.), *An Introduction to the Voluntary Sector.* London and New York: Routledge.

——— and Isabel Vidal (eds.). 1994. *Delivering Welfare. Repositioning Non-Profit and Co-Operative Action in Western European Welfare States.* Barcelone: Centre d'Iniciatives de l'Economia Social.

Pestoff, Victor A. 1994. "Beyond Exit and Voice in Social Services—Citizen as Co-Producers." In Perri 6 and Isabel Vidal (eds.), *Delivering Welfare. Repositioning Non-Profit and Co-Operative Action in Western European Welfare States.* Barcelone: Centre d'Iniciatives de l'Economia Social.

Pollak, Nancy, Kathy Sparrow, Jeff Watts, Steve Collison and Stan de Mello. 1994. *Critical Choices, Turbulent Times. A Community Workbook.* Vancouver: The School of Social Work, University of British Columbia.

Québec. 1992. *La politique de la santé et du bien-être.* Québec: MSSS.

———. 1991. *Loi sur les services de santé et les services sociaux et modifiant diverses dispositions législatives.* In *Lois du Québec.* Chapter 42. Québec: Gouvernement du Québec.

Ranci, Costanzo. 1994. "The Role of the Third Sector in Welfare Policies in Italy." In Perri 6 and Isabel Vidal (eds.), *Delivering Welfare. Repositioning Non-Profit and Co-Operative Action in Western*

*European Welfare States*. Barcelone: Centre d'Iniciatives de l'Economia Social.

Régie régionale de la santé et des services sociaux de l'Estrie. 1994. *Santé et mieux-être: un défi pour l'Estrie. Plan d'action régional 1994-1997*. Sherbrooke: Régie régionale de l'Estrie, octobre.

Régie régionale de la santé et des services sociaux de Montréal-Centre. 1995. *L'atteinte d'un nouvel équilibre. L'organisation des services de santé et des services sociaux sur l'Île de Montréal*. Document de consultation 2, Montréal: Régie régionale de Montréal-Centre, mai.

Renaud, Marc, avec la collaboration de Louise Bouchard. 1994. "Expliquer l'inexpliqué: l'environnement social comme facteur clé de la santé." *Interface* 15 (2): 15-25.

Roeher Institute. 1993. *Social Well-Being. A Paradigm for Reform*. Toronto: Roeher Institute.

Room, Graham and Perri 6. 1994. "Welfare States in Europe and the Third Sector." In Perri 6 and Isabel Vidal (eds.), *Delivering Welfare. Repositioning Non-Profit and Co-Operative Action in Western European Welfare States*. Barcelone: Centre d'Iniciatives de l'Economia Social.

Smith, Justin Davis, Colin Rochester and Rodney Hedley (eds.). 1995. *An Introduction to the Voluntary Sector*. London and New York: Routledge.

Social Planning and Reasearch Council of British Columbia (SPARC of BC) (eds.). 1993. *Well-Being: A Conceptual Framework and Three Literature Reviews*. Vancouver: SPARC of BC.

Stryjan, Yohanan. 1994. "Co-operatives in the Welfare Market: the Swedish Case." In Perri 6 and Isabel Vidal (eds.), *Delivering Welfare. Repositioning Non-Profit and Co-Operative Action in Western European Welfare States*. Barcelone: Centre d'Iniciatives de l'Economia Social.

Taylor, Marilyn and Paul Hoggett. 1994. "Trusting in Networks? The Third Sector and Welfare Change." In Perri 6 and Isabel Vidal (eds.), *Delivering Welfare. Repositioning Non-Profit and Co-Operative Action in Western European Welfare States*. Barcelone: Centre d'Iniciatives de l'Economia Social.

Torjman, Sherri and Ken Battle. 1995a. *The Dangers of Block Funding*. Ottawa: The Caledon Institute of Social Policy, February.

———. 1995b. *Can We Have National Standards?* Ottawa: The Caledon Institute of Social Policy, May.

Vaillancourt, Yves. 1994a. "Pendant que nous surveillons la porte d'en avant, que se passe-t-il du côté de la porte d'en arrière?" *Nouvelles pratiques sociales* 7(1): 229-44.

———. 1994b. "La réforme Axworthy et le Québec." *Nouvelles pratiques sociales* 7(2): 1-12.

———. 1994c. "Éléments de problématique concernant l'arrimage entre le communautaire et le public dans le domaine de la santé et des services sociaux." *Nouvelles pratiques sociales* 7(2): 227-48.

———. 1993a. "Quebec and the Federal Government: The Struggle over Opting Out." In Daniel Glenday (ed.), *Canadian society: Understanding and Surviving in the 1990s*. Toronto: McClelland and Stewart.

———. 1993b. "Trois thèses concernant le renouvellement des pratiques sociales dans le secteur public." *Nouvelles pratiques sociales* 6(1): 1-14.

———. 1992. "Un bilan québécois des quinze premières années du Régime d'assistance publique du Canada (1966-1981): la dimension sociale." *Service social* 41 (2): 19-48.

———. 1991. "Le Régime d'assistance publique du Canada: revue de la littérature québécoise et canadienne." *Canadian Review of Social Policy/Revue canadienne de politique sociale* 27: 20-33.

——— and Murielle Leduc. 1995. *Maîtres ou contremaîtres chez nous?* Rapport d'étape du Groupe de réflexion sur les politiques sociales préparé pour les Partenaires pour la souveraineté, version du 28 avril 1995. Montréal: Partenaires pour la souveraineté.

———, Réjean Mathieu, Christian Jetté and Raymonde Bourque. 1993. *La privatisation des services de santé et des services sociaux au Québec en 1993: Rapport d'étape d'une recherche en cours*. Montréal: Services à la collectivité, UQAM, février.

———, Denis Bourque, Françoise David and Édith Ouellet. 1988. *La privatisation des services sociaux*. Annexe n° 37 au Rapport de la Commission Rochon. Québec: Les Publications du Québec.

# CHAPTER 7

# THE TAX SYSTEM AND SOCIAL POLICY REFORM

*Richard Shillington*

## INTRODUCTION

The tax system's primary purpose is to raise revenue to support government services and activities. It should do this while respecting certain objectives and principles[1]:

- efficiency; spend minimal administrative dollars to collect the tax;
- fairness; implying some sense of progressivity (we return to this below);
- clarity; easy to understand;
- neutrality; does not deter nor distort economic growth.

This being said, tax policy is too often seen as purely an instrument of economic and not social policy. Indeed, in Ottawa, while tax policy is the responsibility of the Department of Finance and social policy is the responsibility of Human Resource Development Canada (HRDC), Finance has been setting both since around 1975. This is done, however, without a clear rationale linking tax and social policy.

As part of social policy research, reviews of the tax system are often difficult because tax policy is complex and much of it is hidden. For these and other reasons, there is much misinformation and mythology surrounding Canadian taxes that can impede or interfere with social policy discussions. Examples of such misinformation include the idea that Canada has a very high rate of taxation and that high income Canadians face extraordinarily high marginal tax rates.

This paper presents information and analysis of the Canadian tax system with a view to advancing informed debate about the system and its role as an instrument of social policy. It begins with an overview of Canada's tax system, including trends of the last twenty to thirty years and comparisons with the tax systems in other Organization for Economic and Co-operative Development (OECD) countries. Several features of Canada's tax system are examined in this overview: the level of taxation; composition of taxes by type of tax (i.e., taxes on income versus profit, property, consumption and wealth); progressivity of the tax system; and tax expenditures[2] and their impact on progressivity. Finally, tax expenditures are compared with direct social spending in terms of the dollars spent and the income distribution of the benefits. Not only is social spending via the tax system large, but the benefits delivered tend to differentially benefit higher income Canadians.

This paper also discusses the role of tax policy as background to the implementation of the social security review (SSR) and the most recent federal budget (February 1995). The argument is advanced that a thorough review of social programs must include tax expenditures. To do otherwise, limits the scope of the review but more importantly biases the analysis by excluding types of social spending which differentially benefit higher income Canadians.

## TOTAL TAX BURDEN: TIME TRENDS AND INTERNATIONAL COMPARISONS

A common misconception about the tax system is that Canadians are over taxed. International comparisons, however, do not bear this out. The data in Table 1 compare Canada's rate (all levels of government) with that of other OECD countries. Canada's rate (36.5 percent of Gross Domestic Product, GDP) is slightly below the twenty-four country OECD average; higher than the United States; but not at all out of line with European rates. Of course, Canadian style social programs cannot be maintained with U.S. style tax rates.

Table 1
**Total Government Tax Rate as a Percent of GDP, 1992**

| | |
|---|---|
| Australia | 25.5 |
| Japan | 29.4 |
| U.S. | 29.4 |
| U.K. | 35.2 |
| **Canada** | **36.5** |
| Germany | 39.6 |
| Austria | 43.5 |
| France | 43.6 |
| Denmark | 49.3 |
| | |
| OECD Average | 38.8 |

Source: Revenue Statistics of OECD Countries 1965, 1993; OECD.

Table 2
**Total Tax Revenue as a Percent of GDP Canada, 1992**

| | |
|---|---|
| 1965 | 25.9 |
| 1970 | 31.3 |
| 1975 | 32.4 |
| 1980 | 31.6 |
| 1985 | 33.1 |
| 1990 | 36.3 |
| 1992 | 36.5 |

Source: Revenue Statistics of OECD Countries 1965, 1993; OECD.

As Table 2 shows, the rate of taxation in Canada increased abruptly between 1965 and 1970, from 25.9 percent of GDP to 31.3 percent. This was a time of significant program

Figure 1
**Share of Government Tax Revenue by Tax Source, 1992**

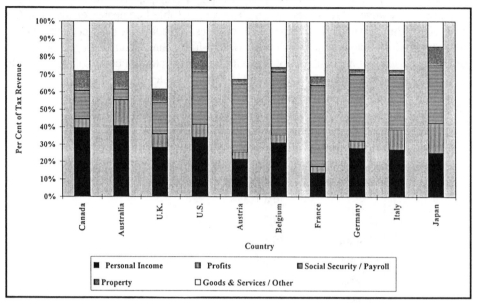

expansion with the introduction of medicare, Canada Assistance Plan (CAP), Guaranteed Income Supplement (GIS) and the Canada Pension Plan (CPP). The rate then stabilized until 1980. It has increased somewhat since 1985, from 33.1 percent to the current level of 36.5 percent. The post-1985 increase has been necessitated by increases in debt services costs.

## TAX MIX

Countries differ not only by virtue of their level of taxation, but also by the composition of taxes or "tax mix." Governments usually tax income, profit, payrolls, consumption and wealth. While Canada may resemble European countries in terms of overall levels of taxation and social services provision, the data in Figure 1 show that Canada is unusual in its composition of taxes. First, Canada relies far more on income taxes than most other countries as a revenue source. Second, our reliance on social security/payroll taxes is much lower than both the United States and European countries. While commentators describe payroll taxes as the "killer of jobs," relatively lower U.S. and European unemployment rates do not support this argument.

Just as Canadian tax rates have changed over time, so too has the tax mix. Table 3 indicates that the reliance on income taxes has almost doubled—from 23 percent of total tax revenue in 1965 to 40 percent of revenue in 1992. On the other hand, the reliance on corporate income taxes dropped by two-thirds—from 15 percent to 5 percent over the same time period. The percentage of revenue coming from payroll taxes has increased and, despite the publicity surrounding the GST, consumption taxes are playing a smaller role in tax revenue than in the past.

It is likely that the misconception of Canada as a high tax country has resulted from the

Table 3
**Per Cent of Government Tax Revenue Canada**

|  | 1965 | 1970 | 1975 | 1980 | 1985 | 1990 | 1992 |
|---|---|---|---|---|---|---|---|
| Personal Income Tax | 22.6 | 32.4 | 32.8 | 34.1 | 35.2 | 41.1 | 39.6 |
| Corporate Income Tax | 14.9 | 11.3 | 13.6 | 11.6 | 8.2 | 7.2 | 4.8 |
| Social Security Contributions | 5.6 | 9.7 | 10.0 | 10.5 | 13.5 | 14.4 | 16.5 |
| Property Taxes | 14.3 | 12.8 | 9.5 | 9.1 | 9.3 | 9.5 | 11.1 |
| Taxes on Goods and Services | 40.5 | 31.7 | 32.0 | 32.6 | 31.8 | 26.0 | 26.1 |
| Other | 1.0 | 1.2 | 1.3 | 1.2 | 1.3 | 1.3 | 1.3 |
| Total | 100.0 | 100.0 | 100.0 | 100.0 | 100.0 | 100.0 | 100.0 |

Source: Revenue Statistics of OECD Countries 1965–1993; OECD.

heavy and increasing reliance on the most *visible* taxes: personal income taxes and consumption taxes. The decline in importance of corporate taxes has received much less attention. This decline has not been due to a reduction in tax rates, but rather the increased utilization of tax shelters and declining corporate profits as a percentage of GDP.

One way Canada's tax system has distinguished itself is in the preferential tax treatment of wealth. Only three OECD countries do not have a wealth transfer tax or an estate/inheritance tax: Canada, New Zealand (just recently) and Australia. Ironically, the U.S. is often used as a comparison bench mark in tax discussions but is not used for wealth taxes. Indeed, the United States collects some $15 billion per year through its estate tax. Without this tax, wealth accumulated in one generation can be passed to the next generation—a windfall to the children—completely free of tax. Canadian's preferential treatment of wealth is truly remarkable when one considers that Canada still has a $500,000 Capital Gains Exemption, and for a decade maintained an even broader Capital Gains Exemption.[3] The absence of a wealth tax explains (at least partially) why we must rely more heavily on income taxes and why middle income Canadians feel "over taxed."

## TAX INCIDENCE AND PROGRESSIVITY

One aspect of the tax system which is poorly understood is its progressivity. Progressive taxes are those in which the burden of taxation, expressed as a percentage of income, increases in relation to income. Progressive taxes apply a higher rate of taxation to higher incomes, a lower rate to lower incomes. Regressive taxes, on the other hand, hit lower income Canadians harder. They typically consist of a flat-rate percentage tax that does not increase as income rises. This is regressive because those with lower incomes spend proportionately more of their income on basic necessities, therefore even a small increase in income (e.g., through a lower rate of taxation) can make a great deal of difference in purchasing power.[4] As income increases, there is a greater "ability to pay" because the "value" of a dollar is less. Progressivity (increasing rates of tax as income rises) in the tax system stems from the principle of "ability to pay."

But most taxes in Canada are not progressive. Of the different types of taxes examined in the previous section, only wealth and income taxes are progressive; payroll taxes tend to be neutral up to the maximum taxable income (maximum insurable earnings for U.I. and

Figure 2
**Total Taxes as a Percent of Broad Income, Canada**

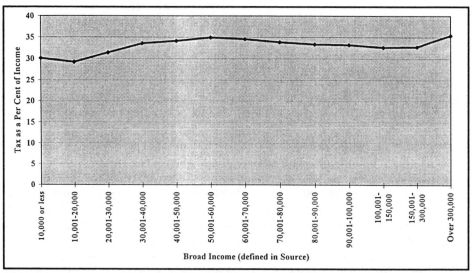

Source: Vermaeten, Gillespie and Vermaeten 1994; Tax Incidence in Canada, Canadian Tax Journal, Vol. 42, No. 2.

maximum pensionable earnings for CPP) and regressive thereafter; consumption taxes, property taxes and lottery revenue are regressive. An important (but difficult) question to answer concerns the degree to which the *combination* of all taxes results in a tax system which is progressive, regressive or proportional.

The answer to this question is provided using *tax incidence* analysis which examines the combined levels of taxation, including taxes on income, profit and consumption. It is a complex analysis because it considers not the initial income distributional impacts of each type of tax, but who ultimately bears the burden for each tax. For example, who ultimately pays increased corporate income tax: is it the shareholders through reduced profits, the employees in reduced wages or the consumer in higher prices? Similar analyses assess the ultimate tax payer for consumption taxes (purchaser, shareholder or employee) and property taxes (landowner or tenant).

Analysis of tax incidence can be used to examine whether the whole system is progressive or not and how the overall tax burden is borne by individuals in different income classes. The findings from the most recent analysis of this type (Vermaeten, Gillespie and Vermaeten 1994) are presented in Figure 2. The results will surprise those who view the tax system as one which demands far more from high income Canadians relative to low and middle income Canadians. The rate of taxation in Canada is essentially flat—between 30 percent and 35 percent of income across the entire income span. Why this happens is the result of a combination of factors:

- most sources of taxation in Canada are regressive; they hit low income Canadians hardest;

- Canada does not have the highly progressive inheritance or wealth taxes prevalent in other countries;
- income taxes, the only Canadian tax which is even nominally progressive, has its progressivity muted by tax expenditures.

In short, if progressivity is a mark of fairness in the tax system, Canada fails.

## PROGRESSIVITY OF THE INCOME TAX SYSTEM

The lack of progressivity in the overall tax system is due, in part, to the effect that tax expenditures have in muting progressivity in the income tax system. How does this work?

The personal income tax system is indeed progressive as far as *statutory* rates are concerned. As Table 4 shows, the statutory federal income tax rate increases from 17 percent to 29 percent in relation to the level of taxable income. When provincial taxes and surtaxes are factored in, the result is a statutory marginal tax rate of around 50 percent for high income Canadians (depending on the province). The impression is left that high income Canadians pay about 50 cents for each additional dollar earned, and that the income tax system is very progressive.

Table 4
**Federal Income Tax Rates, 1992**

| Taxable Income | Federal Marginal Rate | Combined Federal and Provincial Rate |
|---|---|---|
| under $29, 590 | 17% | 27% |
| $29,590 to $59, 180 | 26% | 42% |
| $59, 180 and over | 29% | 46% |

Note: An average provincial rate equal to 60% of basic federal tax is used. These rates exclude temporary surtaxes which will increase the combined income tax rate to about 50%.

But do high income Canadians actually pay 46 cents on every marginal dollar? Table 5 provides the data to answer this question. It shows the average (*actual*, not theoretical) taxes paid by members of different income groups. In 1992, for example, taxpayers with incomes between $80,000 and $90,000 paid an average of $23,981 in federal and provincial income taxes. Those with incomes between $90,000 and $100,000 paid an average of $27,884, which is only $3903 more. Why do individuals who supposedly have a 46 percent marginal tax rate and earn $10,000 of additional income actually pay only $3903 (39 percent) in additional tax? It is because certain types of income receive preferential tax treatment. If the additional marginal income is earned as capital gains or dividends it may be exempt from tax or taxed at a preferential rate. If the income is placed in a registered retirement saving plan (RRSP), or other tax shelter it will not be taxed for years, and then at lower rates in most cases. The result is that marginal income is usually taxed at far below 46 percent. In the above example, the

Table 5
**Average Federal and Provincial Income Taxes Paid**
**Canada, 1992**

| Income Group | Average Income - A - | Average Taxes - B - | Increase in Taxes - C - | Average Tax Rate - D - | Empirical Tax Rate - E - |
|---|---|---|---|---|---|
| $1—$10,000 | $5,500 | $73 | | 1.3% | |
| $10,000—$20,000 | $14,395 | $1,167 | $1,094 | | 12.4% |
| $20,000—$30,000 | $24,786 | $3,723 | $2,557 | 15.0% | 24.6% |
| $30,000—$40,000 | $34,670 | $6,528 | $2,805 | 18.8% | 28.4% |
| $40,000—$50,000 | $44,581 | $10,035 | $3,506 | 22.5% | 35.4% |
| $50,000—$60,000 | $54,511 | $13,528 | $3,493 | 24.8% | 35.2% |
| $60,000—$70,000 | $64,457 | $16,886 | $3,358 | 26.2% | 33.8% |
| $70,000—$80,000 | $74,369 | $20,251 | $3,365 | 27.2% | 33.9% |
| $80,000—$90,000 | $84,589 | $23,981 | $3,730 | 28.3% | 36.5% |
| $90,000—$100,000 | $94,715 | $27,884 | $3,903 | 29.4% | 38.5% |
| $100,000+ | $294,126 | $101,772 | $73,888 | 34.6% | |
| Total | $25,236 | $4,895 | | 19.4% | |

- A - The average income in the income group.
- B - The average federal and provincial taxes paid (federal taxes multiplied by 1.6).
- C - The increase in the average taxes paid between this income group and the previous income group.

Table 6
**Value of Selected Personal Income Tax Expenditures, Canada, 1992**

| | $ Million |
|---|---|
| Non-Taxation of Lottery and Gambling | 900 |
| $100,000 Capital Gains Exemption* | 735 |
| $500,000 Capital Gains Exemption | 1,035 |
| Disability Credit | 265 |
| Medical Expenses Credit | 225 |
| RRSPS | 5,500 |
| Private Pensions | 8,100 |
| Dividend Tax Credit | 640 |
| *Not available after 1994. | |

Source: Selected Personal and Corporate Tax Expenditures, Dept. of Finance, 1994.

*empirical* (actual) marginal tax rate is 39 percent. In other words, the preferential treatment of certain types of income results in an income tax system which is less progressive than statutory tax rates imply.

Understood this way, the nominally progressive income tax system is hardly progressive at all beyond the $40,000 income level. The empirical marginal tax rate, the rate where taxes *actually* increase with additional income, reaches 35 percent for those with incomes in the $40,000–$50,000 range and stays in that range until income is over $150,000. Reference to statutory marginal tax rates can be misleading. The highest income group in Table 5 had a 35 percent average income tax despite having a supposed, or theoretical, 46 percent marginal tax rate on all their income after $59,000. The published or statutory rates of up to 46 percent are theoretical, they do not convey the actual marginal taxes faced by Canadians. The difference between the theoretical and observed is due to "tax expenditures."

## TAX EXPENDITURES

A *tax expenditure* is the technical term for government revenue foregone due to various tax preferences. They include tax credits which are clearly motivated by social policy considerations (e.g., tuition credit, disability credit, credit for medical expenses, spouse and equivalent to spouse), as well as a variety of provisions which are of more questionable social and economic value (e.g., capital gains exemption and research and development tax credits). It is important to clarify one point: *tax expenditures are just as much government spending as direct program spending.* The impact on the balance sheet is identical. The Auditor General has said "a dollar of revenue intentionally foregone or deferred is just as important as a dollar spent."[5] There is no difference between providing $1000 to an individual through a public program and forgiving $1000 of tax that the individual would otherwise owe.

Table 7
**Social Spending Including Social Tax Expenditures; Selected Items**

| Direct Programs 1992—93 | Cost $ billion |
|---|---|
| Old Age Security | 14.4 |
| GIS/SPA | 4.7 |
| U.I. | 19.1 |
| Child Benefits | 5.2 |
| **Social Tax Expenditures 1992** | |
| C/QPP | 2.1 |
| Private Pensions | 8.1 |
| RRSPS | 5.5 |

Source: Federal Spending January 1994, Dept. of Finance; and Selected Personal and Corporate Tax Expenditures, December 1994

An objectionable feature of tax expenditures is that they are largely uncontrolled and unaccountable. While spending through unemployment insurance or Old Age Security is reported annually in the budget and public accounts, indirect spending through the tax system is not reported as completely or routinely. As a result, these tax spending items are not subject to the same level of political scrutiny as direct spending programs.[6]

Tax expenditures should not escape political and public scrutiny, if only because of the substantial sums involved. Just the few tax expenditures alone shown in Table 6 total billions of dollars. The sums are much more substantial when tax expenditures that exist in the corporate and personal income tax systems are counted. Furthermore, as a *method* of spending, tax expenditures have few positive features. They undermine an otherwise progressive income tax system (see previous section), are difficult to control and are largely unaccountable. Given these negative features and the considerable sums of money involved, it is surprising that the priority for the federal government's social security review is the *direct* spending programs and not the tax expenditures.

## SOCIAL SPENDING: DIRECT SPENDING AND SOCIAL TAX EXPENDITURES[7]

It is widely accepted that there is no economic difference between direct spending programs like unemployment insurance (U.I.), Old Age Security (OAS) or Guaranteed Income Supplement (GIS), and social tax expenditures like RRSPS and private pensions. That being said, there are important political differences between these classes of government spending. The discussion below will consider differences in visibility, distributional impacts and implications for size of government.

As noted above, direct program spending is far more visible and accountable than tax expenditures as well as being better understood. The cost figures of direct programs are also more current and readily available than tax expenditures. Table 8 shows that while direct spending programs such as OAS, U.I. and CPP, are targeted to lower and middle income Canadians, many tax expenditures provide more of their benefits to high income Canadians.

Cuts to tax expenditures will have basically the same initial effect on the deficit as a comparable cut in direct program spending yet have different political consequences. A cut in direct spending reduces the size of government which paves the way for a reduction in tax revenue. However, a comparable reduction in tax expenditures increases government revenue and will be seen as increasing the size of government unless other taxes are reduced as a revenue offset.

A social tax expenditure's lack of visibility and complexity (they are generally understood only by tax technicians) explains in part why direct spending is more often targeted for cuts than tax expenditures. Equally important though are the political considerations. Cuts to tax expenditures, as compared to direct spending, will differentially be borne by higher income Canadians and will usually imply greater tax revenue. Thus, cuts to tax expenditures will tend to be supported by those motivated to support low income Canadians and who also usually support an activist role for government. They will be opposed by those who hold a contrary view.

Regardless of impact, social tax expenditures involve sums of money which challenge direct program spending (see Table 7). The foregone federal revenue from pension assistance (private pensions, C/QPP and RRSPS), is almost $16 billion annually, which is not that different from direct support for seniors (OAS, GIS and Spouses' Allowance). By comparison, federal support for social assistance under the Canada Assistance Plan was about $6.7 billion.

The data in Table 8 represent the direct net benefit of social transfers to each taxfiler, after including the effect of taxes owing on the income source and any claw back. As Table 8 demonstrates, social transfers (OAS, Family Allowance, non-taxable income, C/QPP and U.I.) are currently highly targeted. Indeed 84 percent of direct social transfers go to individuals with incomes under $30,000. The tax expenditure associated with private pensions provides little benefit to low income Canadians (about 13 percent). It concentrates its benefit on middle income Canadians where 84 percent of the benefit goes to the 29 percent of taxfilers with incomes between $30,000 and $100,000. RRSPS[8] on the other hand differentially benefit high income Canadians as 12 percent of these benefits are enjoyed by the 1.3 percent of taxfilers with incomes over $100,000.

By contrast, the capital gains exemption (not shown in Table 8) costs the federal government about $1 billion in lost revenue per year currently (much more in 1992 when the $100,000 capital gains exemption still existed), and provides about 71 percent of its benefits to those 1.2 percent of taxfilers with incomes over $100,000. Non-refundable credits include the personal credit and credits for spouse, child (eliminated after 1992), age, disability, medical expenses, U.I. and C/QPP contributions. These credits cover virtually all taxpayers, although they pay no benefit to non-taxpaying poorer Canadians.

## TAX POLICY AND SOCIAL SECURITY REFORM

Social security reform was billed as a review of major social security programs in Canada. Very few analysts would suggest that social programs are optimal and very few would object to improvements in efficiency and effectiveness. But the social security review has all the trappings of a review for cost-cutting purposes and not real reform.

The programs identified for the review were those in Table 8 which are already highly targeted. In the SSR, they were to be studied in order *to increase their targeting*. Social tax expenditures which are poorly targeted and differentially benefit high income Canadians, are not part of the review. Ironically commentators call for even greater targeting of direct programs while defending the existing, poorly targeted tax expenditures.

The exemption of tax policy from the SSR's terms of reference ensured that the reform was not going to be comprehensive. Without a comparable review of benefits delivered through tax policy it is one-sided and has the effect of fighting the deficit solely on the backs of poorer Canadians: the only items from Table 8 included in the social security review were those benefiting lower income Canadians.

Tax policy again played an important role in the federal budget of February 1995. It is clear that deficit reduction was the primary objective. Deficit reduction can be advanced by reductions in program spending or reductions in tax shelters but the federal budget addressed debt reduction almost exclusively through spending cuts. The government put in place certain actions which will:

- maintain tax expenditures for well-off Canadians.
- reduce family security through spending cuts and changes to federal/provincial cost sharing.

Table 8
**Percent of Direct Social Spending and Selected Social Tax Expenditures Benefiting Selected Income Groups, 1992**

|  | under $30,000 | $30,000—$99,999 | over $100,000 |
|---|---|---|---|
| **Taxfilers** | 69.6% | 29.1% | 1.3% |
| **Social Transfers** | | | |
|   **Income Assistance** | 90.5 | 9.2 | 0.2 |
|   OAS | 83.3 | 15.6 | 1.1 |
|   **U.I.** | 82.9 | 16.9 | 0.1 |
|   CPP/QPP | 76.3 | 22.1 | 1.6 |
|   **Child Benefits** | 73.3 | 25.5 | 1.2 |
| **Subtotal:** | 83.6 | 16.1 | 0.2 |
| **Tax Expenditures** | | | |
|   **Non-Refundable Credits** | 65.2 | 32.8 | 2.0 |
|   **Private Pensions** | 12.8 | 83.8 | 3.4 |
|   RRSPS | 19.9 | 68.1 | 11.9 |

Notes: Income Assistance includes Social Assistance, Workers' Compensation and GIS/SPA. Child Benefits includes Family Allowance (FA), and the Child tax Credit. The social transfer subtotal includes the effect of clawing back U.I. and FA. The individual effect of the claw back U.I. and Child Benefits could not be calculated from this source. Average taxfiler income is $26,000

Source: Calculations based on Taxation Statistics 1994—1992 Taxation Year, Revenue Canada.

The option of reducing the deficit through reductions in tax expenditures was virtually ignored in the budget.

## CONCLUSION

We need to add a social perspective to the discussion of tax policy. Too often policy discussions have been dominated by groups representing purely economic points of view. Partly, this is because the tax system is complicated and not well understood by those concentrating on social issues. This paper is intended to add to social policy discussions of our tax system and how it operates.

The findings of this paper are:

- Canada does not have a high tax rate compared to other OECD countries.
- Compared to other countries, Canada relies far more on income taxes and far less on corporate and payroll taxes.
- The share of tax revenue in Canada derived from the corporate sector has fallen

dramatically over recent decades.

- The personal income tax system is not nearly as progressive as one might conclude based on published tax rates. Tax expenditures are responsible for much of the undermining of tax progressivity. The lack of an inheritance tax is also responsible.
- Social spending takes two forms in Canada: visible government spending which tends to benefit lower income Canadians; and invisible tax expenditures which tend to benefit higher income Canadians.
- Any comprehensive social security review must include a review of both direct spending programs like Old Age Security and unemployment insurance as well as the social spending which takes the form of tax expenditures.

It is important that individuals and organizations who track social programs and social spending ensure that tax expenditures are included in their scope. When the next grand social security review is announced or the current review is resuscitated, it should include all social spending, not just the more visible components of program spending.

## NOTES

1. For a complete discussion see Ontario Fair Tax Commission 1993.
2. Tax expenditures refer to the loss of tax revenue to governments due to a tax preference. It may refer to a source of income which is taxed at a preferred rate or exempted from tax. It may refer to a tax deduction or credit. For a full accounting, see Department of Finance 1994.
3. Those who argue that the capital gains tax is itself a wealth tax have confused the terms. A capital gain is a form of income representing only the increased market value (the earning power) of the asset. A wealth tax does not tax the increase but rather the wealth itself.
4. In economic terminology, the marginal utility (satisfaction) of a dollar rises as income decreases and *vice versa*.
5. As reported in the *Financial Post*, March 17, 1995.
6. This is clear in the periodic publication of the *Cost of Selective Tax Expenditures* (Department of Finance). The tables in this publication are punctuated with "NA/Not Available" or "can only be estimated."
7. The term social tax expenditure will be used here to refer to those tax expenditures which are motivated primarily by social policy objectives. They include, but are not limited, to the non-refundable tax credits and the deductions for pensions, child care and medical expenses.
8. The tax expenditures associated with RRSPs and private pensions comes from two sources; first the difference between the taxes collected on pension revenue and deductions; second, the value of the deferral of tax owing on interest earned in pension funds until the pension is paid.

## REFERENCES

Canadian Council of Social Development. 1994. *Submission to the Parliamentary Standing Committee on Finance*. November 15, CCSD.

Department of Finance. 1994. *Selected Personal and Corporate Tax Expenditures*. Government of Canada.

Vermaeten, F., I. Gillespie and A. Vermaeten. 1994. "Tax Incidence in Canada." *Canadian Tax Journal* 42(2).

Ontario Fair Tax Commission. 1993. *Fair Taxation in a Changing World*. Toronto: Government of Ontario.

Organization for Economic and Co-operative Development (OECD). 1994. *Revenue Statistics of OECD Countries*. Paris: OECD.

## PART 3

# SOCIAL SECURITY REFORM, GLOBALIZATION AND LABOUR MARKET RESTRUCTURING

# CHAPTER 8

# NATIONAL SOCIAL POLICY IN AN AGE OF GLOBAL POWER: LESSONS FROM CANADA AND AUSTRALIA

*John Wiseman*

## INTRODUCTION

The aim of this chapter is to explore the implications of globalization and international economic restructuring through a comparative discussion of recent policy developments, outcomes and strategic responses in Canada and Australia. The chapter begins with a discussion of the major themes emerging in theoretical debates about globalization. It argues against overly generalized assumptions about the inevitability of a completely global world economy and society. A more grounded approach to the study of the implications of global economic integration is preferred as is a recognition of the complex interplay between international, national and regional locales and institutions of both state and civil society. The chapter proceeds with a discussion of the similarities and differences in the Canadian and Australian experience of international economic integration during the 1980s and 1990s. In particular it focuses on the outcomes of the 1994 Canadian social security review and the 1994 White Paper on Employment in Australia. The chapter concludes with some reflections on the possibilities and constraints facing relatively vulnerable states, economies and societies such as those of Canada and Australia during the current rapid shift towards globalized economic, social and cultural relations.

The key argument is that, despite significant differences, the recent political and economic histories of Canada and Australia have both been dominated by the impact of globalization. In both countries the central political question has become: how to transform these economies into internationally competitive exporters of high value added goods and services. However the price of the search for competitiveness has been increasing inequality and social polarization as well as growing concern about environmental sustainability and the loss of democratic sovereignty.

This leads to the concluding questions of this paper: Is it true that globalized capital and product markets are inevitable and irreversible? Are there simply no alternatives to the goal of competitiveness at all costs? The recent experience of globalization in Canada and Australia indicates that it has become both harder and more urgent to open up the debate about local, national and international policy alternatives and strategic directions that are consistent with the principles of democratic sovereignty, social justice and environmental sustainability.

## STATE AUTONOMY IN BORDERLESS NATIONS?
## THE USES OF GLOBALIZATION THEORY

The concept of "globalization" has become a much used—and much abused—way of describing and explaining the transformation of institutions and relationships at local, national and international levels in the concluding years of the twentieth century. Too often the language of globalization has been used simplistically to suggest that global corporate power has become an overwhelming juggernaut extinguishing all geographical and historical differences leading inevitably to the creation of a completely global economy and polity. The outcome is an effective end to the sovereignty of nation states and the identity of local cultures.

An alternative view is that globalization implies a more complex and dialectical process of the internationalization and integration of economic, political and cultural relations. Its nature and effects vary in different locales and is subject to ongoing contestation from state and civil society agencies which do retain a degree of relative autonomy. This makes it particularly important to ground debates about the impact of, and alternatives to, globalization in the experience of particular nation states.

The language of globalization can most accurately be used to describe the following political and economic trends: more interdependent national economies and societies; the expansion of international trade, investment, production and financial flows; the growing significance of regional trading blocs and international economic agreements; more influential roles for international financial institutions and transnational corporations; far greater mobility of capital (particularly finance capital) and the overall spread of capitalist, highly commodified and individualized economic, social and cultural relations into ever increasing spheres of human activity (see Costello, Michie and Milne 1989; Featherstone 1990; Drache and Gertler 1991; Glynn and Sutcliffe 1992). These trends have a number of consequences for the sovereignty and relative autonomy of civil societies and state institutions at the sub-national, national and international level (see Hirst and Thompson 1992; Bienefeld 1994; Brecher 1993; Panitch 1994).

First, even supporters of financial deregulation and unfettered capital mobility have discovered that the volatility of globalized money markets creates a climate of escalating economic and political instability which can undermine the creation of efficient and sustainable long-term investment strategies. Thus we see the World Bank noting that deregulated financial markets "tend towards instability and fraud" and the International Monetary Fund (IMF) warning that deregulation may "result in destabilizing and inefficient capital speculation" (World Bank 1989: 4; IMF 1989: 8-9; both cited in Bienefeld 1994: 109).

Second, the fierce pressure to attract footloose capital, expand exports and compete on more open world markets generates a process variously described as "downwards harmonization," "a race to the bottom" (Brecher 1993), "competitive austerity" (Albo 1994) or "the low road to restructuring" (Sengenberger 1991) in which there is constant downward pressure on wages, working conditions, social programs and health and safety standards, and environmental protection. Third, while the gap between richer and poorer nations remains large, there is also a process of polarization within countries. There is a privileged minority with access to highly skilled and well rewarded jobs and a growing majority of less skilled workers excluded to the margins of economic and social relations. As Standing (1989), Yeatman (1992) and Briskin (1994) have shown, this polarization is gendered. Women are being forced into the bottom end of the labour market at the same time as declining expenditure on health and community services increases demands on women to carry out unpaid caring and domestic work in the home. Rising inequalities within and between nations create the context in which large numbers of people are forced to move from rural to urban regions and across national borders in order to avoid poverty and starvation and to find improved living conditions and employment opportunities (Sassen 1990).

Fourth, the relative autonomy and sovereignty of national and sub-national decision-making forums in both state and civil society is undermined by the mobility of capital and the greater bargaining power of international financial institutions. This includes, in particular, the increased power of the international credit rating agencies (see Sinclair 1994). We are still a long way from the complete collapse of national sovereignty. Nevertheless, national economic policy-making has become increasingly difficult within both social democratic and liberal polities. The rising power of transnational corporations and largely unaccountable global institutions such as the IMF and the World Bank also serve to undermine more localized and democratic decision-making forums. Fifth, each of the above tendencies have all led to pressures which, when combined with tensions over cultural and linguistic identities, tend to fragment national states and societies into competing and, at times, conflicting interests.

Three "ideal type" political responses to globalization have emerged in recent years. These responses can be characterized as "champions," "competitors" and "challengers." First, there are those champions of globalization who are fully and unashamedly committed to enhancing the global power of corporations and reducing the legal and political regulatory power of the nation state. I suspect Michael Walker (cited in ECEJ 1992: 8) of the Fraser Institute had this in mind when he candidly reminded us that "a trade deal [such as the North American Free Trade Agreement (NAFTA)] simply limits the ability to which any signatory government may respond to pressure from their citizens." I am quite sure it is what Walter Writson, Chair of Citicorp, was referring to when he enthused that "200,000 monitors in trading rooms all over the world [now conduct] a kind of global plebiscite on the monetary and fiscal policies of the governments issuing currency. . . . There is no way for a nation to opt out" (cited in Brecher 1993: 686).

Second, there is the extensive and influential body of opinion which accepts the inevitability of globalization but focuses on maximizing the competitiveness of national and regional economies. This commonly involves policies designed to reduce costs through labour shedding, wage reductions, deregulating labour markets, improving productivity through technological innovation and improvements in infrastructure, training, production processes, marketing and distribution. Much of the trade union movement in industrialized economies has accepted the inevitability of the competitiveness agenda but has attempted to protect union members through productivity trade offs supposedly designed to minimize job losses and protect working and living conditions (van Liemt 1992). Similarly, as Albo (1994) and Panitch (1994) have argued, social democratic and labour parties have commonly sought alternatives to the policies of "austerity competitiveness." These have pursued strategies of "progressive competitiveness" with the aim of limiting the social dislocation and polarization of economic restructuring through redistributing some of the fruits of export led growth so as to compensate those who have suffered most.

The Conservative and Liberal parties in Canada and the Liberal and Labour parties in Australia have all fundamentally accepted the inevitability of globalization and the need to accelerate export competitiveness. The differences concern the pace of change, not the direction. However there are also a variety of localist, nationalist and internationalist responses which do challenge the fundamental assumptions of the politics of globalization. I will discuss the "challengers," the third ideal type, and some of the alternatives it proposes at the end of the chapter.

## THE PRICE OF COMPETITIVENESS: THE CANADIAN AND AUSTRALIAN EXPERIENCE OF GLOBAL INTEGRATION AND RESTRUCTURING

### THE LEGACIES OF VULNERABILITY

The historical similarities between Canada and Australia have been noted and debated by a wide range of writers and have formed the basis of a number of significant comparative studies (see Boreham et al. 1989; O'Connor 1993; Cooper et al. 1994). Both are geographically large and rich in natural resources such as minerals and timber but have climatic conditions which make agriculture or even the establishment of substantial settlements impossible in much of the country. At the time of European colonization, Canada and Australia were inhabited by indigenous populations and there is therefore a legacy of bitter struggle between indigenous and colonizing interests. Politically, these two nations developed Westminster-style, federal, parliamentary democracies and established a substantial framework of liberal welfare state institutions in the post-war period. Most importantly, the two countries share a common vulnerability to international economic transformations given that both can be characterized as semi-peripheral economies, heavily dependent on the production and export of primary commodities with poorly developed manufacturing sectors and high levels of foreign ownership (Boreham et al. 1989; Drache and Gertler 1991).

There are also important differences between Canada and Australia. First the legacy of the dual French and English colonization of Canada has led to the Canadian federation developing in a more decentralized and fragile way. Centrifugal pressures have been exacerbated by Canada's proximity to the United States. This led to a shift away from an East West, trans-Canada orientation, associated with the export of commodities to Europe and towards the development of North South trading relations with United States markets. By contrast, Australia's geographical and cultural isolation has contributed to the formation of relatively centralized federal state relations including significant Commonwealth control of taxing and spending powers. An overtly racist White Australia immigration policy was also at least partially responsible for a more unified, and more chauvinistic, sense of national identity.

The Australian industrial relations system has been both more centralized and legalized than in Canada (Frenkel 1993). This helps explain the formation and electoral strength of the trade union based Australian Labour Party which has provided the trade union movement with the experience and expectation of direct access to governmental decision-making forums at the national level. Such direct access to national state agencies has not been part of the experience of the Canadian labour movement due to these factors: the limited electoral success of the New Democratic Party; the historical legacies of Gomperism in the international unions linked to the United States; and syndicalism in the Québec labour movement (Heron 1990).

Economically, Australia has remained far more reliant on agricultural exports than Canada which has developed larger and more technologically advanced manufacturing and services industry sectors (Ravenhill 1994; Drache and Gertler 1991). Canadian industrial development has been dominated, however, by U.S. ownership with much of Canadian manufacturing industry operating as branch plant subsidiaries to U.S. parent companies. Canadian trade patterns are also heavily skewed towards the United States whereas Australian trade is far more diverse in terms of both export markets and sources of imports.

The Canadian welfare system has developed in a more redistributive, interventionist and generous manner with an emphasis on universal contributory insurance schemes rather than the more targeted Australian provisions funded from general revenue (O'Connor 1993; Beilharz et al. 1992). In Australia, a "wager earners' welfare state" of high employment levels and wages for male breadwinners has been built behind tariff barriers designed to protect manufacturing investments and employment for male breadwinners. Castles (1988) has usefully described this as a strategy of "domestic defence" rather than "domestic compensation." Until recently, an important consequence of this resulted in comparatively low female workforce participation rates, a stronger assumption of female financial dependency and a sharper sexual division of labour than has existed in Canadian society (O'Connor 1993).

Given their common economic legacies as vulnerable, semi-peripheral and resource dependent nations, it is not surprising that the transition to global integration and post-fordist economic restructuring has been hard and painful in both societies. The aim of the following sections is to explore the Canadian and Australian experience of this restructuring over the period since the mid-1970s.

## DEREGULATED AND RIPPED OFF: COMPETITIVENESS AUSTRALIAN STYLE

At the time of the onset of the 1980-81 recession, the Australian economy remained a highly protected "farm and quarry," heavily reliant on agricultural and mining exports with a small uncompetitive manufacturing sector focused mainly on the domestic market (Bell and Head 1994). The underlying strategy of "domestic defence" was not fundamentally altered by the Whitlam Labour government's abortive efforts between 1972 and 1975 to expand the Australian welfare state and "buy back the farm" through attempts to regain ownership and control of mineral and energy resources. Despite a limited shift in the direction of neoliberal economic policies, the Liberal/National Party government of Malcolm Fraser after 1975 remained committed to protectionism and a resource based economy until it was overwhelmed by the severe recession of the early 1980s.

The immediate aim of the Hawke Labour government, elected in 1983, was to deal with the impact of the recession and to generate economic and employment growth through fiscal expansion while holding down inflation. This latter objective was to be achieved through the establishment of the Accord agreement between the government and the trade union movement. This guaranteed that wages would not rise faster than prices in return for the government's commitment to employment generation and improvements in health and other social programs (Ewer et al. 1991). Trade union access to key governmental decision-making forums and processes was also a central part of the bargain.

The initial burst of neo-Keynesian expansionist policies pursued by Hawke was soon overtaken by international pressure. In December 1983, Treasurer Keating overcame spirited opposition within the parliamentary Labour Party to achieve support for the view that the rising speculative activities and power of international financial institutions meant that it was no longer possible to maintain a managed Australian exchange rate (Kelly 1992). For Keating and his supporters, within both Treasury and the business community, this reform also had the positive effect of ensuring Australia's rapid integration into the harsh realities of global competitiveness. The 1983 decision to float the Australian dollar and abolish exchange rate controls was the first step down the path of financial deregulation. This was completed over the next two years by the removal of interest rate ceilings and the entry of foreign banks.

By 1986, in a climate of economic recovery, the financially deregulated Australian economy faced the problems of rapid currency depreciation and a balance of payments crisis. These arose from the triple pressures of worsening terms of trade, a surge in imports and the servicing of foreign debt, largely the result of private sector borrowing. There was serious talk of IMF intervention and ongoing critical comments from credit rating agencies, such as Moody's, about the over reliance on commodity exports and "economic and structural weaknesses . . . [which] . . . cloud the nation's flexibility for servicing long term external debt" (cited in Kelly 1992: 222). In May 1986, Treasurer Keating provided the famous warning that Australia would become "a banana republic" unless economic restructuring was accelerated to ensure the competitiveness of Australian exports. From that point on, the policy agenda of the Hawke and Keating Labour governments was driven by the view that the central task was to transform Australia from "a farm and a quarry" hinterland into a competitive producer and exporter of high value added manufactured products and services.

Competitiveness has become both the diagnosis and the cure for all kinds of economic and social ills, with the choice of remedies underpinned by the increasingly pervasive dominance of "economic rationalist," neoliberal economic policies (see Pusey 1991). Central themes in the Australian competitiveness strategy have included the deregulation of national and international financial markets, exchange rates and financial institutions; the deregulation of trade through tariff cuts and ongoing efforts to support greater free trade on both a bilateral and multilateral basis; an extensive program of micro-economic reform designed to improve the productivity and competitiveness of Australia's export industries; an ongoing program of tax cuts and reductions in public sector expenditure; and the privatization and commercialization of a wide range of public sector activities such as banking, transport and telecommunications.

The Labour government refused to move as fast or as far down the path towards labour market deregulation as was advocated by business and the Liberal/National Party opposition. Nonetheless, the Accord process became an effective vehicle for reductions in real wages and working conditions (frequently redefined as "restrictive work practices") as well as forming the foundations of movement towards more decentralized enterprise bargaining arrangements (see Ewer et al. 1991, Frenkel 1993). There was also a renewed emphasis on training and skills development through "the Active Society" principle of encouraging (and at times threatening) the unemployed into an expanded range of labour market programs. This policy direction was first articulated through the social security review in 1987 and given further impetus through the White Paper on Full Employment in 1994 (Cass 1987 and Commonwealth of Australia 1994).

The central aim of the entire competitiveness strategy was to provide a supportive climate within which private sector investment would surge into productive export industries. Unfortunately much of the surge was into an orgy of financial speculation as many entrepreneurs used the freedoms of financial deregulation to indulge in "get rich quick" schemes often involving speculation in property, shares and company takeovers (Ravenhill 1994) . Such speculative investment actually made the balance of payments problems worse, as large sums of money were borrowed abroad, leading to a sharp rise in private sector foreign debt. Throughout the latter part of the 1980s, the terms of trade continued to worsen, imports continued to rise and inflation was again becoming a problem. Choosing a policy of high interest rates to slow economic growth accelerated and deepened the recession of the early 1990s.

The Labour government argued that the recession was part of the price Australians had to pay for restructuring the Australian economy so as to make industries internationally competitive. For many the price was bitter indeed. The official rate of unemployment rose to over 11 percent in 1993, the highest level since the depression. Not surprisingly, this situation led to a rising public outcry. Facing a sharply deteriorating electoral situation, the Labor government began to shift from the more extreme rhetoric of "austerity competitiveness" towards a position which can be characterized as "competitiveness with a human face" or "progressive competitiveness" (Albo 1994; Panitch 1994).

The 1993 One Nation statement signalled a rediscovery of the social dimensions of unemployment and some expansion of public expenditure on infrastructure development, education, training and community services. Wrapping himself in the nationalist symbolism of republicanism, Prime Minister Keating managed to stir up sufficient fear about the divisive impact of the Liberal and National parties' fightback platform and its central component of a goods and services tax to win the 1993 election.

After the 1993 election, the Labour government continued to focus on unemployment as a central concern and commissioned a major inquiry into employment options for Australia. This lead to the publication of the White Paper on Employment/Unemployment in May 1994 (Commonwealth of Australia 1994, for a more detailed discussion see Wiseman 1994). The White Paper included an expansion of expenditure on labour market programs as well as some progressive moves to improve the financial independence of women. But the heart of the White Paper proposals remained "business as usual." The answer to unemployment was defined in terms of export growth driven by deregulated financial markets, tariff cuts, free trade, reduced business costs and regulations, the privatization of government business enterprises, enterprise bargaining, training and the active society to improve the "job readiness" of the unemployed. There was also an explicit aim of developing wage subsidy schemes to encourage all workers, particularly women, to take up low wage jobs.

Trade and industry policies continued to be based on the view that

> Australian and international experience make it clear that protectionism, resistance to structural change and avoidance of competition are inimical to growth. . . . An open economy leaves no room for subsidies that prop up uncompetitive firms, nor for detailed prescriptions for industry where government directs the flow of resources. (Commonwealth of Australia 1994: 57)

The White Paper's path to the future is simple and straightforward. "When Australia opted for an open economy, the nation committed itself to succeed in an endless race to become, and remain, globally competitive" (Commonwealth of Australia 1994: 52).

The economic context of policy-making in Australia has been fundamentally changed by the decisions and events of the 1980s and 1990s. The aim has been to turn Australia from a heavily protected primary producing "farm and quarry" into a competitive exporter of manufactured goods and high technology services. Despite some significant social reform measures in areas such as health insurance and Aboriginal land rights, the overall direction has been driven by an economic rationalist faith in the capacity of the free market to deliver competitiveness and prosperity with the benefits trickling down to all sections of the population (Bryson 1994). The government's own Economic Planning and Advisory Council (EPAC) freely admits that while "Australia does not yet have unmanageable levels of the homeless and beggars on the streets . . . even a cursory reading [of the available evidence] . . . suggests that measured income inequality, especially that for market-based earnings has been increasing, or at best has been relatively static" (EPAC 1995: 69, 80).

## UNDERMINED AND OVERWHELMED: COMPETITIVENESS CANADIAN STYLE

Manufacturing exports continue to be more extensive in Canada than in Australia. Nevertheless, Canadian trading and investment relations have been more permeable with higher levels of foreign ownership. Thus Canada also entered the 1980-81 recession as a vulnerable, resource dependent economy (Drache and Gertler 1991; Jenson, Mahon and Bienefeld 1994; McBride and Shields 1993). The onset of the recession followed a decade of conflict between political agendas driven by the goal of a stronger, more interventionist central state and those emphasizing the maintenance of provincial autonomy.

The Nixon administration's protectionist policies in the early 1970s helped provide the rationale for an initial shift towards nationalist and interventionist policies by the Trudeau Liberal government in Canada. The centrepiece of this strategy was the mobilization of Canada's energy resources under the auspices of the National Energy Policy, the Canada Development Corporation and a steady expansion of the social insurance and community service provisions of the Canadian welfare state. The combination of stagflation and rising deficits in the mid-1970s led to a shift away from Keynesianism to monetarism and a winding back of progressive taxation and welfare reforms. However, the commitment to central state intervention in economic management remained. They were tools to both enhance industrial development and strengthen Canadian national identity. Thus in 1980 the recently re-elected Liberal government proposed the creation of a national energy policy designed to channel oil resources into the expansion of export industries. This nationalist strategy collapsed in the face of falling oil prices, high interest rates, rising unemployment and fierce opposition from Canadian and United States capital as well as the oil rich provinces. Canadian capital in particular was keen to gain greater access to United States markets and sources of capital and was intent on a less nationalist, more continentalist, trade and investment policy.

The final two years of the Trudeau government were marked by a sharp turn towards free market economics and a halt to further expansion of the Canadian welfare state. These trends continued under the Mulroney Conservative government elected in 1984. The following ten year period was marked by three related trends: largely unsuccessful attempts to bring about constitutional reforms balancing national and provincial interests; the steady deregulation and winding back of public sector and welfare state activities; and the dramatic internationalization of the Canadian economy through the impact of the FTA and NAFTA.

The Mulroney government's term in office was marked by a series of failed attempts to revise Canadian constitutional arrangements. The reform initiatives of both Meech Lake and Charlottetown were driven by the need to find a compromise which would meet Québec's demands for greater sovereignty while holding together the Canadian federation. But as McBride and Shields (1993) argue, a second significant agenda was to reduce the interventionist authority of the central state by devolving powers, resources and responsibilities to the provinces and, more broadly, to bring about a sharp reduction in financial, environmental and industrial regulation at all levels. The failure of much of this agenda can be attributed to the diverse coalition of opposition forces and the difficulty of brokering complex constitutional reform processes in an increasingly fragmented federation.

The initial agenda of the 1984 Mulroney government combined rhetoric about the need to maintain the "sacred trust" of the Canadian welfare state with a broadly neoliberal economic and social policy agenda based on monetarist financial objectives, the enhancement of competitiveness, the reduction of taxes and government spending, privatization, commercialization and deficit control. As Lightman and Irving (1993) argue, the pace of change was limited to some extent by public opposition and by the difficulty of negotiating change through the relatively decentralized Canadian state. Nonetheless the overall impact was to chip away at the progressivity of the Canadian welfare state through expenditure reductions and the introduction of regressive forms of taxation such as the Goods and Services Tax (GST) (see Evans 1994; Yalnizyan et al. 1994). At the same time, the combination of an ongoing imbalance between revenue and expenditure measures, continuing reliance on high interest rate policies and debt-servicing costs contributed to escalating debt and chronic fiscal policy problems. These have in turn increased the vulnerability of Canadian economic policy-making to international credit rating agencies and other financial institutions.

However, it was only with the election of the Chrétien Liberal government in 1993 that Canada's social policy heritage came under full scale attack. A highly regressive budget in February 1994 cut $5.5 billion, by reducing unemployment insurance benefit entitlements. This was followed in October 1994 by the release of the Axworthy paper, *Agenda: Jobs and Growth. Improving Social Security in Canada* (Human Resources Development Canada 1994). This discussion paper bears a number of startling resemblances to the Australian White Paper on Employment/Unemployment. There is much talk of competitiveness, affordability, targeting the "Active Society" and training incentives as "the answer" (National Anti-Poverty Organization 1995). The proposals are also underpinned by an assumption that traditional levels of social program expenditures are simply no longer affordable given the size of public sector debt.

The Axworthy paper proposes further reductions in unemployment insurance entitlements with a special assault on those people who claim benefits too often. It proposes a two-tiered system of benefits, with people who apply "too often" being paid a reduced rate as well as being required to enrol in training programs (HRDC 1994: 49). An expanded range of transition to work wage supplements and training wages are also put forward. These were explicitly intended to subsidize the growing number of low wage jobs, many of which are occupied by women. Indeed, the overall package should be seen in the context of the same rapid growth in low paid, casualized and part-time female employment which has characterized the recent development of the Australian labour market. This also led the Australian White Paper to emphasize the subsidization of low wage female employment.

Drawing on data contained in *Improving Social Security in Canada* (HRDC 1994) and internal Treasury Board information, the Ecumenical Coalition for Economic Justice (ECEJ 1994a: 1) calculated that a total of $15 billion is to be taken out of unemployment insurance (U.I.), the Canada Assistance Plan (CAP) and the post-secondary education component of Established Programs Financing (EPF-PSE) between 1995 and 1999. This is on top of a previous $7 billion cut between 1990 and 1993. When combined with reductions in funding for the Canadian health care system, it is likely that around a quarter of Canada's expenditure on social programs will be lost over the next five years.

There are three sets of arguments driving the Canadian social policy reform process. First, there is the official line that the reforms are designed to "improve" income security arrangements. These improvements tend to involve making benefits less generous, harder to get and more tightly linked to participation in labour market programs. Second, there is the debt argument. The Canadian government argues that previous levels of benefits are no longer affordable due to high levels of debt. Witness Finance Minister Paul Martin who argues that the elimination of the deficit depends on the reform of Canada's social safety net (Department of Finance 1994: 71). The Canadian debt problem is real but is largely a product of high interest rates and reductions in corporate tax rather than rising social expenditures. In Canada, as in Australia, there is a constant need to challenge the use of public sector debt figures as the basis for asserting that deeper and deeper cuts in social expenditure are both inevitable and non-negotiable. This increasingly common political assertion fails to recognize that there are always alternative ways of managing debt in terms of both the time frames used for debt reduction and the fair distribution of the costs of debt-servicing.

However the most powerful and most disturbing explanation for the severity of the assault on Canada's welfare state traditions is the downward pressure on wages, working conditions and social programs arising from the internationalization of the Canadian economy and, in particular, the impact of so-called free trade agreements with the United States, and more recently, Mexico. Indeed as Lightman and Irving (1993: 82) argue "free trade may deliver the ultimate blows to the values of the welfare state in Canada [for] . . . the new language of global competitiveness and the logic of the economic market has arguably posed a far greater threat to the Canadian welfare state than has any neoliberal ideological attack."

The roots of the FTA and NAFTA treaties can be traced back to the early 1970s with Canadian business interests becoming increasingly concerned about limited access to U.S. markets and U.S. corporations wanting to ensure access to Canadian resources and, increasingly, cheap Mexican labour (Clarkson 1991). Canadian business also correctly identified trade agreements as powerful mechanisms for challenging comparatively high Canadian wages, working conditions, social policy provisions, environmental, health and safety standards. However, it was not until after its victory in the fiercely contested 1988 election that the Mulroney government was able to pass the FTA. A further six year period of debate and deep divisions led to the ratification of NAFTA by the Chrétien Liberal government in 1994, despite earlier Liberal election promises to renegotiate the agreement.

The key to understanding the full significance of NAFTA is a recognition that it is far more than a free trade agreement. As many critics have pointed out, the most important single feature of NAFTA is its role as a surrogate constitution or "corporate bill of rights" protecting the unrestricted and unregulated mobility of capital (Drache and Gertler 1991; Grinspun and Cameron 1993; Barlow 1994). As Clarkson (1991: 116) argues, "Canadian–American 'free trade' can . . . be seen less as an expression of an export-led economy than as an arrangement assuring mobility for their capital to American and Canadian transnational corporations."

Signatories to NAFTA are expressly forbidden to discriminate against foreign investment. This means far more than just the removal of tariffs and restrictions on the movement of finance and investment capital. It means that governments are forbidden to construct "non tariff" barriers such as subsidies or regulatory standards which might benefit national companies or in any way limit the investment and trade decisions of domestic and foreign corporations. The national state is legally obliged to intervene to prevent provincial govern-ments from preventing or regulating capital mobility. Public sector enterprises must operate commercially and be open to competition from private sector companies. Once a function or service is privatized it must be governed by NAFTA rules of national treatment. It cannot be returned to the public sector without compensation to companies which are or even might be involved in this area.

United States corporations have made it quite clear that they regard the Canadian health, tertiary education and income security systems as "unfair" economic subsidies. The Canadian government is under ongoing pressure to ensure the "downward harmonization" of social policy provisions to the generally much lower United States standards. Similar downward pressures have also been applied to environmental, health and safety regulations.

The impact of NAFTA and the broader processes of globalization have contributed to the creation of a climate in which there is a strong public perception that the overriding priority is to appease the god of "international competitiveness" and that this requires the sacrifice of citizens and geographical regions deemed uncompetitive and therefore expendable. This has provided a powerful weapon to those, such as Tom Courchene of the C.D. Howe Institute, who have sought to convince the Canadian population that the Canadian welfare state must now be dismantled because it is no longer affordable: "social policy must facilitate and assist the occupational, industrial and even geographical relocation that the new worlds economic order is requiring of the present generation of Canadians" (Courchene 1987: 179). This is in the context of overwhelming evidence of an ongoing increase in the inequality of Canadian income and wealth distribution and of rising poverty (see McBride and Shields 1993; Canadian Centre for Policy Alternatives 1995; Campaign 2000 1994; Ross et al. 1994).

Similarly, residents of regions, such as the fishing communities of Newfoundland and the Maritime provinces, have been told that it is now too expensive to provide employment opportunities or services in these areas. They will simply have to move. For many citizens of Canada, as in the United States and Mexico, free trade in the post-NAFTA world has meant learning to survive in a "race to the bottom" in which corporations attempt to play one group of workers off against another by lowering wages, working conditions, social provisions and environmental standards.

## THE CANADIAN AND AUSTRALIAN EXPERIENCE
## OF GLOBALIZATION AND COMPETITIVENESS

The recent impact and experience of globalization in both Canada and Australia has been remarkably similar. In Australia, the influential former head of Nissan and Channel 7, Ivan Deveson (1993: 27), has argued "there is no doubt that we cannot afford the 'social net' that we have—that the size of the net must be linked to the economy—that to some degree our commitment to an efficient economy has been weakened by some excessive dependency on social support." In Canada, the head of the Canadian Manufacturers Association (CMA) argues that

> ... all Canadian governments must test all their polices to determine whether or not they reinforce or impeded competitiveness. If a policy is anti competitive, dump it.
> ... The social programs we've come to depend on ... we're going to have to abandon.
> We're gong to be shutting down hospitals, like it or lump it. (cited in ECEJ 1994b)

Sovereignty over political decision-making has also been a casualty. In Australia it has become almost impossible to talk about higher levels of public sector expenditure or progressive taxation without being drowned out by commentators shouting that, not only would this make Australian business uncompetitive but, in a deregulated financial system, the international financial markets and credit rating agencies would never permit such policies to be implemented. This has led to a profound form of political self-censorship with even the most progressive of Labour politicians simply refusing to talk about alternatives to current economic policy settings because, it is argued, there is no point in talking about things which simply cannot happen.

The deregulation of the Canadian financial system has not been as complete as in Australia, but this has been more than offset by the impact of the FTA and NAFTA in determining the direction of fiscal and monetary policy. The Canadian political situation has also been complicated by the failure of the Meech Lake and Charlottetown constitutional negotiations and the centrifugal pressures of the impending decisions about Québec. This has led to a trend towards a more fragmented political system and a fertile climate for capital to pursue divide and rule tactics, playing off one provincial government against another. The Keating Labour government has pursued an aggressively nationalist strategy with a stronger focus on national standards in relation to key social programs and policy areas such as Aboriginal land rights. On the other hand, Australia has had to deal with the special problem of geographical, economic and political marginalization from the major regional trading blocs.

The Canadian trade union movement has tended to remain more autonomous from state policy-making and more critical of free trade agreements and global integration than the Australian Council of Trade Unions (ACTU). This helps explain the far more active public debate about free trade and globalization in Canada than in Australia as well as the more extensive alliances established between Canadian unions and other social movement groupings such as the Action Canada Network (ACN). Most Australian trade unions have been prepared to temper overt criticisms of Labour government policies in relation to financial deregulation, free trade and enterprise bargaining in return for the access to decision-making provided through the Accord process. There is a price to be paid for political influence, just as there is a price to be paid for political autonomy.

There are important differences but the central question is similar in both societies. How can resource based, highly vulnerable economies such as Australia and Canada survive in a deregulated and globalized international economy without sacrificing the values of democracy, sovereignty and social justice which have been central to their historical development?

## Room to Move: National Strategies in an Age of Global Power?

It is relatively easy to mount a critique of the social, political and economic consequences of globalization and competitiveness. The critical question is whether it is possible to envisage or implement alternative policies and strategies. As Sam Gindin (1992: 22) of the Canadian Auto Workers rightly notes:

> . . . the issue isn't whether an efficient and dynamic economy is important—it obviously is. The issue is whether labour and the left want to engage in this debate on the corporations' terms of competitiveness, and allow them to define their interest as the national interest, or whether it is possible to define an independent, alternative

way of looking at economic needs: call it a democratic approach to the development of our productive capacities.

This section of the paper considers the "challengers," the third ideal type political response to globalization, identified earlier. Questions about alternative responses to the politics of globalization have international, national and local dimensions. Internationalist strategies have tended to focus on the creation of alternative political, financial and legal global institutions which can form a democratic counterweight to the power of transnational capital (Sweeney 1994). If corporate power has shifted to the global arena then global trade unions, environmental agencies, community organizations and governmental institutions are the proposed remedy. Such organizations can then provide the base for the creation of international corporate codes of conduct, controls over financial transactions and the construction of new forms of international governance including the possibility of international corporate taxes (Walker 1993).

Increasing attention is also being paid to the enshrinement of trade union and human rights principles in international trade agreements and the creation of multilateral and bilateral social charters specifying minimum standards of living and standards of social service provision. However, the limited effectiveness of the social charter and trade union rights agreements under both the NAFTA and European Union suggests that it would be unwise to place too much faith in internationalist strategies on their own.

Other critics of globalization, such as Ekins (1992) and Brecher et al. (1993), have emphasized localist responses involving the "Lilliputian tactic" of tying down the corporate "giants" of global corporate power. This achieved with thousands of interconnected local grassroots movements and struggles, including the creation of international alliances between local trade unions, community organizations and social movements and the opening up of new channels for organizing previously unorganized groups within and across national borders. Part of the aim here is to create the conditions for an "upward" rather than "downward" harmonization in which workers and citizens with lower wages and working conditions are lifted upwards rather than driving down the living standards of workers in more prosperous economies. Paradoxically too, the globalization of corporate power is likely to lead to renewed focus on the fostering of local economic networks and local community relationships as significant arenas within which identity and difference can be protected, solidarity and mutuality nurtured and ecological values sustained (see Liepitz 1989).

As the rhetoric of "think global: act local" becomes more pervasive, it is tempting to accept that the room to move at the nation state level has effectively disappeared. Ongoing threats to national sovereignty and autonomy have certainly provided fertile ground for populist and chauvinist movements such as the Canadian Reform Party or the resurgent fascist parties in Europe. But while the very idea of national political identity may have been opened to question by the internationalization of capital, it has in fact become more important than ever to reconsider the relationship between social movements, labour movements and nation states.

As Mahon (1993: 13-14) correctly points out, it is unnecessary and unhelpful to

> ... fall back into the icy void of world systems theory: the world has more depth than a global network of economic power extending from the centre(s) to the periphery.

To problematise the coherence and durability of national societies and states, however, does call for new ways of thinking about the way that social space is organised and reorganised over time. . . . [T]he nation state is not dead but strategic horizons have to be expanded to render visible other layers of action.

If we lose democratic control over the key decision-making forums and processes of the national and regional state, then we lose everything, for all real decision-making power in relation to capital formation, production and distribution will have been effectively corporatized. But at the same time, we need to imagine and create new local, national and international decision-making structures and processes. These must link labour movements, social movements and civil society community organizations in ways which reaffirm and give substance to the values of sustainability, social justice and democracy in an age of global power.

In writing about the impact of NAFTA on her country, Margaret Atwood (1993) has commented on the traditional belief that beavers will bite off their own testicles and throw them to their pursuers when threatened. As the Australia Labour and Liberal parties march together down the path towards new trade and investment agreements in the Asia Pacific region, it is to be hoped that the same metaphor does not apply to the kangaroo. Beavers also have a unique capacity for invention and creativity. And kangaroos are fierce fighters when cornered. It is beyond time to reopen public debate about the questions: who benefits from the politics of globalization and competitiveness? And how can those Canadians and Australians, who do not accept the inevitability of the race to the bottom, create the room to move and continue to search for democratic, fair and sustainable sources of political and economic ideas and institutions?

## References

Albo, G. 1994. "Competitive Austerity and the Impasse of Capitalist Employment Policy." In S. Miliband and L. Panitch (eds.), *Between Globalism and Nationalism: Socialist Register 1994*. London: Merlin Press.

Atwood, M. 1993. "Blind Faith and Free Trade." In *The Case Against Free Trade*. San Francisco: Earth Island Press.

Barlow, M. 1994. "NAFTAmath: How Free Trade is Restructuring Canada." *Canadian Perspectives* (Autumn) 12.

Bell, S. and B. Head (eds.). 1994. *State, Economy and Public Policy in Australia*. Melbourne: Oxford University Press.

Beilharz, P., M. Considineand and R. Watts. 1992. *Arguing About the Welfare State*. Sydney, NSW: Allen and Unwin.

Bienefeld, M. 1994. "Capitalism and the Nation State in the Dog Days of the Twentieth Century." In R. Miliband and L. Panitch (eds.), *Between Globalism and Nationalism*. London: Merlin Press.

Boreham, P., S. Clegg, J. Emmison, G. Marks and J. Western. 1989. "Semi Peripheries or Particular Pathways: The Case of Australia, New Zealand and Canada as Class Formations." *International Sociology* 4 (1): 67-90.

Brecher, J. 1993. "After NAFTA: Global Village or Global Pillage?" *The Nation* (December 6): 685-89.

———, J. Childs and J. Cutler (eds.). 1993. *Global Visions: Beyond the New World Order*. Montreal: Black Rose Books.

Briskin, L. 1994. "Equity and Economic Restructuring in the Canadian Labour Movement." *Economic and Industrial Democracy* 15: 89-112.

Bryson, L. 1994. "The Welfare State and Economic Adjustment." In S. Bell and B. Head (eds.), *State, Economy and Public Policy in Australia*. Melbourne: Oxford University Press.

Campaign 2000. 1994. *Child Poverty in Canada: Report Card 1994*. Toronto: Campaign 2000.

Canadian Centre for Policy Alternatives. 1995. *CCPA Monitor*. Ottawa: March.

Cass, B. 1987. *Income Support for the Unemployed in Australia: Towards A More Active Society*. Social Security Review Issues Paper No. 4. Canberra: AGPS.

Castles, F. 1988. *Australian Public Policy and Economic Vulnerability*. Sydney, NSW: Allen and Unwin.

Clarkson, S. 1991. "Disjunctions: Free Trade and the Paradox of Canadian Development." In D. Drache and M. Gertler (eds.), *The New Era of Global Competition: State Policy and Market Power*. Montreal: McGill-Queen's University Press.

Commonwealth of Australia. 1994. *Working Nation: Policies and Programs*. Canberra: AGPS.

Cooper, A., R. Higgott and K. Nossal. 1994. *Relocating Middle Powers: Australia and Canada in a Changing World Order*. Vancouver: UBC Press.

Costello, N., J. Michie and S. Milne. 1989. *Beyond the Casino Economy*. London: Verso.

Courchene, T. 1987. *Social Policy in the 1990s*. Toronto: C.D. Howe Institute.

Department of Finance. 1994. *Agenda: Jobs and Growth. A New Framework for Economic Policy*. Ottawa: Department of Finance.

Deveson, I. 1993. "The Challenge of Change for Australians." *Business Council Bulletin* May: 26-29.

Drache, D. and M. Gertler (eds.). 1991. *The New Era of Global Competition: State Policy and Market Power*. Montreal: McGill-Queen's University Press.

Economic Planning and Advisory Council (EPAC). 1995. *Income Distribution in Australia: Recent Trends and Research*. Commission Paper No. 7. Canberra: AGPS.

Ecumenical Coalition for Economic Justice (ECEJ). 1994a. *Economic Justice Report*. 5 (3), October.

———. 1994b. *Economic Integration of the Americas: An Education and Action Kit*. Toronto: Routledge.

———. 1992. "NAFTA: A New Economic Constitution for North America." *Economic Justice Report*, 3 (3) October: 1-8.

Ekins, P. 1992. *A New World Order: Grassroots Movements for Social Change*. London: Routledge.

Evans, P. 1994. "Eroding Canadian Social Welfare: The Mulroney Legacy 1984-1993." *Social Policy and Administration* 28 (2): 107-19.

Ewer, P., I. Hampson, C. Lloyd, J. Rainford, S. Rix and M. Smith. 1991. *Politics and the Accord*. Sydney: Pluto Press.

Featherstone, M. (ed.). 1990. *Global Culture: Nationalism, Globalization and Modernity*. A Theory, Culture and Society Special Issue. London: Sage.

Frenkel, S. (ed.). 1993. *Organized Labor in the Asia-Pacific Region*. Ithaca, New York: ILR Press.

Gindin, S. 1992. "Putting the Con Back in the Economy." *This Magazine* May: 17-22.

Glynn, A. and B. Sutcliffe. 1992. "Global but Leaderless? The New Capitalist Order." *Socialist Register*, 76-95.

Grinspun, R and M. Cameron (eds.). 1993. *The Political Economy of North American Free Trade*. Montreal: McGill-Queen's University Press.

Heron, C. 1990. *The Canadian Labour Movement: A Short History*. Toronto: Lorimer.

Hirst, P. and G. Thompson. 1992. "The Problem of 'Globalization': International Economic Relations, National Economic Management and the Formation of Trading Blocs." *Economy and Society* 21 (4): 357-96.

Human Resources Development Canada (HRDC). 1994. *Agenda: Jobs and Growth. Improving Social Security in Canada*. Ottawa: Minister of Supply and Services.

IMF. 1989. *Staff Studies for the World Economic Outlook*. Washington, D.C.: IMF.

Jenson, J., R. Mahon and M. Beinefeld. 1994. *Production, Space, Identity: Political Economy Faces the 21st Century*. Toronto: Canadian Scholars' Press.

Kelly, P. 1992. *The End of Certainty*. Melbourne: Penguin.

Liepitz, A. 1989. *Towards a New Economic Order: Postfordism, Ecology and Democracy*. Oxford: Polity Press.

Lightman, E. and A. Irving. 1993. "Restructuring Canada's Welfare State." *Journal of Social Policy* 20 (1): 65-86.

Mahon, R. 1993. "The 'New' Canadian Political Economy Revisited: Production, Space, Identity." In J. Jensen et al., *Production, Space, Identity: Political Economy Faces the 21st Century*. Toronto: Canadian Scholars' Press.

McBride, S. and J. Shields. 1993. *Dismantling a Nation: Canada and the New World Order*. Halifax: Fernwood.

National Anti Poverty Organization (NAPO). 1995. *NAPO's Response to the Federal Discussion Paper "Improving Social Security in Canada"*. Ottawa: NAPO.

O'Connor, J. 1993. "Citizenship, Class, Gender and Labour Market Participation in Canada and Australia." In S. Shaver (ed.), *Gender, Citizenship and the Labour Market: The Australian and Canadian Welfare States*. Sydney: University of New South Wales, Social Policy Research Centre Reports and Proceedings No. 109.

Panitch, L. 1994. "Globalisation and the State." In R. Miliband and L. Panitch (eds.), *Between Globalism and Nationalism*. London: Merlin Press.

Pusey, M. 1991. *Economic Rationalism in Canberra*. Cambridge: Cambridge University Press.

Ravenhill, J. 1994. "Australia and the Global Economy." In S. Bell and B. Head (eds.), *State, Economy and Public Policy in Australia*. Melbourne: Oxford University Press.

Ross, D., E. Shillington and C. Lochhead. 1994. *The Canadian Fact Book on Poverty*. Ottawa: Canadian Council on Social Development.

Sassen, S. 1990. *The Mobility of Labor and Capital: A Study in International Investment and Labor Flow*. Cambridge: Cambridge University Press.

Saunders, P. 1994. *Welfare and Inequality: National and International Perspectives on the Australian Welfare State*. Melbourne, Cambridge University Press

Sengenberger, W. 1991. "The Role of Labour Market Regulation in Industrial Restructuring." In G. Standing and V. Tokman (eds.), *Towards Social Adjustment: Labour Market Issues in Structural Adjustment*. Geneva, ILO: 235-50.

Sinclair. T. 1994. "Passing Judgement: Credit Rating Processes as Regulatory Mechanisms of Governance in the Emerging World Order." *Review of International Political Economy* 1:1 (Spring); 133-58.

Standing, G. 1989. "Global Feminization Through Flexible Labour." *World Development* 17(7): 1077-95.

Sweeney, S. 1994. "What is the 'New Labor Internationalism'? Comments on Upward Harmonization, Social Chapters and Globalization from Below." Paper Presented to the Sixteenth Annual North American Labor History Conference on International and Comparative Labor History, October 27-29, Wayne State University Detroit.

van Liemt, G. 1992. "Economic Globalisation: Labour Options and Business Strategies in High Labour Cost Countries." *International Labour Review* 131 (4-5): 453-70.

Walker, M. 1993. "Global Taxation Paying for Peace." *World Policy Journal* 10 (2) Summer: 7-12.

Wiseman, J. 1994. "After Working Nation: The Future of the Work Debate." *Labour and Industry*. 6 (1) October.

World Bank. 1989. *World Development Report 1989*. Washington, D.C.: World Bank.

Yalnizyan, A., T. Ide Ran and A. Cordell. 1994. *Shifting Time: Social Policy and the Future of Work*. Toronto: Between the Lines.

Yeatman, A. 1992. "Women's Citizenship Claims, Labour Market Policy and Globalisation." *Australian Journal of Political Science* 27: 449-61.

# CHAPTER 9

# DISCIPLINE, INSECURITY AND PRODUCTIVITY: THE ECONOMICS BEHIND LABOUR MARKET "FLEXIBILITY"

*Jim Stanford[1]*

## INTRODUCTION

One important and oft-stated goal of the federal government's social policy reform exercise is to promote greater "flexibility" in the functioning of Canada's labour market. The government's Green Paper, *Agenda: Jobs and Growth. Improving Social Security in Canada* (Human Resources Development Canada [HRDC] 1994a: 30, 60, 54) is full of references to "fostering labour mobility," finding "ways to increase the flexibility of the system" and promoting "flexible work arrangements." It argues that the Canadian labour market has been too slow to adapt to the changes that have swept the Canadian and global economies.

The belief that chronic unemployment results from government policies and regulations which have made the labour market too "inflexible" rests on a particular set of economic assumptions. These theoretical underpinnings are only rarely identified by those who are arguing in favour of greater flexibility. And the concrete empirical evidence that Canada's labour market is indeed inflexible in any real economic sense is questionable at best.

This chapter explores some of the theoretical and empirical dimensions of flexibility-enhancing labour market and social policy proposals. It considers more precisely what flexibility means, as used by the proponents of greater flexibility. It compares empirical evidence regarding the actual flexibility of employment in Canada and the U.S. It explores the free-market, neoclassical economic assumptions on which the flexibility agenda is based and compares those assumptions with alternative views regarding how the labour market actually operates. Finally, it considers whether or not greater labour market flexibility is indeed likely to reduce unemployment and enhance the efficiency of work in Canada.

## THE FLEXIBILITY AGENDA

Adopting an almost trite, futuristic jargon, the Green Paper repeatedly stresses the notion that Canada's existing social security system has somehow produced an inflexible, maladapted workforce:

> The world has changed faster than our programs. In the last decade especially, the sheer relentless force of technological, economic and social change has reshaped our lives and our livelihoods. Government policies and approaches have been too slow in responding. (HRDC 1994a: 7)
>
> No one is sheltered from the changes sweeping through the economy. (HRDC 1994a: 18)
>
> The [social security] system is geared to help people where change was the exception, not the rule, so it does too little to help people adjust to change. (HRDC 1994a: 21)

The centre-piece of this reform must be helping people to prepare themselves for work in a changing world. (HRDC 1994a: 29)

The UI program is out of date. . . . It does not work well for the growing number of Canadians who need help adjusting to changes in the labour market, at a time when adjustment to change is essential. (HRDC 1994a: 42)

The notion that Canadian social programs, and the workforce behaviours which they have influenced, have led to a general ossification of the labour market is very widespread throughout the debate over social policy reform. Indeed, other political leaders and policy analysts also have been most explicit about the potential benefits of flexibility-enhancing labour market policies.

For example, the Finance Minister's pre-budget discussion document, *Agenda: Jobs and Growth. A New Framework for Economic Policy*, the so-called "purple book," (Department of Finance 1994: 37, 21) speaks of the importance of "encouraging Canadians to adapt to change." It asserts, in language more blunt than that of the Green Paper, that labour market regulations (such as measures governing arbitrary dismissal and other employment security laws) have "reduce[d] the willingness of many employers to take the risk of hiring a new employee." The Governor of the Bank of Canada has echoed these sentiments, suggesting in his semi-annual review of monetary policy (Bank of Canada 1995) that unemployment would drop in Canada if government took various measures (including reducing the payroll taxes that fund U.I. and other social programs) to enhance labour market flexibility. The editors of the *Globe and Mail* (1994: A18) concluded that the optimal employment strategy for Canada is to "undo the rigidities that prevent labour markets from doing their job, which is to see that all available labour is employed in its best use."

The call for labour market flexibility is an international one. Many Canadian commentators have taken their cue from the Organization for Economic Co-operation and Development [OECD] *Jobs Study* (1994a), which was released just a few months before the Green Paper and which won a strong public endorsement from Human Resources Minister Axworthy. The OECD report presented a menu of flexibility-enhancing policy changes (including restricting U.I. benefits, removing regulations governing retirement and employment security, reassessing minimum wages and reopening collective agreements to facilitate wage reductions) that would presumably enhance labour market flexibility. The *Jobs Study* followed an earlier OECD study on the particular institutional features of Canada's labour market (OECD 1991: 100) which found that the U.I. system and other programs tend to "impede labour market efficiency" and "reduce mobility incentives."

In international comparisons of labour market flexibility, the U.S. economy is generally seen to possess the most flexible and hence "efficient" labour market, and consequently enjoys a low rate of unemployment (compared to most other industrialized countries). Chronic high unemployment in Europe is seen as a symptom of an "over-regulated" labour market. Canada's experience is usually characterized as falling somewhere in between these two prototypes—although leaning increasingly toward the European model.

## WHAT EXACTLY IS LABOUR MARKET FLEXIBILITY?
Despite the importance attached by these social and economic policy-makers to the goal of labour market flexibility, their proposals and policies are often vague as to precisely what type

of flexibility is actually being promoted. Apart from imprecise references to an ongoing need to "adapt to change," it is not clear exactly what type of flexibility is desired. Of course, the choice of language is not accidental: like "free" trade or investor "confidence," Canadians may not know exactly what labour market "flexibility" implies, but clearly it is a good thing. Who could oppose flexibility?

The implication of this vagueness is that somehow Canada's economy is being prevented from utilizing labour most efficiently. Employment and work are not adjusting adequately to change: presumably workers are being kept in jobs (by unions or by government rules perhaps) that are less efficient, and being prevented from applying for or moving to the more efficient jobs that are presumably being opened up by the inexorable process of "change." Inflexibility results in higher unemployment, and the economy is held back from its productive frontier.

This portrait of inflexibility and resistance to change will come as a surprise to many workers in the Canadian economy: those who have lost their jobs or have a very real fear of losing their jobs as a result of ongoing economic change, and those who have gone to great lengths (including retraining and relocation) to attempt to take advantage of what new employment opportunities have been generated. In this era of relentless downsizing in both the private and the public sectors, how many Canadians are in fact allowed to hold on to jobs that are no longer needed by the economy by taking advantage of rigidities in the labour market? And how many new job vacancies are actually going unfilled because of those same rigidities?

If flexibility is defined, in the commonly understood sense, as the ability to change, then labour market flexibility can be defined as the ability to move labour from one occupation or form of employment to another—that is, to allocate and reallocate labour to different uses at different times, according to the economy's changing demands for labour inputs. In this commonsense understanding, Canada's labour market has actually become *hyper-flexible* in recent years. The degree of employment volatility has clearly increased, the security of job tenure has been almost universally weakened, and the expansion of non-standard work arrangements has added an extra dimension of flexibility to the allocation of labour. In short, Canada has developed a "just-in-time" labour market: labour is increasingly hired precisely when and where it is needed and discarded immediately upon becoming redundant.

There is ample empirical evidence of this enhanced degree of flexibility—indeed volatility—in employment in Canada. More than 20 percent of all Canadian workers lose or change their jobs each year (Department of Finance 1994: 23), a historically high pace of turnover. Indeed, during the last recession, the rate of total job turnover in Canada (jobs created and destroyed as a share of total employment) was among the highest of all industrialized economies (OECD 1994b). Further evidence suggests that the pace of job turnover in Canada accelerated during the 1980s, relative to the 1970s, at the same time as wage differentials increased significantly (Baldwin and Rafiquzzaman 1994). This trend toward increasing job volatility has almost certainly continued during the 1990s.

It is not just that Canadians are changing jobs more frequently; it is also that the conditions of employment have become more volatile and flexible, thanks to the growth of non-standard work arrangements such as sub-contracting, home work, part-time work, and overtime. Fully one-half of the new jobs created in Canada during the 1980s were non-standard: that is, jobs that were not full-time, were not year round, or involved working for more than a single employer (Economic Council of Canada 1990). The federal government's Advisory Group on Working Time found that non-standard work has contributed greatly to the flexibility of production in numerous rapidly changing industries, but at the expense of the employment security and standards of their workers:

> This flexibility is often gained by reducing the number of core, permanent, full-time workers to a minimum, making the regular hours of work more variable, or increasing reliance on people whose hours of work can be easily changed: temporary workers, part-time workers without fixed hours, or so-called self-employed contractors such as homeworkers. (HRDC 1994b: 29)

The number of Canadians working part-time hours has increased—but so, ironically, has the number of overtime hours worked by full-time employees, resulting in a polarization of the labour market between those who cannot find enough hours of work, and those who are working too many. The share of Canadians working a "normal" work week (between 35 and 40 hours per week) has declined from 71 percent in 1976 to 61 percent in 1993 (Sunter and Morissette 1994). Firms, as a result, seem better able to structure working hours to fit their particular circumstances. Those which require a stable, core workforce, and hence must offer relatively better wages and benefits, reduce the fixed unit cost of their core workforce by working a smaller number of workers for greater hours; overtime can be cut back to reduce labour costs when product demand is slower. Other firms, meanwhile, prefer the flexibility that comes with maintaining a roster of available part-time workers; declining product demand is met by reducing the number of employees called in to work. Either way, employment is increasingly responsive to the precise demand conditions affecting the employer.

Osberg (1994) has argued that this growth in non-standard work arrangements is actually self-reinforcing. By reducing the number of standard full-time jobs available in the economy, the trend to flexible work arrangements has increased the supply of workers who are available to accept part-time or irregular work; this in turn encourages more firms to adopt these hiring strategies, since they face less of a risk of being unable to find sufficient workers during busy times. In turn, this *further* reduces the number of full-time jobs—creating a circle of cumulative causation characterized by ever-greater numbers of non-standard jobs, and ever-greater numbers of unemployed or underemployed Canadians available to fill those jobs.

What about the oft-discussed "skills mismatch" between the capabilities of available Canadian workers and the requirements of Canadian jobs? Could there be some rigidity in the education and training process which is impeding our economy's ability to allocate labour to emerging high technology jobs? Canada's record in advanced education is actually very good, relative to other OECD economies: we spend more on post-secondary education, as a share of GDP, than any other economy (HRDC 1994a: 57), and a comparatively high share of our population has received post-secondary training. Yet a very large proportion of the new jobs being generated in the economy continue to require quite *low* levels of skill and training. For example, federal projections suggest that almost one-half of the new jobs expected to be created between 1995 and 2000 will require only a high school education or less (HRDC 1995).[2] The evidence is sparse that, apart from a few narrow technical occupations, there are jobs that are difficult to fill because of a lack of skills among Canadian workers. At the same time, there is growing evidence of a process of "credential inflation," whereby Canadians are investing in additional training largely for purposes of job-market queuing. To increase their chances of attaining employment, even jobs for which their skills are not entirely necessary, the real economic return (in aggregate *social* terms, rather than from the personal perspective of those who use education to advance their position in the queue) of many educational investments is somewhat questionable.

## EMPIRICAL COMPARISONS OF LABOUR MARKET FLEXIBILITY IN CANADA AND THE U.S.

The preceding evidence suggests that it is difficult to conclude that Canada's labour market has indeed become inflexible (in the practical economic sense defined above: its ability to allocate and reallocate labour to jobs at different times and in different paces). But how does Canada's labour market flexibility compare to that of our leading economic competitors?

Table 1
**The Volatility of Sectoral Employment—Canada and the U.S., 1983—1994**
(37 industries at 2-digit level)

|  | Total Period | 1983-1988 | 1989-1994 |
|---|---|---|---|
| *Arithmetic Mean, Normalized Standard Deviation of Employment*[1] |  |  |  |
| Canada | 10.01% | 6.14% | 8.71% |
| U.S. | 7.54% | 5.53% | 4.10% |
| *Weighted Average, Normalized Standard Deviation of Employment*[1] |  |  |  |
| Canada | 8.65% | 5.87% | 6.25% |
| U.S. | 7.77% | 5.43% | 3.72% |
| *Industries in Which Volatility Was Greater in Canada (out of 37)* | 27 | 26 | 29 |

NOTE: 1. Normalized standard deviation equals the standard deviation as a percentage of the sample mean.

An examination of employment data suggests, in fact, that not only has Canada's labour market become more flexible over time, it is in fact *more* flexible than that of the U.S. which is often presented as possessing the prototypically flexible labour market. For example, Table 1 presents measures of the volatility of sectoral employment in Canada and the U.S. based on employment patterns since 1983 in thirty-seven different industries.[3] A normalized standard

Figure 1
**Output amd Employment Through a Recession**
**Canada and the U.S., 1981 and 1990**

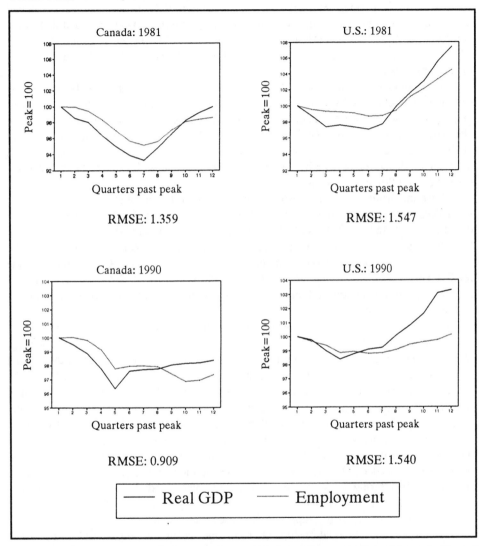

deviation of employment is calculated for each industry[4] as an index of the volatility of employment. For the total twelve-year period from 1983 to 1994, average sectoral employment volatility in Canada was notably higher than in the U.S., whether calculated on an arithmetic or a weighted-average basis.[5]

What is even more interesting is the differing direction of change in the two countries. In Canada, employment became more volatile during the second half of the sample (from 1989 to 1994, coinciding with the introduction of the free trade agreement and the sharp recession of the early 1990s), whereas in the U.S. the opposite occurred. Employment volatility in Canada was greater than in the U.S. during both the first half and the second half of the sample but the difference between the two countries became much larger during the 1990s. On an arithmetic-mean basis, sectoral employment in Canada was more than twice as variable during the period 1989-94 than was sectoral employment in the U.S. Over the second half of the sample, the variability of sectoral employment in Canada exceeded that of the comparable U.S. sector in twenty-nine of thirty-seven cases.[6] Therefore, not only is Canada's labour market more flexible (in the sense defined above) than that of the U.S., but the size of the difference is increasing.

Further evidence on the relative flexibility of Canada's labour market can be obtained by examining the relationship between employment and real output. Figure 1 plots an index of employment and an index of real output (real GDP) for Canada and the U.S. during each of the last two economic recessions (beginning in 1981 and 1990, respectively). These indices start at 100 for the quarter in which the pre-recessionary output peak was attained in each country. They then indicate the change in both employment and output during the twelve quarters (three years) following that peak.

One immediately noteworthy aspect of these graphs is the fact that both recessions were much deeper and longer lasting in Canada than they were in the U.S. This immediately casts doubt on one oft-stated conclusion of the advocates of labour market flexibility: namely that Canada's unemployment has increased relative to the U.S. in recent years because of the greater importance here of labour market regulations and rigidities. Clearly much of the relative rise in Canadian unemployment can be explained by the less fortuitous macro-economic environment here and, in particular, by the impacts of trade-related restructuring and higher real interest rates.

But it is also interesting to compare the relationship *between* output and employment over the business cycle in the two economies. Generally, there is a lag between an initial downturn in output and the subsequent downturn in employment as employers recognize the coming recession and take the necessary steps to reduce their workforces; presumably this lag will be longer, the more rigid and burdensome are the rules and laws that constrain employers' ability to lay off their workers. This lag period was shorter in Canada than in the U.S. during the 1981 recession, and became notably shorter still in Canada during the 1991 recession. There is an increasingly close and immediate relationship between employment and output in Canada which reinforces the conclusion that employers are able to hire labour when it is needed, and *only* when it is needed. The implication that firms are forced by burdensome labour market rules to continue hiring workers when they are no longer needed, and that this regulatory burden imposes a significant disincentive to new employment (as suggested above by the Department of Finance), is not supported by the empirical evidence.

The closeness of the relationship between employment and output can be empirically tested in a variety of manners. One method is to measure the size of the gap that may emerge between employment and output over the course of the business cycle. We therefore calculate the root mean square error (RMSE) of the difference between the employment and GDP indices over the twelve quarters reported.[7] As indicated in Figure 1 and reported in Table 2, not only is the RMSE between the two series smaller for Canada than in the U.S. over both recessions, but the relationship between employment and output becomes notably closer for Canada in the 1990s while the corresponding relationship in the U.S. has remained more or less stable. Thus the gap between Canada and the U.S. increases notably.

Table 2
**Output and Employment Through a Recession**
**Canada and U.S., 1981 and 1990[1]**

| | | RMSE of Indices[2] | Regression Results | | | | | |
|---|---|---|---|---|---|---|---|---|
| | | | Change GDP | | Constant | | Adj. $R^2$ |
| | | | Coeff. | T-Stat | Coeff. | T-Stat | |
| Canada | 1981 | 1.359 | .607 | 5.916 | -.126 | -.947 | .773 |
| | 1990 | 0.909 | .481 | 2.901 | -.171 | -1.451 | .426 |
| U.S. | 1981 | 1.547 | .484 | 5.307 | .085 | .636 | .731 |
| | 1990 | 1.540 | .338 | 3.647 | -.087 | -1.247 | .508 |

| NOTES: | 1. | Comparison of indices of employment and GDP (GNP for U.S. in 1981) for the twelve quarters beginning with the quarter in which the pre-recessionary peak in GDP was encountered (1981:2 and 1990:1 in Canada, and 1981:3 and 1990:2 in the U.S.). Indices calculated so that starting point equals 100. |
|---|---|---|
| | 2. | Root mean square error of the difference between the employment and GDP indices over the twelve quarters. |
| | 3. | First-difference regression of the change in employment on the change in GDP and a constant (ie. time trend); 11 observations. |

Another empirical test involves attempting to utilize the change in output to *predict* the change in employment, thus verifying whether or not firms are somehow prevented or inhibited from changing their employment patterns in response to changes in product demand. We thus regress the first difference of the employment index (that is, the proportional change in employment) on the first difference of the output index and a constant (reflecting, in a first difference context, a time trend in employment); these results are also reported in Table 2. Of particular interest here is the coefficient on the output index: it is higher in Canada than in the U.S. in both time periods, and the relative size of the difference increases from the 1981 recession to the 1990 recession.[8] This suggests, again, that employment is particularly flexible in Canada with respect to real economic activity, and that Canada's "flexibility advantage" relative to the U.S. has actually increased.[9]

## FALLING WAGES AND THE DEREGULATION OF LABOUR MARKETS
The preceding comparison of the actual performance of the Canadian and U.S. economies suggests that Canada's labour market is relatively and increasingly flexible in terms of its ability to move labour in and out of different kinds of employment in response to changes in the demand for that labour. To what, then, do the advocates of flexibility refer when they claim that Canada's labour market is too rigid? A clue to this paradox is provided by one labour market outcome which differs radically between Canada and the U.S.

Real hourly wages (relative to changes in the consumer price index) for production workers in the U.S. have declined by almost 15 percent in the two decades since their peak in 1973.[10] Real wages are now lower than they were in 1964—even though real productivity in the U.S. economy (measured by real GDP per person employed) has since grown by some 28 percent. This is evidence of a rather socially perverse form of labour market flexibility:

American workers are producing more and more each year, but getting paid less and less for it.

In contrast, real hourly wages in Canada (again relative to consumer prices) have increased by as much as 5 percent since 1973 (versus a 15 percent drop in the U.S.), and have been more or less constant since the early 1980s. This is relatively modest in comparison to the approximate 12 percent gain in real output per employed worker since 1973.[11] But there is little doubt that Canadian workers have managed to defend their economic position in the midst of the economic turbulence of the past two decades more successfully than their American counterparts.

There are a number of factors behind the decline in U.S. wages, including the rising cost of non-wage employment benefits (such as private health care premiums) and the polarization of income distribution between production workers and skilled managers and technicians. But undoubtedly one important factor has been the *deregulation* of the U.S. labour market over this same time period. There has been a substantial weakening of the whole range of institutional and social controls over labour market outcomes. Symptoms of this deregulation include the precipitous decline in trade union representation (the private sector unionization rate is approaching 10 percent in the U.S. versus some 30 percent in Canada), the erosion of the real minimum wage (relative to consumer prices) and the widespread failure to enforce labour standards regulations.

Perhaps this is the type of flexibility that policy-makers have in mind for the Canadian labour market. As suggested above, this process is better described by the term *deregulation*. The key difference between the Canadian and U.S. labour markets is not that employment is somehow inflexible in Canada, but rather that there is a much greater degree of social regulation over key employment outcomes (including, but not restricted to, various forms of wage regulation such as collective bargaining, minimum wages and pay equity regulation). By abandoning these attempts to consciously guide labour market outcomes and adopting a more *laissez-faire* labour market strategy, it is argued that lower unemployment and greater labour market efficiency will result; what is not usually stated is that the primary operative mechanism through which this efficiency is achieved is via a significant and secular decline in the economic return to labour.

It is not surprising, therefore, that the benign euphemism of labour market flexibility is adopted to describe this policy agenda. It could more accurately (but certainly less palatably) be described as a wide-ranging agenda of deregulation, one which aims to institutionally disempower employees in their general dealings with employers and bring about a significant reduction in average labour incomes. This sounds considerably less pleasant than merely trying to help Canadian workers adapt to change.

## THE ECONOMIC ASSUMPTIONS BEHIND THE DEREGULATED LABOUR MARKET

The notion that labour market deregulation will indeed reduce unemployment rates and result in a more efficient allocation of labour depends on several usually unstated economic assumptions. Several of these assumptions and corresponding policy conclusions are summarized in Table 3. The deregulation model is derived from a neoclassical understanding of both the functioning of the labour market and the determination of overall macro-economic performance.

The neoclassical model assumes that market-clearing pressures, reflected in flexible prices, will clear the markets for all productive inputs. In the case of the labour market, wages should adjust up or down until a perfect balance is obtained between the number of workers available and the number of jobs offered by employers. The resulting wage will itself be determined by the real productivity of labour; competition between employers will ensure that each worker is paid exactly the value of his or her productivity. The only constraint ultimately holding back the level of employment in the economy is the number of workers available (that is, the level of labour supply); wage flexibility and market-clearing will ensure that all available workers can indeed find work. As for "demand-side" factors (where the demand for workers may be insufficient to absorb labour supply), the neoclassical model admits their relevance only in the *short run,* due to macro-economic shocks, such as temporary recessions. In the long run, the economy will automatically settle at its full employment level of output. Any unemployment that appears to exist at that equilibrium position (the so-called "natural" rate of unemployment) is actually disguised voluntary unemployment, and results largely from individuals choosing to collect social benefits rather than effectively offering their labour services to the market.

The policy conclusions of this model are clear. Regulations and policies which interfere with the crucial market-clearing process should be relaxed. Minimum wages and collective bargaining should be abandoned or at least weakened, allowing the wage to fall to market-clearing levels (as illustrated in Figure 2). Social programs which facilitate excessively long job search or discourage geographic mobility should be reformed to reduce voluntary unemployment. Skills training, work incentives and other measures should be adopted to enhance the effective supply of labour to the market (the supply of motivated and appropriately trained workers). Any concern that the resulting free market wage may be too low to be consistent with social goals (such as eliminating poverty) should be addressed by trying to enhance the free market value of individual workers (by increasing their education level, also known as their "human capital") rather than by trying to interfere with the market process itself.

Underlying all these conclusions is the assumption that, left to its own devices, a competitive labour market will indeed ensure that all willing workers are employed and that the resulting market-clearing wage will, in some essential sense, be a fair one (in that it automatically reflects labour productivity). There is a competing model of how the labour market actually functions, however, in which these assumptions are not accepted as valid. The assumptions of this alternative, structuralist model are also summarized in Table 3.[12]

Rather than assuming that income distribution is determined solely by market-clearing processes, this model also recognizes the importance of socio-economic institutions in determining the balance of economic power between competing economic interests. The model thus adopts a vision of explicit or implicit conflict and bargaining between economic agents (such as between employers and employees) in which the relative economic and institutional power of the two sides is a key variable. For a variety of reasons, full employment will not be generated autonomously in the labour market, even in the long run. In the first place, the influence of economic and social structures may prevent the wage from settling at its market-clearing level. More importantly, the level of unemployment is itself an important determinant of the relative bargaining power of the two sides in the employment relationship: when unemployment is very low, the bargaining power of workers (over both wages and day-to-day work practices) is greatly enhanced. As a result, wages may increase and effective

Table 3

**Neoclassical and Structuralist Models of the Labour Market: Key Assumptions and Policy Implications**

|  | *Neoclassical Model* | *Structuralist Model* |
|---|---|---|
| **Theoretical Assumptions** | | |
| Determination of income distribution | Market-clearing; marginal productivity | Bargaining power; social and institutional structures |
| Labour market constraint | Labour supply (supply-side) | Labour demand (demand-side) |
| Long run unemployment | Natural unemployment is voluntary, and reflects labour market rigidities | Equilibrium unemployment is voluntary, and is recreated to ensure productivity and profitability |
| Macro-economic constraint | Short run shocks only; aggregate economy settles at full employment | Demand constraint is a usual, long run feature of the aggregate economy |
| **Policy Conclusions** | | |
| How to reduce unemployment | Increase *effective* labour supply (ie. supply skilled, motivated workers) | Relax the demand constraint (ie. create jobs) |
| How to reduce poverty | Encourage accumulation of human capital | Regulate labour market outcomes; stimulate aggregate demand |
| Source of weakened work incentive | Generous social programs | Stagnant wages |

productivity may decrease to a point where it is less profitable for firms to expand their investments and employment. Indeed, it will generally be to employers' advantage to maintain a certain level of equilibrium unemployment in the system. The subsequent risk posed to workers (of losing work and joining the ranks of the unemployed) both moderates their wage demands and enforces desirable discipline in the workplace.

Figure 2
**Labour Market "Flexibility" Neoclassical Case**

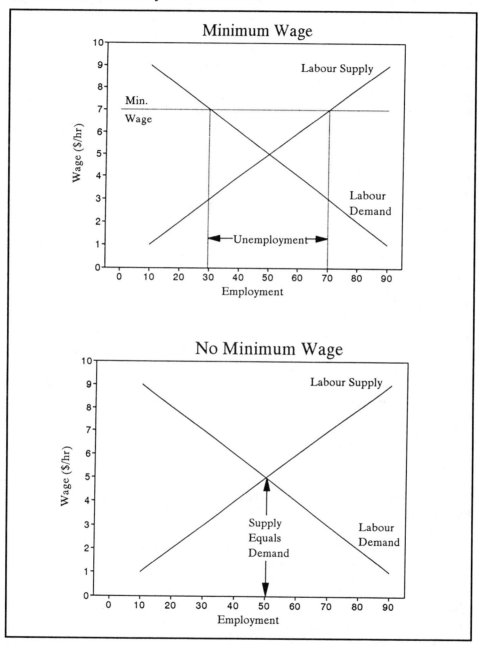

## WILL UNEMPLOYMENT FALL IN THE "FREE" LABOUR MARKET?

This structuralist approach casts doubt on the benign outcomes of labour market deregulation predicted by a neoclassical analysis. Yes, wages can be expected to fall as a result of deregulation. Wage regulation, collective bargaining institutions and income-replacing and income-supplementing social programs underwrite wage demands by supplementing the relative importance of continued employment to the living standards of workers.[13] Therefore, the erosion of these practices and institutions will weaken considerably the bargaining position of labour within the implicit or explicit bargaining conflict over income distribution. But this decline in wages will not clear the labour market or eliminate unemployment. In general, employment is limited by labour demand (that is, by the availability of jobs) rather than by labour supply. Indeed, some degree of unemployment is an essential precondition for profit-driven economic activity, and unemployment will be autonomously recreated even within a deregulated labour market.[14] Labour market deregulation will shift bargaining power and hence income toward employers, enhancing profitability. This may indeed create some jobs, if profit-driven firms step up their activity in response to enhanced profit rates. But it may also undermine aggregate demand conditions in the macro-economy by reducing the volume of consumer spending (thanks to both lower wages and to cutbacks in income support programs). The net effect is uncertain—even if unemployment does ultimately fall, this victory may be made hollow by the social hardship and polarization which accompanies it.

Figure 3 summarizes the complex and contradictory employment effects of labour market deregulation, when the full employment, supply-side assumptions of the neoclassical model are abandoned. A number of chains of causation point toward lower unemployment as a result of deregulation, especially in an open economy where both investment and exports are more sensitive to the relative cost competitiveness of domestic production. Weaker labour market regulations, by enhancing the bargaining position of employers, generate both lower wages and higher productivity (thanks to the greater flexibility allowed employers in organizing and disciplining work practices)[15] and hence create a two-fold reduction in unit labour costs (that is, wages per unit of output). Greater profitability and competitiveness stimulates investment and exports with consequent macro-economic spin-offs. The central bank may be encouraged by the weakness of wage demands to lower its interest rate (at any given level of unemployment), thus stimulating even more economic activity.[16] Finally, one additional but socially perverse channel of influence would see the unemployment rate fall simply because cuts in social programs and income supports chase discouraged workers from the official labour force (since their incentive to report that they are actively looking for work has disappeared).

On the other hand, low wages and reduced income support programs will cut deeply into consumption demand because working and poor households spend a higher proportion of their total income on consumption than do higher income households. This single chain of causation could conceivably result in a net negative impact on employment since domestic consumption is still the largest single source of aggregate demand in the macro-economy.[17] In an increasingly open economy, however (in which investment and exports are highly sensitive to labour cost competitiveness), the net impact of lower unit labour costs on employment is more likely to be marginally positive, since any ultimate increase in employment is attained at the expense of declining living standards and the associated adverse macro-economic multiplier effects.[18]

Figure 3
**Employment Effects of Labour Market Deregulation**

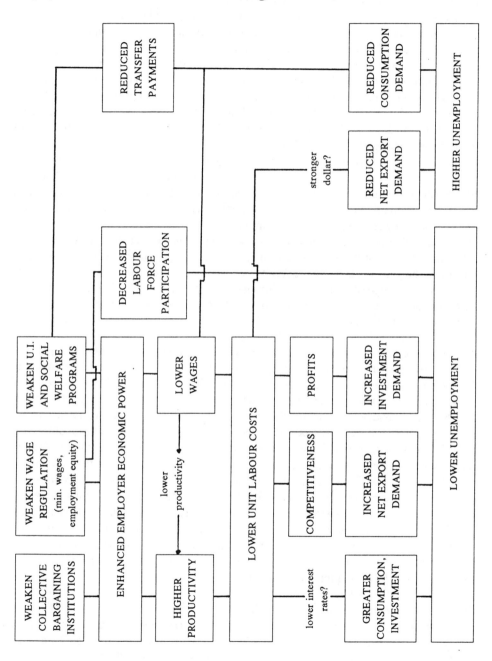

## THE RISING COST OF JOB LOSS
## AND THE INSECURITY OF CANADIAN WORKERS

From a perspective which stresses the importance of conflict and relative bargaining power rather than the automatic clearing of competitive markets, the focus in the current social policy reform exercise on scaling back unemployment insurance (U.I.) and other "passive" income support programs takes on a new significance. It is not that these programs inhibit the concrete allocation and reallocation of labour in Canada. More meaningfully, they have assisted Canadian labour in retaining a certain degree of bargaining power and defending its economic position, despite the integration of Canada into a global economy characterized increasingly by downward pressure on costs and wages. Scaling back income support programs in Canada, along with other labour market deregulation initiatives proposed at various levels of government (most radically by provincial governments in Alberta and Ontario), can be seen as part of a broader strategy to forcibly harmonize Canada's labour market outcomes with those of our trading partners (especially the U.S.). The reforms aim to enhance the international competitiveness of Canada's economy on a low wage basis; this goal is achieved by deliberately increasing the economic insecurity facing Canadian workers, hence moderating their wage demands and disciplining their behaviour in the workplace.

Indeed, the extent to which income support has been undermined, and the consequent increase in the general economic insecurity of Canadian workers, is already visible on the basis of policy changes that preceded the formal social security review. Figure 4 summarizes the historical evolution of different measures which together affect the extent of income security offered by Canada's U.I. system. The need for greater income security is obvious, given the increase in both the rate and the duration of unemployment since the mid-1970s.[19] However, the extent of U.I. protection for unemployed workers has deteriorated steadily (as measured by the share of officially unemployed workers who qualify for U.I. benefits). The decline in U.I. coverage has been especially rapid in the 1990s, in the wake of the series of cutbacks in benefits implemented by the present and previous federal governments. Indeed, the 1995 federal budget, abandoning the lofty reform language of the Green Paper, simply announced another straight cutback in benefits of at least 10 percent (Department of Finance 1995: 56), indicating perhaps that the government is more interested in simply reducing income supports than in genuinely reforming them. By spring of 1995, less than one-half of officially unemployed Canadians qualified for any U.I. benefits whatsoever.[20] In contrast, the level of benefits (for those who qualify for them) has remained relatively stable as a share of average wages since 1971 (when benefit levels were increased as part of the 1971 U.I. reform).

The diminishing chance of receiving U.I. benefits, together with the increasing duration of unemployment, have both contributed to a large increase in the degree of economic insecurity facing Canadian workers, even those who are employed. One way of measuring this insecurity is through a measure called the "cost of job loss" (CJL). This measures the income that an individual can expect to lose, on average, if they lose their job. It will be higher if it takes longer to find another job, if it is difficult to qualify for U.I. coverage, or if the level of benefits (assuming that an unemployed person qualifies) is lower.[21] When the CJL is high, workers are less willing to take actions in defense of their broader economic position (such as opposing wage concessions, going on strike or resisting speed-up practices in the workplace) if these actions might in some way threaten their continued employment. As

Figure 4

**The Erosion of U.I. Protection Canada, 1960—1995**

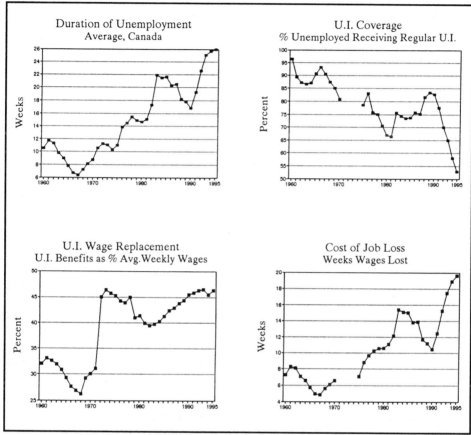

indicated in Figure 4, the average CJL facing Canadian workers has approximately tripled since the mid-1970s. The consequently weakened bargaining position of labour, not surprisingly, has corresponded with stagnant wages and with the popularity of workplace restructuring initiatives which may enhance productivity but which have often undermined the safety and quality of work life.

It is interesting to compare the rise in the CJL in Canada with a similar rise that has occurred in the U.S. (see Figure 5). The Canadian U.I. system is still roughly twice as generous as its American counterpart, taking into account both higher benefits and a higher coverage ratio. Despite this, however, Canadian workers have recently become even more insecure than workers in the U.S., due to the much longer average duration of unemployment in Canada. As shown in Figure 5, the CJL in the two countries has been remarkably similar, despite their dramatically different social programs. In the wake of recent U.I. cuts, for the first time Canada's CJL now significantly exceeds that of the U.S.[22]

Figure 5
**Cost of Job Loss in Canada and the U.S., 1960–1995**

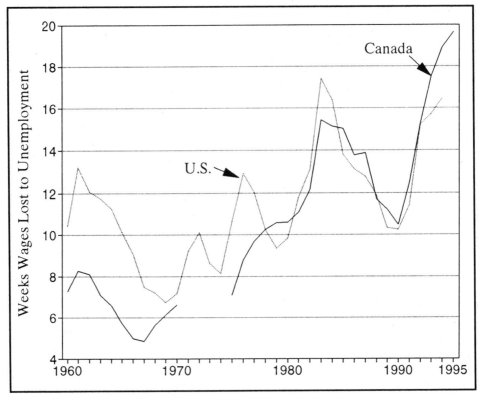

The observed "harmonization of insecurity" between the two countries casts further doubt on the assumption that Canada's labour market is inflexible. It is also consistent with the structuralist model of the labour market outlined above. Profit-seeking employers require a certain degree of unemployment-driven insecurity as a normal labour market outcome, in order to elicit workplace discipline and to moderate wage demands. Attempts to alleviate that insecurity solely by expanding income security programs may be offset partially or even fully by an autonomous labour market adjustment producing higher unemployment. Employers need unemployment to discipline labour; but when the social safety net is very weak, relatively less unemployment is required to achieve the same amount of discipline. The federal government seems to wish to trade in the Canadian version of economic insecurity (more generous programs combined with higher unemployment) for the U.S. version (very weak programs and somewhat lower unemployment). Workers will not become any less insecure as a result, and significant unemployment will continue to be an ongoing outcome of the labour market; but the government will spend less money and the economic bargaining position of employers will be enhanced considerably.

## Conclusion

The social security review process has been infused with lofty language about the need to assist Canadians in adapting to change. Advocates of greater flexibility in the functioning of Canada's labour market promise that this flexibility will produce lower unemployment and greater mobility in the world of work. Their menu of policy reforms includes the restructuring and scaling back of income support programs, more market-sensitive training initiatives and various other policies which fall outside the federal policy review (such as changes to minimum wage and collective bargaining legislation at the provincial level).

The real empirical evidence on flexibility in Canadian employment patterns suggests, however, that Canada's labour market is in fact highly flexible, in relation both to previous time periods and to the labour market outcomes of our trading partners. An important effect of the undoing of much of Canada's income security system will less likely be any observed increase in real flexibility, nor a change in the behaviour of unemployed persons, but rather a notable decline in the wages of employed persons. Under free market neoclassical assumptions, this wage decline is expected to eliminate unemployment. Under more realistic assumptions regarding the operation of labour markets, however, large scale unemployment will continue to exist and unemployment rates may not fall significantly at all.

Canadian workers are not particularly secure, despite the expensive U.I. system which they co-fund, since average received benefits are offsetting a diminishing portion of the rising cost of unemployment. Ultimately, therefore, a more effective set of income security policies must also address the demand-side constraint that continues to limit the labour market, no matter how flexible it becomes. Government must pro-actively focus on job creation initiatives (through measures such as pro-growth macro-economic policies, investment stimulus and others), in addition to providing decent income security for intervening periods of unemployment. Otherwise, tax-weary Canadians are as likely to opt for a cheaper, privatized U.S.-style version of insecurity instead of the more expensive Canadian variety.

## Notes

1. Views expressed are those of the author alone and should not be attributed to the CAW.
2. Of the 1.4 million new jobs expected by the federal government's Canadian Occupational Projection System by 2000, some 640,000 fall within Skill Levels C and D (requiring secondary education or less).
3. The thirty-seven industries are at the two-digit level of sectoral disaggregation. Data are reported in Statistics Canada Catalogue 72F-002, *Annual Estimates of Employment, Earnings and Hours*, and January issues of the U.S. Department of Labor, Bureau of Labor Statistics publication, *Employment and Earnings*. Some minor adjustments were required to ensure comparability between the sector definitions utilized in the two sources; data are available from the author on request. The data analysis begins in 1983—the first year of Statistics Canada's establishment-based Survey of Employment, Payrolls and Hours.
4. This normalized standard deviation equals the sample standard deviation for each industry as a percentage of the sample mean.
5. The weighted-average index of volatility is lower than the arithmetic average index for Canada because the relatively larger industries tended to be somewhat less volatile. In the U.S., on the other hand, large and small industries tended to be roughly equally volatile, so the two measures are similar.
6. It is interesting to note that, of the eight sectors in which the U.S. industry experienced greater

variability of employment, four corresponded to public sector activities (the three levels of government employment and health care services). Thus of the thirty-three private-sector industries included in the sample, Canadian employment was more variable in twenty-nine (or 88 percent). The notion that Canada's *private* sector is prevented by rigidities from allocating or reallocating labour is therefore especially questionable.

7.   The root mean square error measures the square root of the average squared deviation between the two series.

8.   The coefficient on change in GDP is 25 percent higher for Canada than the U.S. in the sample beginning in 1981, but over 40 percent higher in the sample beginning in 1990.

9.   In both countries, the size of the coefficient on GDP change decreased from the first data set to the second; this reflects the relatively "jobless" nature of the recent economic recovery in both countries in which advances in economic output were not accompanied by gains in employment. Of incidental interest in the regressions reported in Table 2 are the sign and size of the coefficients on the constant term. A negative coefficient indicates an ongoing positive growth in labour productivity; that is, the amount of labour required to produce a certain volume of output declines over time. The Canadian regressions have much larger negative constant terms than the U.S. and the term becomes more negative in the 1990s data sample, suggesting that the Canadian economy has experienced greater productivity shifts (resulting from trade-related restructuring, for example). This is another potential explanation for the relative rise of Canada's unemployment rate: not only has the Canadian economy suffered deeper recessions that the U.S. (resulting in less output produced), but it has also experienced greater ongoing productivity shifts (resulting in a need for even fewer workers to produce that lower volume of output). Since none of the constant terms are statistically significant, however, too much importance should not be attached to this result.

10.   Data from the Council of Economic Advisors (1994), *Economic Report of the President*, Table B-45.

11.   Data from Statistics Canada (1995), *Canadian Economic Observer, Historical Statistical Supplement*.

12.   The terms "structural" or "structuralist" have different meanings in different disciplines of the social sciences. In economics, they refer to the core idea that social and economic institutions, or "social structures," will affect patterns of both income distribution and labour relations, in contrast to the market-clearing pressures emphasized by neoclassical models. As a result, aggregate demand factors take on a new and lasting importance. See Bowles, Gordon and Weisskopf (1989) or Taylor (1991) for representative examples of structuralist economic analysis.

13.   In the terminology of Esping-Andersen (1989), social programs offer workers some opportunity for "decommodification": their subsistence becomes somewhat independent from their status as suppliers of a commodity (labour services).

14.   In this conclusion, the structuralist approach finds an important theoretical pedigree in the work of Kalecki (1971)—a contemporary of Keynes, who developed a very similar model of the importance of demand-side conditions in macro-economics, but who emphasized the resistance that full employment strategies would likely encounter from business groups for exactly this reason.

15.   This productivity-enhancing effect is offset somewhat by a negative impact on productivity resulting from the decline in wages; "efficiency wage" theory predicts that workers will exert greater effort in return for higher wages. The net effect of deregulation on labour intensity, however, is almost certainly positive.

16.   At the same time, however, the dollar may rise in response to enhanced profitability and the consequent inflow of foreign capital, thus undercutting some of the gain in export competitiveness that would otherwise be expected.

17.   In Canada, domestic consumption (both public and private) accounts for 80 percent of total aggregate demand. In 1994, this was by far the weakest component of an otherwise vibrant

recovery—growing by just 2.1 percent, compared to a 5.3 percent increase in private investment and a staggering 20 percent increase in exports. Stagnant wages and constrained transfer payments are important factors behind the sluggishness of domestic consumption.

18. Stanford (1995) conducts macro-econometric simulations of the effects of lower wages and higher productivity, using a twenty-equation time series model of the Canadian economy. Under neoclassical assumptions, a decline in wages is found (as expected) to increase employment; the adverse demand-side impacts of lower wages are ignored. Under alternative, structuralist assumptions, lower wages and transfer payments cause a significant decline in consumption demand. This largely (but not wholly) outweighs the positive stimulus to exports and investment in an open-economy setting, so that overall GDP rises slightly. The net employment effect of lower wages is slightly positive, but the net employment effect of higher productivity is negative.

19. The top left graph in Figure 4 illustrates the duration of unemployment in weeks. Prior to 1976, Statistics Canada did not collect data on the duration of unemployment. However, duration is closely associated with current and lagged levels of the unemployment rate. The pre-1976 data in Figure 4, therefore, is estimated on the basis of fitted values from a regression of unemployment duration on current and lagged unemployment rates and a quadratic time trend; this regression obtained an $R^2$ value of .970 over the 1976-94 sample. Nevertheless, the pre-1976 values for unemployment duration and hence for cost of job loss should be interpreted cautiously.

20. See top right graph in Figure 4. Measures which make it harder to qualify to collect U.I., and measures which reduce the duration of benefit payments, have both reduced the average U.I. coverage ratio. The data series on coverage presented in Figure 4 is incomplete; no consistent data is available for the 1971-74 period. This causes a corresponding gap in the cost of job loss series presented below.

21. The CJL is measured in weeks of lost wages, and can be summarized by the following formula:

$$\text{CJL} = \frac{\text{Avg. wage - (Avg. U.I. Benefit * U.I. Coverage Ratio)}}{\text{Avg. wage}} * \text{Duration of Unemployment}$$

This is a highly simplified measure (it does not account for the value of non-wage employment benefits, or the different rates of U.I. coverage for new job losers compared to existing unemployed persons), but it nevertheless reflects the overall trend in the general degree of economic insecurity in the economy. The concept of CJL arose within the structuralist economic literature on the "labour extraction" problem; see especially Bowles (1985) and Weisskopf, Bowles and Gordon (1983).

22. It should be noted that since this simplified CJL measure excludes non-wage employment benefits, it may underestimate the relative CJL in the U.S. (where employer-supplied health insurance is an important component of overall compensation). Note also that a complete CJL measure should consider other social security programs in addition to U.I. (such as welfare); we have focused in this discussion on the erosion of U.I., but welfare programs play an increasingly important role in backstopping income security for employed workers in the wake of the erosion of U.I. Social welfare is less generous and accessible in the U.S., and so our relative CJL estimate for the U.S. may be further underestimated.

## REFERENCES

Baldwin, John and M. Rafiquzzaman. 1994. "Structural Change in Employment and Wage Differentials." *Canadian Business Economics* 2 (4): 22-35.

Bank of Canada. 1995. *Monetary Policy Report, May 1995*. Ottawa: Bank of Canada.

Bowles, Samuel. 1985. "The Production Process in a Competitive Economy: Walrasian, Hobbesian and Marxian Models." *American Economic Review* 75 (1): 16-36.

———, David M. Gordon and Thomas E. Weisskopf. 1989. "Business Ascendancy and Economic

Impasse: A Structuralist Retrospective on Conservative Economics, 1979-87." *Journal of Economic Perspectives* 3 (1): 107-34.

Council of Economic Advisors. 1994. *Economic Report of the President*. Washington: Council of Economic Advisors.

Department of Finance. 1995. *Budget Plan*. Ottawa: Department of Finance.

————. 1994. *A New Framework for Economic Policy*. Ottawa: Department of Finance.

Economic Council of Canada. 1990. *Good Jobs, Bad Jobs*. Ottawa: Economic Council of Canada.

Esping-Andersen, Gosta. 1989. "The Three Political-Economies of the Welfare State." *Canadian Review of Sociology and Anthropology* 26 (1): 10-35.

*Globe and Mail*. 1994. "Liberating Labour." Editorial. March 16: A18.

Human Resources Development Canada. 1995. *Preliminary Demand Estimates from the Canadian Occupational Projection System*. Mimeo. Ottawa: Human Resources Development Canada.

————. 1994a. *Agenda: Jobs and Growth. Improving Social Security in Canada: A Discussion Paper*. Ottawa: Minister of Supply and Services.

————. 1994b. *Report of the Advisory Group on Working Time and the Distribution of Work*. Ottawa: Minister of Supply and Services.

Kalecki, Michael. 1971. "Class Struggle and the Distribution of Income." *Kyklos* 24 (1): 1-9.

Organization for Economic Co-operation and Development. 1994a. *The OECD Jobs Study*. Paris: Organization for Economic Co-operation and Development.

————. 1994b. *OECD Employment Outlook*. Paris: Organization for Economic Co-operation and Development.

————. 1991. "Labour Market Performance and Policy." In *OECD Economic Surveys: Canada*. Paris: Organization for Economic Co-operation and Development.

Osberg, Lars. 1994. *Concepts of Unemployment and the Structure of Unemployment*. Mimeo. Halifax: Economics Department, Dalhousie University.

Stanford, Jim. 1995. *The Grim Economy: Theoretical and Empirical Perspectives on Growth and Equity in an Open Economy*. Mimeo. Toronto: Canadian Auto Workers.

Statistics Canada. 1995. *Canadian Economic Observer, Historical Statistical Supplement*. Ottawa: Minister of Supply and Services.

Sunter, Deborah and Rene Morissette. 1994. "The Hours People Work." *Perspectives on Labour and Income* 6 (3): 8-13.

Taylor, Lance. 1991. *Income Distribution, Inflation, and Growth: Lectures on Structuralist Macroeconomic Theory*. Cambridge, Mass.: MIT Press.

Weisskopf, Thomas J., Samuel Bowles and David M. Gordon. 1983. "Hearts and Minds: A Social Model of U.S. Productivity Growth." *Brookings Papers on Economic Activity* 2: 381-441.

# CHAPTER 10

# DIVERSITY IN RETIREMENT AND THE FINANCIAL SECURITY OF OLDER WORKERS

*Grant Schellenberg*

## INTRODUCTION

The retirement transition has become increasingly diverse over the past fifteen years. Change in the "normal" retirement age is the most widely recognized component of this shift, with the majority of Canadians now retiring from the labour force before age sixty-five, and a considerable portion retiring before age sixty. Expectations of early retirement are also widespread; most Canadians still in the labour force expect to retire before age sixty-five, and many expect to do so before age sixty (Schellenberg 1994: 20-21). But not only is the *timing* of retirement changing, so too is the *process* of retirement.

People are leaving the labour force through different pathways and for different reasons than in the past. As firms pare down their workforces and reorganize their operations, older workers are being offered early retirement packages and financial incentives to encourage them to leave their jobs. For many, this provides a welcome opportunity to leave the labour force at an early age. Others have not fared so well in the restructuring process. Unemployment rates among older workers are at their highest point since the Second World War and, for many people, retirement is simply a disguised form of joblessness (Organization for Economic Co-operation and Development 1992: 205-13).

Labour force exit through these different pathways is associated with variations in the financial well-being of older workers. Those voluntarily leaving paid employment are more likely to have adequate retirement income than those displaced by job loss and health problems. This reflects differences in earnings prior to leaving the labour force, as well as differing access to certain income sources after labour force exit, most notably private pensions. This raises concern regarding the financial security of some older workers, particularly as they are displaced from the labour force at younger ages and struggle to bridge financially the time span between the age of labour force exit and the age of public pension eligibility.

## THE CHANGING AGE OF RETIREMENT

The exit of workers from the labour force at younger ages has been one of the most striking economic trends since the Second World War. This trend has long been evident among men aged sixty-five and over, with the labour force participation rate of this group declining from 47.5 to 11.0 percent between 1947 and 1994 (McDonald and Chen 1993: 88; Statistics Canada 1995: B-7). But increasingly, labour force exit has grown among younger age groups. For example, among men aged sixty to sixty-four, the labour force participation rate dropped by almost 20 percentage points—from 68.3 to 47.2—between 1981 and 1994. For those aged fifty-five to fifty-nine there was a drop of 10 percentage points—from 83.9 to 72.7—over the same period (see Table 1). Labour force exit now appears to be occurring among even younger men with the first signs of declining participation among forty-five to fifty-four year olds appearing in the 1990s. The participation rate of this age group remained around 91 to 92 percent through the 1970s and 1980s, but dropped to 89.8 percent in 1994. This decline is slight, to be sure, but may well be the precursor of a more significant shift out of the labour force among men in their early fifties and late forties.

Among women there has also been a marked trend toward retirement at younger ages, although this is not reflected in their labour force participation rates. This is because changes in their rate reflects the interplay of two forces. On the one hand, women's labour force participation rate has been pushed upward by the widespread entry of women into the paid labour force through the post-war period; and on the other hand, it has been pushed downward by the general tendency towards early retirement (OECD 1992: 201-02).

Table 1

**Labour Force Participation Rates by Age Group and Sex, Canada 1971—1994**

|  | MEN | | | WOMEN | | |
|---|---|---|---|---|---|---|
|  | Age 55-59 | Age 60-64 | Age 65 & over | Age 55-59 | Age 60-64 | Age 65 & over |
| 1971 | 84.9 | 74.1 | 20.0 | 38.7 | 29.1 | 5.1 |
| 1976 | 82.4 | 69.0 | 16.0 | 39.2 | 27.3 | 4.2 |
| 1981 | 83.9 | 68.3 | 14.1 | 41.7 | 28.1 | 4.5 |
| 1986 | 80.7 | 59.3 | 11.8 | 44.3 | 27.2 | 3.7 |
| 1991 | 77.8 | 53.6 | 11.3 | 49.7 | 27.9 | 3.5 |
| 1994 | 72.7 | 47.2 | 11.0 | 49.2 | 25.3 | 3.5 |

Source: Statistics Canada, *Labour Force Annual Averages 1975-1981, 1981-1988* and *1989-1994*, Cat.71-529 and Statistics Canada *The Nation: Labour Force Activity*. Cat. 93-324, March 1993.

Nonetheless, the prevalence of early retirement among women (and men) is evident in their ages of retirement. As shown in Figure 1, among retired Canadians, 38 percent of women and 27 percent of men left the labour force before age sixty, and almost 70 percent of women and 60 percent of men left before age sixty-five. No longer do most people retire at or around age sixty-five as they did in previous decades (Kohli and Rein 1991: 6). Retirement now occurs across an age span of fifteen years or more, from the early fifties to the mid-sixties. This has a number of implications.

The "destandardization" of the retirement age is altering our understanding of the life course. In the earlier post-war period, retirement and old age were almost synonymous. Exit from the labour force and entry into "old age" were two sides of the same transition (Guillemard 1991: 211). At the same time, eligibility for government programs, such as Old Age Security (OAS) and Canada/Quebec Pension Plans (C/QPP), signified the official boundary between adulthood and old age. But with many people now retiring in their fifties—well before they can be considered elderly in any sense of the word—the link between retirement, old age and eligibility for public "old age" programs is disintegrating. This is transforming our views of what it means to be "retired" and to be "old." It also raises an important policy consideration.

Figure 1
**Retired Men and Women: Age at Retirement, Canada, 1991**

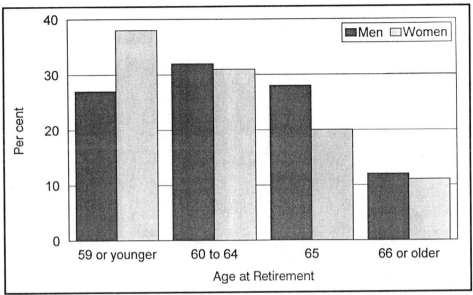

Source: Prepared by the Centre for International Statistics, using *Survey on Aging and Independence* microdata, 1991.

Old age programs remain based on the assumption that retired people and old people are part of the same group. This is no longer the case and programs serving the elderly no longer serve all retired people. This raises the question of whether some retirees, particularly those involuntarily displaced from the labour force at relatively young ages, are becoming more economically vulnerable. As will be shown shortly, this is indeed the case.

Finally, along with the destandardization of retirement comes uncertainty. It is difficult for people to foresee at what age and under what conditions they will leave the labour force given the increasing range of possibilities. Among employed persons aged forty-five to fifty-four, about one-quarter are unable to state the age at which they expect to retire. This is not surprising considering that retirement is ten to fifteen years in the future for many of these individuals. Yet even among people aged fifty-five to sixty-four, more than one-fifth are uncertain about their plans (Schellenberg 1994: 35-37). Economic insecurity is an important factor in this regard as people with low incomes, no employer pension coverage, shorter job tenure, employment in semi-skilled and unskilled occupations and low levels of education are most likely to be uncertain about their retirement age.

## The Changing Process of Retirement

Not only is the age of retirement becoming more diverse, so too is the process of retirement. People are now retiring in different ways and for different reasons than they did in the past. This is due in large part to the transformation of the retirement transition brought about by the process of economic restructuring undertaken by firms through the 1980s and 1990s.

International trade and competition have intensified with the emergence of newly industrializing countries, the formation of new trading blocs and the globalization of consumer markets.
The speed and variability of business operations have also increased with the introduction of
new technologies and the growing pace of international capital transactions. In this changing
economic climate, businesses have been forced to adapt or face elimination. In response they
have reorganized processes of production and distribution, downsized their workforces,
reduced layers in the managerial hierarchy and employed labour on new terms and arrangements.

Retirement has played an important part in this reorganization. It is being used as a
mechanism for workforce adjustment as firms pare down their workforces and reorganize
their operations. Many firms are offering older workers financial incentives, such as early
pension benefits and "cashouts" to encourage them to leave their jobs. For example, Jason
Siroonian (1993: 10) reports that between 1990 and 1992, 43,000 people who retired earlier
than planned cited the receipt of a cashout or early retirement package as their main reason
for doing so. This was up 28 percent over the previous three-year period (1987-89). Evidence
from the *Survey on Aging and Independence* (Statistics Canada 1991) points to a similar trend.
Of all the retirees who left the labour force prior to 1982, only 8 percent mention early
retirement policies as a motivating factor. Among those who retired between 1986 and 1989,
17 percent cite early retirement policies, while this is the case for 23 percent of those who
retired in 1990 and 1991. In short, early retirement policies have become increasingly
prevalent over the last fifteen years. This is also apparent in Revenue Canada's Taxation
Statistics. As shown in Table 2, the proportion of taxfilers aged fifty-five to fifty-nine and
sixty to sixty-four reporting income from employer pensions and superannuations increased
through the 1980s. This increase is particularly striking among men, with almost a 100 percent
increase between 1981 and 1992.

Table 2

**Taxfilers Receiving Income from Employer Pensions or Superannuation by Age and
Sex, Canada selected years (percent)**

|  | 1981 | 1985 | 1992 |
|---|---|---|---|
| **Men** | | | |
| **Aged 55 to 59** | 8.3 | 11.5 | 16.8 |
| **Aged 60 to 64** | 19.8 | 27.9 | 35.5 |
| **Women** | | | |
| **Aged 55 to 59** | 7.4 | 7.4 | 10.3 |
| **Aged 60 to 64** | 18.5 | 19.4 | 23.3 |

Source: Prepared by the Centre for International Statistics using Revenue Canada, *Taxation
Statistics,* selected years.

For many workers, these developments have no doubt provided a welcome opportunity to leave the labour market. Indeed, having adequate income and a desire to stop working are the two most frequently mentioned reasons for retirement among retirees in their fifties and early sixties.

But there is another side to this story. Not all older workers leaving the labour force have done so voluntarily or because they were offered financial incentives. Many have been pushed out by job loss and older workers have been far from immune to persistently high unemployment rates. The rate of unemployment among Canadians aged fifty-five to sixty-four, like the rate for the entire labour force, increased dramatically during the last two recessionary periods (see Figure 2). And in spite of the economic recovery of the late 1980s, the unemployment rate among older workers did not return to its pre-recession level. Moreover, job loss among older workers appears to be worsening. In the recessionary period of the early 1980s, their unemployment rate peaked at 7.8 percent (1984) but, in the more recent downturn, it peaked at 9.6 percent (1993)—two percentage points higher. Such an increase was not evident among the broader labour force.

Figure 2
**Unemployment Rates by Selected Age Groups, Canada 1981-1994**

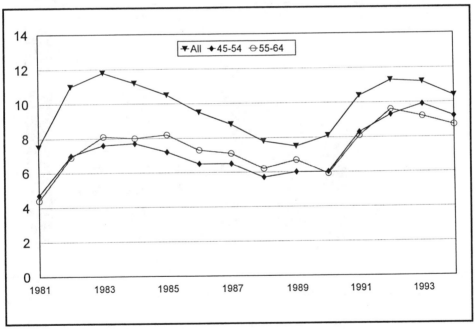

Source: Prepared by the Centre for International Statistics using *Labour Force Annual Averages 1981-1988* and *1989-1994*. Cat. 71-529.

To understand the impact of job loss on the retirement transition, it is useful to consider the characteristics of unemployment among older workers. While the unemployment rate among these workers is lower than the labour force average, a fact attributable in part to their longer job tenure and greater job seniority, older workers who lose their jobs face particular difficulties finding new ones. As shown in Figure 3, the average duration of unemployment for this groups is much longer than for the labour force as a whole.

This duration increased through the 1980s. For men aged forty-five and over, it rose from eighteen weeks in 1976 to a high of thirty-two weeks in 1985, declining slightly during the economic recovery of the latter 1980s. But by 1994, the average duration of unemployment among older men reached thirty-five weeks. Among men aged fifteen to twenty-four it was seventeen weeks.

It is also important to note that these figures likely underestimate the true scope of unemployment among older Canadians, since "discouraged workers" are not counted. These are individuals who have looked for a job within the last six months, but given up their search because they believe that no jobs are available. Older workers are particularly likely to be in this group.

Figure 3
**Unemployed Workers: Average Duration of Unemployment by Age Groups, Selected Years**

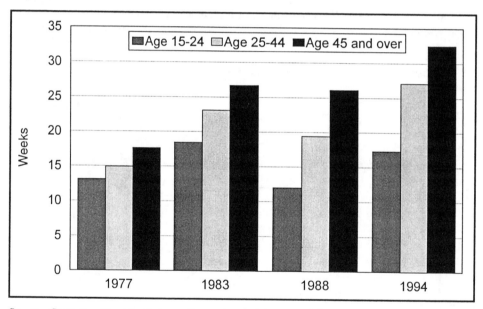

Source: Statistics Canada, *Labour Force Annual Averages,* Cat. 71-529, selected years.

One result of these changes is that unemployment has become a pathway leading from the labour market into "retirement." Ernest Akyeampong (1987: 107) of Statistics Canada examined the circumstances of workers who were permanently laid off because of plant closures, work load reductions and similar reasons during the 1981-84 recessionary period. He found that only 39 percent of workers aged fifty-five to sixty-four had found employment by 1986, compared to 65 percent of workers aged twenty-five to fifty-four. "Moreover, about 41 percent of the older workers had left the labour force; only 14 percent of the younger ones had done so." The recession of the early 1990s had a similar effect. During the 1990-92 period, the number of workers who retired earlier than planned because of lay-offs or plant closures (45,000) " . . . was more than double the number for the 1987-89 period (20,000)" (Siroonian 1993: 10). Again, the recession was particularly hard on older workers, with job loss and unemployment forcing many into retirement.

## "Retirees" or "Displaced Workers"?

In the context of the rapidly changing labour market, a number of empirical questions arise: how many older people who are no longer in the labour force are "retirees" and how many are "displaced workers"? What factors are associated with being one or the other? And what are the financial implications of leaving the labour force through these different pathways? It is to these questions we now turn.

Given the growing prevalence of early retirement, the following analysis is limited to people aged fifty-five to sixty-four. Moreover, the analysis focuses on "recent labour force leavers"—people who are no longer in the labour force but who left their last jobs within the previous five years. This subgroup was chosen because detailed information on why they left the labour force is available; such information is not available for people who left the labour force more than five years previously. Data are drawn from the Survey of Consumer Finances (scf) microdata. The 1992 and 1993 scfs (which contain data on the 1991 and 1992 calendar years) have been combined for the analysis to ensure adequate sample size for the fifty-five to sixty-four year age group. All income amounts have been adjusted to 1992 dollars, and the survey weights have been adjusted to provide population estimates averaged over the two years.

As shown in Figure 4, the largest share of recent labour force leavers retired from their last job. This is the case for 59 percent of the men and 40 percent of the women. Nonetheless, many recent labour force leavers are displaced workers, with about one-quarter having left their last job because of lay-off or job loss. Many of these people, particularly men, were unemployed for part of the previous year, suggesting they wanted to stay in the labour force, and left their previous job involuntarily. Health problems resulted in the labour force exit of 12 percent of men and 17 percent of women, while smaller proportions left for other reasons.

If "displaced workers" are defined as those who left the labour force within the previous five years because of lay-off or job loss, there were approximately 125,000 such workers (aged fifty-five to sixty-four) in 1991-92. One might also add to this total the long-term unemployed (not shown in Figure 4) since those in older age groups face particular obstacles in their job search and often become discouraged workers. If these people are included, the number of displaced workers rises to about 180,000. Finally, if one also counts the people who left their jobs within the previous five years because of illness or disability, the number of displaced workers rises to almost 250,000. One might speculate that at least some were displaced by lay-offs or other economic factors, particularly in the wake of the recession of the early 1980s, but the extent of this cannot be measured.

Overall, while retirement still constitutes the main pathway out of the labour force, displacement by job loss and health problems affects a substantial number of older workers. Over the past fifteen years, the different pathways have become more prevalent. Between 1981 and 1992, the number of recent labour force leavers displaced from the labour force by job loss and lay-off increased by 72 percent (from 105,000 to 181,000 workers), while the

Figure 4
**Recent Labour Force Leavers\*: Reason for Leaving Last Job, by Sex
Canada, 1991-1992**

Men Age
55-64

Laid off/lost job
Health
Retired
Other

Women
Age 55-64

\*Refers to persons not in the labour force who left last job within previous 5 years.

Source: Prepared by the Centre for International Statistics, using the *Survey of Consumer Finances* microdata, 1992-93.

number of those retiring increased by 68 percent (from 167,000 to 281,000). The number of recent labour force leavers citing illness and disability related factors declined slightly over the same period.

With the growing prevalence of these diverse pathways out of the labour force, the circumstances and characteristics of individuals are increasingly important in the retirement transition. Not all individuals are equally able to benefit, or protect themselves, from changes in the labour force. Some are more vulnerable to lay-off and unemployment, while others are better able to afford retirement at early ages. In short, patterns of labour force exit vary substantially across socio-economic status (Lackzo 1989: 24-54). As shown in Table 3, workers displaced by job loss and health problems tend to have lower levels of education than retirees. Among men, for example, two-thirds of those displaced from their jobs had not completed high school, compared with about half of retirees. In terms of occupation, a relatively large share of retirees were previously employed in professional and managerial occupations, while displaced workers were more likely to have been employed in blue collar jobs. Finally, retirees are likely to have had higher paying jobs than displaced workers while they were still in the labour force. Of the people in Table 3 who had paid employment during the previous year, the average weekly earnings of those who subsequently retired were several hundred dollars higher than those who were subsequently displaced by job loss or health problems. In other words, the people most vulnerable to involuntary labour force exit tend to be those least able to afford it.

Overall, the range of socio-economic inequality in Canadian society is reflected in patterns of labour force exit. People with adequate financial resources are better able to exercise control over the timing of their retirement and to retire early if they wish. Those without such resources work until they are eligible for a public pension or, as we have seen here, they are pushed out of the labour force by factors beyond their control. Trends that foster inequality, such as high unemployment and increasing earnings polarization, are likely to be reflected in future retirement patterns.

Table 3
**Recent Labour Force Leavers\*: Education, Prior Occupation and by Prior Earnings, by Sex and Reason for Leaving Last Job  Canada 1991-1992**

| | Men Aged 55 to 64 | | | Women Aged 55 to 64 | | |
|---|---|---|---|---|---|---|
| | Retired[1] | Displaced by job loss | Displaced by health | Retired | Displaced by job loss | Displaced by health |
| **EDUCATION** | | | | | | |
| Less than high school | 48 | 68 | 66 | 42 | 53 | 65 |
| High school/ some post-secondary | 22 | 15 | 19 | 30 | 23 | 16 |
| Completed post-secondary | 30 | 17 | 16 | 29 | 25 | 19 |
| Total | 100% | 100% | 100% | 100% | 100% | 100% |
| **PRIOR OCCUPATION** | | | | | | |
| Prof./Managerial | 30 | 11 | - | 31 | 14 | 20 |
| Clerical | - | - | - | 25 | 31 | - |
| Sales/Service | 17 | 15 | 17q | 31 | 29 | 52 |
| Blue collar | 48 | 67 | 68 | 13 | 26 | - |
| Total | 100% | 100% | 100% | 100% | 100% | 100% |
| **PRIOR AVERAGE WEEKLY EARNING[2]** | $ 940 | $ 600 | $ 630 | $ 510 | $ 310 | $ 400 |

\* This includes people who are no longer in the labour force and who left their last paid job within the previous five years.
[1] Retirees include people who left the labour to retire, as well as those who left for other reasons.
[2] Average weekly earnings (wages, salaries and self-employed earnings) of respondents who had employment during the previous calendar year. Dollar amounts have been rounded to the nearest 10.
- Sample size too small to provide reliable estimate.

Source: Prepared by the Centre for International Statistics using Survey of Consumer Finances microdata, 1992 and 1993.

## THE FINANCIAL PROFILES OF RETIREES AND DISPLACED WORKERS

The transition out of the labour force has important financial implications for Canadians. Older workers displaced from the labour force before they are ready to leave are less likely than others to be adequately financially (or emotionally) prepared for retirement. For those not included in an employer pension plan, job displacement may mean the depletion of personal savings in the attempt to bridge the gap financially between the age of labour force exit and age of public pension eligibility. This issue is particularly troublesome since this gap is widening. This raises the spectre of growing financial insecurity among today's near-senior population, as well as among tomorrow's elderly.

There are large differences in the financial profiles of people leaving the labour force in different ways. As shown in Table 4, retired men have average incomes of about $34,000 while men displaced by job loss or health problems have average incomes about $12,000 less. The same pattern is evident among women, with the average income of displaced workers about $4000 less than that of retirees. In slightly different terms, men and women displaced from the labour force have average incomes 35 to 40 percent lower than those of retirees.[1]

Table 4
**Recent Labour Force Leavers\*: Average Income by Sex, Age Group and Reason for Leaving Last Job, Canada 1992-1992**

|  | Men Aged 55 to 64 | | | Women Aged 55 to 64 | | |
|---|---|---|---|---|---|---|
|  | Retired | Displaced by job loss | Displaced by health | Retired | Displaced by job loss | Displaced by health |
| Private Sources | 29,700 | 17,100 | 15,300 | 10,900 | 6,800 | 5,600 |
| Public Sources | 4,300 | 6,000 | 6,400 | 2,800 | 2,800 | 4,200 |
| All Sources | 34,000 | 23,100 | 21,700 | 13,700 | 9,600 | 9,700 |

\* This includes people who are no longer in the labour force and who left their last paid job within the previous five years. Income data refers to the previous calendar year during which respondents may have had employment earnings. Amounts have been rounded to the nearest 100.

Source: Prepared by the Centre for International Statistics using Survey of Consumer Finances microdata, 1992 and 1993

In part, this variation reflects differences in the earnings profiles of people prior to leaving the labour force, with displaced workers likely to have had lower weekly earnings than retirees. But it also reflects the different sources of income received by retirees and displaced workers once they have left the labour force. Table 5 shows the proportion of total aggregate income received from different sources by recent labour force leavers: employer pensions; investments; c/QPP; etc. Quite clearly, a much larger proportion of the total aggregate income received by retired men and women comes from employer pensions than is the case among displaced workers. Indeed, 61 percent of the total aggregate income received by retired men was derived from this source compared with 37 percent received by men displaced by lay-off and job loss. The same pattern is evident among women, although they derive a smaller share of their income from this source than men, reflecting their lower rate of pension coverage. Not surprisingly, a relatively large share of the income received by workers displaced by lay-off is from unemployment insurance; similarly, displaced workers receive a larger share of their income from social assistance.

The same story emerges if individual rather than aggregate income is examined. For example, 62 percent of retired men received employer pension income and the average amount received was $21,700. In contrast, about half as many men displaced from the labour force received income from such pensions, and of those who did, the average amount received was about 36 percent lower. The pattern is the same among women but, again, women in all three groups are less likely than men to receive income from this source. Similarly, displaced men and women are much more likely than their retired counterparts to receive income from unemployment insurance, social assistance and other government programs.

Table 5
**Labour Force Leavers[1]: Proportion of Total Aggregate Income from Specific Sources, by Sex and Reason for Leaving Last Job, Canada 1991-1992**

|  | Men Aged 55 to 64 | | | Women Aged 55 to 64 | | |
|---|---|---|---|---|---|---|
|  | Retired | Displaced by lay-off | Displaced by health | Retired | Displaced by lay-off | Displaced by health |
| Earnings | 1 | 1 | 1 | 1 | - | 3 |
| Employer-pensions | 61 | 37 | 30 | 41 | 16 | 15 |
| Investments | 15 | 13 | 9 | 24 | 21 | 18 |
| Other private* | 4 | 6 | 13 | 4 | 6 | 6 |
| Total Private | 82 | 56 | 53 | 70 | 43 | 42 |
| Unemploy. Insurance | 1 | 17 | 4 | 3 | 12 | 2 |
| Social Assistance | 3 | 9 | 8 | 3 | 7 | 15 |
| CPP/QPP | 11 | 11 | 26 | 19 | 17 | 29 |
| Other public** | 3 | 7 | 10 | 5 | 21 | 12 |
| Total Public | 18 | 44 | 48 | 30 | 57 | 58 |
| TOTAL | 100% | 100% | 100% | 100% | 100% | 100% |

[1] Includes respondents who are no longer in the labour force and who left their jobs within the previous five years. Respondents with one or more weeks of paid employment in the previous calendar year are excluded from these estimates. This was done to estimate the relative importance of income sources aside from wages, salariesand self-employed earnings.
* Includes income from inheritance, alimony, severance pay or retiring allowance, strike and sick pay from unions, royalties and other private sources.
** Includes income from Spouse's Allowance, Veteran's Allowance, Goods & Services Tax Credit, provincial tax credits, Child Tax Credits, Family and Youth Allowance and other public programs.

Source: Prepared by the Centre for International Statistics using Survey of Consumer Finances microdata, 1992 and 1993.

The diversity of pathways out of the labour force raises concerns regarding the financial well-being of some groups within the near-senior population. Older workers who are displaced from the labour force have few financial options open to them: they tend to come from low paying jobs and are less likely to have investment income than other workers; they are less likely to be included in employer pensions; and they are often displaced from their jobs before they are eligible for even a partial public pension at age sixty. One consequence is that these people are more likely than others their age to live in families which fall below Statistics Canada's Low Income Cut-Off (LICO) (see Table 6). This is particularly the case for those who did not have paid employment during the previous year, indicating that as displaced workers are out of the labour force for longer periods, they become more susceptible to poverty. Retirees, who are more likely to have made adequate financial preparations for their labour force withdrawal, are less likely to face this situation. If trends continue to erode the economic security that older workers derive from the labour market, greater pressure may well be placed on public income security programs, such as the Guaranteed Income Supplement, in the years to come. Unfortunately, current trends in public policy, with their emphasis on decreasing public expenditures and reducing the size of governments, will make it increasingly difficult to meet this growing need for income support.

Table 6

**Recent Labour Force Leavers: Percent in Families Below LICO\* by Sex and Reason for Leaving Last Job, Canada 1991-1992 (percent)**

|  | Men Aged 55 to 64 | | | Women Aged 55 to 64 | | |
|---|---|---|---|---|---|---|
|  | Retired | Displaced by job loss | Displaced by health | Retired | Displaced by job loss | Displaced by health |
| All respondents | 12 | 18 | 20 | 17 | 16 | 27 |
| Respondents with no employment in previous year | 14 | 29 | 24 | 20 | 23 | 32 |

\* Refers to Statistics Canada's 1986 Low Income Cut-Off

Source: Prepared by the Centre for International Statistics using Survey of Consumer Finances microdata, 1992 and 1993.

## POLICY IMPLICATIONS OF THE DIVERSE ROADS TO RETIREMENT

Overall, voluntary retirement is still the dominant pathway out of the labour force taken by older workers. Nonetheless, labour force displacement by job loss and health problems affects a significant number of older workers and raises questions regarding the ability of existing programs and policies to deal adequately with the circumstances faced by these workers. A number of proposals regarding the reform of the Canada/Quebec Pension Plans and other income security programs have been advanced in recent years, several of which have particular implications for displaced workers aged fifty-five to sixty-four.

### REFORM OF THE CANADA/QUEBEC PENSION PLANS

The diverse financial profiles of older workers raise a number of implications for reform of the Canada/Quebec Pension Plans (C/QPP), soon to top the federal government's social policy review agenda. A number of proposals have been made in recent years, several concerning the age of public pension eligibility (National Council of Welfare 1990; Canadian Institute of Actuaries 1995).

Given the aging of the population and the inevitable increase in the number of people who will be receiving benefits relative to the number who will be making contributions, concerns regarding the financial viability of these programs are prevalent. To alleviate the mounting financial pressure on the programs, raising the eligibility age for benefits is one policy option that has been suggested. This could be implemented in a number of ways. The current ages for partial and full retirement benefits could be kept in place but actuarial adjustments made to impose greater penalties on people taking benefits before the "normal" age of sixty-five. Currently, partial C/QPP retirement benefits may be received as early as age sixty, but benefits are reduced by one-half of one percent for every month they are taken before the recipient's sixty-fifth birthday. Consequently, an older worker opting for benefits at age sixty has his or her total pension benefit reduced by 30 percent with this reduction remaining in effect even after the pensioner reaches age sixty-five. By increasing the penalty associated with early benefit take-up, the argument goes, early retirement would be discouraged and program expenditures decreased. Towards the same end, the age of eligibility for partial benefits could be raised from age sixty to, say, age sixty-four, and eligibility for full benefits could be raised from age sixty-five to age sixty-nine or seventy.

While these proposals could substantially reduce program expenditures, they do face a number of shortcomings. Labour markets are clearly moving in the opposite direction as older workers leave their jobs at younger ages on both a voluntary and involuntary basis. Given high rates of unemployment, age discrimination in hiring and training practices, and downsizing in both the public and private sectors, it is likely that many older workers will be unable to remain in the labour force even if they wanted to do so. Restricting access to public pensions would simply impose greater financial hardship on them without altering their labour market opportunities. In many cases, such hardships would be shouldered by the more disadvantaged workers, since it is those from lower paying and less skilled jobs who are most vulnerable to lay-off and unemployment. It should be noted that in the United States, where the public pension eligibility age is already being increased, there have been only modest changes in the retirement decisions of older workers. Studies show that "[r]aising the standard retirement age by two years leads to an estimated increase in the average retirement age by two months or less" (OECD 1988: 81). In other words, even in the face of a considerable loss of retirement benefits, people's retirement decisions change little. As the OECD points out, "the results predict that workers will not give up much leisure if the standard retirement age is increased, but they will be made poorer (OECD 1988: 81)."

Another potential shortcoming of raising the age of public pension eligibility is the added pressure that likely would be exerted on other public programs like unemployment insurance, social assistance and disability pensions. The last of these has been of particular concern given the dramatic increases in take-up rates in recent years. Between 1980 and 1993, the number of men aged fifty-five to sixty-four receiving a C/QPP disability pension more than doubled, rising from 55,000 to 115,000. The number of female beneficiaries more than tripled over this period, rising from 20,000 to 61,000 (Schellenberg 1994: 89). These increases are attributed to a number of factors including: high unemployment rates and displacement of older workers from the labour market; greater awareness and recognition of mental health disabilities; a shifting of clients from provincial programs, such as worker's compensation to the federal C/QPP disability pension; and less reassessment of the medical condition of disability pension claimants because of limited staff resources (McOuat 1995). It could well be expected that restrictions on C/QPP retirement pension benefits would place further pressure on disability pensions as well as other programs, resulting in a shifting of public expenditures rather than an actual reduction.

From quite a different perspective, arguments have been made for lowering the age of public pension eligibility. The National Council of Welfare (NCW) has argued that C/QPP retirement pensions should be made available to workers at age sixty *without penalty,* provided workers have made forty years of contributions and do not use the general drop-out provision in the calculation of their benefits (1990: 29-31). The drop-out provision allows workers to exclude certain periods of low or no earnings in the calculation of pension benefits. The NCWS argument is that C/QPP provisions are unfair to blue collar workers who enter the labour force immediately after high school and work until they are age sixty-five. These workers make contributions for forty-seven years before they are eligible for benefits without penalty at age sixty-five. In contrast, professionals who go to university and enter the labour force at age twenty-five make contributions for forty years before being eligible for such benefits. They are able to disregard the seven years of non-contribution using the drop-out provisions. By making all workers with forty years of contributions eligible for a full pension, these discrepancies would be eliminated.

This change would also make the public pension system more comparable to private sector plans. Many of the latter use the "rule of 86" or the "90 factor" in calculating benefits, with workers eligible for full pensions once their age plus years of service equal 86 or 90. The c/QPP are premised on the idea that people work from age eighteen (the age at which contributions are first deducted) to age sixty-five—a period of forty-seven years. Even taking into account the drop-out provisions allowing people to exclude up to seven years of low or no earnings in their benefit calculation, the public system assumes careers last forty years. Forty years of service plus benefits without penalty at age 65 adds up to the "rule of 105." The NCW argues that these provisions are unduly strict.

In terms of displaced workers, eligibility for full benefits at age sixty would eliminate the financial penalty incurred by many of those forced to take early c/QPP. Since many displaced workers do not have private pensions, removal of the 30 percent penalty (at age sixty) would mean a significant increase in retirement income. It should also be noted that workers who enter the labour force while in their teens are those most likely to be employed in physically demanding blue collar occupations. These are also the workers most likely to experience labour force displacement because of poor health or job loss and for whom early retirement is likely to be particularly appealing. The financial situation of these workers could be improved by this option. However, some displaced older workers still may not benefit. Those who have been on the margins of the labour force throughout their lifetimes, facing repeated bouts of unemployment or low wage work, may not have accumulated the forty years of contributions necessary for full benefits at age sixty. They would still face a penalty for taking early c/QPP, raising the question of whether the advantages of earlier eligibility would be available to those most in need.

Other shortcomings of earlier eligibility must also be recognized. Cost is an obvious consideration. Even under the current benefit rules, c/QPP contribution rates are forecast to rise from 5.4 percent in 1995 to about 10 percent in the year 2015, and to over 13 percent by the year 2030 (Chief Actuary, Office of the Superintendent of Financial Institutions, cited in Coyne 1994). Extending full benefits to eligible workers at age sixty would increase benefit expenditures and decrease contribution revenues, thereby exerting further financial pressure on the programs. This would likely be augmented by an increase in the trend toward early retirement, since earlier benefit entitlement would give older workers more financial incentive to leave the labour force.

Finally, expanding public pension eligibility to address the immediate labour market problems of older workers could also be difficult to reverse at a later period, should labour market conditions change. As the OECD notes, "[i]f such schemes are instituted in response to a short-term problem, such as a rise in unemployment, it becomes difficult to limit them to . . . one particular group of older workers" (1992: 196). In political terms, it undoubtedly would be easier to expand pension eligibility to meet current exigencies than to restrict eligibility to meet future ones.

## REFORM OF OLD AGE SECURITY, THE GUARANTEED INCOME SUPPLEMENT AND THE SPOUSE'S ALLOWANCE

In addition to the Canada/Quebec Pension Plans, a review of the other income security programs for the elderly is also on the policy agenda. These programs include Old Age Security (OAS), the Guaranteed Income Supplement (GIS), and the Spouse's Allowance (SPA). These programs are designed to ensure that all seniors have a basic level of income; eligibility is not conditional on past contributions or previous paid employment. Old Age Security is the major component of this income security system. All persons aged sixty-five and over who meet eligibility requirements receive OAS benefits, although people with higher incomes have their benefits "clawed back" through the tax system. The GIS is an income-tested supplement for people aged sixty-five and over who receive OAS but little or no other income, while the SPA is an income-tested benefit paid to low income widow(er)s aged sixty to sixty-four and to low income spouses (aged sixty to sixty-four) of OAS pensioners. Space does not permit a detailed review of these programs here, but one policy option currently being debated warrants consideration.

The Caledon Institute of Social Policy has proposed that the OAS, GIS and SPA be rolled together into a single income-tested benefit designed to assist low and moderate income Canadians aged sixty and over (Caledon 1993: 1-3). Benefits from this "super-GIS" would be available to all individuals with incomes below a set minimum and adjusted each year to reflect increases in the cost of living. Partial and diminishing benefits would be available to middle income Canadians, up to a point where benefits would be phased out altogether. The income threshold at which benefits would be reduced would be fully indexed to inflation so that the financial protection offered by the program would not be eroded over time.

A number of reasons are offered in defence of the super-GIS. First, the option of retaining the current Old Age Security program is viewed as untenable given demographic trends. In 1993, 3.3 million seniors received $14.9 billion in OAS benefits. The Caledon estimates that by the year 2036, 8.6 million seniors could be receiving OAS with total expenditures reaching as much as $38 billion (in 1993 dollars) (Caledon 1993: 2). Some of this expenditure would be recovered through taxation (OAS benefits are taxable) and through the claw back but the projected cost increase is still considerable.

The erosion of OAS benefits through the claw back is another reason for moving to the super-GIS. When first introduced in 1952, OAS was a universal program including all Canadians aged sixty-five and over who met residency requirements. In 1989 this universality was eliminated. An increasing portion of the OAS benefit is now clawed back once people's income exceeds a set amount ($53,215 in 1995), up to a point where all benefits are lost ($84,195 in 1995). While this may not sound too regressive, the insidious aspect of the claw back is that the threshold levels are only partially indexed. This means that in years when inflation is at or below 3 percent, no adjustments are made to the threshold levels, and in years when inflation is above 3 percent, these levels are increased only by the amount of inflation above the 3 percent limit. One consequence is that if inflation persists at 3 percent for the next twenty-five years, the claw back will apply to people with incomes of $25,400 (in 1995 dollars). Many middle income Canadians who are expecting OAS to comprise part of their retirement income may be surprised to find they are not eligible for benefits. By making the super-GIS more transparent, people approaching retirement would better know where they stand.

The super-GIS program would also eliminate the current limitations of the Spouse's Allowance. Benefits from this program are available to widowed and married individuals, but not to people who separated, divorced or never married. Three court challenges have been launched, alleging that the program discriminates on the basis of marital status and violates equality rights guaranteed under the Canadian Charter of Rights and Freedoms. By discontinuing the SPA and implementing the super-GIS, this uneven treatment of people would be eliminated.

Finally, from the standpoint of displaced older workers, the super-GIS would ensure an adequate level of income for those aged sixty to sixty-four. Many of these workers do not qualify for the Spouse's Allowance and are likely to be reluctant to apply for social assistance (welfare) given the stigma attached to these programs and the low benefits paid. The current Guaranteed Income Supplement is also unavailable to them since applicants must be aged sixty-five or older. The proposed super-GIS would improve the financial security of people aged sixty to sixty-four, particularly those with little income except modest C/QPP benefits resulting from low lifetime contributions and the penalty for early take-up.

Despite its advantages, it is important to recognize this option would constitute a substantial reduction in the role of government in ensuring income security for retirees. When implemented in the mid-1960s, the C/QPP was designed to replace 25 percent of the income of the average worker upon retirement. This was far below the 60 to 70 percent replacement rate deemed necessary to ensure an adequate standard of living, but the OAS was designed to contribute a further 15 percent of the average wage. Together C/QPP and OAS replace 40 percent of the average wage upon retirement, with workers expected to use private pensions, RRSPs and other sources to come up with the balance. This mix of public and private sources remained in place from the mid-1960s to 1989, when the OAS claw back was implemented. With the slow elimination of OAS through the claw back, the share of retirement income that middle class Canadians will derive from public sources will decline from 40 percent to 25 percent and they will be forced to rely more heavily on private sources of income. The situation would be the same under the super-GIS. Middle income Canadians would be ineligible for program benefits and would be forced to rely on private sources for a larger share of their retirement income. For many, this would involve a considerable change in retirement planning: in 1992, about one-half of people with incomes between $40,000 and $50,000 contributed to an RRSP—the rest did not—and less than one-half (47 percent) contributed to a registered pension plan (Revenue Canada 1994: 64-65). If the super-GIS were targetted to low income Canadians, then even people with modest incomes would have to make their own retirement preparations, despite their limited financial ability to do so. In 1992, only one-third of taxfilers with incomes between $25,000 and $30,000 contributed to an RRSP and slightly less contributed to a registered pension plan. In a context of debt, deficits and cost-cutting rhetoric, pressure to limit the super-GIS to only the poorest of Canadians could result, leaving modest and middle income earners to fend for themselves.

## Partial Retirement

Clearly, Canadians face difficult choices and as this short overview underscores, all policy options have their advantages and disadvantages. If we are to deal effectively with the aging of the population and labour market changes, it will be necessary to assess critically our traditional views of employment, retirement and "old age," and to seek creative policy options. Strategies that encourage partial or flexible retirement may be one alternative.

The retirement transition is generally viewed in terms of a clearly demarcated exit out of the labour force. However, as noted earlier, this transition is being transformed along a number of dimensions and it is necessary to rethink our traditional views. Rather than being an abrupt end to paid employment, retirement could be reshaped to allow a gradual or partial withdrawal from paid employment. This could be done by reducing the number of hours worked each week, for example by moving to part-time or flexible schedules; or by reducing the number of weeks worked in the year, for example by extending holidays and leaves of absence on a paid, unpaid or self-funded basis. Job sharing is another option. Measures encouraging partial retirement would afford older workers greater opportunity to ease out of the workforce step-by-step and provide a less costly alternative to complete withdrawal. Adequacy of income would be better ensured with earnings from employment comprising part of the retirement income package.

Partial retirement would also offer benefits to employers, allowing them to keep highly experienced workers on the job and reducing their loss of human capital investment. Employers (and employees) would also benefit from an inter-generational transfer of skills and expertise from older to younger workers that could be facilitated by partial retirement and mentoring arrangements. Broader societal benefits would include lower unemployment rates. The federal government's Advisory Group on Working Time and the Distribution of Work (Human Resources Development Canada 1994:49) reports that flexible retirement (and early retirement) has " . . . a small but significant potential for job creation or preservation, as well as for enhancing the choice and quality of life for those affected." Government balance sheets would also be improved given the increased pool of taxable income and reduced expenditures on unemployment insurance, social assistance and other programs.

The main obstacle to partial retirement is the loss of income faced by workers in the short term (as fewer hours are worked) and, more importantly, in the long term. If partial retirement reduces earnings below the maximum pensionable earnings limit under the c/QPP, then workers will receive a smaller public retirement pension than they would have if they continued working full-time. Future benefits under private plans would also be reduced. Often benefits are calculated on the basis of the worker's highest earning years with their employer. If a significant period elapses between the point at which these highest earnings are reached and the point at which benefits are calculated (a gap attributable to partial retirement and the resulting reduction in hours of work and earnings), the pension benefit would be reduced by the rate of inflation. If pension benefits are calculated on the basis of the workers last five years of employment, then the benefit reduction would be even greater. Workers who would otherwise be willing to reduce their work hours and take partial retirement, may be unwilling to do so given the longer-term financial costs. Elimination of these penalties would be an important step in encouraging a process of gradual retirement. One policy option would be to give employees the options of reducing their hours of work, while maintaining or even increasing pension premiums so that reduction in benefits over the long term would be avoided.

The implications of these findings for the SSR and the recently announced review of retirement benefits seems clear. Governments cannot consider these benefits in isolation from labour market trends. Those with uninterrupted employment and private employee-based pensions will have better access to the income resources required for retirement. Those pushed out of the labour market and retirees with a history of unemployment, underemployment and interrupted work experiences will have limited private pension investment and will need access to other sources of secure retirement income. While programs of the future may vary and take on different forms, the provision of public pensions will become more important as labour market retirement incomes diminish in value and/or become less certain.

## NOTE

1.  Some of the respondents included in Table 4 were employed for part of the previous year and consequently received a portion of their income from wages, salaries and self-employed earnings. If the analysis is limited to people who did not have any paid employment during the year, average incomes are lower, but the income difference between retirees and displaced workers remains about the same.

## REFERENCES

Akyeampong, Ernest. (1987). "Job Loss and Labour Market Adjustment." *The Labour Force*. Ottawa: Minister of Supply and Services.

Caledon Institute of Social Policy. 1993. *Thinking the Unthinkable: A Targeted, Not Universal Old Age Pension*. Ottawa: Caledon Institute of Social Policy.

Canadian Institute of Actuaries. 1995. *Troubled Tomorrows: The Report of the Canadian Institute of Actuaries' Task Force on Retirement Savings*. Ottawa: Canadian Institute of Actuaries.

Ciffin, S. and J. Martin. 1977. *Retirement in Canada, Volume 1: When and Why People Retire*. Staff Working Paper SWP-7704. Ottawa: Policy Research and Long Range Planning Branch, Department of National Health and Welfare.

Coyne, Andrew. 1994. "The Burden of our Pensions." *Globe and Mail* August 15: A8.

Guillemard, Anne-Marie. 1991. "International Perspectives on Early Withdrawal from the Labour Force." In John Myles and Jill Quadagno (eds.), *States, Labor Markets, and the Future of Old-Age Policy*. Philadelphia: University Press.

———— and Herman van Gunsteren. 1991. "Pathways and Their Prospects: A Comparative Interpretation of the Meaning of Early Retirement." In Martin Kohli et al. (eds.), *Time for Retirement: Comparative Studies of Early Exit from the Labour Force*. Cambridge: Cambridge University Press.

Health and Welfare Canada. Selected Years. *Canada Pension Plan/Old Age Security: Statistical Bulletin*. Ottawa: Health and Welfare Canada.

Human Resources Development Canada. 1994. *Report of the Advisory Group on Working Time and the Distribution of Work*. Ottawa: Minister of Supply and Services.

Kohli, Martin and Martin Rein. 1991. "The Changing Balance of Work and Retirement." In Martin Kohli et al. (eds.), *Time for Retirement: Comparative Studies of Early Exit from the Labour Force*. Cambridge: Cambridge University Press.

Laczko, Frank. 1989. "Between Work and Retirement, Becoming 'Old' in the 1980s." In Bill Bytheway et al. (eds.), *Becoming and Being Old: Sociological Approaches to Later Life*. London: Sage Publications.

McDonald, Lynn and Mervin Chen. 1993. "The Youth Freeze and the Retirement Bulge, Older Workers and the Impending Labour Shortage." *Journal of Canadian Studies* 28 (1): 75-101.

McOuat, E. Representative of the Canada Pension Plan. 1995. Presentation at the Experts Roundtable on Pension Reform, hosted by the Caledon Institute of Social Policy. June 5, Ottawa.

Myles, John. 1994. *Old Wine in New Bottles: Privatizing Old Age Pensions*. Ottawa: Caledon Institute of Social Policy.

National Council of Welfare (NCW). 1990. *Pension Reform*. Ottawa: National Council of Welfare.

Organization for Economic Co-operation and Development (OECD). 1992. "Labour Market Participation and Retirement of Older Workers." *Employment Outlook, July 1992*. Paris: OECD.

———. 1988. *Reforming Public Pensions*. Paris: OECD.

Revenue Canada. 1994. *Taxation Statistics: Analyzing the Returns of Individuals for the 1992 Taxation Year and Miscellaneous Statistics*. Cat. RV 44-1994. Ottawa: Minister of Supply and Services.

Schellenberg, Grant. 1994. *The Road to Retirement: Demographic and Economic Changes in the '90s*. Ottawa: The Canadian Council on Social Development.

Siroonian, Jason. 1993. "A Note on the Recession and Early Retirement." *Perspectives on Labour and Income* 5 (4): 9-11.

Statistics Canada. 1995. *Labour Force Annual Averages, 1989-1994*. Ottawa: Minister of Industry, Science and Technology.

———. 1991. *National Survey on Ageing and Independence*. Ottawa: Statistics Canada.

———. 1989. *Labour Force Annual Averages, 1981-1989*. Ottawa: Minister of Supply and Services.

## PART 4

# WORKFARE, TRAINING, EDUCATION AND SOCIAL SECURITY REFORM

# CHAPTER 11

# AUSTRALIAN RESPONSES TO UNEMPLOYMENT: EXPANDING THE OPTIONS FOR SOCIAL SECURITY REFORM IN CANADA?

*Graham Riches*

## INTRODUCTION

On returning to Canada from Australia in late 1994, it was still possible to believe, despite premonitions to the contrary, that progressive social policy debate and reform were on the political agenda. The Axworthy social security (HRDC 1994) reform proposals were being discussed across the country and, judging by the advice that was being presented to the Standing Committee on Human Resources Development (House of Commons 1995), it appeared that serious debate could be engaged about strengthening the Canadian social safety net. After all, the Liberal Party was again in power in Ottawa, the party which a generation earlier had presided over the development of Canada's welfare state and which, in its years in opposition between 1984 and 1993, had fought the neoconservatism of the Mulroney government. How wrong one can be!

It is now widely recognized that any hopes for progressive and comprehensive reform of Canada's social security system which might have emanated from the federal government's agenda for change as set out in the discussion papers of the fall of 1994, and the public consultations engaged by the House of Common's Standing Committee on Human Resources Development, have largely been derailed. A full employment goal, strengthened commitments to the social rights of citizenship, positive redefinitions of work and its more equitable distribution, adequate incomes and social security benefits, concern for environmental sustainability and the eradication of poverty are conspicuous by their absence in official proposals for reform.

Finance Minister Paul Martin's February 1995 deficit obsessed budget, guided by the economic policy considerations of the previous neoconservative Progressive Conservative administration and spurred on at the last moment by Moody's public warning concerning Canada's credit worthiness, is the ideological flag marker and the real blueprint for social security reform. The federal government's strengthened commitment to deficit reduction, private sector led economic growth and international competitiveness has brought continued labour market reform and deregulation; massive public sector job cuts; health, education and welfare spending cutbacks including the repeal of the Canada Assistance Plan and the further off-loading of social costs onto the provinces following the implementation of the newly proposed Canada Health and Social Transfer. In other words, while comprehensive reform may be on the agenda, progressive reform is not. The dismantling of Canada's welfare state is well under way.

More worrying perhaps is that there is no effective parliamentary opposition to the Liberal government's proposals for change, nor mouthpiece for debate and alternative reform. The Bloc Québécois is more concerned with the break-up of Canada and the Reform Party would urge even deeper restraint and more punitive welfare measures. Indeed the landslide victory (in terms of seats won) of the Progressive Conservatives in the June 1995 Ontario election on an anti-welfare and tax cutting platform with only 45 percent of the popular vote suggests that parliamentary democracy is in trouble. Even the NDP, provincially, appears swept along on the tide of conventional economic ideas and restrictive welfare policies. These are neither propitious times for social policy reform in Canada nor even for debating the issues. Democratic debate is at a premium as the non-government sector and advocacy groups wishing to promote progressive policy reform are marginalized through funding cutbacks (Delacourt 1995: D1, D5), appear not to have their views reported in the media or else have difficulty acting sufficiently in concert with others to make their voices heard.

Also missing from the current social policy debate in Canada is an analysis of how other countries are responding to the issues of high unemployment, labour market restructuring and social security reform in the context of the New World Order.[1] Canada is not the only country in the 1990s to be confronting the related issues of economic restructuring, mass unemployment, income and work polarization, inadequate education and labour market programs and a crumbling social safety net. Nor is it alone in developing an agenda for reform. In May 1994, in response to similar circumstances and prior to the Canadian government's proposals, the Australian Commonwealth (federal) government released its own White Paper, *Working Nation*, containing broad ranging reforms focusing particularly on the needs of the long-term unemployed. Whether there is still room for debate about the possibility for progressive social security reform in Canada, certainly in the lifetime of the current Parliament and in light of the "commonsense" revolution in Ontario, is an open question. Assuming the federal and provincial governments are still willing to listen, however, the opportunity to learn from overseas experience should not be lost.

This paper therefore seeks to draw lessons for the Canadian welfare reform agenda through exploring and commenting upon proposals for policy change in Australia. In adopting a comparative perspective, it examines the proposals for labour market and social security reform with particular reference to unemployment announced in the Australian government's White Paper, *Working Nation*. It compares these proposals, and the process which was engaged in their development, with those presented to the Canadian Parliament in the January 1995 Report of the Standing Committee on Human Resources' *Development Security, Opportunities and Fairness: Canadians Renewing their Social Programs*. It examines the principles which underlie the Australian reform agenda, its specific policy proposals relating to unemployment, and the politics of reform-making or ways in which the debate about unemployment and social policy has been engaged Down Under in terms of the consultation process and the role of the non-government sector. In conclusion, the paper will assess the benefits of the Australian experience to the Canadian debate about unemployment and welfare reform in terms of lessons to be disregarded and to be learned: first, by commenting on the relevance of specific policies being developed Down Under and second, by asking why, despite the many similarities between the welfare reform agendas of both countries, the possibility for progressive reform seems more likely in Australia than in the Canada of today.

## COMPARATIVE ANALYSIS AND "LESSONS FROM ABROAD"

As Jones (1985: 3) argues there are three main reasons why cross national studies are of significance in the study of social welfare:

> comparative study promotes a better understanding of the home social policy environment; it helps broaden ideas as to what may be done in response to particular issues or problems and may even suggest 'lessons from abroad'; it opens the doors to a greater breadth and variety of case material, such as may further the development of theoretical constructs about social policy formation and development to an extent that could not be possible on the basis of home country experience and material alone.

This paper concentrates its attention on learning from overseas bearing in mind that the benefits of comparison lie not only in identifying initiatives as yet untried in the home country, but also in recognizing similarly failing policies. With respect to labour market and social security reform both are on offer in Australia.

There are of course limitations to the "lessons from abroad" argument and cross national analysis. Policy proposals cannot simply be transplanted from one country, or culture, to another. As Jones (1985: 5) observes "social policies do not exist in a vacuum apart from each other and independent of the society within which and as part of which they have developed. They are not therefore available for export 'with satisfaction guaranteed'." Ginsburg (1993: 18) likewise warns that the very suggestion of 'comparative' analysis of social policy is problematic because it conjures up the hope that social scientists have developed rigorous methods and established schools of thought for comparing welfare states. Nothing could be further from the truth."

In spite of this admonition, Ginsburg (1993: 23) advances arguments for both quantitative and qualitative comparative analysis and himself adopts "a 'structured diversity' approach, which emphasizes the diversity or even the uniqueness of each welfare state in its national and historical context." In advocating this approach, he quotes Castles (1989: 12-13) who argues that the

> investigation of particular cases is not a return to the particularistic over determination of single nation histories. . . . [T]he logic of comparative explanation does not suddenly disappear when we are treating intentional, institutional and historical variables. Learning from a particular national experience will always take particular forms, but patterns of human action and purposes, especially as molded by the fact of living in societies constrained by common structural parameters, are likely to manifest intrinsic similarities as well as residual differences.

In comparing Australian and Canadian unemployment policies and welfare reform, the "common structural parameters" of which Ginsburg speaks set a context in which the policy responses can be seen to flow in the main from broadly similar institutions and principles but which also exhibit distinct features. Both countries share common histories as invader/settler societies and as former colonies of the British Crown. Though the initial reasons for invasion and settlement differed, they both subjugated indigenous peoples and are still having to come to terms with the constitutional, social and economic consequences of such acts. Aboriginal and Torres Strait Islander peoples in Australia, like First Nations peoples in Canada, have the highest rates of unemployment and suffer most from inadequate economic and social policy.

Both countries have relatively small populations (Australia—17.6 million, Canada—29 million) in large resource rich land masses, and historically have been able to trade their natural resources and agricultural products supported by protective trade and agricultural policies to sustain their high standards of living. However, times are changing and pressures for reform are keenly felt as a consequence of global economic change. The governments of Australia and Canada today share ideological preferences for free trade and international competitiveness, labour market deregulation, public sector cutbacks and the view that economic growth through a private sector led recovery is the path to future prosperity.

In terms of governance, both countries have common traditions of Westminster–style parliamentary democracy at both state/provincial and federal levels though there are some interesting differences. Each state in Australia, with the exception of Queensland, has an elected senate (proportional representation) as does the federal Parliament. Voting in Australia is compulsory and based on a preferential (House of Representatives), not first past the post, system as in Canada (McAllister et al. 1990: 56-57). Despite some pretensions in Western Australia favouring separation, there is no immediate or longer-term threat to the break-up of the Australian state as is posed by Québec in Canada. Both countries are concerned about their national identities partly as a function of post-Second World War patterns of immigration but more fundamentally as a function of their geo-political situations: Australia in terms of its proximity to Asia and the rapidly expanding economies of Southeast Asia, and Canada in terms of United States trade and cultural imperialism.

As federal states, Australia and Canada share the complexities of social policy-making and implementation in the context of divided jurisdictions. Australia historically has favoured a more selective, less universalistic approach to social security than Canada (at least until recently). The Australian government exerts its constitutional and financial powers more strongly than does Ottawa with respect to labour market policy, post-secondary education and social security. National wage arbitration and pay awards cover significant numbers of Australian workers, though the recent pursuit of economic rationalism and the development of local enterprise bargaining is threatening this centralized approach. Since the mid-1980s, the Commonwealth's Department of Employment, Education and Training has enforced a major and highly centralized reform (some would say revolution) of post-secondary education of which the latest round is the Quality Assurance Review of all universities. While Australia has no federal unemployment insurance program (in Canada a key target of Axworthy's reforms), the Department of Social Security in Canberra has federal responsibility for both unemployment benefits (recently renamed New Start and Job Search Allowances) and a full range of income- and means-tested social security benefits. Policy change might therefore be easier to introduce than in Canada where provincial powers (as in social assistance) and Québec nationalism present strong countervailing forces.

It is argued that Australia and Canada typify "liberal" as opposed to conservative or socialist regimes (Esping-Andersen 1990; Ginsburg 1993). In terms of Esping-Andersen's de-commodification index, which ranks welfare states according to the degree to which a person's right to a service or to maintain a livelihood can be achieved without reliance on the market (or as a trade-off for her or his labour power), Australia and Canada are ranked along with the United States as liberal welfare states (Esping-Andersen 1990: 21-27). In other words, people's social rights of citizenship are conditional upon their performance in and relationship to the labour market. As Ginsburg (1993) comments "liberal welfare states tend to have benefit systems in which stigmatized means-tested assistance has a central role, social insurance benefits are modest and private benefits are promoted by the state." In other words, both welfare states make it difficult for the aged, sick and unemployed workers to survive economically outside the labour market. In this context it can then be expected that welfare reform in both Australia and Canada will be informed by liberal ideology and its preference for the market economy and, following Titmuss (1974: 31), a handmaiden role for the state in relation to the social costs of change.

Lastly, in terms of "common structural parameters," there is a striking similarity in the social and economic issues confronting both Australia and Canada. In Australia, official unemployment hovers about the 10 percent mark with nearly one million people out of work. More than 350,000 Australians are classified as long-term unemployed (jobless for more than a year) and a new acronym "VLTU" (very long-term unemployed) is now applied to those out of work for more than two years. Youth joblessness, the plight of retrenched older workers, female unemployment and the significant exclusion of Aboriginal peoples from mainstream economic and social life are crucial issues. Well paid manufacturing jobs have given way, on the whole, to less well paid service sector employment, the value of real wages has been declining for fifteen years, and low paid part-time work shows the fastest growth. High rates of job creation have failed to make any significant reduction in chronic and structural unemployment. Welfare benefits are generally inadequate, emergency relief runs out and food banks in Sydney, Melbourne, Perth and Brisbane are a growing phenomenon. Pressures for labour market and social security reform are being increasingly dictated by global markets and the dictates of international competitiveness rather than by an Australian sense of a "fair go" or social justice. This is not to romanticize the Australian welfare state and its claimed egalitarian ethic, but rather to underline a decline in national sovereignty in terms of welfare policy formulation and development.

Many Canadians would have little difficulty recognizing this scenario. In the past three decades average rates of unemployment have been steadily rising and currently top 10 percent (Department of Finance 1994: 19). Long-term unemployment has likewise increased significantly. In 1993 more than 13 percent of those without jobs, or 200,000 Canadians, had been unemployed for over a year and the increase in the unemployment rate, according to the Minister of Finance (Department of Finance 1994: 22) is completely accounted for by a rising trend in the average length of jobless spells. The phenomenon of the rise of the one third/two thirds society is well documented in Canada (Ternowetsky and Riches 1993: 1-28) as is the growing plight of other marginalized groups. Poverty continues to increase. In 1993 nearly one in seven families and one in five children lived below the poverty line (Nation Council of Welfare (NCW), 1995: 8, 12). As in Australia such changes have occurred despite the fact that during the 1980s jobs were being created at very fast rates. The demise of Canada's social safety net during this time is also well documented (Riches 1986; NCW 1987). As in Australia, labour market restructuring and social security reform are being pursued as a necessary complement to deficit reduction, economic growth and job creation as the best guarantors of future well-being. Not unsurprisingly, the "structural adjustment" policies of the free trade agenda are determining social policy and, in the process, undermining national sovereignty.

## CANADIAN WELFARE REFORM: IMPROVING SOCIAL SECURITY IN CANADA AND SECURITY, OPPORTUNITIES AND FAIRNESS

### *POLICY-MAKING AND THE CONSULTATION PROCESS*

In Canada the federal government's response to these issues has been the release of a series of discussion papers on economic and social policy released in October 1994 under the rubric of an *Agenda for Jobs and Growth* followed by the federal budget in February 1995. One of the Minister of Finance's papers, *A New Framework for Economic Policy* (Department of Finance 1994), prepared the groundwork for the budget. Meanwhile, the Minister of Human Resources Development's discussion paper, *Agenda: Jobs and Growth. Improving Social Security in Canada* (commonly referred to as the Axworthy proposals) (HRDC 1994), was the basis of extensive consultation across the country. This resulted, just prior to the February 1995 budget, in the report of the House of Commons Standing Committee on Human Resource Development, *Security, Opportunities and Fairness: Canadians Renewing their Social Programs* (House of Commons 1995). The committee's inquiry was conducted in two phases. Phase one involved extensive public hearings in early 1994 and produced a discussion paper or Green Book. Later that year the committee travelled across Canada and held public hearings in twenty communities. It received over 1200 submissions from individuals and groups and heard 637 witnesses. It also sought the responses of Canadians through a workbook entitled *Have Your Say* which invited respondents to submit their preferences for reform. Over 25,000 responses were received. Consultations were certainly held but the degree to which they were taken into account by the Standing Committee's report and the federal budget is open to question. For example, Canada has now repealed the Canada Assistance Plan (Bill C-76) and will introduce block funding for welfare transfer payments in opposition to the stated preferences of a significant majority of community and welfare interest groups who appeared at the hearings.

### *POLICY PROPOSALS*

At the time of writing, the precise status of the recommendations of this report are unknown. What is clear is that the parameters for social security reform in Canada have been established by the government's economic reform agenda. The Minister of Finance's (Department of Finance 1994: 35-38) stated economic strategy

> is to foster the creation of more and better jobs for Canadians. This goal can only be achieved through sustained economic growth flowing from increased productivity and complemented by measures to reverse the decades-long rise in Canada's core unemployment rate. The economic growth and job creation strategy is based on five broad themes:
> * helping Canadians acquire skills (e.g., better basic education, improving school to work transition, culture of lifelong learning);
> * encouraging Canadians to adapt to new opportunities (e.g., flexible job markets, active social security systems promoting training and work incentives);
> * getting government right (e.g., governance, labour market deregulation, social security reform);
> * providing leadership in the economy (e.g., strengthening the private sector,

building public infrastructure, promotion of new technology and foreign trade);
- creating a healthy fiscal and monetary climate (e.g., debt and deficit reduction).

They are, as the minister himself points out, entirely consistent with the recommendations of international bodies of the jobs conference in Detroit in 1994 and the Naples G-7 Summit meeting.

The welfare reform policy recommendations of the Standing Committee on Human Resources Development need to be understood within this framework and in the context of the 1995 federal budget (Department of Finance 1995). This established deficit reduction as the prime national goal and included the laying off of 45,000 federal civil servants, the repeal of the Canada Assistance Plan and the elimination of cost shared funding, and further cuts of $7 billion (in addition to the $5 billion imposed in the 1994 budget) in health, post-secondary education and welfare spending. These changes represent the retreat of the federal government from its long established policy of using its spending power to promote national standards in welfare policy in favour of increased provincial jurisdiction (pace Québec). While the committee's (House of Commons 1995: 19) view remains that the best social policy is a job and the best strategy is economic growth, its stated welfare reform agenda comprises three key themes: caring for Canada's children; investing in people; and enhancing security and fairness. These translate into a number of specific recommendations:

## CARING FOR CHILDREN
- a working income supplement for parents in low wage jobs which would increase the attractiveness of work to those receiving unemployment insurance or social assistance;
- more effectively targeted child tax benefits;
- increased child care funding (since ruled out by the February budget);
- tightening the regulations regarding child support payments.

## INVESTING IN PEOPLE
- more effective training and the elimination of federal/provincial duplication with more effective partnership with community stakeholders and the private sector;
- more effective employment development services with more individualized attention, community involvement and attention to the needs of those with disabilities (including Independent Living) and First Nations peoples; and the development of nationally recognized standards;
- active labour market policies: voluntary schemes rather than the coercive measures of workfare program (though of course the scrapping of CAP will enable the provinces to introduce workfare);
- the introduction of universal income contingent loans for post-secondary education (along the lines of the Australian Higher Education Contribution Scheme) and other learning opportunities.

## ENSURING GREATER SECURITY AND EQUITY
- a reduction of unemployment insurance benefits and/or an increase in eligibility requirements and inclusion of part-time and contract workers;
- tax expenditures;

- more flexible work arrangements for those in the federal civil service (for those who are left) and initiatives to measure unwaged work and estimate its economic value;
- reform of the Canada Assistance Plan from a cost shared to a block funding transfer;
- that further study be given to the question of tax expenditures;
- that the social security reform program should be subjected to gender analysis;
- that the workforce reflect the diversity of Canada's population;
- and that the Aboriginal Strategic Initiatives Program be continued.

While the Canadian social security reform agenda remains subject to continued federal-provincial discussions and the immediacy of Québec referendum politics, it is clear they are guided by the global parameters of structural adjustment and the promotion of active, as opposed to passive, welfare systems. Deficit reduction, economic growth, international competitiveness and private sector job creation are the backdrop against which the carrot and stick approach of work incentives and workfare are being re-introduced and reinforced. In light of federal social spending cutbacks and the absence of any mention of the idea of full employment, it is difficult not to conclude that Canada's social security reforms are fundamentally designed to promote and discipline a low wage economy with diminished rights to social security and to oversee the more efficient management of long-term structural unemployment.

## Australian Welfare Reform:
### Restoring Full Employment and Working Nation

As Canadians debate their government's proposed social security reforms, we might want to ask whether there is anything to be learned from the Australian welfare reform proposals, particularly in light of Wiseman's comment that the Canadian "income security policy discussion paper bears a number of startling resemblances to the recent Australian White Paper (*Working Nation*)" (Wiseman 1995: 2). While this is correct, it is also of interest that welfare reform Down Under has been introduced by an avowedly Labour government.

First, in terms of the Australian policy environment of 1993-94, it is important to recognize that welfare reform is a key element of the Commonwealth government's strategy of economic reform, social justice and political rejuvenation (referred to as the One Nation Policy). This represents the ideas and commitments of a federal Labour government seeking to revitalize itself after ten years in office during which it actively pursued the New World Order agenda of structural adjustment: deregulation, privatization and public spending restraint known in Australia as "economic rationalism." Prior to the 1993 federal election Paul Keating, the current Prime Minister and erstwhile treasurer (Finance Minister), was held most responsible for Australia's 10 percent unemployment and increasing inequality. He came within a whisker of losing power to the National Liberal Party in 1993 and was only saved by the opposition campaigning to introduce a Goods and Services Tax, a policy which ironically, Keating, as treasurer, had once endorsed.

In light of Canada's ongoing constitutional debates about national sovereignty with Québec, the Western provinces and the First Nations, it is important to note that One Nation is also about recasting Australia's sense of national identity. Its commitment is to the establishment of a republic preferably by the year 2001 which will mark the centenary of Australian federation; to advance national reconciliation with Aboriginal peoples through constitutional recognition of Native land title; and to promote economic renewal through free trade and increased international competitiveness in the Asia-Pacific region. Combating unemployment and forging a new social contract are seen to be essential to these efforts. The Keating government's labour market and social security reform policies are one attempt to distance Labour from its past and to prevent the further slide into an increasingly divided society.

## POLICY-MAKING AND THE CONSULTATION PROCESS

Following the re-election to federal government of the Australian Labour Party in 1993, Prime Minister Keating appointed a high powered Committee on Employment Opportunities to "begin fashioning an effective response to the problem of unemployment" in the form of a Green Paper. Keating (Commonwealth of Australia 1993: xiii) himself posed the question: "If unemployment is a national responsibility, how best do we all share in solving it?" There was strong central direction both in terms of the consultation and the policies which ensued.

The committee was chaired by the secretary to the Cabinet and comprised four senior bureaucrats and three academics (two economists and a social worker). Its brief was to review Australia's economic outlook and the implications for the labour market, including a review of developments since the 1960s, and to bring forward a range of policy options with regard to labour market and social security reform. Of immediate concern were the needs and prospects of the unemployed and particularly the long-term unemployed. Deficit reduction by 1996-97 was identified by the government as a key referent for the commissioners. Public input was invited and in December 1993 the committee published its Green Paper provocatively entitled *Restoring Full Employment*. Further public consultations were held and in May 1994 the government released its White Paper entitled *Working Nation*, setting out its economic and welfare reform agenda.

The processes of policy consultation in Australia and Canada were very similar, including skepticism about their openness. As Stilwell (1994: 122) observes regarding the Australian experience, despite the fact that more than 2200 responses were received to the Green Paper, including 430 meetings with a range of interest groups, the Green Paper itself did not present options for discussion and the process engaged was "more like a public testing of the water." He also points to the lack of an environmental critique of economic growth despite the fact that "submissions arguing this point were put to the government by the Democrats, Green and various environmental groups" (Stilwell 1994: 115). Of course, without a detailed analysis of all the briefs submitted, it is difficult to claim that the government paid little or no attention to the advice it received, particularly when the White Paper itself, like its Canadian counterpart to follow, claims to present the views of what the commissioners heard from the public. In terms of the Canadian Report of the Standing Committee on Human Resources Development (House of Commons 1995), the jury must also remain out as to whether policies which it puts forward fully represent the advice contained in the briefs and the public consultations.

## POLICY PROPOSALS

The key elements of the policies set out in the White Paper, now being implemented by the Commonwealth government, have been noted by Stilwell (1994: 111-12). They comprise:

- a target unemployment rate of around 5 percent by the year 2000;
- a reliance on economic growth in the private sector to generate most of the approximately two million jobs needed to hit the target;
- a reassertion that current policy settings and the micro-economic reforms already in place provide the basis to generate that growth;
- special policies to create job opportunities for the long-term unemployed (the "jobs compact"), and restructured and partly privatized employment services;
- reform of other aspects of labour market assistance and training, including more funding for entry level training (including a Youth Training Allowance) and some specific measures targeted at Aboriginal and Torres Strait Islanders, people from non-English speaking backgrounds, women and people with a disability;
- changes to social security arrangements to eliminate disincentives for unemployed people, particularly unemployed couples, to take on part-time employment, including a new Parenting Allowance available to the spouses of unemployed and low income people who are caring for children, and a reduction in the allowance income test for those on welfare who are working (from a 100 percent to a 70 percent withdrawal rate);
- some modest initiatives in regard to industry policy and regional policy; and an expenditure commitment totaling $6.5 billion over three years to cover these policies; but coupled with a commitment to reduce the budgetary deficit to around 1 percent of GDP by 1996-97.

In considering these proposals it is first important to recognize that, despite Keating's concern not to leave the jobless behind, the White Paper, like its Canadian counterpart, contains no specific commitment to full employment. The Australian Green Paper had held out the prospect of restoring full employment (at least in its title), but the White Paper's most optimistic scenario is a 5 percent unemployment rate by the year 2000. While this might seem an impressive commitment, it could only be achieved if part-time jobs and low paid full-time employment are endorsed as the way of the future. This is a path which the Australian government proposes to follow but which is judged, by informed commentators, to be unattainable.

Second, the White Paper's key principle is its explicit commitment to private sector led economic growth and international competitiveness. As Stilwell (1994: 114) notes, Australia views economic growth as its panacea. Australia's Labour government continues to look to the private sector to generate the necessary jobs and training. Public sector employment is disregarded. This familiar recipe is well known in Canada. In Australia, government remains committed to economic rationalism. One problem of course, as in Canada, is that growth rates will not be high enough to generate the necessary numbers of jobs (and adequate incomes). Moreover, there is little evidence that strong growth is a necessary guarantor of low joblessness. Between 1974-1992 Australia and Canada were high growth Organization for Economic Cooperation and Development (OECD) countries but they also had some of the highest unemployment rates (Dow 1993: 44). As Stilwell (1994: 114-15) suggests, there are other problems associated with the growth scenario: no substantial new policies are proposed to generate the faster economic growth; it assumes freedom from the constraints which have operated in the past; the strategy further locks the nation into the international capitalist economy and thereby increases its vulnerability to internationally induced economic cycles;

it fails to recognize that unemployment is now a long-run structural phenomenon, not merely a feature of economic recession, and there is little consideration of the environmental critique of economic growth.

Yet the White Paper reforms and the 1994 budget received general public approval (Stilwell 1994: 112). There was a sense from labour, business and welfare groups that the government was taking some steps to deal with the problem of long-term unemployment. Indeed specific aspects of the Jobs Compact for the long-term unemployed (e.g., the guarantee of a job for six to twelve months), the proposals supporting married women in their search for paid employment, the introduction of the Parenting Allowance enabling them or their spouses to be home caring for their children as well as the reforms to the Commonwealth Employment Service, might well be commended, despite reservations, to Canadian policy-makers.

The Job Compact for the long-term unemployed as the centerpiece of the White Paper reforms provides evidence of this. Indeed, given the Axworthy proposals for a two-tiered unemployment insurance program in Canada, distinguishing between the needs of occasional and more frequent users of the program (now set aside in favour of reduced benefits and tighter eligibility criteria), this Australian initiative is worth considering both for its commitment to the chronically jobless as well as the policy dilemmas it raises.

The Job Compact is designed to move those out of work for more than eighteen months back into the work force as quickly as possible in order to prevent the development of a permanent "underclass" of unemployable people. The program comprises:

- individual and more intensive case management;
- training and support to ensure job readiness;
- a job for six to twelve months (primarily in the private sector);
- a training wage which combines employment with training leading to recognized and transferable skills;
- additional funding to support job development in areas of high unemployment;
- intensive job search assistance and referral to suitable vacancies at the end of the Job Compact placement to maximize the employment outcomes for those assisted;
- stronger penalties for job seekers who do not meet their obligations under the Job Compact.

The training and employment guarantees of this policy are attractive and represent a real commitment to the long-term unemployed and the recognition that "economic growth will not quickly help the people who are long term unemployed" (Commonwealth of Australia 1994). Yet informing this initiative is the "active society" principle of reciprocal obligations which means that, if you do not accept training or a reasonable job offer, penalties will be imposed and benefits will be denied for specific periods. *Working Nation* does not introduce workfare into Australian social security (such requirements already exist) but does demand stronger penalties for non-compliance or breaches. Arguments favouring workfare, whether advanced in Australia or North America, hold little attraction despite the triumph of the "commonsense" revolution in the June 1995 Ontario election. As Lightman (1995: 180-81) persuasively argues, workfare is punitive and contradicts an established Canadian norm that people are entitled to a minimum level of income: "that as long as unemployment remains at double digit levels, no incentives of any sort are likely to lead to substantial overall employment gains."

Guaranteed employment for the chronically jobless is certainly to be welcomed, especially if it is freely chosen work but, if they are to become the new deserving poor, what will be the consequences for those only recently out of work who will be subjected to lengthier waiting periods? They will become the new class of undeserving unemployed. While some will undoubtedly benefit, the failure of government to create the necessary jobs means many more will simply be reshuffled and remain in the dole queues as a reminder to part-time workers and the low paid not to press their luck too far. The burden of unemployment will continue to rest with the individual.

The Australian White Paper also revisits the principle of less eligibility to inform its social security reforms. It explicitly argues that the gap between welfare benefits and low wages in Australia should be widened to encourage (require) people to accept "reasonable job offers" and that by reducing work disincentives for those on unemployment benefits they will be better off in part-time work or in low paid full-time employment (Commonwealth of Australia 1994: 146, 158). In one sense the intent appears admirable in that it stresses the importance of people finding and maintaining work experience. Yet the principle which is being endorsed is that of the 1834 English Poor Law doctrine of less eligibility which demands that no one on welfare should receive more than the lowest paid wage earner. Its purpose in the administration of public relief is to regulate labour and maintain the work ethic by using the spur of poverty to ensure people accept low paid employment. Similar proposals are being advanced in Canada in terms of the Working Income Supplement which is designed to make low wage work more attractive than welfare and to provide wage subsidies to business.

The Australian proposals supporting married women in their search for paid employment and the introduction of the proposed Parenting Allowance enabling them or their spouses to be at home caring for their children are worth considering. So too are the new policies to allow those on welfare who are working to retain a higher proportion of their earnings. Yet one might ask what will be the consequences of increasing the attractiveness of low paid and part-time work unless large numbers of well paying jobs come on line. It remains likely that women and minority groups will continue to be frustrated as they seek well paid and secure employment. What is the policy logic of encouraging people back into the labour force during a period of mass unemployment if government cannot guarantee jobs?

## THE LESSONS TO BE LEARNED

The Australian government's proposals for labour market and social security reform and the country's debate about unemployment and welfare reform suggest a number of lessons for Canada; some should be disregarded and others given thoughtful consideration.

Canada should not be repeating the mistakes which Australia's Labour government is making: its over reliance on the market and placing private sector led economic growth before a commitment to full employment and significant public sector job creation; its support of the active society principle of reciprocal obligations in a situation of high unemployment; and its advancement of less eligibility through work incentive policies which widen the low income/benefit gap, promote low wage work, and reinforce distinctions between the deserving and undeserving unemployed. Even leaving aside the moral arguments against enforced work, there is little evidence that economic growth will provide sufficient jobs to employ those engaged in mandatory work and training schemes. Such structural adjustment policies are not designed to create a full employment society but rather to manage more efficiently continuing high levels of unemployment, underemployment and an increasingly divided society in the interests of capital not people. In this sense Canada has nothing to learn from Australia, given that its own labour market and social security reforms are already pursuing such policies. Indeed the similarity of their welfare reform strategies confirm their status as liberal welfare state regimes.

In light of such conclusions, is it reasonable to argue that the possibility for progressive welfare reform somehow seems more likely in Australia than in Canada? Are there any lessons which Canadians should be learning? The answer is a qualified yes. First there are a number of commitments and policy proposals which, with qualification, merit consideration. Second there is a debate underway in Australia about citizenship, full employment and an alternative economic agenda which appears to have greater public legitimacy than similar discussions in Canada.

The key elements of the Australian reform package which merit further debate are the focus on chronic and structural unemployment and the idea of guaranteed work and training through the Job Compact. Setting aside the workfare principle which informs it, given that it is just as likely to succeed as a voluntary undertaking by jobless people, the commitment to a real job for up to twelve months is a significant opportunity for those out of work. It suggests that the Commonwealth government is willing to invest the necessary public funds to create jobs either directly or through the private sector. This goes to the heart of the matter and answers the criticisms of those who rightly say that no amount of workfare and work incentives will succeed unless there is significant public sector job creation. Whether this is the intention of the Commonwealth government is another matter but at least in Australia there is an intellectual, human and political grasp of the real nature of the problem. Indeed the guarantee of socially useful employment (including the raising of children and the care of the elderly and those with disabilities) could pick up on the ideas of those such as Daly and Cobb (1990: 313) and Lipietz (1992: 99-106) who argue for minimum wage community employment underwritten by a universal basic allowance or guaranteed annual income.

There is also in Australia, or at least there was in the period following the election of the Keating government, a sense that the country is going somewhere. Not only will it be at the centre of world attention in the year 2000 when it hosts the Olympic Games but, more significantly, it is currently engaged in a debate about affirming national identity by shaking off its constitutional ties to the United Kingdom and becoming a republic. This is perhaps only germane to the debate about welfare reform in that the idea of One Nation had to meet the criticisms of the constitutional monarchists by laying out an inclusive vision for all Australians, including the unemployed and other marginalized groups. While *Working Nation*, informed as it is by market principles, falls far short of being an economic and social charter, at least the debate about unemployment is set within a forward looking context. In Canada it is a defensive debate with Ottawa being seduced by neoconservatism and seeking to placate not only Québec, but the western led Reform movement and resurgent forces of the Progressive Conservatives in Ontario as well. Moreover, Ottawa is engaged in divesting itself of powers which guarantee for those most vulnerable the social rights of Canadian citizenship. The dismantling of Canada's welfare state, first by stealth under the Mulroney regime and now more blatantly by the Chrétien government, can only lead to deeper divisions and increasing inequality.

In Australia there is a more assertive federal government than in Canada. In terms of governance it is taking a more directive role in relation to labour market and social security reform. While the economic and social rights of citizenship may not be adequately addressed, at least the prospect is better than in Canada where the commitments of territorial justice are giving way to provincial rights and local autonomy. *Working Nation* appears not to be a device for off-loading Commonwealth government responsibilities onto the states. It seems more likely that, in the context of One Nation, national standards in social security have a greater prospect of being safeguarded than by the block funding proposals being implemented in Canada. This is not to argue that provincial autonomy or state rights should not be defended. With respect to personal social services, perhaps they are to be preferred. However, in terms of income security and labour market programs, given their central place in meeting basic needs in a wage economy where the levers of monetary and fiscal power are centrally controlled, it is essential that comprehensive policies are developed which guarantee the rights of all Canadians, wherever they may live, to paid employment, adequate incomes and social security benefits. This, of course, is a key feature of Australia's central wage bargaining and arbitration system which unfortunately the current Commonwealth government is attempting to unravel. What is required in Canada is a federal system of income security in which national standards, supported by the revenue generating power of the federal government and the social justice arguments of One Nation, could prevail. Perhaps this is a lesson which Australia might teach. It clearly was the lesson of the Great Depression of the 1930s, and of the Canada Assistance Plan in 1966, but one which Canadians have now chosen to forget.

What is required is a national agenda of full employment. This agenda should redefine work, its remuneration and distribution (and the reduction of working time), explicitly commit itself to progressive tax reform, engage the question of adequate incomes and benefits, and call for a strong role for the public sector. What the Australian White Paper makes clear is that no amount of labour market and social security reform will work if jobs are not created. The same lesson is true for Canada. Canada's safety net collapsed in the 1980s. It will not be successfully rebuilt unless or until the federal and provincial governments set about the task of creating a full employment society and sustainable economic welfare.

It is true that neither country is seriously considering such an alternative economic agenda. Stilwell (1994: 115) makes the point that, despite briefs submitted to the Committee on Employment Opportunities in Australia, ecologically sustainable welfare is not discussed in the Green or White Papers. As in Canada, welfare reform is driven by deficit reduction, productivity and economic growth. Economics for community or "sustainable economic welfare," to use Daly and Cobb's term (1990: 443), is not a part of official discussion. Yet in both countries these debates are being increasingly engaged by progressive analysts, non-government organizations and popular movements.

In Australia groups such as the Australian Council of Social Service (ACOSS) and their state counterparts, the Other Economic Summit, Reworking Australia, the Whitlam Institute for Social and Economic Research and Uniya (a Christian Centre for Social Research and Action sponsored by the Jesuits) have been contributing to a lively debate about an alternative economic agenda. This is not to suggest that a similar debate is not occurring in Canada but it seems to have greater difficulty in engaging mainstream public debate. In Australia, however, this is more possible given the fact that the left faction of the Australian Labour Party is represented in Parliament and the Democrats and the Greens have elected representatives in the Senate where they hold the balance of power.

Finally it should be noted that ACOSS (1995: 11) has recently established a Future of Work Commission charged with

> examining pathways and barriers to moving into and out of paid work throughout the life cycle; the implications of changing patterns of participation in paid work; access to income within and outside paid work; and, the public policy changes needed to establish a full employment objective relevant to emerging social and economic conditions, and to achieve that objective.

The importance of such a commission, whose membership is broadly representative, lies in the fact that ACOSS is the peak social welfare organization in Australia; it has strong ties to the community and can bring influence to bear on government. It is highly significant that full employment remains on the public agenda in Australia.

In terms of the remaking of Canadian social policy, the establishment of such a commission should recommend itself to the Canadian welfare community. It would present an opportunity for an alternative social and economic agenda to be developed, particularly one which engaged the environmental critique. It would allow for full discussion of the many briefs that were presented to the Standing Committee on Human Resources Development and whose conclusions seem in the main not to have been accepted. Further, it would define an alternative agenda which could inform political debate. It would allow a range of advocacy groups to work together to develop a strong alternative voice and to translate their message into public action. At the very least there needs to be an antidote to the conventional economic wisdom which is adhered to by all political parties in Canada today. This is not to say that either Australia or Canada will easily move beyond the liberal ideas which consistently have informed their economic and social welfare policy, but it would be a much needed contribution to the debate.

## NOTE

1.   The exceptions are the constant media references to the Contract with America and the dismantling of federal welfare programs in the United States and the occasional reference to New Zealand (which is held up as a model to be emulated).

## REFERENCES

ACOSS. 1995. "Future of Work Commission Successfully Launched." *Impact.* News monthly of the Australian Council of Social Service. March.

Canberra: Australian Government Publication Service.

Castles, F. (ed.). 1989. *Comparative History of Public Policies.* Cambridge: Polity Press.

Commonwealth of Australia. 1994. *Working Nation: Policies and Programs.*

———. 1993. *Restoring Full Employment: A Discussion Paper.* Committee on Employment Opportunities. Canberra: Australian Government Publication Service.

Coombs, H.C. 1994. *From Curtin to Keating: The 1945 and 1994 White Papers on Employment. A Better Environment for Human and Economic Diversity?* Darwin: North Australia Research Unit, Australian National Research University.

Daly, H.E. and J.B. Cobb Jnr. 1990. *For the Common Good.* Boston: Beacon Press.

Delacourt, S. 1995. "Losing Interest." *Globe and Mail* April 1: D1, D5.

Department of Finance. 1995. *Budget Speech*. Ottawa: Department of Finance.

———. 1994. *A New Framework for Economic Policy*. Ottawa: Department of Finance.

Dow, G. 1993. "What Do We Know about Unemployment, Full Employment and the Role of Politics?" In P. Smyth (ed.), *The Employment White Paper: A New Social Charter*. Canberra: Uniya.

Esping-Andersen, G. 1990. *The Three Worlds of Welfare Capitalism*. Cambridge: Polity Press.

Ginsburg, N. 1993. *Divisions of Welfare*. London: Sage Publications.

House of Commons. 1995. *Security, Opportunities and Fairness: Canadians Renewing Their Social Programs*. Ottawa: Queen's Printer.

Human Resources Development Canada (HRDC). 1994. *Improving Social Security in Canada: A Discussion Paper*. Ottawa: Minister of Supply and Services.

Jones, C. 1985. *Patterns of Social Policy*. London: Tavistock.

Lightman, E.S. 1995. "You Can Lead a Horse to Water, but...: The Case Against Workfare in Canada." In J. Richards et al. (eds.), *Helping the Poor. A Qualified Case for "Workfare."* The Social Policy Challenge Series. Toronto: C.D. Howe Institute.

Lipietz, A. 1992. *Towards a New Economic Order*. Cambridge: Polity Press.

McAllister, I., M. Mackerras, A. Ascui and S. Moss. 1990. *Australian Political Facts*. Melbourne: Longman Cheshire.

National Council of Welfare (NCW). 1995. *Poverty Profile 1993*. Ottawa: Minister of Supply and Services.

———. 1987. *Welfare in Canada: The Tangled Safety Net*. Report of the National Council of Welfare. Ottawa: Minister of Supply and Services.

Riches, G. 1995. "Lessons from Down Under." In Caledon Institute of Social Policy, *Critical Commentaries of the Social Security Review*. Ottawa: Renouf.

———. 1986. *Food Banks and the Welfare Crisis*. Ottawa: Canadian Council on Social Development.

Stilwell, F. 1994. "Working Nation: From Green to White Paper." *Journal of Australian Political Economy* 33 (June): 110-23.

Ternowetsky, G. and G. Riches. 1993. *Labour Market Restructuring and the Public Safety Net: Current Trends in the Australian and Canadian Welfare States*. SARU Working Paper Series (9): 1-28. University of Regina: Faculty of Social Work.

Titmuss, R. 1974. *Social Policy: An Introduction*. London: Allen and Unwin.

Wiseman, J. 1995. "The Price of Competition? Lessons for Australia in the Dismantling of Canada's Welfare State." *Just Policy* (March): 54-56.

# CHAPTER 12

# WIDE OF THE MARK:
# USING "TARGETING" AND WORK INCENTIVES TO
# DIRECT SOCIAL ASSISTANCE TO SINGLE PARENTS

*William Low*

## INTRODUCTION

Over the last two decades, single parents increasingly have been the target of special incentives to move them off social assistance and into full-time work.

> Since the mid-seventies, the majority of provinces have redefined the expectation of work for single mothers on income maintenance programs. . . . The emergence of the work incentive for this group, and their redefinition as employable, is one of the most significant developments to take place in social assistance policies in recent years. (Evans 1988: 126)

Rein (1973) outlines three forms of work incentives which use the carrot and stick to varying degrees:

1) a *financial* strategy which increases the monetary rewards from low paid work;
2) a *service* strategy which provides support to reduce obstacles to employment; and
3) a *restrictive* strategy which forces employment by imposing work requirements and/or implicit measures such as eroding the value of benefits.

This paper will focus on the financial and restrictive strategies, illustrating the weakness of both voluntary financial incentives and restrictive mandatory work-for-welfare rules.[1]

While the aftermath of the 1995 federal budget signaled that Axworthy's social security reform would take a backseat to tackling the country's fiscal problems, some of his provincial counterparts are heading a drive for social welfare reform tied to fiscal restraint.[2] Workfare programs have been rejected in the past by Manitoba and Alberta (Lightman 1991) but Ontario, with the election of Mike Harris, is now poised to bring in work-for-welfare policies in order to reduce welfare rolls and the public bill for social assistance.

Evans (1988) illustrates how converging factors led to the emergence of work incentives targeted at single parents. Section 2, (A Woman's Work is Never Done) of this paper expands this to examine the rationale behind the shift to the restrictive strategy being observed today in Canada. The need for compulsion is criticized on three grounds:

The author wishes to thank the B.C. Ministry of Social Services and the Social Demonstration and Research Corporation for access to information about their programs. Thanks also to participants at the conference and the editors of this volume for valuable comments.

1) there is limited empirical evidence that single parents prefer not to work[3];
2) jobs in an increasingly segmented labour market will not themselves foster independence from social assistance; and
3) the direct welfare of the children in single-parent families is effectively ignored in market-oriented policies.

Section 3 (Financial Incentive Programs) uses two voluntary programs in B.C. to illustrate the first point above. Evidence from both programs indicates that single parents respond to financial incentives and take on work if it pays. Given this pervasive willingness to work, the paper argues in Section 4 (The Job Market: Snakes and Ladders) that both financial and restrictive strategies are inadequate methods for addressing broader issues of welfare since they rely on a narrow market-oriented economic perspective. Both approaches are likely to fall far short of the ultimate goal of independence from welfare because they ignore elements of the transition from welfare to work which go beyond individual choice. These are the nature of the job market and the "social infrastructure" needed to support families.

Finally, this paper addresses the concern over child poverty that has contributed to the trend in work incentive programs targeted at single mothers. Along with greater access to "social goods," it is argued that policy reforms should provide "in-kind" benefits targeted directly at children. A more direct approach to improve the children's lives must complement welfare-to-work programs targeted at their parent.

## A Woman's Work is Never Done

Social security programs were conceived as adjuncts to economic policies which stressed full employment. As Glennerster (1990: 12) puts it:

> Probably the most important social policy of the post-war period was never formulated as legislation . . . the [British] welfare state of the 1940s had twin pillars—a commitment to full employment *and* the range of social legislation that came immediately afterwards. (original emphasis)

Underpinned by a commitment to high and stable levels of employment, social security programs were envisaged as providing short-term support to a relatively small portion of the population.

However, the availability of work also meant an expectation that recipients seek and take work; principles of the old "Poor Laws" prevailed. Single mothers were one of the few groups which did not face a stringent work expectation. Commenting on Canada, Evans and McIntyre (1987: 103) note that provincial legislation after 1945 even discouraged part-time work outside the home. The 1970s saw this principle eroded so that there is now an expectation of paid work, in addition to the work of caring for children. As one single mother in Ontario commented regarding the pending welfare changes: "I don't think anyone can say that I'm not working when I'm raising four children" (Gallagher 1995: A9).

The days of full employment as the basis of social policy have also faded. As the Axworthy report (Human Resources Development Canada 1994: 16) states:

> . . . work is becoming less permanent, providing less security. Indeed much of the

job creation over the past fifteen years has been part-time. Today, about four in every ten jobs in Canada fall outside the traditional, 40 hours a week mold. This contrasts with the situation as recently as 1976 when over 70 per cent of jobs offered standard work hours.

These changes are not natural or inevitable results of market forces in the economy. Public policy has actively undercut the commitment to full employment from two sides: by concentrating on reducing government spending and public debt; and by attempting to restructure the economy, especially through "flexible" labour markets, to improve international competitiveness. This new wind blowing through economic policy circles signals a colder climate for social welfare policy.

This is illustrated by Evans (1988: 128) who cites three convergent and interrelated trends leading to work incentive programs for single mothers during the 1970s: financial restraint felt by governments; a shift in political attention away from the working poor and towards those on social assistance; and the growth in the numbers of single parents in society more generally and on assistance in particular.

The crucial catalyst translating these trends into social welfare policy has been the emergence of economic thinking as a dominant force in public policy formation. The "economist's" view of work incentives and single parents is neatly summed up by Allen (1993: S201): "It is probably fair to say that most economists agree that needs-tested aid to able-bodied individuals discourages work and encourages marital breakdown." The principle of a cold calculus of individual self-interest and a belief in market forces underpins the economic approach not only to matters of finance, savings, work and leisure but have also been extended to marriage, divorce and child bearing (see Becker 1981). American social policy writers such as Charles Murray (1984) have been prominent in synthesizing these beliefs to argue that lower work incentives resulting from social assistance benefits lead to a cycle of "welfare dependence" with consequent lower productivity and economic growth.

Canada is often criticized for becoming increasingly American and this trend has been evident in many social welfare policy circles. The strong views on work incentives and self-reliance, cornerstones of American social welfare policy so fashionable today, have their antecedents in the debate over reforming the Poor Law in 1830s Britain: low benefit levels *and* the system of administration ensured that recipients were worse off than the employed (the principle of "less eligibility"; see Lightman 1991).

One manifestation of this is workfare. This entails compulsory rules regarding work in exchange for benefits, though training and unpaid work experience or community service programs are substituted. In a review of U.S. welfare-to-work programs, Gueron and Pauly (1991: 5) write:

> . . . one major element of all recent proposals to redesign welfare [is] the goal of encouraging self-support and reducing long-term welfare receipt: requiring people on welfare to participate in employment-directed services. Programs and proposals have varied in their emphasis on carrots and sticks, but the basic vision of recent reforms is to change AFDC [Aid for Families with Dependent Children] from a means-tested entitlement (where benefits depend only on income and assets) toward a reciprocal obligation.

Work obligations inevitably run into the wall of work availability. Caught in the middle are the recipients of income security programs who, by and large, are struggling to avoid both welfare dependence and working poverty. The overlap between low earnings and receipt of public assistance (the working poor) makes the "solution" to welfare dependence all the more difficult to define. Nonetheless, the trend towards workfare continues apace. A recent volume published by the C.D. Howe Institute (Richards et al. 1995: xvi) concludes "government programs could more effectively reduce poverty if they were to *increase* the obligation on social assistance recipients to engage in work and/or training in exchange for benefits, and *decrease* the availability of long-term untied benefits (original emphasis)."[4] Newly elected Ontario Premier Mike Harris is poised to wield just such an ax in Ontario.

## FINANCIAL INCENTIVE PROGRAMS

Implicit in the appeal of compulsory rules requiring work and/or training is the notion that social assistance recipients do not want to work.[5] At its crudest level, this is manifested in a belief that "welfare bums" stay on assistance because they prefer a life of "leisure" at the public's expense, hence the growth in long-term welfare dependence. A related belief, though at odds with the notion of a lack of work effort, is that "welfare cheats" fraudulently draw assistance while also working. A more thoughtful explanation argues that the social assistance system produces perverse incentives which may or may not draw people into welfare but once there keeps them in a poverty trap where people are marginally better off on welfare than taking on low paid work. The instances where social assistance recipients lose benefits such as medical/dental benefits or subsidized housing are oft-cited examples of the poverty trap (Evans and McIntyre 1987). Similarly, the principle of "less eligibility" traditionally imposes a dollar-for-dollar reduction of benefits if the person takes on paid work (but still earns below the cut-off level for assistance).

One popular financial strategy for moving single parents off welfare and into work is to grant earnings exemptions so that some money from work can be kept without any reduction in benefits. Economists suggest a symmetrical response of labour supply to "tax changes" of this type. When benefit rates (BR) fall, theory suggests that work effort should rise for the individual already in the program.

The reverse should apply if the BR rises. However, the lower tax rate also raises the break-even level below which a person becomes eligible for benefits. Some people may feel, notwithstanding stigma and other costs, that they will be better off in the program and begin to claim benefits. They may or may not change their work behaviour but are most likely to lower their work effort. Further, some people who would not qualify even under the new break-even level might reduce their work effort in order to qualify. Therefore, the aggregate net effect on work effort is ambiguous despite the intention of raising work effort through a lower "tax-back" of benefits. (Economists refer to a substitution effect and an income effect.)

Note the emphasis on the financial rewards of working. Traditionally, economists have focused on the monetary incentives to work; people have a reservation wage below which one chooses not to work because wages do not offset the disutility (effort, discomfort) of work. The higher the level of social assistance benefits, the higher the reservation (alternative) wage and so the lower the incentive to work. A few economists have begun to explore the positive utility of work: satisfaction, human interaction, sense of accomplishment and fulfilment of human potential (Lane 1991).

Table 1
**Number of People Benefiting from the Enhanced Earnings Exemption Rule Changes**

| (June 1986—December 1987) | Single Parents | All categories of recepient |
|---|---|---|
| June 1986* | 2294 | 5990 |
| July* | 2361 | 5976 |
| August* | 2393 | 5950 |
| September | 2619 | 5914 |
| October | 2786 | 6136 |
| November | 3084 | 6730 |
| December | 3190 | 6880 |
| January 1987 | 3140 | 6551 |
| February | 3260 | 6839 |
| March | 3344 | 7120 |
| April | 3373 | 7317 |
| May | 3565 | 7673 |
| June | 3523 | 7825 |
| July | 3877 | 8185 |
| August | 3892 | 8003 |
| September | 3954 | 8037 |
| October | 3893 | 7713 |
| November | 4225 | 8137 |
| December | 4336 | 8134 |

* People who would have qualified for earnings exemptions under the new rules that started in September 1986

Source: Calculations by author based on administrative records in the G.P.S. records system of the B.C. Ministry of Social Services.

Most provinces in Canada have used earnings exemption programs to create work incentives for social assistance recipients (see Seguin 1987, Evans and McIntyre 1987 for inter-provincial comparisons).[6] B.C.'s Ministry of Social Services introduced its Enhanced Earnings Exemption program in 1986 recognizing "the initiative and self-motivation of the ministry's clients." The objectives of the program are as follows:

> The end result would be that a client could gradually work his way out of the need for income assistance. The enhanced earnings exemption would act as an incentive for greater numbers of income assistance recipients to achieve independence of the system. (Ministry of Human Resources 1986: 1)

All employable recipients were eligible. In practice, however, the program was targeted at lone parents because a single person could not work full-time even at minimum wage without earning above the cut-off level for income assistance.

The program had two separate components. First, it shortened the waiting period for eligibility to an existing exemption from nine months to four months of consecutive benefits.[7] Second, recipients could also keep twenty-five cents of each dollar earned above this "flat rate exemption," the enhanced exemption. Social assistance recipients are eligible for the exemption for a maximum of eighteen months in a three year period but can qualify for the program again. The effect of the program is assessed by comparing earnings in the three months prior to the introduction of the policy with the sixteen month period immediately thereafter up to December 1987. One outcome is the sizable number of social assistance recipients declaring earned income, even in the face of 100 percent benefit reduction. Roughly 10 percent of the caseload declared earnings in each of the three months prior to September 1986. Among single parent families, about 15 percent of those who stood to benefit from the new rules were already declaring earnings in August 1986.

Table 1 shows the number of people on social assistance in B.C. who either would have benefited if the enhanced earnings exemption rules had been in effect in June, July and August 1986, and the number who actually benefited in each month thereafter, up to December 1987. Our baseline for comparison is roughly 6000 social assistance recipients who had earnings in each of the three months prior to the introduction of the new rules and met the criteria of eligibility. With the introduction of the enhanced earnings exemption the number of recipients actually fell slightly; some people opted to be declared "unemployable" and so received an additional benefit payment due to the rule changes. Thereafter, the number of benefiting recipients continued to grow until leveling off in July 1987.

Those receiving an earnings exemption peaked (for our period of analysis) at 8185 cases in July 1987, a growth of 2271 cases or about 40 percent higher than when the program was introduced. Such a large change is presented as evidence of a direct effect of the program, rather than from other factors. Note also that, unlike the AFDC experience in the U.S., the caseload (generally and for single parents) did not grow but actually fell in this period, arguably because a four month waiting period discouraged people from leaving work to take social assistance and subsequently taking on work again.

The majority of the rise in benefiting cases occurs among families with children. This is not surprising since the level of benefits and hence the cut-off level for families is higher than for single people on social assistance. Only parents can work full-time at minimum wage and still qualify for benefits. The number of single parent families taking advantage of the new rules rises from roughly 1500 at the start of the program to over 4000 by the end of 1987. Table 2 shows that, at its peak in 1988, over a quarter of single parents eligible to receive an earnings exemption under the new rules were indeed working, up from only 15 percent before the program commenced.

The timing of this peak should not surprise us, since it was during the economic upswing experienced across western economies in the late 1980s. The overall responsiveness of social assistance recipients to the macro-economic climate is illustrated by Figure 1. The top line shows the benefiting cases as a proportion of the potential benefiting cases from January 1990 through December 1992. The bottom line shows the corresponding (seasonally unadjusted) unemployment rate in each month. Note the almost perfect mirror image of the two lines

Table 2
**Number of Benefiting Families as a Proportion of Those Eligible**

| (August of Each Year) | | |
| --- | --- | --- |
| | Two Parents | Single Parents |
| 1986* | 18.1 | 14.8 |
| 1987 | 24.0 | 23.4 |
| 1988 | 26.8 | 27.5 |
| 1989 | 28.0 | 25.5 |
| 1990 | 27.8 | 26.5 |
| 1991 | 26.2 | 23.7 |
| 1992 | 29.3 | 22.3 |

\* Families which would have qualified for earnings exemptions under the new rules that started in September 1986

Source: Calculations by author based on administrative records in the G.P.S. records system of the B.C. Ministry of Social Services.

(excluding the first three months of 1990). Thus, as employment prospects improve (the bottom line falls) the proportion of benefiting cases rises and vice versa.

In conclusion, we emphasize two points. First, even in the face of a 100 percent benefit reduction rate, a meaningful (10 percent) proportion of B.C.'s social assistance recipients choose to work during the mid-1980s. Second, the considerable labour force response of single parents on social assistance to a relatively minor financial incentive further demonstrates a willingness to work on the part of recipients. Remember that the implicit "marginal tax rate" on earnings remained at 75 percent under the program. The rationale behind this willingness to work under the new rules may be obvious, even a little more income can make a great deal of difference to those who start with very little, a perspective probably lost on many researchers. (In fancy terminology, the marginal utility of income might be very high for people on social assistance.)

The issue whether "work pays" leads us to the alternative financial strategy of wage supplements if single parents take on full-time employment and simultaneously leave social assistance.[8] The "self-sufficiency" projects (ssp) in B.C. and New Brunswick[9] are much more complex than the earnings exemption rules described above. We highlight some of the crucial components:

1.  **Long-term recipients**: The projects are open to single parents who have been on social

Figure 1
**Cyclical Nature of Employment: Enhanced Earnings Exemption Recipients**

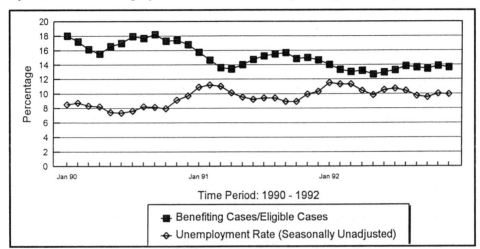

assistance for over one year, reflecting the concern over "welfare dependence." The supplement lasts for up to three years.

2. **Earnings-based Supplements**: The supplement is one-half the difference between actual and benchmark earnings: benchmark earnings in New Brunswick and B.C. were $30,000 and $37,000 respectively. Thus, a single mother in B.C at minimum wage ($6 per hour, 40 hours per week, 50 weeks per year) could double her earned income of $12,000 ($37,000—$12,000 = $25,000 /2 = $12,500).

3. **Voluntary and Experimental**: Eligible recipients are approached and offered the opportunity to participate but participation is voluntary and refusal does not affect benefits. However, only half those approached are offered the wage supplement; participants are randomly assigned to a control and an experimental group. The latter have one year in which to find a full-time job and leave social assistance.

The projects are modeled on a number of large scale social experiments or "demonstration projects" run in the U.S. Funding comes from the "Innovations" branch of Human Resources Development Canada (HRDC) and is administered by a non-profit company established specifically for this project.[10]

To date, the projects have been relatively successful in recruiting participants and those people have been finding full-time work. Table 3 shows that, as of February 1994, 24 percent of those eligible for earnings supplements had found full-time work and left social assistance (22 percent in B.C. and 28 percent in New Brunswick), though this is likely to rise as many participants still had at least three months in which to find a full-time job. Roughly one-third of those taking advantage of the supplement in B.C. and almost one-half of New Brunswick participants were earning minimum wage: average hourly wage for participants was considerably higher in B.C. than in New Brunswick ($8.29 and $6.30, respectively). As a result of the low average wages being earned, the average monthly supplements are effectively the same as the monthly social assistance payments these women would have received (just over

Table 3
**Summary of the Self-sufficiency Project**

| (Data up to February 1994) | B.C. | N.B. |
|---|---|---|
| Sample size (eligible for supplement) | 714 | 352 |
| Number of claiming supplement | 155 | 100 |
| Percent of eligible claiming supplement | 22 | 28 |
| Average hourly wage | $8.29 | $6.30 |
| Average monthly earnings | $1,200 | $944 |
| Average monthly supplement | $828 | $723 |

Source: Lui-Gurr, S, S. Currie Vernon and T. Mijanovich. 1994. *Making Work Pay Better Than Welfare*. Vancouver: SRDC, Table 4.

$800 in B.C. and just over $700 in New Brunswick). Income from both earnings and supplements resulted in an average pre-tax annualized income of $24,336 in B.C. and $20,004 in New Brunswick.

Thirty percent of "supplement eligible" participants finding work may or may not be deemed success. Many women refer to barriers to working even with the spur of more money: waiting for children to attend school; health problems; limited training and education; providing primary care for children or other family members (see Lui-Gurr et al. 1994). Further there are limited simultaneous "service" strategies being used to encourage or assist these women in their job search.[11] It is still too early to say what the long-term effects of this wage supplementation program will be but the intended effect is obvious: full-time work, even at low wages will help lead to "independence" after the supplementation ends. We turn now to this issue.

## THE JOB MARKET: SNAKES AND LADDERS

The goal of any of the three strategies, financial, service or restrictive, is to create long-term "independence" from welfare. While the evidence presented above is quite compelling that single mothers respond to financial incentives, there is little evidence that long-term "independence" results. The enhanced earnings exemption program was too limited in scope and the Self-sufficiency Projects cannot yet be assessed. However, neither is explicitly designed to create "independence."

Implicitly, both strategies assume a "job ladder" where low paid, possibly part-time, work leads to well paid full-time work. Yet the context in which the Axworthy report envisages social welfare reform both acknowledges and seeks to develop further the "flexible" segmented labour market of the twenty-first century. The children's board game Snakes and Ladders is a fitting analogy for the current labour market into which social assistance recipients may be thrown through workfare. Encountering a snake sends the player tumbling down the board into a worse-off position. Advancing is slow unless one comes upon a ladder which allows the player to climb up quickly towards a winning position. Either event occurs randomly, a literal roll of the dice. The restructuring of labour markets with the growth of low paid, part-time, non-standard employment indicate that, unlike the random chance in Snakes and Ladders, opportunity for moving upward is declining.

The job market facing social assistance recipients can be characterized by at least three segments: a "casual jobs" market, a "bad jobs" market and a "good jobs" market. Social assistance recipients who work mostly operate in the casual jobs market characterized by infrequent work and very low weekly hours, such as a day of dishwashing in a restaurant or moving boxes in a warehouse. Those who work longer hours operate in the "bad jobs" segment, characterized by low hourly wages, few benefits (such as medical and pensions schemes) and high job insecurity. Only in the "good jobs" segment can one hope to enjoy long-term independence from welfare.

It is unclear whether there are ladders out of the casual jobs market; often people are working sporadically due to physical/mental disability. Financial strategies may provide the needed ladder, but possibly only into the "bad jobs" market. Job insecurity in this segment ensures the snakes are many and the ladders short and few. Indeed, if we believe the rhetoric about the job market of the future (increasing levels of technical training from increased years of formal education will be required), the long ladder to get from the "bad jobs" to the "good jobs" market will be increasingly elusive. This is a major criticism of workfare programs: they fail to recognize the gap in training between those employed and those entering workfare or learnfare programs (Lightman 1995). Therefore, however successful either earnings exemption or wage supplementation programs may be in reducing welfare rolls and government debt levels, they do not provide automatic routes out of the poverty trap. The Ontario proposals to cut benefit levels by 20 percent threaten social assistance recipients with a long slide downwards while work requirements offer relatively few ladders and even further snakes (lower or out-right loss of benefits) if they fail to find work.

Faith in job ladders persists largely because of the belief in a "virtuous circle" of work at a macro-economic level.[12] The concept of a "virtuous circle" of work assumes a pool of people willing to work for low wages allowing the economy to grow and ultimately generating a flow of high paid work. Access to social assistance benefits is seen to be cutting off the stream of workers willing to work for low wages and pricing western economies out of the marketplace. The notion that all boats are ultimately lifted by a rising tide is prevalent but the process is essentially unexplained. Even to economists who purport to study the market, it remains largely a black box.

## PAY NOW AND PAY LATER

A third reasoning is used to justify policies targeted at single parents: concern over the future of children in single parent families, in terms of the immediate effects of poverty but also the potential for long-term welfare "dependence." The underlying philosophy is again narrowly market-oriented: higher income (sufficient to take the family out of eligibility for social assistance) provides the means by which single mothers meet the needs of their families. In part this is true by definition, more money gives greater choice over the range and quantity of goods and services. Goods which are conventionally defined as purely "private" (e.g., food and clothing) are quite well supplied by the market to those with the necessary income in developed wealthy countries. More telling is the ability of the market to provide a range of services such as day care, housing or transportation. For working single parents on the margins of poverty, adequacy, affordability and flexibility of these services will be crucial to the well-being of their families as well as their own aspirations to remain off public assistance. As we move away from goods which are conventionally defined as purely "private" towards goods with many "social" elements, the market is arguably less good at matching demand and supply.

Consider the problem of day care for people on minimum wage. The arithmetic is as discomforting as it is simple. Full-time work at minimum wage (for example 40 hours per week at $6.00 per hour) yields pre-tax income of roughly $960 per month. Full-time daycare in licensed family daycare costs more than $400 a month. Further, low paid work often involves shifts, overtime, unsociable hours, weekends, etc., which do not conform to the "normal" hours of most day care providers. Day care policy must go beyond subsidies because increasing funds once again rely on the market-oriented solution of demand and supply. The Axworthy report (HRDC 1994: 53) devotes two of its ninety pages to the issue of day care which is argued to lie "at the heart of the three areas addressed by [the] Discussion Paper." The report recognizes the need for more subsidized day care spaces and suggests further integration of day care and early child development. Affordable housing and transportation fall into the same rubric. Public policy in these areas is increasingly market-driven and hence unlikely to meet the needs of the poor.

What alternatives or complements exist to achieve broad goals of improving single parent families' welfare? A number of strategies are possible. First, the problem of single mothers and work is no different than it is for the rest of the population. What is required are sufficient numbers of secure, well paid jobs. The issue of job progression must be more clearly understood in this era of global competitiveness and technological change. Some starting points would be improved employment services, as suggested in the Axworthy report, as well as career planning and development, and follow-up access to training programs. Single parents may need additional help with "life skills," self-esteem and parenting skills to help them cope with the challenges of raising children alone and finding rewarding work. However, without the availability of jobs and employment the impacts of these individual skill based initiatives will be negligible.

Second, if child poverty is a primary concern, a more direct approach should complement the "trickle down" of resources through the family unit. Social welfare policies have tried to address concerns over how resources are spent within the household through "earmarked" transfers such as housing subsidies, medical benefits and, in the U.S., food stamps. A strong element of moral concern over inappropriate spending (e.g., alcohol or drugs) underlies these policies. Currie (1993) assesses programs designed to provide cash benefits to single mothers versus programs providing in-kind benefits directly to children. Programs such as school lunches, extended school hours and Head Start are found to have significant effects on the health, education and well-being of children from poor families.[13] Still, in-kind transfers are not a solution as long as people are trapped in poverty with inadequate welfare payments.

Third, earnings exemptions and wage supplements skirt the obvious issue that jobs paying minimum wage (or even just above) do not meet the needs of many single parent families on social assistance. The individual supplements provided by SSP are clearly quite high; Table 3 shows that it averaged over $800 per month in B.C., or almost $6.00 per hour of work based on a thirty-five hour week. Even a fifty cent per hour rise in the minimum wage in B.C. recently was contested hotly so an across-the-board change of the magnitude provided by SSP is clearly out of the question. The standard reasoning for not raising minimum wages is that employers will hire fewer people if they must pay more. However, this received wisdom is being challenged by a number of economists (Card and Krueger 1995).

## Conclusions

This paper argues that programs targeted at single mothers on social assistance have been wide of the mark for several reasons. It may be "commonsense," as the Ontario Conservatives' campaign slogan implied, to believe that single mothers are on welfare because they do not want to work. The empirical evidence is lacking even if economic theory seems compelling. Our evidence shows quite strong willingness to respond to financial incentives which belies the "commonsense" belief.

Financial and restrictive strategies in social assistance programs do little to overcome both the general lack of employment and the increasingly segmented nature of the labour market so that the "choice" open to single mothers is usually poverty from welfare dependence or poverty from low paid insecure work. It is a fundamental contradiction to design public policy to create a more flexible labour market and to punish those who end up depending on social assistance, either "frequent" U.I. users or "dependent" welfare recipients. Workfare is likely to increase the snakes the working poor encounter in the labour market without increasing the number of ladders.

There is a well known dilemma, which we will call the "universal dilemma": choose any two of the following—fast, cheap, good: the parallel in social welfare policy reform would be: choose any three of the following—fast, cheap, fair, long-lasting. Social welfare policies for single mothers which hold out greater promise of success than either financial incentives alone or work/training requirements are unlikely to be fast or cheap. A broadly defined social welfare policy should consider the "social infrastructure" needed to raise a family as well as the nature of the job market and pay structures.

The social policy pendulum has swung sharply to the right at the moment. The policies of the Alberta and Ontario Conservatives signal that social welfare reform will be a major component of provincial politics across Canada. Bills C-65 and C-76 open the door for further moves towards workfare by the provinces since it removes the monetary leverage the federal government had to prevent compulsion. As this paper argues, increasingly restrictive strategies for reducing the welfare rolls follow from an adherence to market-oriented economic and social theory. The two main crucibles of neoconservative ideology in the 1980s—Britain and New Zealand—show mixed and limited "success" in economic terms from radically tearing down the structures of the welfare state; the human cost is much less discussed. Canadian social welfare policy reform should heed this omission and give the human costs of reform due consideration.

## NOTES

1.  Service strategies have been particularly widespread in provincial social assistance programs since the Four Corners Agreement signed in 1985 between the federal and provincial governments. These include the highly controversial and highly expensive NB Works program (see Milne 1995). Some comments are made regarding the need for expanded employment services but this paper does not examine specific programs.

2.  The federal cabinet is still debating reforms which will cut back eligibility to and duration of U.I. programs, including reduced benefits for "frequent" users (Greenspon 1995: A1).

3.  The largest body of empirical evidence about single parents is drawn from the U.S. Aid to Families with Dependent Children (AFDC) program, and most of these studies were done prior to 1980. It shows a possible 30 percent reduction in work effort due to the availability of welfare benefits. However, Moffit (1992) also concludes that 95 percent of beneficiaries would have been eligible for AFDC even if they had worked an additional 30 percent, since weekly hours and rates of pay were so low. The general concern that welfare benefits displace work effort is strongly influenced by analysis of the U.S. Negative Income Tax experiments which showed a potential 2-5 percent reduction in labour supply from a guaranteed annual income.

4.  All the analysts in the report save one are economists, and only one dissenting voice, Ernie Lightman's, is heard.

5.  Lightman (1981, 1994) is careful to emphasize that workfare constitutes programs which either explicitly require work for benefits, or set conditions so onerous as to make refusing work impossible. Hence, compulsion and voluntarism are clouded. (See also Evans 1993).

6.  Such a program was tried in the U.S. for the Aid for Families with Dependent Children (AFDC) program. Lone mothers were able to retain the first $30 in earnings and 33 cents of each additional dollar without offsetting reduction in benefits. Hard evidence on work incentive effects is especially difficult to obtain since very few participants of AFDC actually work (less than 6 percent in 1987; see Moffitt 1992). However, what is available is not comforting for those who believe in work incentives from lower BR.

7.  In 1986, this flat-rate exemption was $100 for families or a single recipient designated as "handicapped," and $50 for a single person. It has since doubled to $200 and $100, respectively.

8.  Leaving social assistance is a requirement since, as noted above, they might qualify to stay on assistance if their earnings after exemptions are below the cut-off level. However, as we will see, the supplement simply replaces the benefits cheque in most cases to date.

9.  Note that there are two separate programs running in New Brunswick, NB Works and the Self-suffiency Project. Both are funded by HRDC but the former uses a service strategy and the latter uses a financial strategy. There are no formal links between the two projects.

10. The Social Research and Demonstration Corporation (SRDC), established to oversee the projects, is currently also running a wage supplementation scheme for U.I. recipients in seven provinces. Clearly governments, both federal and provincial, are looking at these schemes as one method for tackling long-term "dependence" on social assistance.

11. There may be some overlap between SSP and NB Works but no specific program of support was designed for SSP. A concession was granted to SSP participants so that the supplement income is not counted in calculating eligibility to social housing.

12. This is not simply a neoconservative belief. The concept is rooted in the principle of multiplier effects from any rise in aggregate expenditure in the economy.

13. Similar programs run across Canada; the Axworthy report makes brief mention of a Head Start program for Aboriginal children to help their future progress in schooling.

## REFERENCES

Allen, Douglas. 1993. "Welfare and the Family: The Canadian Experience." *Journal of Labor Economics* 11 (1), Part 2: S201-23.

Becker, Gary. 1981. *A Treatise on the Family*. Cambridge: Harvard University Press.

Card, David and Alan Krueger. 1995. *Myth and Measurement: The New Economics of the Minimum Wage*. Princeton: Princeton University Press.

Currie, Janet. 1993. "Welfare and Well-being of Children: The Relative Effectiveness of Cash and In-kind Transfers." In James Poterba (ed.), *Tax Policy and the Economy Vol. 8*. Cambridge: MIT Press for NBER.

Evans, Patricia. 1993. "From Workfare to the Social Contract: Implications for Canada of Recent US Welfare Reforms." *Canadian Public Policy* 19 (1): 53-67.

———. 1988. "Work Incentives and the Single Mother: Dilemmas of Reform." *Canadian Public Policy* 14 (2): 125-36.

——— and Ellen McIntyre. 1987. "Welfare, Work Incentives and the Single Mother: an International Comparison." In J. Ismael (ed.), *The Canadian Welfare State: Evolution and Transition*. Edmonton: University of Alberta Press.

Gallagher, Beth. 1995. "Single Moms Start to Panic." *Vancouver Sun* June 17: A9.

Glennerster, Howard. 1990. "Social Policy Since the Second World War." In J. Hills (ed.), *The State of Welfare: The Welfare State in Britain since 1974*. Oxford: Clarendon Press.

Greenspon, Edward. 1995. New U.I. Plan Would Cut Benefits." *Globe and Mail* June 10: A1.

Gueron, Judith and H. Pauly. 1991. *From Welfare to Work*. New York: Russell Sage Foundation.

Human Resources Development Canada (HRDC). 1994. *Improving Social Security in Canada: A Discussion Paper*. Ottawa: Minister of Supply and Services.

Lane, Robert E. 1991. *The Market Experience*. New York: Cambridge University Press.

Lightman, Ernie. 1995. "You Can Lead a Horse to Water, but...: The Case Against Workfare in Canada." In John Richards and William Watson (eds.), *Helping the Poor: A Qualified Case for "Workfare."* Toronto: C.D. Howe Institute.

———. 1991. "Work Incentives Across Canada." *Journal of Canadian Studies* 26 (1): 120-37.

Lui-Gurr, Susanna, Sheila Currie Vernon and Tod Mijanovich. 1994. *Making Work Pay Better Than Welfare: An Early Look at the Self-sufficiency Project*. Vancouver: Social Research and Demonstration Corporation.

Milne, William J. 1995. "Revising Income Assistance Programs in New Brunswick: A Look at the Demonstration Projects." In John Richards and William Watson (eds.), *Helping the Poor: A Qualified Case for "Workfare."* Toronto: C.D. Howe Institute.

Ministry of Human Resources (British Columbia). 1986. "Proposed Enhanced Earnings Exemption for Income Assistance Clients." *News Release 86:03*. April 7: 1.

Moffitt, Robert. 1992. "Incentive Effects of the U.S. Welfare System: A Review." *Journal of Economic Literature* 30 (1): 1-61.

Murray, Charles 1984. *Losing Ground: American Social Policy 1950-1980*. New York: Basic Books.

Rein, Martin. 1973. "Work Incentives and Welfare Reform in Britain and the United States." In Bruno Stein and S.M. Miller (eds.), *Incentives and Planning in Social Policy*. Chicago: Aldine Publishing.

Richards, John and William Watson. 1995. *Helping the Poor: A Qualified Case for "Workfare."* Toronto: C.D. Howe Institute.

Seguin, Gilles. 1987. "Descriptive Overview of Selected Provincial Income Supplementation and Work Incentive Initiatives." In J. Ismael (ed.), *The Canadian Welfare State: Evolution and Transition*. Edmonton: University of Alberta Press.

# CHAPTER 13

# NB WORKS: IMAGE VS. REALITY

*Joan McFarland and Robert Mullaly*

## INTRODUCTION

> You want to get off income assistance!
> You want to work and be financially independent!
> You want a brighter future for you and your family!
> You know that getting a job takes education and training—that employers look for
> people who are confident and have some experience in the workplace!
> You realize that you don't have these qualifications.
> And, you're ready to do something about it!
> NB Works is designed for people like you.
> (NB Works brochure "The Future is Yours!" 1993)

NB Works is a Phase II Social Assistance Recipient (SAR) Agreement program developed under the 1985 federal-provincial "Agreement on Enhancement of Employment Opportunities for Social Assistance Recipients." The agreement was designed "to promote the self-sufficiency of social assistance recipients and to reduce their dependence upon federal and provincial income support programs by enhancing their employability through the application of appropriate employment and training measures" (Employment and Immigration Canada 1987, cited in ERN 1991). Although a number of employability enhancement projects were signed by New Brunswick and the federal government, NB Works has been the showpiece that has received the most attention from the media and the most praise from prominent federal politicians such as Jean Chrétien and Lloyd Axworthy. Its stated primary goal is "to ensure that the participants achieve a level of educational/skill proficiency and obtain relevant work experiences that will allow them the opportunity to achieve permanent labour force attachment" (Departments of Advanced Education and Labour and Income Assistance, DAEL and DIA 1992).

The purpose of this paper is to examine the gap between the image and reality of NB Works. We shall do this by describing the program; introducing a four quadrant model to consider NB Works in relation to workfare programs; examining the image of NB Works and how it has been created; and considering the reality of NB Works as experienced by a group of NB Works participants. We will offer our own analysis of the program in the concluding section of the paper.

---

We wish to acknowledge the contributions of the following: CLC Atlantic and CUPE Local 1190 for their support; the sixteen NB Works participants for allowing us to interview them for this study; the NB Works program staff for sharing information and giving generously of their time; Dr. Sandra Wachholz, for her valued research assistance; and Dale Dassett and Jeananne Knox for transforming our notes and other hieroglyphics into acceptable form and format.

## DESCRIPTION OF NB WORKS

Canada and New Brunswick signed their first Employability Enhancement Agreement in January 1987. Commonly referred to as the SAR Agreement, it resulted in the development of various cost shared employability enhancement demonstration projects. After a second SAR Agreement was signed in May 1992, those projects which were waiting for signing, including NB Works, were immediately approved.

Human Resources Development New Brunswick is responsible for the direct operation of NB Works, but it is managed by a joint federal-provincial committee with representatives from Human Resources Development Canada and the provincial departments of Advanced Education and Labour and Human Resources Development. The funding arrangement for the project is as follows:

| | |
|---|---|
| Province of New Brunswick | $ 25,381,812.00 |
| (wages for job exposure) | |
| Canada Assistance Plan (HRDC) | 5,807,505.00 |
| (supplementals and top-up) | |
| Developmental Funds (HRDC) | 81,243,877.00 |
| (U.I. training allowances) | |
| Training and Development Fund (CAP) | 64,685,946.00 |
| (course purchase) | |
| | $ 177,119,140.00 |

Source: DAEL and DIA 1992: np and information from HRDC

The target population for NB Works are those persons who[1]:

- have been in receipt of social assistance for at least six months;
- are entitled to higher ranges of income support (single mothers and two parent families);
- have limited education (less than grade twelve but at least grade seven);
- have little or no labour force attachment;
- are assessed as having the greatest potential for success in the program.

The initial objective was to accept 3000 persons into the project by having three intakes of approximately 1000 each in 1992, 1993 and 1994. By the time the final group had made its way through NB Works, it would have been a six year project. However, a fourth intake was added in January 1995, funded by money that accrued from drop-outs from other intakes.

Participation in NB Works is advertised as completely voluntary. Potential participants are identified from the social assistance caseloads and invited to attend information sessions to learn about NB Works. Interested persons are administered an achievement test to determine their level of education, and must be eligible to enter intermediate or senior level academic upgrading. A pre-employment session is then given where, in addition to job preparation counselling, an assessment is made of the candidate's motivation and attitude to a long-term commitment to NB Works. A "case management model" is utilized whereby participants are offered a range of training and work experiences as they move through the following continuum of services: orientation, case plan development, job placement (five months), extra-mural high school (maximum twenty-four months), skills training (maximum nine months), job experience search (maximum three months) and an optional eight month subsidized private sector job placement. The various services within the continuum are based on each participant's case plan and the completion of all case plans is the responsibility of the provincial Department of Human Resource Development. Other than the initial job placement of five months, the time allotted for each component may be less than the maximum expressed and some components may be repeated or omitted depending on the individual's needs.

Participants receive a wage during the job placement phase from the provincial government departments involved along with child care benefits, a clothing allowance and a health card from CAP funds. During the training phases, participants receive the unemployment insurance training allowance (from the U.I. Developmental Fund) along with additional benefits from CAP funds which include child care expenses, a transportation allowance (for more than forty-eight kilometres), a "top-up" to ensure that participants do not fall below the basic rate of income assistance and a health card. The provision of other benefits is at the discretion of the participant's case worker who manages the case plan. The courses are purchased using funds from the Training and Development Fund, a diversion of CAP funds allowed under the 1985 Employability Enhancement Agreement, and thus shared on a 50:50 basis by the province and federal government.

## NB WORKS: IS IT WORKFARE?
There have been many definitions of workfare but perhaps we can start with the general definition that workfare "includes a variety of job related activities that may be required as a condition of social assistance" (Evans 1993: 56). The key words here are "required as a condition of" and "job related activities." It must be noted however that, in the United States, the terms mandatory and voluntary workfare (and learnfare) have been adopted (ERN 1991: 3). In this paper, when we speak about workfare, we mean mandatory workfare. Voluntary workfare (and learnfare) correspond to what we refer to as "employability enhancement programs."

Ernie Lightman (1991: 123), under the rubric of work incentive strategies, has created a chart to depict some of these ideas. The chart (see Figure 1) looks at the continuum from voluntary to compulsory participation in programs as well as the ideological continuum from the "right to benefit" (or "entitlement") to that of "responsibilities and obligations" on the part of participants in the programs.

We have developed an expanded version of the Lightman chart (see Figure 2) which we hope might help clarify some of the issues around these programs and enable us to better explain the "reality" of NB Works. Our depiction puts the employability concept at the centre. We see the concept as both the symbol and the reality of the changes that are taking place in social assistance programs.

We look at three continuums rather than just two. In addition to the voluntary/compulsory and right/obligations aspects, we add the passive/active aspect of such programs. In addition, we include the role of such measures as earnings exemptions, tax-back rates, service and financial strategies and guaranteed annual income schemes. We also try to incorporate such

Figure 1
**Entitlement to Social Assistance—A Continuum of Work-related Qualifications**

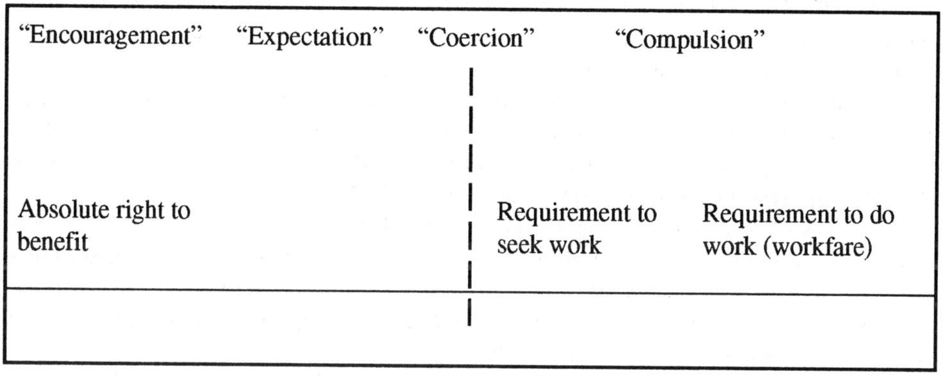

| "Encouragement"   "Expectation"   "Coercion"        "Compulsion" |
|---|
| Absolute right to<br>benefit |
|  |

Source: Lightman 1991, 123

Figure 2
**Employability and Workfare Programs**

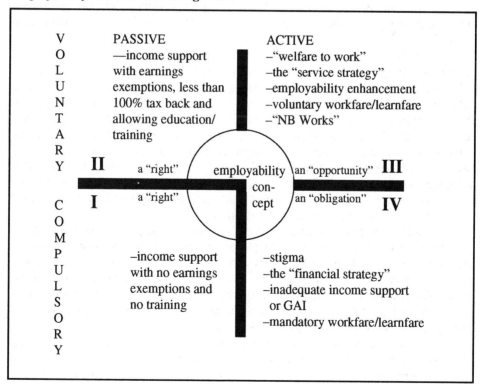

issues as the role of full employment policies, the cost of the programs and the creation of a low wage labour force for employers.

The three basic dimensions of our chart are the voluntary/compulsory continuum, shown vertically; the passive/active continuum, shown horizontally; and the rights/obligation continuum, shown diagonally. There are four quadrants.

An income support system based on a right to benefit principle which allows no earnings exemptions and no education or training would be found in quadrant I, at the bottom left. In this quadrant the concept of "employability" has no place (unless the recipient seeks to enhance employability on his/her own) and so is blacked out.

Social assistance, as we have known it in the 1960s-1980s under CAP, would be in quadrant II, at the top left. The right to benefit principle exists but there is some limited "encouragement," a term used by Lightman along the voluntary/compulsory continuum, to earn income. The "encouragement" is in the form of an earnings exemption and a less than 100 percent tax-back on earnings beyond that.

We would place programs like NB Works in quadrant III, at the top right. The program is officially voluntary. It involves work and training and is therefore active along the passive/active continuum. It is based on the concept of "opportunity" as contrasted to that of either a "right" or "obligation" of participants. Such programs have been referred to by some as "welfare to work" (Evans 1993: 56); "programs of attitudinal and psychological support, T-groups, education, and training activity" (Rein 1983 cited in Lightman 1991) or employability enhancement programs, characterized by Evans (1993: 62) as "carrots" as opposed to "sticks."

Mandatory workfare appears in quadrant IV. Mandatory workfare is compulsory, active and involves obligations and responsibilities on the part of participants. However, workfare is just one of the types of programs that belongs in quadrant IV. Mandatory learnfare, the obligation to take further education or training to receive benefits, would also be in quadrant IV. The "financial strategy," described by Lightman (1991: 124) as "the manipulation of financial rewards" such as the raising or lowering of benefits based on participation in training or the labour force, also makes programs compulsory if the benefits otherwise received would be too low for survival. A guaranteed annual income which sets basic rates too low for survival without labour force participation would put it in quadrant IV. The stigma attached to "not working or learning," especially if there is a lot of public rhetoric around this idea, can itself add a compulsory aspect to participation in a program.

Quadrant IV programs, such as financial strategies, inadequate income support or a guaranteed annual income which force people into the labour market, would only be possible in a full employment economy. Full employment is not required in order to put on mandatory workfare/learnfare programs or the programs in quadrant III. Governments can create "make-work" jobs for these. However, for mandatory workfare/learnfare or quadrant III programs *to succeed*, full employment is required. Such programs cannot be judged successful if participants are not able to find a job at completion.

In terms of the cost of active programs, in general, it decreases as we move down the chart from quadrant III to IV. Training and support programs are very expensive. The size of a low cost labour force increases, however, as we move from quadrant III to IV. With a guaranteed annual income, employers get subsidized workers. With workfare, they can get virtually free workers, the supply of which can be continuously replenished.

Figure 3 puts employability and workfare programs in context by emphasizing the macro variables which determine the possibility of welfare recipients' transition from assistance to work. These are policies which promote such goals as full employment, higher minimum wages, fair taxes, universal day care, pay equity, support of unions and the redefinition of work and work sharing (Swanson 1994: 23).

Figure 3
**The Macro Context**

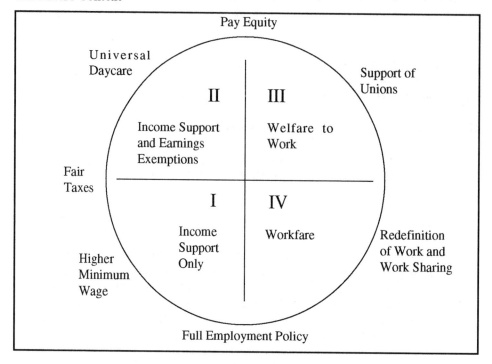

## THE IMAGE OF NB WORKS, ITS SOCIAL CONSTRUCTION AND REALITY

NB Works has received considerable national attention for a number of reasons. First, it is a national demonstration project that was sold to the federal government to "act as a guide for future SAR programming at a national level" (*NB Works Update*, November 1993: 1). Second, there is Frank McKenna, a very high profile politician being groomed, some say, for leadership of the national Liberals and hence given a lot of "goodies" from Ottawa (Higgins 1994: 7). And third, there is the program's communications strategy, outlined in its own documents, to "identify central messages which should come out of NB Works" (*NB Works: Annual Report*: 12). A communications committee has been established and a full-time communications officer hired. They publish a quarterly newsletter entitled, *NB Works Update*. As well, a NB Works video containing glowing testimonials from selected NB Works participants has been produced for distribution.

As part of the communications strategy for NB Works, the national media, especially the *Globe and Mail* and CBC, are invited to New Brunswick, shown around the project and

introduced to selected participants. Prominent federal politicians are also invited to visit NB Works. For example, Jean Chrétien was a recent visitor and called the project "a model for reforming the (Canadian) social welfare system" (York 1993: A1). With respect to the image of NB Works, what are the central messages that the communications strategy is attempting to convey? From NB Works documents, the emphasis seems to be on the innovativeness of the program, its generosity in opportunities offered to participants, the success of the program for participants and the efficiency of its delivery through the cooperation of two levels of government. It would be an understatement to say that the messages emphasize the positive. Take, for example, this account of media attention in one issue of *NB Works Update* (1993: 4):

> NB Works was recently featured on the CBC radio program *Sunday Morning*. The fifteen minute segment looked at the project's *success* to date from participants, administration, and academic perspectives (emphasis added).

The strategy is to use the words of enthusiastic participants:

> Communications will be focusing efforts to promote understanding of the participants who are reaping dramatic benefits from involvement in the project.
> (*NB Works Update*, June 1994: 3)

For example,

> I don't like to even think about what would have happened with my life and with my family's life without NB Works. So many positive things have happened to us because of NB Works. I'm going to get my grade 12, my wife's back in school to do with NB Works, everything's coming together. It's been a long time coming. We've had hard times. I don't like to think about where my life would be right now without NB Works because I know it wouldn't be nice.
> David Nye, NB Works participant and father of two.
> (*NB Works: Annual Report 1992-93*: 16)

The above then is a brief overview of the image of NB Works and how it has been constructed. It is interesting to contrast the image of NB Works projected by the government's communications strategy with the following official goals of the program found in the *NB Works Update* project profiles:

1) To develop the human resource and employment potential of the social assistance caseload.
2) To begin to change the attitude that may exist that income assistance is an end in itself.
3) To save social assistance dollars through the move of persons from caseload to workforce.

Clearly the advertising and promotional objectives used to sell NB Works to the public are different from the official goals of saving money and reducing work disincentives.

## The Reality: The Participants' Experience of NB Works

NB Works is conceptualized as a program based on "opportunity." This is in contrast to previous labour force re-entry programs which were conceptualized more on a "bridging" model. In earlier programs, "overcoming barriers" was a major focus of the design with such aspects as counselling and life skills playing a major role. In an "opportunities" approach, which is more market-oriented, opportunities are presented and it is largely up to the participant to take advantage of them. Support services are minimal, or at least play a lesser role.

### The Interviews

This section of the paper discusses the "opportunities" presented by NB Works as perceived and experienced by a group of participants in the program. We interviewed sixteen NB Works participants who were referred to us by various community groups.

It is recognized that sixteen is a small sample and that our means of locating participants could potentially lead to bias, although we believe that we found a heterogeneous group. This approach was used for a specific reason. If participants were referred to us by program managers, the sample might be biased in another direction. We would likely get the "stars" who are being used in the communications strategy. Also, it is worth noting that the program itself has carried out a case study of thirty participants but has not released the results. Hence we did not have access to that data.

Participants from each of the four intake groups were represented among the sixteen we interviewed as well as New Brunswick's major centres: Fredericton, Moncton and Saint John. There were no Francophones in the sample. Otherwise, the interviewees' personal profiles closely fit the target group for NB Works. Fifteen were female, one was male. Almost all were single mothers in their late twenties or early thirties with minimal previous labour force experience. The male was a single father with experience in the labour force, employed and unemployed.

In general, these participants perceived the program as an opportunity. On entering the program, they understood that they would be able to set goals for a career; they would get their grade twelve; they would get skills training of their choice; and when they graduated from the program, they would be "competitive" in the job market.

However, their experiences were somewhat different. In fact, they found that the program entailed sacrifices on their part in terms of money and family. In addition, it involved a number of serious frustrations for them caused by the program's organizational difficulties and the situations in which some found themselves. These included being unable to complete the upgrading; facing the possibility of dropping out or expulsion; and not having any hope for a decent job in the end.

The discussion which follows is organized around these experiences. First, the issues from the participants' point of view with regard to case management, work exposure, upgrading, skills training and jobs is presented. Second, the impact of the program on participants' lives is examined. This involves the financial impact as well as that on their

family life and self-esteem. Also the drop-out/expulsion problem which participants face is discussed. Finally, a contrast is made between how the participants view the concept of NB Works with the success of the actual program.

## CASE MANAGEMENT

The goal of NB Works, for the program designers, was to produce "a seamless continuum" for participants using an individualized case management approach. However, there were continual problems and hitches in the running of the program. Only some of these were or could be corrected as the program went along. In fact, when we asked participants about what they would change about the program, "better organization" was one of the most frequently made suggestions.

Our understanding of NB Works was that the participants would meet with their case managers and plan their three years in the program. When we checked this out with participants, they seemed to have no idea what we were talking about. This was not their perception of the process at all. Almost all felt that they had no "plan" and had had no such discussions with their case managers. For them, the case manager was just like their worker under income assistance. They saw the case manager's role as being supportive, helping them get what they needed and sticking up for them in case meetings.

## WORK EXPOSURE

In the early days of NB Works, there were many public criticisms of the work exposure phase of the program: it was poorly planned; the jobs, mainly cutting brush for NB Power, were unsuitable and poorly supervised; participants were subjected to sexual harassment; and working conditions were dangerous. NB Works was seen as exploitative. The work was being financed by the province and the employers basically paid nothing. Finally, its real purpose was not so much to give job exposure as to get recipients off normal income assistance rolls and onto unemployment insurance (PGF Consultants 1993b).

Actually, the participants we interviewed seemed relatively satisfied with this phase of the project. A number of them "liked" or even "loved" cutting brush, especially those that had a rural background. Many of the others worked as teaching assistants. They spoke positively of the experience, especially of the kindness and respect that they received from teachers. In the summer, some worked as janitors in the schools, a job which did not receive such a positive rating. Others worked as secretaries for schools or other non-profit organizations.

The complaints that we heard about this phase of the program concerned the lack of options and money received. Their job exposure experience was not related to their career goals. There were few choices available. They were paid $6.25 per hour (the NB minimum wage is $5) which some claimed meant lower take-home pay than they had been receiving on income assistance.

## UPGRADING

When we asked participants their main objective in joining NB Works, nine of the sixteen said that it was to get their upgrading. Yet the upgrading proved to be one of the most problematic phases of the program. This is despite some very dedicated and caring teachers (although there were also some who were not, the participants told us).

For some of the women[2], it was not possible to complete the upgrading in the time allotted. Participants with educational levels as low as grade seven were accepted into NB Works and expected to complete an academic grade twelve program in a maximum of two years. Although the program has accommodated these students by creating a computer training program for them to transfer into, they felt tremendous disappointment.

Other participants believed that they were getting more upgrading than they really needed. Some already had their GED or high school diploma when they started. However, on completing required testing, they were found to have a lower level of academic competence than their credentials indicated and were asked to do remedial work. Understandably, they found this frustrating and humiliating.

## Skills Training

The skills training portion of the program, most of which is given in the New Brunswick community college system, takes place in different locations in the province. This often means a move with or without family. Either way, the move can be difficult and stressful for the participant.

## Jobs

None of the participants we interviewed were either ready for the job search or in a job. In fact, very few have reached these levels. Information we were given verbally by HRDNB for January 1995 was that thirty-nine of the 3000 original participants were at the job search stage and sixteen "job ready." No official figures on employment will be collected until twelve months after graduation.

One of the issues is whether participants will find a job at the end of the program. While a job is not officially promised, it is implied. In fact, the very term "self-sufficiency" implies a job. How else would NB Works participants possibly attain "self-sufficiency"?

The participants we interviewed were not optimistic in their outlook. A number of them expressed the idea that "there will be no jobs once you are done" or in the end "we will be a bunch of educated bums." One woman pointed out that participants lost all hope of being able to stay on with their work exposure employers when "they figured out that it cost the company only $1.25 per hour for this person." She went on:

> When you are out on your work placement, even if you try hard, you know that there are hundreds of people behind you in NB Works that can work in your same job. Even if you try really hard to impress them, they will not hire you as they can hire a NB Works student.

## Impact of the Program

Participants were promised that they would be no worse off financially while in the NB Works program than they had been on income assistance. This was not exactly true and was an issue of great concern to those in the program.

What we found was that the actual money received was greater only if child care monies were included and the participant had more than one child. This was so because they were allowed to keep any monies not used for child care. However, this posed a dilemma for the mother. If she used the money for a good day care program, then she and her family had to survive on less than she had been receiving with income assistance. On the other hand, if she found a cheaper babysitter (often a family member or friend) and pocketed the extra money, she felt guilty for depriving her child(ren) of an enriched day care experience. Furthermore, if she did take this option, she had to claim the extra money for income tax purposes. This was a scary prospect for a number of the women.

In all, the women we talked with felt that being on NB Works was a considerable financial sacrifice for them. In addition, the payment arrangements under NB Works differed from those under income assistance. In some cases, payment was delayed, such as when the source of funding changed from income assistance to wages (i.e., during the work exposure phase) to unemployment insurance (during the upgrading and skills training phases). For example, in the initial transition, participants received only one-half of their regular income assistance cheques because their wages were about to start. However, the wages were not to be paid until the end of the two week period. The result was that several recruits dropped out of the program because they had no resources to get them to the end of the month.

## IMPACT ON CHILDREN

> After years of not even talking about school, single parents are now doing homework with their children at the kitchen table. It becomes a family goal that they all get their education. (Karen Mann, a senior official in the NB Department of Income Assistance, quoted in *Globe and Mail*, December 17, 1993: A1)

The picture painted in the publicity surrounding NB Works is that the program is great for the children in the families involved. Again, we were provided a somewhat different version. Some women did describe their children as being "proud" of their mothers and the program as "having mostly a positive impact" on their children. However, many felt that the program had been "hard" on their kids and "hard" on them as mothers. It was "hard" on the family because of the lack of time to spend together, the mother not being able to give the kids enough attention, the mother "racing around in the morning," the mother being tired when she came home and losing her patience and her temper in the evening. One mother described it as "heartbreaking" and another of "going and crying in her room about it." A child's illness was a particularly serious problem. Without a medical certificate, participants were docked money for their absences and in some cases asked to leave the program because of too many such absences.

## IMPACT ON SELF-ESTEEM

Another selling point of NB Works was the effect it would have on participants' self-esteem. Again, we found a mixed picture. Some participants concurred that it did have this effect saying such things as "it gave me a life" or "it was a sort of awakening for me." But one group of participants we spoke with claimed it had caused their self-esteem "to decline by about ninety percent." This occurred because of serious problems they were having in completing certain components of the program.

In general, self-esteem was related to the amount of time the participant had been in the program. Just after acceptance to the program, self-esteem was very high. After that, self-esteem was related to successful completion of each stage of the program. We have already noted that our interviews did not include any participants who were at the job search phase of the program. However, if the experience of university graduates in the current New Brunswick job market is any guide, this phase could be the ultimate self-esteem destroyer.

## Drop-Outs

NB Works has experienced very significant drop-out rates. As of January 1995, after thirty of the total thirty-five months had passed, only 33 percent of the original intake participants were still in the program. In other words, 67 percent had exited from the program. It is not known what happened to all of them, but 39 percent of the original intake participants were back on social assistance. The percentages for the other intakes, when prorated for the lesser amount of time spent in the program, are similar. (See Table 2 in Appendix 1 for detailed drop-out figures.)

The myth is that participants drop out because they lack the "work ethic" or are "lazy," that they would rather sit at home and watch soap operas than get out and take advantage of opportunities to change their situations. A recent *NB Works Update* (September 1994: 4), based on a recent evaluation not yet released, suggests other reasons for NB Works drop-outs such as "illness, substance addiction or abuse, little or no self-esteem, history of failure in school" concluding that "self-sufficiency is not necessarily something they are ready for." But the *Update* also defends the program pointing out that drop-outs in other educational institutions, e.g., universities, are just as high.

What we found was that "drop-outs" are, in fact, of two kinds: those that drop out themselves and those that are expelled or dismissed. The drop-outs we spoke with did so because of insurmountable barriers in terms of their personal circumstances, almost always family related, that the program could not accommodate. The reasons given to participants for their expulsions or dismissals were "too many absences," sometimes combined with "an attitude problem."

The expulsions are an aspect of the program which has received very little public attention. We were told that a participant's performance is regularly reviewed in case meetings of caseworkers and instructors and that appeals are heard before appeals boards whose members make the final decision on a participant's status. This strict attendance policy, or "lack of flexibility" as viewed from the participants' eyes, seems to suggest that the "lack of work ethic" plays a significant role in the decisions affecting the status of participants.

## Participants' View of the Concept of NB Works

One question we asked the interviewees was what they thought of "the concept" of NB Works. In general, their responses to the concept were positive: "good idea," "wonderful if people can get off welfare." However, when we asked them if NB Works was a success, their responses were quite different. According to them, NB Works could have been good but for the following reasons:

> "It needs more organization . . . ."
> "We need more help with career goals . . . ."
> "It needs a more realistic time frame . . . ."

"The program should screen better . . . ."
"Upgrading was a waste . . . ."
"Participants are not getting enough reward . . . ."
"It needs to recognize people's family problems . . . ."

It seems to us that the participants approved of the program as it had been presented (the rhetoric of NB Works) but had quite a different view of its reality.

One particular aspect of the rhetoric that emerged in the women's stories was the issue of the future generation. The women said that they were in NB Works "for the sake of the kids" or "to prove to her kids and herself that she can do it." This is also what the government is saying. But by buying into this idea, the women are putting even more pressure on themselves and are going to take an even harder fall if they are not able to "succeed" according to the program's definition of success: "self sufficiency."

## CRITIQUE AND CONCLUSIONS

In this paper we have tried to present both the image and reality of NB Works, the communications strategy, the way NB Works was set up, how it relates to the concept of workfare, the political context for the program and the experiences of sixteen participants. In this final section, we will give our own analysis and critique. We will divide our discussion into three levels of inquiry: conceptual, operational and political.

Conceptually, even if the image were reality, we see a number of problems with NB Works. Although it has been toned down considerably, the project initially was about changing the work ethic of New Brunswickers on income assistance. Both Bernard Valcourt, the federal minister of employment at the time of the signing of the NB Works agreement, and Frank McKenna made numerous statements to this effect. There is little doubt that such work ethic rhetoric benefits employers who through training, work exposure and workfare programs get low or no cost workers. In fact, the participants in NB Works have shown themselves to be anything but lazy. Our researcher described the women she interviewed as "stoic" and "amazingly persevering" under sometimes quite adverse conditions.

The case management approach is a centrepiece of NB Works yet conceptually its appropriateness needs to be questioned. Case management is an individualized, market-oriented approach to service delivery. Its advantage is supposed to be efficiency in both cost savings and the delivery of the "seamless continuum" of programs. This is in direct contrast to a bridging style of program delivery that uses a group approach, focuses on helping participants overcome barriers and gives maximum support to participants in the programs they undertake. While it is recognized that barriers are the most important causes for dropouts in programs such as NB Works (Holt 1994), the case management approach seems to give minimal attention to them. What is considered to be the competing employability program in New Brunswick, the Self-sufficiency Project, goes much further in this direction than even NB Works.

NB Works is based on "targeting." A very narrow group of people are eligible for participation in the program, those who are deemed most able to successfully complete it. Again this is for efficiency and cost saving reasons. However, if it is a program of opportunity then such targeting is inherently unfair. We noted in our visits to NB Works program sites considerable jealousy of NB Works participants by others who were in upgrading and skills training but were paying for the same courses, not to mention by the unemployed who believed that NB Works participants (in the job exposure phase) were taking away jobs. Again it should be noted that the Self-sufficiency Project is even more narrowly targeted.

If success is measured in job placements of participants, a program such as NB Works cannot possibly succeed in an economy with high unemployment. Frank McKenna took a calculated risk when he introduced NB Works in a high unemployment economy. He knew that the successful job placement of program graduates would be all but impossible in these conditions. His stated strategy was to use the trained work force from NB Works to attract business to the province (Freeman 1993: B8.) However, one must question the soundness of this strategy. How can one expect adults with a grade seven education and heavy family responsibilities to carry the burden of the province's economic development?

As well, such a program is highly unlikely to succeed in an economy with a low minimum wage. Participants in NB Works (especially those with more than one child) will not be able to survive if all they can earn is low wages and so be forced to return to social assistance. Furthermore, in a high unemployment economy, even if a participant finds a job, it will be a job that another unemployed person does not get. Such a shuffle of jobs really does not improve the overall situation. Unless McKenna's strategy of bringing investment to the province succeeds, NB Works will not increase the number of jobs, it will only increase the competition for scarce jobs.

Operationally, NB Works suffers from organizational and flexibility problems. Also, the quality of the program is dependent on the quality of its case managers, career counsellors and teachers. While many of these are committed to the program and the participants, there are also some "bad apples" who have spoiled the program for some participants. On the other hand, the team that put together NB Works has shown an amazing ability to respond in a positive manner to many of the problems that occurred in the program's early stages. For example, after the initial evaluation which took place several months into the program, participants' financial problems were responded to by the introduction of a top-up allowance that was to ensure that they did not receive less than they did on welfare. An orientation program was also introduced to explain the program to new participants after some complained of being baffled as to what the whole thing was about. As well, more training was offered to the case managers and career counsellors. The team seemed to be sensitive to the potential effect of displacement on those already employed or unemployed. However, given a program that is conceptually flawed in the first place, with its market orientation, case management and targeting, there is little that a committed team of professional service providers can do for the long term.

Politically, there is the question of the communications strategy which seems to be deliberately misleading. It highlights the successes but appears to operate under a "gag order" on problems and failures. This is possible because the evaluations are controlled by a joint government committee that can (and has) delayed the release of results. We have been told that job placement outcomes may not be made available until after the year 2000. Also, case study data have been collected and analyzed but not released.

It is our view that, for the politicians, the reality of NB Works is just as much about ideology, saving money and appearing to be doing something about cleaning up the welfare mess as it is about providing opportunities to welfare recipients. New Brunswick has one of the highest rates of unemployment in the country and pays the lowest welfare rates. Recent social welfare legislation in the province is based on neoconservative assumptions and ideas that harken back to the Poor Laws which guided the treatment of the poor in New Brunswick up until 1960 (Mullaly and Weinman 1994). We find a statement by Premier McKenna (*Daily Gleaner*, June 15, 1993) to be especially telling with respect to attitudes about social programs and the people who must rely on them. He referred to income assistance programs as those "which foster dependency, which make it *comfortable* for people to do nothing and learn nothing" (emphasis added). In other words, social programs themselves are seen to be the problem. It is social programs, not economic need, that purportedly brings the people to the doors of social service agencies in the first place. Such victim-blaming diverts attention from the real problem which is unemployment.

In addition to focusing the blame for poverty and unemployment on the unemployed, NB Works is also used to reduce welfare costs (one of the stated goals of the program). People are transferred from welfare to NB Works which reduces the number of people on welfare by potentially three thousand after two years of operation. As the federal government is responsible for most of the project's funding, the provincial government experiences reduced welfare costs. When the government announced a decrease in the social assistance caseload in 1994, the total decrease was about the same as the number of people in NB Works (Llewellyn 1995). However, the perception among the public is that the government is cleaning up the welfare mess because there are fewer people in receipt of assistance. To ensure that NB Works does not lose sight of its cost-cutting function, top civil servants from the province's Board of Management (which develops cost-cutting strategies for the government) have been strategically placed as administrative heads (i.e. deputy ministers) of the provincial departments involved with NB Works. Of course, reduced spending serves politicians better than it does welfare recipients.

## THE FUTURE

Perhaps of most concern is the question of what happens in the future. As we tried to show in the four quadrant model (see Figure 2), NB Works is not presently a mandatory workfare program. However, it would not take much to make it so. With the end of CAP in 1996, it would be possible for provinces to require income recipients to participate in a program like NB Works. Such a program would be a quadrant IV program in Figure 2, e.g., a mandatory workfare/learnfare program. The New Brunswick government seems to be moving in this direction. In its 1993 document, *Creating New Options, The Future of Income Support and Employment Related Services*, the issue of mandatory participation is given a prominent role.

Also, the fact that NB Works is a demonstration project, a very expensive one, is cause for concern. There is little likelihood that, in the future, it or a similar program will be offered to persons with low levels of education such as those targeted by NB Works. The province has recently made grade twelve a prerequisite for almost all further training. The only alternative at the present time is New Brunswick's Community Academic Service Program (CASP), a community based program operated on a shoestring budget by the Department of Advanced Education and Labour (MacKeracher 1994: 47). CASP is free for participants but offers only literacy and basic education programs. It is dependent on community and business funding. It is taught by less qualified teachers than are found in the community college system. If this is to become the alternative, no wonder participants believe that NB Works, whatever its problems, is an opportunity too good to pass up. As one participant told us:

Table 1
**Profile of NB Works Participants**

|  |  | Intake 1 | Intake 2 | Intake 3 |
|---|---|---|---|---|
| **Age Groups** |  |  |  |  |
| Under 25 |  | 10% | 13% | 21% |
| 25 - 34 |  | 60% | 51% | 42% |
| 35 - 44 |  | 27% | 34% | 33% |
| 45 - 54 |  | 3% | 2% | 4% |
| **Average Age at time of Intake** |  | 30 yrs | 31 yrs | 32 yrs |
| **Gender** |  |  |  |  |
| Women |  | 86% | 83% | 82% |
| Men |  | 14% | 17% | 18% |
| **Education Level Completed at Time of Intake** |  |  |  |  |
| Grades 1 - 6 |  | 4% | 4% | 3% |
| Grades 7 - 9 |  | 51% | 42% | 44% |
| Grades 10, 11, 12 |  | 34% | 39% | 35% |
| High School Diploma/GED |  | 10% | 16% | 16% |
| Post Secondary |  | 2% | 4% | 3% |
| **Number of Children Needing Care Within Household** | **Total** |  |  |  |
| One | 53.4% | 50.5% | 45.5% | 54.2% |
| Two | 33.6% | 36.9% | 39.2% | 30.8% |
| Three | 10.2% | 10.8% | 12.8% | 10.5% |
| Four or more | 2.7% | 1.8% | 2.5% | 4.5% |
| **Types of Child Care Used (Multiple Mentions Possible)** |  |  |  |  |
| Before/After School | 4.5% | 2.7% | 7.0% | 4.7% |
| Day Care | 18.0% | 14.9% | 12.8% | 20.7% |
| Relative in Home | 35.5% | 21.2% | 24.2% | 33.8% |
| Non-relative in Home | 32.2% | 23.4% | 24.0% | 34.4% |

Source: Data supplied by HRDNB

Table 2
**Exit Report as of January, 1995**

|  | Began NB Works | Total Remaining In NB Works (%) | | Exits (%) | | Exited Not On SA (%) | | Exited & Returned To SA (%) | |
|---|---|---|---|---|---|---|---|---|---|
| INTAKE 1 | 1030 | 342 | (33%) | 688 | | 276 | | 412 | (39%) |
| INTAKE 2 | 959 | 539 | (56%) | 420 | | 155 | | 265 | (26%) |
| INTAKE 3 | 909 | 107 | (78%) | 202 | | 67 | | 135 | (15%) |
| TOTAL | 2898 | 1588 | (55%) | 1310 (44%) | | 498 | (17%) | 812 | (28%) |

Source: Data supplied by HRDNB

> You'd be crazy not to participate. There's never going to be another program like this in the future.

However, with the ending of the CAP there may be more programs like this, only with far less funding and based on mandatory participation.

## NOTES

1. The actual profiles of participants in each of the three intakes (explained in the text) are given in Appendix 1, Table 1.
2. Since more than 80% of the participants are women, we will refer to them as such for convenience of expression.

## REFERENCES

Departments of Advanced Education and Labour and Income Assistance (DAEL and DIA). 1992. *NB Works*. Fredericton: Province of New Brunswick. May.

ERN (Employability Resources Network). 1991. "Enhancing Employability of Welfare Recipients: Literature Review." Winter. Ottawa: Canadian Council on Social Development.

Evans, Patricia M. 1993. "From Workfare to the Social Contract; Implications for Canada of Recent US Welfare Reforms." *Canadian Public Policy* 19 (1): 53-67.

Freeman, Alan. 1993. "New Brunswick Hits Books After Years of Hard Knocks." *Globe and Mail* January 16: B8.

Gherson, Giles. 1992. "N.B. Means New Business." *Reader's Digest*. Westmount, Quebec. December, 103-08. Condensed from *Financial Times of Canada,* July 16, 1992.

Higgins, Mark. 1994. "Volunteer–or Else! New Brunswick Sets the Stage for Workfare." *This Magazine*. August: 6-7.

Holt, Margaret R. 1994. *Women's Experience of Early Discontinuation*. Unpublished Masters of Education Thesis. Fredericton: University of New Brunswick.

Lightman, Ernie S. 1995. "You Can Lead a Horse to Water, but . . . : The Case against Workfare in Canada." In John Richard and Aidan Vining et al., *Helping the Poor: A Qualified Case for Workfare*. Toronto: C.D. Howe Institute.

———. 1991. "Work Incentives Across Canada." *Journal of Canadian Studies* 20 (1): 120-37.

Llewellyn, Stephen. 1995. "Welfare Reforms Criticized." *Daily Gleaner*, March 25.

MacKeracher, Dorothy. 1994. "CASP! Do You Really Want One in Your Neighbourhood?" *Women's Education des femmes*. Spring 11 (1): 47-52.

McFarland, Joan. 1994. "Combining Economic and Social Policy through Work and Welfare." In *Papers on Economic Equality prepared for the Economic Equality Workshop*. Ottawa: Status of Women Canada.

Milne, William J. 1995. "Attachment to the Labour Market: The Status of NB Works." Paper Presented at CERF "Re-tooling the Workforce" Conference. Fredericton, March 31-April 1.

Mullaly, Robert and Joan Weinman. 1994. "A Response to the New Brunswick Government's Social Reform Paper 'Creating New Options.'" *Canadian Review of Social Policy* Winter (34): 94-99.

*NB Works: Annual Report, March 1992 to March 1993*. Fredericton: NB Works Communications.

*NB Works Brochure*. 1993. "The Future is Yours!" August 8. Fredericton: NB Works Communications.

*NB Works Updates*. November 1993, June 1994 and September 1994. Fredericton: NB Works Communications.

New Brunswick, Department of Income Assistance. 1993. *Creating New Options: The Future of Income Support and Employment Related Services*. December.

New Brunswick, Departments of Advanced Education and Labour, and Income Assistance. 1992. "NB Works." May.

PGF Consultants. 1993a. *New Brunswick Works: Report on Evaluative Research Surveying Drop-outs, Case-study Managers and Teachers*. January 5.

———. 1993b. *New Brunswick Works: A Report on Participants' Evaluation*. March 31.

Rein, Martin. 1983. "Work Incentives and Welfare Reform in Britain and the United States." In Bruno Stein and S.M. Miller (eds.), *Incentives and Planning in Social Policy*. Chicago: Aldine.

Swanson, Jean. 1993. "Cheating the Poor." *Canadian Forum* April: 20-23.

———. 1993. *Daily Gleaner*. June 15. Editorial.

York, Geoffrey. 1993. "Ottawa Starts Re-weaving Safety Net: New Brunswick Gives New Life to Those at End of the Road." *Globe and Mail* December 17: A1.

# CHAPTER 14

# HEDGING YOUR DEBTS:
## AN ANALYSIS OF RECENT FEDERAL INITIATIVES IN HIGHER EDUCATION IN CANADA

*Jonathan Greene*

## INTRODUCTION

"Now, more than ever, education means opportunity" (Porter 1965: 167). These words, written in the midst of post-secondary expansion in Canada, are no less true today than they were three decades ago. Today, it is estimated that nearly one-half of the new jobs created in the future will require a post-secondary degree. In 1993, unemployment figures for university graduates equaled 5.7 percent. In contrast, community college graduates and individuals without post-secondary education were twice as likely to be unemployed (9.4 percent and 11.2 percent respectively) (Human Resources Development Canada (HRDC) 1994b: 12). In addition to the differences in employment opportunities, there are sharp discrepancies in income based on levels of educational attainment. Post-secondary graduates, on average, earn almost 50 percent more than those with no "post-secondary qualifications" and university graduates alone earn over 50 percent more than the average Canadian (HRDC 1994b: 12). A recent Organization for Economic Co-operation and Development (OECD) document reported that, in English speaking countries, wage differentials between low and high skilled workers widened over the 1980s. In Canada, "the widening of wage differentials was associated with actual falls in real wages for low-skilled workers" (OECD 1994: 22). Seen in this light, those without the opportunity for a higher education can expect their quality of life to decrease, relative to the rest of the country. What this all leads to is a recognition of the fact that creating access to post-secondary education is an important and indispensable mechanism in the distribution of wealth in contemporary capitalist societies.

As a result of the role the university plays in creating and maintaining a stratified society, gaining access to the university becomes critical in allowing individuals to gain upward income and occupational mobility. If Canada accepts the "liberal" paradigm based on merit, having as one of its main tenets the right to equal opportunity, it is essential that all Canadians have access to a post-secondary institution of their choosing. In the 1960s and '70s, post-secondary education in Canada went through an era of expansion and democratization. Tuition fees were kept at relatively low levels and enrolment patterns consistently were on the rise. Ironically, however, the disparities that existed in attendance at universities between individuals from lower and higher income classes seemed to have only marginally changed (Porter and Jasmin 1987; Pike 1981: 5). Another aspect of this expansion was the growth of

I would like to thank the members of my family, both near and far, who have assisted me by reading draft copies of the paper, pushing and helping me to meet deadlines, and mental support. I would also like to thank the students and others who attended the conference for your energy and for providing me with new insight. Special thanks to Margaret Little for reading draft copies of the paper, providing an ear, mind and mouth when solicited, and for her relentless encouragement.

community and technical colleges in Canada. While the advent of community colleges has been a positive force in creating more choice for students, it is argued that the community college system has the effect of creating a two-tiered post-secondary educational system which maintains social-class divisions within society. Community colleges have lower tuition fees, draw a larger proportion of students from working class homes and, on average, lead to less prestigious occupations with lower incomes (HRDC 1994b: 10; Pike 1981: 6; Statistics Canada 1992-93: 174, 179). During the 1980s, much of the growth in post-secondary enrolments came about due to the fact that women began entering post-secondary institutions in greater numbers. While this went a long way in breaking down divisions based on sex, it was ineffective in reducing the disparities based on income class, since most of these women have come from middle and upper class homes (Guppy and Pendakur 1989: 60).

Over the last three decades tuition fees have been relatively low and the quality of post-secondary education has enabled Canadians to compete within the international economy. However, in recent years the federal government's commitment to the effective maintenance of quality and accessibility has been waning. Since 1982, there has been consistent reductions in the rate of growth of federal fiscal transfers to the provinces on behalf of post-secondary education. Since 1990, federal funding of post-secondary institutions has been frozen. Coinciding with this fiscal "prudence" has been a new emphasis on the role of the "individual" as the main beneficiary of a university education. This has allowed for a new dialogue to take place which seeks to place a larger share of the costs of education on the individual attending university.

The purpose of this paper is to continue the dialogue that began among Canadians during the social security review (SSR) process concerning the future role of the federal government in ensuring quality of, and access to, post-secondary education in Canada. This will be done through an analysis of recent federal initiatives in higher education. The paper is divided into two main sections. The first section will review and analyze the two main proposals put forward by the federal government during the social security review. The second section will examine briefly the possible effects of the changes to the funding arrangements for post-secondary education as laid down in the 1995 federal *Budget Plan*. The conclusion reached is that these initiatives threaten the future viability of creating the conditions for equal access to a higher education. In addition, in concurrence with earlier analyses both in Canada and elsewhere, it has been found that while tuition fees are essential for creating accessibility, low tuition fees by themselves will not achieve the maximum result. It is necessary to utilize a "holistic" approach which seeks to include and address other factors that play a role in educational choice.

## THE SOCIAL SECURITY REVIEW

Two policy proposal documents released by the federal government between October 1994 and January 1995 formed the basis for the debate that ensued during the four months of the social security review process. *Improving Social Security In Canada: A Discussion Paper* (HRDC 1994a) was the first of these documents, released on October 5, 1994. Chapter Three, "Learning: Making Lifelong Learning A Way of Life," dealt exclusively with post-secondary education and training, unveiling the federal government's two options which would form the basis of a new era of federal involvement in post-secondary education. The second document, *Federal Support to Post-Secondary Education: A Supplementary Paper*, was released four months later to "provide Canadians with more detailed information about the current system and the options outlined in the *Discussion Paper*" (HRDC 1994b: Preface). This document dealt exclusively with post-secondary education reform. In both publications there is a shift from the collective provision of educational opportunity to one where the individual as the main benefactor assumes more responsibility. This is explicit in the Department of Finance's *Economic and Fiscal Update*:

> And while society gains collectively from the skills of its citizens, the greatest beneficiaries of investment in human capital are individuals themselves, in terms of both life time financial return and potential for personal development (Department of Finance 1994: 42).

One of the options presented is to maintain the current federal-provincial funding arrangement under Established Programs Financing–Post-Secondary Education (EPF-PSE). Beginning in 1996-97, this plan would restore the EPF-PSE transfer to the 1993-94 level which was about $6.1 billion in total. The transfer would then be frozen at this level until such time as the cash portion of the transfer became zero, estimated to be in about ten years (HRDC 1994a: 25). (See Table 1 in the Appendix that summarizes changes in federal provincial arrangements for post-secondary funding from 1977-95.)

Adoption of this option would be detrimental to the continued viability of the post-secondary education sector as it exists today. Because the costs of maintaining the post-secondary education system have been increasing on an annual basis, the continual freeze on the total transfer would mean that the disparity between public expenditures and costs would continue to grow. Subsequently, post-secondary institutions would have to react in one of two ways, or a combination of both. Tuition fees could be raised on an annual basis to meet the rising costs, or the institutions could take measures to save costs, which would affect the quality of education. In essence, it would be an acceptance of the current scenario and the methods that have been used to cope with the fiscal crisis through the last decade. Throughout the 1980s, tuition fees increased on an annual basis (Martinson 1994: 36), more part-time and sessional lecturers were hired compared to full-time faculty (Rajagopal and Farr 1992: 322-27), and the infrastructures of the universities have been allowed to deteriorate (AUCC 1991: 19; Duhamel 1992: 5-6). If this continues, access to university will be reduced as a result of the tuition increases, consequently the ability of Canadian students to achieve academic excellence and compete on an international stage will be sharply curtailed due to a decreased quality of education.

The second proposal is to replace the current EPF arrangement with a new system of loans based on the income contingency principle. Beginning in 1996-97, the federal government would replace the declining cash transfer with two billion dollars in loans to be phased in over a period of five years. By the end of a decade there would be an extra two billion dollars in the post-secondary sector because the tax points that would remain with the provinces will increase to the point where they would be worth over six billion dollars. This is about what the total frozen transfer is worth at this time under EPF. The amount of money allocated for the program would be capped at two billion dollars. Consequently, it would be essential to either set limits on the loans, relate loan amounts to the cost of tuition, and/or create a strict set of guidelines for which schools and programs would be eligible for the loan to ensure that the number of users would not exceed the total amount available. The new loan program would operate independently from the current Canada Student Loan Program (CSLP) and obtaining a loan under this system would not be based on "need." CSLP would supposedly act as a complement to the new program, remaining as a loan program for those in "need."

There are two main components of the federal plan which could have an effect on access to post-secondary education. First, the plan involves the elimination of the cash transfer portion of the EPF-PSE total transfer. As this takes place, tuition begins to increase out of the necessity to replace the lost revenue from the declining cash transfer. By the time the total transfer is eliminated, tuition would have at least doubled and would continue to rise thereafter at a rate of between 7 and 10 percent a year (HRDC 1994b: 32). Second, a new Income Contingent Loan Repayment Plan (ICLRP) would be implemented with interest accumulating on the loan from the moment the loan transaction takes place, at market interest rates. This is in contrast to the current policy of forgiving the interest on the loan until after an individual completes his/her education. In order to fully understand the effects of these changes, it is necessary to analyze each component in isolation. It should be recognized, however, that within the federal plan these two components went "hand in hand." In other words, the income contingent loan plan acted as a mechanism for the government to curtail its transfers for post-secondary education.

One factor common to many proponents of increasing tuition fees is the assumption that low tuition fees have little or no correlation with increasing access to university (AUCC 1991: 95; Government of Canada 1987; Levin 1990: 53; Stager 1989). Evidence is provided by citing the fact that, even though tuition fees have been relatively low, the socio-economic demographics of universities in Canada have not changed to any great extent. On this basis, maintaining low tuition fees, through the use of general tax revenue, amounts to a regressive economic policy (AUCC 1991: 95; Levin 1990: 53). David Stager concurs (1989: 52) with this argument, adding that it should not be "surprising" that changes in fees have a small impact on enrolment since the tuition fee is a small fraction of the student's total cost of university, accounting for only about 15 percent of the total cost. These arguments have led some observers to the belief that, even if tuition were free, there would not be a corresponding increase in enrolment among individuals from the lower income classes (AUCC 1991: 95; Government of Canada 1987: 47).

There is evidence that suggests the opposite, however. A recent study undertaken in the United States found that there is a correlation between tuition charges and a student's decision to enrol.[1] "For students from low income families, grant amounts were significant and positively associated with enrollment, while tuition was significant and negative" (St. John 1990: 169). When all variables were held constant, increases in grants and decreases in tuition had the largest probabilities of increasing enrolment (St. John 1990: 169). David Stager (1989: 52-53) addresses this issue in his study, *Focus on Fees*, citing an "excellent review of twenty-five studies" to the effect that it was found that a 10 percent increase in tuition fees results in a decrease in enrolment of 6 percent. Several other studies find that "enrollment response to tuition changes differs according to student ability, family income and other factors. Students with high ability, or from high income families, were the least responsive to tuition changes."

Based on these analyses, it seems difficult to conclude that tuition changes have a relatively small impact on enrolment, particularly in the context of the proposals outlined during the social security review. Considering that the 6 percent of individuals who would be affected by the tuition changes would come disproportionately from lower income classes, we can conclude that there is a class bias in any plan that seeks to increase tuition fees. It must also be remembered that the 6 percent affected represents a decrease from the population that already attends a post-secondary institution, excluding the entire population who currently does not attend a post-secondary institution. In this light, the policy would not only be regressive, but it would also be a passive policy in that it is absent in any of the programs to ameliorate the current disparities that already exist.

Looked at in another way, maintaining low tuition fees, with no other programs to increase access in place, has not been completely fruitless. There has been some movement among lower income groups into university. Porter and Jasmin (1987: 23) found that in 1983 26 percent of undergraduates in university came from the lowest income background studied ($0-$22,000). Therefore, while the movement is small, it has not been entirely absent. If approached in this manner, without even considering what the effect would be on future generations of prospective students, the question that must be answered is what affect tuition increases have on those individuals from lower income backgrounds who are currently attending university?

Present indications suggest that over the last decade there has been an increase in the number of students who live in poverty resulting from increases in tuition fees. For example, over the last eight years five post-secondary institutions in Manitoba have opened up food banks on campus. "Food bank volunteers stressed increased costs of tuition and books as a major factor behind food bank use" (Winnipeg Harvest 1994). In 1990 and 1991 tuition increased at a rate three times that of inflation. In 1992 and 1993 inflation increased by less than 2 percent while tuition increased by over 8 and 9 percent respectively (Beauchesne 1994: C3). What appears to have taken place, partially as a result of tuition increases, is not a reduction in enrolment, as would be expected, but an increase in impoverishment among university students. This suggests that we must view tuition fees not as a single cost compartment but as a single component of the overall cost.

Students have a single pool of money that is utilized for all purposes. If the cost of one area is increased, for example tuition fees, then the individual is automatically forced to take money out of another area of expenditure, such as food, shelter or clothing to pay for the increased costs of tuition. As Noami Stoakes (Canadian Federation of Students 1991: 36) points out, tuition costs are the most difficult to manipulate because they are a "fixed" cost. Living costs, while being "fixed" by owners of production and merchants, are more easily controlled by the individual because they can simply "choose" to go without or reduce their consumption. Thus, it may be useful to analyze what drives these individuals to forgo a sustainable living in order to attend university, when we know that a majority of individuals from lower income classes do not even attend university. As will be seen later in the paper, this may be partially explained by variables other than the rate of tuition.

## THE TUITION FEE DISCOURSE[2]

A positive by product that has resulted from the current tuition fee discourse has been re-focusing the debate onto other areas. This is essentially a re-examination based on an acceptance of the findings of earlier studies (Pike 1970; Porter et al. 1973). These studies name other factors, mainly economic and environmental, affecting individuals early in life, as having an impact on academic choices (AUCC 1991: 96; Government of Canada 1987: 48; Levin 1990; Porter et al. 1973). Based on these findings, Edward St. John (1990: 173) concludes there is a three stage model that explains the college choice process:

> First, students develop a predisposition to attend college, based on their backgrounds and early school experiences. This predisposition to attend could develop as early as the ninth grade. Then, in high-school, students begin their college search, which is influenced by the high school experience and search activities, resulting in a choice set. Choices about which school to attend of the institutions a student applies to—and whether to attend—come only as the final stage in the process. Responsiveness to changes in tuition charges and aid amounts are most likely to have an impact in the final stage of the college choice process. Therefore, the number of potential college applicants is limited by the time students reach their senior year in high school. In fact, whether a student will apply to college can be predicted with greater accuracy than whether an applicant will attend.

The new discourse seeks to focus on the first and second phases. Frances Stage and Don Hossler (1989) note there are four factors that play a role in whether an individual will attend university. These include family income, parental levels of education, student academic achievement and parental encouragement. Evidence in Canada seems to support this contention. Porter and Jasmin (1987: 21-23) found that individuals from families where the father worked in an occupation classified as "skilled," "semi-skilled," or "crafts and trades" were almost twice as likely to be in a career program at a community college than were those whose father was in a "managerial," "semi-professional" or "professional occupation." In sharp contrast, only between 2 and 3 percent of all post-secondary students came from families whose father was classified as a "labourer." The disparities were even more dramatic when parental education was taken into account. Students with parents who had not achieved a high school degree were five times as likely to attend a community college than were those whose parents had a university degree (Porter and Jasmin 1987: 21).

There is also reason to believe that the problems may extend beyond the family situation into the institutional system of public education itself. Those working within the school may serve to "dampen the ambition" of individuals with certain ascribed characteristics (Pike 1980: 9). The Economic Council of Canada has noted that socio-economic status affects both a student's performance at school and the types of courses s/he will take. Two important factors in creating, maintaining and eradicating this situation are the "atmosphere of the school and the attitudes of the teachers and principles" (ECC 1992: 8). Accordingly, any study of barriers towards attending university in the first and second phase of decision-making, must take into account not only the effects of an individual's socio-economic status, but also the way in which the system itself may be geared to differentiate between the classes.

A shortcoming in this new discourse is that it tends to take as a given that students think consciously about attending a post-secondary institution early on in life. In reality, it seems more likely that for many individuals the thought of attending a post-secondary institution, whether it be university or college, has not even entered the equation. A growing proportion of the population in Canada is living in poverty. Given the fact that these people are unable to provide for basic living needs, it would not be surprising to find that these individuals have never even considered the possibility of attending a post-secondary institution. More emphasis must be placed on those individuals who do not make it through the first phase of St. John's model. Consequently, it becomes necessary to discuss access in terms of a much broader picture of the entire welfare state and its function within Canada as a provider of opportunity. By ensuring access to post-secondary education, it might be found that poverty is reduced. However, only by eradicating poverty and the institutional biases that affect the future direction of children will equal opportunity to attend a post-secondary institution will be created. Fifteen years ago Robert Pike (1980: 134) made this point quite succinctly:

> ... it is reasonable to suggest that if a country does not make major efforts to foster a greater equality of income and living conditions, but attempts rather to remove educational inequalities solely through the resources of the school, then the policy-makers stand to be branded as hypocrites for their unwillingness to seek to remedy the economic determinants of educational inequalities at the source. They are bound to fail in their school-related measures because of the primacy of family and neighborhood in the process of socialization.

It is important to recognize that within the Canadian context the acceptance of the new discourse on access, while being valuable, has often come at the expense of the need to maintain accessible tuition fees. In this sense, we must be watchful of those who advocate a "multi-faceted" approach because it tends to mean addressing certain factors at the expense of others. This has led some people to believe that simply offering increased loan amounts through a more progressive loan system, in conjunction with an increased emphasis on early age factors, will be sufficient. Hence, the propagation of an income contingent loan repayment plan.

## THE INCOME CONTINGENT LOAN PLAN

Numerous variations of an income contingent loan plan have been put forward. However, the concept appears to be based, indeed praised, on one universal principle—that it is progressive. The program is considered progressive because it is grounded in the principle that individuals will pay according to their earnings, therefore reducing the risk that fixed payment loan plans place on low income earners. Accessibility to university is then increased because the loan will be more palatable to prospective students who will not have to worry about being burdened by unmanageable payments when their income is low (West 1993: 27). Some argue that by placing the economic burden more squarely on the individual recipients of higher education, a financial burden is lifted from the public treasury and the regressive components of a low tuition policy are eliminated (Stager 1989: 118). As loans are to be collected through the income tax system, their collection becomes more administratively efficient removing the default problems associated with the CSLP (AUCC 1991: 96; Friedman 1955: 140; West 1993: 29-30).

The federal government's new loan plan would coincide with a reduction in fiscal transfers. This will place upward pressure on tuition fees but "may be a necessary price to pay to put in place a permanent system for ensuring accessibility for post-secondary education" (HRDC 1994a: 63). Graduates who have borrowed money through the program would pay back a portion of the loan on an annual basis. The rate of repayment would be based on a percentage of the individual's annual income. The less money one earns the lower the rate of repayment. Repayment would take place through the income tax system and, while low income earners (below $15,000) would be protected from making payments, they would not be protected from accumulating increasing amounts of debt as the interest would continue to accrue until the loan was paid in full or forgiven. It was mentioned that there could be a ceiling on repayment, either at a certain debt level or age, but this was tempered by reminding us that "the cost of providing such measures could of course be substantial" (HRDC 1994b: 40).

As a concept, an income contingent loan repayment plan does have the potential to be progressive. By its nature repayment would be based on how much one earns. This should mean that those who earn less income would pay less of the costs of their loan overall, in comparison to higher income earners. However, under the federal government's plan and, other income contingency schemes, the lower income earner would not pay less overall, but would pay less on an annual basis. This has led one commentator to describe the program as "income-sensitive," rather than "income-contingent" (Hauptman 1990: 48). Low income earners would pay more overall because they would be paying less on an annual basis, accumulating more debt from interest than an individual who earns a higher income and who pays off the loan at a quicker pace. Once the increases in tuition and the accompanying accumulating interest charges are taken into account, students earning lower or no income could be accepting a lifelong debt.

There is reason to believe that, psychologically, people do not want to burden themselves with large amounts of debt. The Smith Commission (AUCC 1991: 195) acknowledged this in its final report when it noted that "the prospects of large amounts of indebtedness has been shown to be especially daunting to people who come from less affluent families." The St. John (1990: 169) study also found that increasing loan limits and availability had no affect on enrolment among students from lower income families. Even with an income contingent loan plan, where supposedly the risks are reduced, there is cause for concern. Peter Leslie (1980: 345) raised some important points on the topic in his 1980 study for the AUCC:

> This is a scheme which is far from being unattractive, but any optimism that an all-loan program would have little adverse effect on accessibility must be doubted. One's guide on these matters should not be abstract reasoning, but the abundant sociological evidence which reveals the unwillingness of young people, particularly from lower income levels, to assume heavy long-term debt. The contingent repayment idea is of course designed precisely to overcome such "loan aversion" by eliminating the risk involved in borrowing, but the truth is that we cannot predict how young people would react to a plan based on the contingent repayment principle. The mere fact that it is labeled a "loan," and the terms are complex, is likely to constitute a real if "merely" psychological barrier.

There appears to be enough evidence which supports the existence of psychological barriers to schemes seeking to place a larger economic burden on students to raise doubts about the utility of the plan. In the absence of any evidence to allay these fears, accepting an income contingency policy would be like taking a "stab in the dark" and "hoping for a bulls eye." Canada has the resources to be more careful in developing its policies through a careful analysis of the situation and a participatory and democratic process. Implementing programs that are not based on any firm foundation is to accept a long-term policy that may or may not meet its stated goal.

The income contingent program is also regressive because there is an element of discrimination built into the program based on gender and race. Women continue to be under-represented in a number of areas that have the potential to produce larger incomes and, in most occupational fields, women graduates earn lower average incomes than men (Statistics Canada 1992-93: 50, 52, 56, 174, 179). As a result women would be more likely to assume lower rates of repayment. Hence they will pay for a longer period of time and, as a result, pay more overall. Similarly, it has been argued recently that, while visible minorities have attained an equal status in educational and occupational attainment with "whites" and "white minorities," they have yet to receive comparable income status (Herberg 1990). The effects of this are the same as that for women. It will take them longer to pay off their debt, therefore they will also pay much more than their counterparts of equal educational and occupational status.

There is one more issue that must be addressed concerning an income contingency program. It may have the effect of relegating low income earners to a life of poverty as members of the "working poor." In the event that an individual completes university and is unable to find a job, s/he would be shielded from making payments at that time. However, when the individual gains employment that provides a relatively low income, but not low enough to be below the threshold level, the individual must begin making payments on the loan. It is possible that making these payments could result in the individual not having enough money to sustain him or herself. Therefore, although individuals have been able to find employment, loan repayment schedules relegate them to the ranks of the "working poor."

## THE 1995 FEDERAL BUDGET PLAN

The changes outlined in the federal government's *1995 Budget Plan* (Department of Finance 1995) released in February effectively terminated any of the post-secondary education proposals and discussions undertaken during the social security review. The budget calls for the consolidation of the two programs, EPF and the Canada Assistance Plan (CAP), into one monetarily reduced block transfer, the Canada Health and Social Transfer (CHST). In exchange for the fiscal reductions, the provinces were given increased decision-making power to decide in what proportion the transfer would be allocated to each of the three programs: health, post-secondary education and social assistance. In relation to post-secondary education, the budget has a two-fold effect. First, because the provinces have been given less money to spend on social programs as a whole, post-secondary education will certainly face cutbacks in transfers from provincial governments. This will result in a combination of increased tuition fees and a reduced quality of education. Second, any hope of maintaining comparable standards across the provinces of quality and tuition fee levels could be lost, without a concerted effort by the provinces to maintain such a system.

According to the budget, "the reduction in transfers to provinces in 1996-97 compared to 1994-95 is 4.4 percent" (Department of Finance 1995: 54). This figure is misleading because it takes into account the value of the CHST, beginning in 1996-97, plus equalization. Under the budget the equalization formula has not been changed, so the value of equalization payments will increase, offsetting part of the effect of the reduced fiscal transfer under the CHST. However, if all the current fiscal arrangements had remained in place, the equalization payments would have increased regardless; thus, including them in the analysis regarding revenue loss by the provinces serves to lessen the extent of reduction that has taken place. When the CHST replaces EPF and CAP in 1996-97, without taking into account the increase in equalization, there will be an 8.42 percent reduction across the board for the three programs. There will be a reduction in transfers equaling about 15 percent for each program over the two year period 1996-98.[3]

In the past, although the transfers for post-secondary education have always been unconditional under EPF, there was a sense of certainty that there would be a reliable amount of money for higher education because a specific portion of the total EPF transfer was "earmarked" for this function.[4] While this has not produced equality, it has allowed the system to maintain a certain amount of parity between the provinces in offering post-secondary education. Tuition levels have not deviated to any great extent between provinces and the quality of education has been relatively even. Differences in quality appear mainly at the graduate levels which, in large part, have to do with professorial research, academic resources, number of course offerings, availability of teaching and research assistantships, and money for students to attend the institution.

The relative parity that has existed between universities has now been undermined by the ability of the provinces to fund universities as they see fit. One province may choose to allocate more resources to post-secondary education than others. In a similar fashion, some governments may choose to focus more heavily on community and technical colleges rather than universities, or vice versa. Both of these situations will create a disparity across the country in access and quality. This raises questions concerning the federal role in higher education, particularly as an arbiter of the creation and maintenance of "national" standards. Because access and quality are concerns, two long-standing arguments for a federal presence remain cogent.

First, the provinces do not have the same revenue raising capacities. Any federal reduction in fiscal transfers to the provinces has uneven consequences across the country. It has recently been estimated that for every dollar reduction in EPF transfers, the tax effort required to replace the dollar is between 17 and 39 percent greater in the "have not" provinces than it is for the three "have" provinces (Hobson and St-Hilaire 1993: 39). This being the case, the wealthy provinces, if they are willing, will find it easier to maintain higher expenditures on post-secondary education, creating a further balkanization of the post-secondary system.

The second issue, "spillovers," refers to the fact that the benefits of provincial expenditure in one area may provide economic benefits to other provinces, at no cost to the other provinces. This is the case with higher education when individuals who are trained in one province utilize their skills in another province. In his study of inter-provincial migration, Alan Maslove (1992) found that mobility between provinces increases steadily with increased educational attainment. However, the benefits of this migration are unevenly distributed between the provinces. Only Ontario and British Columbia are net recipients of individuals within the three highest educational groups studied and only Ontario, B.C. and Alberta have a positive inflow of individuals with at least one university degree. As a result of these externalities, those provinces who are net "losers" may be inclined to "underspend" on education because the total benefits from that educated workforce will not equal the expenditures to train those individuals (Hobson and St-Hilaire 1993: 17). Maslove (1992: 70) concurs with this analysis, concluding that his results "suggest that the mobility of individuals with post-secondary education, particularly under the age 45, is potentially large enough to affect provincial government decisions on PSE expenditures." Federal intrusion is thus necessary to ensure that there are "national" standards of educational access and quality.

If the provinces are left solely responsible for determining PSE expenditures the end result could be that the Canadian post-secondary education system will mirror that of their American counterparts. In the United States the massive growth of private universities has created a large gap between the best and worst universities. As a consequence, the already enormous competition between individuals for acceptance to the better universities will most likely be compounded and, as a result, will have a discriminatory effect on those individuals who have been accepted to higher quality institutions in another province, but do not have the economic resources to attend. Potentially qualified students will then be relegated to accepting a second or third class education. In addition, the Canadian economy will suffer if disparities in quality reach a certain magnitude. Canadians will not be as well trained as their international counterparts to compete in the technologically advanced global economy.

Access to, and the quality of, education are already being compromised as a result of the budget. First, the Canada Scholarship Program (CSP) is being eliminated. The CSP provides up to 2500 renewable tuition scholarships worth $2500 dollars to eligible students in math, science and engineering programs. As part of the program, half of the scholarships were targeted and awarded to women in an effort to bolster their numbers in these programs. In terms of sheer numbers the program appears to have been successful. According to Peggy Berkowitz (1995: 7) between 1988 and 1993 women's enrolment in science and engineering disciplines, traditionally a preserve of men, increased by 37 percent at the same time overall female enrolment only increased by 15 percent. Second, the Social Sciences and Humanities Research Council of Canada (SSHRC) and the Natural Sciences and Engineering Research Council (NSERC) will see their funding reduced by $77 million over the next three years (Department of Finance 1995: 100). This could hurt students both directly, if part of that lost funding comes from fellowships and, indirectly, because their professors will have less opportunity to conduct research that allows them to be on the "cutting edge" of their fields which often translates into a more knowledgeable staff and a better education. Research also brings prestige to a university—equally important because a degree from a prestigious university can result in more employment opportunities. NSERC has already begun to eliminate programs. One of the first targets has been undergraduate scholarships for large universities.[5]

Third, numerous universities and colleges have once again announced tuition increases for the 1995-96 academic year. As a result of this we can infer, based on prior experience, that either enrolment will be reduced, more students will be forced to rely on campus food banks or both. Whatever the outcome, the effects of these increases will not be neutral. They will have a disproportionate affect on individuals from lower socio-economic classes.

## CONCLUSION

Access to a post-secondary education is one of the keystones to upward socio-economic mobility in Canada. Throughout the 1960s and 1970s, although tuition remained relatively low and enrolment continued to rise, the socio-demographics of the university changed little. The one bright spot for those interested in breaking down class barriers has been the increase in the proportion of women who attend university and community colleges. However, beginning in the 1980s the federal commitment to maintaining access to a quality post-secondary education, like many other social services, has been reduced as a result of the current fiscal "crunch."

With this new era of "fiscal management" has come a new and revitalized discussion concerning the role of the state as a provider of publicly subsidized higher education. Whereas in the 1960s and '70s there was little question that society was the main benefactor of an educated population, today there is a reversal where the individual is seen as the main benefactor of a higher education. This was the starting point for the federal government at the outset of the social security review. From this point of view, then, it should not be surprising that the options outlined by the federal government during the review had as their aim the elimination of federal transfers to the provinces. The two proposals were quite similar. They would have effectively eliminated the federal government from direct subsidization of higher education. The first option, maintaining EPF, would have made the process long and drawn out as the effects would creep up slowly as they have in this last decade. The second option, replacing the cash transfer with the new income contingent loan program, would have achieved the same result but much more quickly. Both options are regressive because they make it more difficult for low income earners to attend post-secondary institutions. As a rule, whenever a fee is raised for entrance to an institution, it becomes more exclusionary.

The federal budget plan following the review process set out a program that effectively allowed the government to achieve part of the goal set out in the discussion paper (HRDC 1994a) because it decreased the value of the fiscal transfers to the provinces. Indeed, the federal government was able to decrease the transfers without installing more money for loans. In this way, they had achieved much of what they had hoped for while, at the same time, disencumbering themselves of a political "hot potato." The budget, however, not only decreases the fiscal transfers but places the future of higher education in the hands of ten provincial governments who, in spite of their similarities still maintain different electorates, different agendas and varying financial resources. With both the federal reductions and the complete decentralization of power, it is fair to say that the possibilities for parity across provincial borders seem in danger, as does public subsidization of higher education.

If anything has been gained from these two recent initiatives, it has been a greater understanding of the difficulties in creating accessibility for higher education. Access does not begin with low tuition fees. As St. John noted, low tuition fees come into play in the last phase of the entire college choice process. Creating opportunity begins with the alleviation of poverty and the breakdown of institutional and systemic barriers which seem to serve the vested interests of a stratified society by eliminating the competition. Therefore, as one group of commentators put it, while "we may espouse equality of opportunity through open admissions standards for higher education, we do not follow through by providing the conditions whereby people experience equal opportunity to benefit" (Corman, Barr and Caputo 1992: 24). The important aspect of any approach is to recognize that both economic and environmental factors, including tuition rates, play a role in determining access. What is needed is a "holistic" approach in an effort to create universal access. Only when there is a concerted effort to eliminate these barriers will Canadians be able to speak freely and truthfully about accessibility to higher education.

## APPENDIX

### Table 1
Summary of federal-provincial programs and initiatives
for post-secondary education 1977-1995

| Year | Program/Proposal | Commentary |
|---|---|---|
| 1977 | Established Programs Financing (EPF) | Falls under the terms of the Federal-Provincial Fiscal Arrangements and Established Programs Financing Act, encompassing both health care and post-secondary education. EPF provides an equal per capita, unconditional, block funded grant to the provinces. The post-secondary portion of the transfer is known as EPF-PSE, comprising 32.1 percent of the total EPF grant. The initial grant was set at about fifty percent of the per capita expenditures for PSE in the top two provinces in 1976-77, multiplied by population. The total grant is transferred through the twin mechanisms of a cash transfer and a transfer of equalized personal and corporate income tax points. An additional two tax points were transferred as a replacement for the lost revenue guarantee under the previous arrangement. Annual cash transfer increases equal the average growth of the gross national product (GNP) for the previous three years, multiplied by population. The value of the tax points are independent of the GNP escalator.

Cash Transfer = Total Transfer - Equalized Tax Points |
| 1982 | EPF-PSE: revised | The GNP escalator is changed to include both the cash and tax transfer. The cash transfer equals the difference between the total transfer and the equalized tax points. The federal government also recoups from the provinces the two extra tax points given in 1977. |
| 1983 | EPF-PSE: revised | Federal transfers are limited to increases of six percent in 1983-84 and five percent in 1984-85. |
| 1986 | EPF-PSE: revised | GNP escalator is changed from the growth of GNP to the growth of GNP - 2 percent. |
| 1989 | EPF-PSE: revised | The GNP escalator is reduced to GNP - 3 percent. |

| 1990 | EPF-PSE: revised | The total federal transfer is frozen at the 1989 per capita level for two years. Increases for population growth are maintained. |
|---|---|---|
| 1991 | EPF-PSE: revised | The freeze on the per capita payments is extended until 1994-95. |
| 1994 | EPF-PSE: proposal | Two options were put forth by the federal government during the social security review in 1994-95. One called for the renewal of the freeze on the total EPF-PSE transfer, resulting in the elimination of the cash transfer. Each year the economy grows, the value of the tax points increases. As the tax points increase, the cash transfer decreases by an equal amount. Due to the freeze, it was been estimated that the cash transfer would reach zero within a decade. |
| 1994 | Income Contingent Loan Repayment Plan (ICLRP): Proposal | ICLRP was the second option put forth by the federal government during the social security review. The program involved the elimination of the cash transfer portion of EPF within one to five years, to be replaced with $2 billion dollars in loans under the principles of ICLRP. The components of ICLRP were as follows:<br>— Interest would have begun to accrue on the loan at market interest rates immediately upon negotiation of the loan, continuing until the loan was paid in full or forgiven.<br>— Repayment is based as a percentage of an individual's annual income. The lower the income, the lower the annual rate of repayment. If an individual's income fell below a stated level s/he would not be expected to make payments. During the time that payments were not made interest would have continued to accrue on the outstanding debt.<br>— Loan repayments would take place through the income tax system.<br>— Possibility of a repayment ceiling on the loan. After a certain number of years if the loan had not yet been fully repaid the loan would be forgiven.<br>— The program would have been available for all students regardless of "need," acting as a complement to the "needs" based Canada Students Loan Program. |
| 1995 | Canada Health and Social Transfer (CHST) | Program outlined in the 1995 federal budget. Begin- |

ning in 1996-97, EPF and the Canada Assistance Plan (a federal-provincial cost sharing program) will be amalgamated into one block funded program, the CHST. CHST will remain in force through 1997-98. The provinces have been given a total two-year fiscal transfer reduction of about $4.5 billion dollars for these programs than would have been the case if both EPF and CAP remained in place. In return, the provinces have been given complete control over how this money will be divided between the three major programs, health, post-secondary education, social assistance and welfare services. Until CHST comes into effect in 1996-97, the current arrangements for these programs will remain in force. In 1998-99, if no new funding arrangement is completed, EPF will again become effective, utilizing the GNP - 3 percent escalator.

## NOTES

1.  Earlier studies in Canada have suggested that there may be a link between an individual's socio-economic status, tuition fees and a student's decision to enrol in a post-secondary institution (Porter et al. 1973: 34, 80-81, 129; Pike 1970: 106).

2.  An important factor in understanding statements concerning access is to understand the methodology utilized for that purpose. Researchers and policy-makers should be "wary" about relying too heavily on the use of statistical data as a measure of the role of tuition fees as an indicator of access. Utilizing statistical analysis has played an important role in assessing who attends university and providing researchers with "focus" groups for attention. However, statistical data that seeks to compartmentalize the effects of certain factors, in this case tuition fees, does so at the expense of seeing the role that numerous factors play in tandem with one another. This has possibly led to misconceptions about the role of tuition in creating access. According to recent analyses, increases in tuition should result in a corresponding decrease in enrolment. Yet, we know that although tuition has increased by over 100 percent, enrolment has also continued to rise (Lynd 1994: 13; Martinson 1994: 36). Therefore, a simple analysis of the statistics does not give us further insight into the current problems; indeed it masks the problems and underplays the possible effects of tuition increases.

3.  For analytical purposes, these figures are based on the assumption that each program will receive an equal share of the reductions.

4.  It has been argued that some of the provinces did not allocate all of the money earmarked for post-secondary education into education. Tim Sale, in a report prepared for the Economic Council of Canada, found that between 1977-78 and 1985-86, an increasing proportion of the transfer allotted for post-secondary education had been diverted to health care (Sale 1992: 16-17).

5.  For further information on the current changes in program funding at NSERC see page 19 of the February 1995 edition of *University Affairs*. Ottawa: Association of Universities and Colleges of Canada and Canadian Universities Foundation.

## REFERENCES

Association of Universities and Colleges of Canada (AUCC). 1991. *Report: Commission of Inquiry on Canadian University Education.* Ottawa: Association of Universities and Colleges of Canada.

Beauchesne, Eric. 1994. "Inflation Low, Tuition Soaring Stats Can Says." *Toronto Star,* October 15: C3.

Berkowitz, Peggy. 1995. "Wooing Women to Science: Who Will Pay?" *University Affairs* February: 6-8.

Canadian Federation of Students. 1991. *Compromising Access: A Critical Analysis of Income Contingent Loan and Post-Secondary Education Funding Schemes.* Ottawa: Canadian Federation of Students.

Corman, June, Lynn Barr and Tullio Caputo. 1992. "Unpacking Attrition: A Change of Emphasis." *The Canadian Journal of Higher Education* 22 (3): 15-27.

Department of Finance. 1995. *Budget Plan 1995.* Ottawa: Minister of Supply and Services

————. 1994. *Creating a Healthy Fiscal Climate: The Economic and Fiscal Update.* Ottawa: Minister of Supply and Services.

Duhamel, Ronald. 1992. *The Federal Role in Education: A Policy Document.* Ottawa: Liberal Party of Canada.

Economic Council of Canada (EEC). 1992. *A Lot to Learn: Education and Training in Canada.* Ottawa: Economic Council of Canada.

Friedman, Milton. 1955. "The Role of Government in Education." In R.A. Solo (ed.), *Economics and the Public Interest.* New Brunswick: Rutgers University Press.

Government of Canada. 1987. *Report of the Standing Senate Committee on National Finance: Federal Policy on Post-Secondary Education.* Ottawa: Government of Canada.

Guppy, Neil and Krishna Pendakur. 1989. "The Effects of Gender and Parental Education on Participation Within Post-Secondary Education in the 1970s and 1980s." *The Canadian Journal of Higher Education* 19 (1): 49-62.

Hauptman, Arthur M. 1990. *The Tuition Dilemma: Assessing New Ways to Pay for College.* Washington, D.C.: The Brookings Institution.

Herberg, Edward N. 1990. "The Ethno-Racial Socio-Economic Hierarchy in Canada: Theory and Analysis of the New Vertical Mosaic." *International Journal of Comparative Sociology* 31 (3-4): 206-21.

Hobson, Paul A.R. and Frances St-Hilaire. 1993. *Reforming Federal–Provincial Fiscal Arrangements: Towards Sustainable Federalism.* Montreal: Institute for Research on Public Policy.

Human Resources Development Canada. 1994a. *Improving Social Security in Canada: A Discussion Paper.* Ottawa: Minister of Supply and Services.

————. 1994b. *Federal Support to Post-Secondary Education in Canada: A Supplementary Paper.* Ottawa: Minister of Supply and Services.

Leslie, Peter M. 1980. *Canadian Universities 1980 and Beyond: Enrolment, Structural Change and Finance.* Ottawa: Association of Universities and Colleges of Canada.

Levin, Benjamin. 1990. "Tuition Fees and University Accessibility." *Canadian Public Policy* 16 (1): 51-59.

Lynd, Doug J. 1994. "Increases in University Enrolment: Increased Access or Increased Retention." *Education Quarterly Review* 1 (1): 12-21.

Martinson, Mariem. 1994. "University Enrolment and Tuition Fees." *Education Quarterly Review* 1 (4): 36-43.

Maslove, Alan. 1992. "Reconstructing Fiscal Federalism." In Frances Abele (ed.), *How Ottawa Spends: The Politics of Competitiveness 1992-93.* Ottawa: Carleton University Press.

OECD. 1994. *The OECD Jobs Study: Facts, Analysis, Strategies.* Paris: OECD.

Pike, Robert M. 1981. Sociological Research on Higher Education in English Canada 1970-1980: A Thematic Review." *The Canadian Journal of Higher Education* 11 (2): 1-25.

————. 1980. "Education, Class, and Power in Canada." In Richard J. Ossenberg (ed.), *Power and Change in Canada.* Toronto: McClelland and Stewart.

————. 1970. *Who Doesn't Get to University . . . and Why: A Study on Accessibility to Higher Education in Canada.* Ottawa: Association of Universities and Colleges of Canada.

Porter, John. 1965. *The Vertical Mosaic: An Analysis of Social Class and Power in Canada.* Ottawa: University of Toronto Press.

Porter, Marion R. and Gilles Jasmin. 1987. *A Profile of Post-Secondary Students in Canada.* Ottawa: Education Support Sector, Department of the Secretary of State.

————, John Porter and Bernard R. Blishen. 1973. *Does Money Matter?: Prospects for Higher Education in Ontario.* Ottawa: Macmillan.

Rajagopal, Indhu, and William D. Farr. 1992. "Hidden Academics: The Part-Time Faculty in Canada." *Higher Education* 24: 317-31.

Sale, Tim. 1992. *The Funding of Post-Secondary Education in Canada: Can the Dilemma be Resolved?* Ottawa: Economic Council of Canada.

St. John, Edward. 1990. "Price Response in Enrollment Decisions: An Analysis of the High School and Beyond Sophomore Cohort." *Research in Higher Education* 31 (2): 161-76.

Stage, Frances K. and Don Hossler. 1989. "Differences in Family Influences on College Attendance Plans for Male and Female Ninth Graders." *Research in Higher Education* 30 (3): 301-15.

Stager, David. 1989. *Focus on Fees: Alternative Policies for University Tuition Fees.* Toronto: Council of Ontario Universities.

Statistics Canada. 1992-93. *Education in Canada: A Statistical Review for 1992-93.* Ottawa: Statistics Canada.

West, Edwin. 1993. *Ending the Squeeze on Universities.* Montreal: Institute for Research on Public Policy.

Winnipeg Harvest. 1994. "Student Poverty and Food Banks." *Winnipeg Harvest Newsletter,* Fall.

## PART 5

# WOMEN AND THE SOCIAL SECURITY REVIEW

# CHAPTER 15

# THE FEDERAL SOCIAL SECURITY REVIEW: A GENDER-SENSITIVE CRITIQUE

*Therese Jennissen*

## INTRODUCTION

For more than a year the current federal government has been engaged in a process of reviewing Canada's social security system. During this time various documents and background papers were circulated, consultations for public input were held, a task force was set up to advise the Minister of Human Resources Development Canada (HRDC), and a final report by the Standing Committee on Human Resources Development was tabled in the House of Commons. On February 27, 1995 in the budget speech, the Finance Minister presented the future role of the federal government in social welfare policy in unequivocal terms (Department of Finance 1995b). The budget speech, and subsequently Bill C-76,[1] called for a significant reduction in federal social spending and a substantially modified role for the federal government in the social security of the country. Although this direction is not entirely new, it now officially forms the basis for future policy development, thereby paving the way for a fundamentally altered social security system in Canada.

This paper is a critique of the social security review (SSR) from a gender-sensitive perspective.[2] It argues that the federal government structured the framework for the debates over the future of social security in Canada without considering gender differences. This means that there were no formal provisions for discussion of issues of particular concern to women and issues of concern to specific groups of marginalized women, including women with disabilities, Aboriginal women, women of colour, older women and impoverished women. It should come as no surprise, therefore, that the options, recommendations, and directives put forward by the federal government do little in the way of advancing women's equality and, in some respects, serve to set it back.

In the past, the federal government has committed itself to gender equality through the Canadian Charter of Rights and Freedoms: international covenants such as the Nairobi Forward-Looking Strategies for the Advancement of Women; the Convention on the Elimination of All Forms of Discrimination Against Women; and, more recently, through its participation in the Fourth World Conference on Women held in China in September 1995. But the prognosis for the advancement of women's equality in the near future is not healthy. The effects of economic restructuring on women's employment opportunities, cuts to funding women's programs, cuts to the public service sector, the demise of the Canadian Advisory Council on the Status of Women, and the direction of the social security review tend toward undermining women's equality. This paper begins from the premise that social policy should advance people's welfare, including women's equality. By ignoring gender differences in the SSR, the federal government has, in fact, undermined its commitment to advancing women's equality.

The paper focuses on the potential impact on women of a number of policy options and recommendations raised in the SSR, some of which were further articulated in the federal budget and Bill C-76. It addresses both the general direction of the review and specific policy proposals. Although the federal budget in some ways pre-empts the SSR, the debates in the review are relevant for this paper to the extent that they inform us about "government thinking" on social policy. They also educate us about the concerns expressed by Canadian women and women's groups, and serve as a baseline against which to measure the degree to which the federal government is prepared to include in policy issues that Canadian women identify as important.

## THE IMPORTANCE OF GENDER SENSITIVITY IN SOCIAL POLICY

Gender *in*sensitivity means "ignoring sex as a socially important variable" (Eichler 1991: 7). Margrit Eichler identifies gender insensitivity as one particular type of sexism that is often found in research (Eichler 1991: 66-71). Gender insensitivity can occur in a number of ways. Two examples include when data have been collected in aggregate form rather than by sex, or when data are simply used in aggregate form even though they have been collected by sex. In the case of the social security review it appears that the latter applies. Data that point to the relative status of Canadian women in the workplace, the home, the family and the community are readily available[3] and clearly indicate that, in general, the majority of women occupy a status that is subordinate to men. Moreover, there are data available that speak to the differential impact that various social policies have on women (including the impact on specific categories of women) in relation to men.[4] The designers of the framework for the social security review, however, did not take this into account and instead focused on non-gendered categories such as "the family," "the household," and "the labour force"—terms which effectively obfuscate the unequal status of women relative to men in Canadian society.

The failure to address gender differences with regard to social policy can have serious implications for women, as this paper will illustrate. According to Eichler, "failing to analyze data by sex when they have been collected on both sexes may . . . severely limit the utility of any findings and may, in fact, hide some of the most important aspects of a phenomenon" (Eichler 1991: 73). She adds that "[t]his would be true for all cases in which there is significant social difference between the sexes" (Eichler 1991: 73). Ironically, the differences between the sexes are pronounced in the three areas the federal government chose to review: employment, education and security. This paper assesses the "most important aspects" of the social security review (and, to some extent, the budget and Bill C-76). It demonstrates how the structure of these deliberations differentially affect women and ultimately lead to inhibiting, and in some cases reversing, equality for Canadian women.[5]

## THE SOCIAL SECURITY REVIEW (SSR)

### A. CONTEXT AND PROCESS OF THE SOCIAL SECURITY REVIEW

Although this paper centres on the social security review launched by HRDC Minister Lloyd Axworthy in January 1994 (the Axworthy review), it recognizes that the SSR is one important part of a much larger restructuring process that is occurring in Canada. Over the past decade governments of Canada have become increasingly preoccupied with the debt and deficit reduction and our ability to compete in a global economy. The Finance Department has been developing an economic strategy that cannot be separated from the SSR.[6] The pre-budget consultation hearings by the Standing Committee on Finance, in fact, were held at the same time as the second set of hearings of the SSR. Other relevant reviews have been, and continue to be, taking place in various departments of government.[7] The social security system has been identified as one important area where both cost containment and a "reshaping" of the workforce will occur.

The home base for the SSR is the federal Department of Human Resources Development Canada which established an all-party Standing Committee directed to analyze and make recommendations on the future of social security in Canada. The discussion paper (1994e) and supporting documents produced by HRDC reflect the position of the Liberal government. The Standing Committee on Human Resources Development, which produced the interim and final reports, was comprised of members of the Liberal, Bloc Québécois and Reform parties. The complex relationship between the various departments, the structure of committees, the relationship between committees and the government, and federal-provincial dynamics play important roles in how policy discussions are ultimately played out.

The federal government made strong appeals for public participation in the SSR and stressed the need to hear from individual Canadians. Numerous individuals and groups appeared before the Standing Committee and/or sent written briefs. Public input was limited, however, by serious time constraints. For example, phase one of the review occurred over a six week period which gave individuals and organizations appearing before the committee, or submitting briefs, very little preparation time. The second round of hearings was also short. In spite of these drawbacks, individuals and organizations made compelling arguments to the committee.

## B. CONTENT OF THE SOCIAL SECURITY REVIEW

### i. Developing the initial framework for review

On January 18, 1994 the federal government announced its intention to reform, within a two year period, Canada's social security infrastructure (House of Commons 1994a: 10). From the time Axworthy introduced his motion, a great deal of attention was paid to the important role the Canadian public was to play in charting the future of Canada's social security system. Canadians were invited "to join in the rebuilding of the social security, labour market, and learning framework of this country" (House of Commons 1994b: 609).

Although the review was billed as an opportunity for the average Canadian to help shape the future of social policy, the parameters of the debate were already clearly determined and outlined in both Axworthy's motion to establish the review and in the focus paper available to the public. In other words, the public's input was circumscribed by the limits of the review agenda; an agenda which failed to include immigration, health, housing and pensions.

Nonetheless, a number of women's groups pushed the parameters of the debate by encouraging members of the Standing Committee and the Task Force to incorporate a gender-sensitive perspective in the SSR.[8] In a brief to the Task Force on Social Security, for example, the Canadian Advisory Council on the Status of Women (CACSW) stated that ". . . the CACSW's position is that Canada's domestic and international commitments to women's equality *require* governments and their advisors to adopt a gender-sensitive framework for all aspects of their work" (1994: 2).

These requests were largely ignored and gender sensitivity is not reflected in the interim report which established the framework for the SSR. For example, none of the eight guiding principles for the social security review make reference to the promotion of women's equality. Moreover, the report concludes with a list of priorities directed toward three distinct populations—Canadian families, particularly Canadian children living in poverty, youth, and unemployed and underemployed adults. The unique status of women within these categories is not acknowledged.

In essence, the interim report, did not make a link between gender and structural inequality in Canadian society. This absence of gender sensitivity obscures the fact that women are over-represented among the poor; that sole-support mothers, women with disabilities, Aboriginal women and old women are among the poorest members of Canadian society; women are disproportionately represented in part-time and non-standard work; and women perform most of the child care and family responsibilities. Moreover, it does not recognize that women, by virtue of their subordinate status in society, are differentially affected by the social security system (Lero and Johnson 1994; Baines, Evans and Neysmith 1991).

### ii. Options,[9] recommendations[10] and actions[11]

Since the tabling of the interim report in March 1994, the social security review has gone through a series of stages. On October 5, 1994 HRDC Minister Axworthy tabled in Parliament a paper entitled *Agenda: Jobs and Growth. Improving Social Security in Canada: A Discussion Paper*. This document was intended to provide Canadians with a framework for participating in the reform of the social security system. The discussion paper[12] categorized the options for reform into three broad themes: working, learning and security. A series of supplementary papers followed the release of the discussion paper and provided additional details "to encourage more informed participation in the debate" (HRDC 1994b: 1). Following another round of hearings and submissions in the second half of 1994, the Standing Committee on Human Resources Development finally released its recommendations to government in February 1995.[13] Shortly thereafter, the federal budget speech identified some clear directions for the future of social policy in Canada.

As the following section of this paper illustrates the discussion paper, like the interim report, offers only a superficial analysis of the impact of the proposed social policy changes on women. However, the final report of the Standing Committee on Human Resources Development, noted the significance that women's groups placed on the need for a gender analysis in the SSR. The committee made four recommendations specifically related to the question of alleviating women's poverty, providing access to education and training programs, and the importance of linking violence, inequality and poverty to ensure that social security programs meet the specific needs of women. The committee also recommended that "the reform of social security programs be subjected to a gender analysis to ensure women's increased and equal social and economic participation in the paid labour market" (House of Commons 1995b: 100-01).

Of the fifty-two recommendations made by the committee, however, those dealing with women's equality (alongside recommendations directed at Aboriginal peoples and ethnic and visible minority populations) comprised the last eight recommendations in the report (House of Commons 1995b: 100-04).

It is not entirely clear how the federal government intends to act on all of the social issues reviewed but, given the nature of the changes emanating from the federal budget, it is unlikely that gender sensitivity will be a priority in the restructuring the future social security system.

The following five social policies or policy areas were central to the SSR are currently being discussed and have important implications for women.

## A. EMPLOYMENT DEVELOPMENT SERVICES

The discussion paper acknowledges that having a job is one of the most important forms of social welfare. Training people to find and keep jobs is therefore a centerpiece of the social security review (HRDC 1994e: 29). The paper proposes a wide range of "employment development services" such as personal career counselling, job search strategies, provision of labour market and job information, classroom and on-the-job training, work experience projects and earnings supplementation (HRDC 1994e: 29-30).

To build a new and effective model of employment development services, the discussion paper suggests there needs to be a shift toward coordination of the activities of all partners within a flexible, locally managed, community based structure (HRDC 1994e: 32). This requires improvements in the tools and management of the system. Improved tools would include (1) enhanced needs assessment and counselling tailored to meet individual needs drawing upon federal, provincial and municipal services; (2) a centralized labour market information system (e.g., the "electronic hiring hall"); (3) enhancement of basic literacy and numeracy skills; (4) the possible expansion of varied training formats such as classroom, on-the-job, computer based training and distance education; (5) workplace training; and (6) innovative approaches to employment which could include income supplements, self-employment assistance or "wages for unemployed workers to perform useful work in their communities," commonly referred to as "workfare" (HRDC 1994e: 33-38).

The final report of the Standing Committee on Human Resources Development, *Security, Opportunities and Fairness: Canadians renewing their social programs*, generally supports the points raised in the discussion paper underscoring the importance of local training, more provincial responsibility and collaboration with labour and the private sector. The final report also recommends that "particular access and accommodation needs of women, Aboriginal peoples, persons with disabilities, ethnocultural groups, and visible minorities be considered in the design and delivery of employment development services" (House of Commons 1995b: 80).

### Potential effects on women

The labour market is one of the most frequently cited examples of systemic inequality that persists between women and men in Canada. It is common knowledge that, on average, women earn less than men, are over-represented in the secondary labour market and in non-standard work, perform the bulk of unpaid labour, are adversely and disproportionately affected by economic restructuring, and continue to be used as a reserve army of labour.[14] The discussion of employment development services makes no mention of these general disparities between the situation of female and male workers. This means that the policy options for training and education discussed in the SSR, and reiterated in the budget speech, will simply perpetuate these disparities.

This also suggests that the particular education and training needs of women will be overlooked. The National Association of Women and the Law (NAWL) argued that the first requirement for training programs for women is accessibility. In a brief to the Standing Committee of the Human Resources Development, NAWL stated:

> For women, access means equal spending on job training for women—training in the form of programs which are accessible to all women, including immigrant and

linguistic minority women, women with disabilities, and aboriginal women, all of whom face particular barriers in gaining access to current employment training programs. Access also means readily available and up-to-date information; programs which are locally available and community based; necessary support services including subsidized child care, transportation and training allowances; non-exclusionary eligibility criteria, and bridging programs (National Association of Women and the Law 1994: 18-19).

Although the Standing Committee on Human Resources Development recommended that the access and accommodation needs of women, particularly the needs of Aboriginal women, women with disabilities, ethnocultural and visible minority women, be considered in designing and delivering employment development services, it remains to be seen if this will become government policy.

The focus around employment in the SSR is on education and training which, in themselves, do not create jobs. Education and training are meaningful only if there are good jobs available after the completion of the training.

## B. UNEMPLOYMENT/EMPLOYMENT INSURANCE

Unemployment insurance reform has been a central focus of the SSR. The federal government intends to have draft legislation in place this fall and a revised act ready by July 1, 1996 (Department of Finance 1995b). A number of options for reform have been circulating. The discussion paper proposed two possible measures. One was to keep the existing system but to tighten it through a combination of more stringent requirements for eligibility, lower benefit levels and/or shorter periods of eligibility. A more drastic option was to develop a two-tiered employment insurance program consisting of a "basic insurance" for occasional users of U.I., and an "adjustment insurance" for frequent claimants. Basic insurance would be designed for infrequent users of the U.I. system and would continue in the same form as it currently exists (HRDC 1994e: 43-47).

After an initial number of claims under the basic insurance program, frequent claimants (for example, those who make three or more claims in five years) would be switched to the adjustment insurance and receive "expanded access to a broader range of employment development programs" (HRDC 1994e: 46). The adjustment insurance program "could be paid at a lower rate than basic insurance, it could be subject to an income test, or it could have a different duration" (HRDC 1994e: 45). One of the suggestions for income testing was to base it on family income.

The Standing Committee on Human Resources Development recommended against the two-tiered system on the basis that it would be "unduly harsh for seasonal workers and may tend to stigmatize them" (House of Commons 1995b: 88). It was also against making benefits conditional on family income and reducing the entitlement period. Among a number of other recommendations, the Standing Committee called for government to reduce unemployment insurance benefits and/or increase eligibility requirements, and to extend U.I. coverage to part-time and contract workers.

Discussion of U.I. in the budget speech centred on cutting costs, removing disincentives to work and generally simplifying the system. In the budget plan, the government indicated that U.I. reform "will reduce the overall size of the U.I. program by a minimum of 10 percent.

This overall reform, combined with the improvements in the administration of the U.I. program . . . will secure savings for tax payers of $700 million in 1996-97" (Department of Finance 1995a). According to the Budget Plan, the "key job for unemployment insurance in the future must be to help Canadians stay off unemployment insurance" (Department of Finance 1995b).

Although the exact content of the impending U.I. legislation is not entirely clear, according to recent newspaper reports, HRDC Minister Axworthy has abandoned the notion of the two-tiered system. Apparently, one direction currently being discussed is tying the level of U.I. benefits more closely to how much work an applicant has done and how much U.I. the applicant has collected in the past (Greenspon 1995a). The objectives of the new "employment" legislation are to simplify the system, remove disincentives to work, lower costs and provide training (Toulin 1995).

More recently, documents obtained by the *Globe and Mail* suggest that Lloyd Axworthy has presented to Cabinet a set of far-reaching reform proposals that would effectively raise the threshold for U.I. qualification, cut the duration for collecting insurance, reduce disincentive to take on additional work and penalize previous claimants. More specifically, the plans appear to include a reduction in overall benefits (10 percent or $1.6 billion). The formula for collecting U.I. would be based on number of hours worked instead of total number of weeks. Benefits would be based on average earnings during a fixed twenty-two week period whether or not the applicant worked in all of these weeks instead of on average earnings of all weeks worked. The minimum requirement to qualify for U.I. would be raised from twelve weeks at fifteen hours a week (180 hours) to 455 hours, and the maximum duration of benefits would be cut from fifty weeks to forty weeks. Benefit rates would remain at 55 percent of insured earnings for most workers but low income claimants with dependents would be bumped up to 65 percent of insured earnings. Claimants who have collected U.I. previously would find their claims drop by one percentage point for every fifteen weeks previously collected (Greenspon 1995a, 1995b).

*Potential effects on women*
The proposed changes to U.I. outlined in the discussion paper and the budget are regressive measures which would have a negative impact on the majority of Canadian women and men who would come to rely on this system.[15] However, given the subordinate status of women generally in the Canadian labour force, these measures will have a disproportionately negative impact on women. The reasons for this assertion are illustrated below.

U.I. reform is driven by the idea that this program encourages dependence and discourages job creation. It completely ignores the pattern of women's employment in Canada. Women move in and out of the workforce because of "bad jobs," child bearing functions, the absence of affordable, quality child care and because jobs are being cut. For example, although women make up one third of the employees in the manufacturing sector, overall they have lost more jobs than men in recent years because women in manufacturing are concentrated in those jobs most affected by foreign competition (Lindgren 1994).

Further restricting eligibility requirements for U.I. will not change the employment patterns of women but will only penalize them further for the structural inequalities that exist for them in the labour market and in society generally. Shortening the eligibility period, as proposed in the discussion paper, would simply mean less income for women. It is well established that when family income decreases, the domestic work of women increases (Townson 1994: 5). Decreasing benefit levels will also have a differential impact on women because, as a group, they are concentrated in the lower paying, less stable jobs. On average, women earn 72 percent of what men earn (Lero and Johnson 1994: 6), an earnings differential that is played out in different U.I. benefit levels available to men and women. In 1993, 69 percent of part-time workers were women (Townson 1994: 5). Non-standard work (part-time, casual, part-year, multiple jobs, telework, contracted-out work and self-employment) is increasing and, as the supplementary paper on unemployment insurance acknowledges, the exclusion of non-standard work from U.I. coverage is also increasing (HRDC 1994c: 73). It appears unlikely that future U.I. policy will be extended to cover part-time and other types of non-standard work.

The notion of tying benefits of frequent claimants to family income or household income in multiple-earner families was raised in both the discussion paper and the supplementary paper on U.I. The Standing Committee recommended against this notion and it appears that the federal government is moving away from this idea. This option would have devastating effects on women's autonomy and equality. Since men, on average, earn more than women, it is more likely for a woman to lose her benefits. Two dangerous assumptions underlie this option. The first assumption is that money is evenly redistributed in families and households, although evidence shows the contrary.[16] Second is the assumption that women should be prepared to become economically dependent on their partners. These assumptions transgress the basis of women's equality—economic independence, autonomy and self-determination.

## C. CHILD CARE

A highlight of the SSR was its recognition of the importance of child care. The discussion paper stated that the federal government "sees child care as a priority for the reform of social security programs, lying at the heart of the three areas addressed by the Discussion paper" (HRDC 1994e: 53). The document suggests that the Liberal government will follow through on its commitment to create 150,000 new day care spaces and to spend $720 million over three years (to begin after a year of 3 percent economic growth and pending agreement with the provincial and territorial governments). Although this amount is still low, it represents a commitment, in principle, to the need for child care.

The SSR's commitment to child care was encouraging, particularly the acknowledgment of the urgent need for child care for Aboriginal communities, rural regions, children with disabilities, and for more flexible child care arrangements to accommodate the changing nature of work. Consistent with the government's position in the discussion paper, the report of the Human Resource Development Standing Committee put forward a number of recommendations on child care (House of Commons 1995b: 74). However, there was no mention of child care in the budget and the move toward block funding and away from cost shared programs most likely spells the end of any possibility of a national day care program.

### Potential effects on women

The initial discussion of child care reflected in the discussion paper attempted to address it as a gender-neutral subject. The document focused on the "needs of working parents" and "most Canadian parents—including lone parents," without any mention of the particular significance of child care to women (HRDC 1994e: 53). In the supplementary paper (HRDC

1994b: 7-9) however, direct reference was made to "mothers" bearing the most responsibility and stress in finding child care and in leaving their jobs because of inadequate child care arrangements (HRDC 1994b: 3). Moreover, the supplementary paper identified access to child care as "an important measure to promote women's economic independence" (HRDC 1994b: 3). Though there appeared to be a strong commitment to child care in the SSR, its future is now uncertain if not unlikely given the block funding arrangements introduced in Bill C-76, the Canada Health and Social Transfer.

## D. LEARNING

Learning is identified in the SSR as the best way to ensure national development in a global economy. According to the discussion paper, learning must be a continuous and ongoing process if we want to want to be internationally competitive (Remus 1994: 1). Although post-secondary education (PSE) is a provincial responsibility, the federal government has played an important role in financing education, particularly since the Second World War. One of the federal government's roles has been to provide cash transfers and tax points to the provinces to help cover the costs of PSE. This arrangement is made through the Established Programs Financing (EPF). Currently the cash portion of the transfer is frozen. The diminishing cash transfers to the provinces for PSE means that less money has been going to the provinces (and will eventually disappear) even though tax points have been transferred from the federal to provincial governments.

Two options for financing PSE are outlined: (1) "either maintain the EPF arrangement at a total no higher than the 1993-94 level" or "find a better approach that would entail creating more stable alternative forms of support..." (HRDC 1995: 25). In both options the cash portion of the transfer will disappear. In the first option, it will simply run out and the federal contribution will be only in tax points. The second option proposes an expanded student loan which would be repaid through an Income Contingent Repayment (ICR) loan (HRDC 1995: 37-40). The basic principle underlying the ICR loan is that it would be repayable after the borrower had left the university and entered into the workforce. Unlike current student loans, however, the repayment schedule for ICR loan would be adjusted to the former student's income level. The discussion paper suggests that loan repayment could be attached to the income tax system and deducted, at source, from a person's pay cheque.

The discussion paper also raises the idea of encouraging people to save money for further education through "savings investment vehicles" such as registered savings plans (RSP). It identifies a number of ways that the federal and provincial governments could work together to promote "lifelong" learning. Priority areas would include: (1) school-to-work transition which would focus on ensuring that young people acquire needed skills to enter the workplace; (2) making learning more portable so job-to-job transition would be easier (the development of a Learning Passport); (3) developing innovative approaches to distance education and computer assisted learning; and finally (4) enhancing international educational opportunities so Canadian students can acquire skills offered in foreign countries.

The report of the Standing Committee on Human Resources Development made a number of recommendations concerning education, including support for the ICR loan.

*Potential effects on women*

There is no reference to gender in either the discussion paper or the supplementary paper dealing with PSE, yet the proposed changes would seriously set back women's equality. Cuts to federal funding and the options provided in the documents clearly indicate that the consumers of education will be filling in the funding gaps. The increasing financial pressure on the provinces means that PSE will increasingly be turned over to the private sector and/or tuition fees increased.

Both of the options provided in the discussion paper and in the supplementary paper will mean higher costs for consumers. The effects of this will be detrimental to most working class Canadians but will be felt disproportionately by women who occupy most of the low paying jobs and are over-represented among the impoverished. Higher tuition may simply become a barrier to access for women, who generally have less money and who may have extra expenses such as child care. Restricted access to post-secondary education means that women's opportunities for better paying jobs will become even more restricted. Without access to higher education, women's chances of equitable employment are seriously compromised.

Women will also be disproportionately affected by the ICR loan. On average, women's earning power is lower than that of men, women's attachment to the labour market is often interrupted with child bearing/rearing functions, and women in colleges and universities generally incur more debts than men (Canadian Federation of Students 1995). These factors contribute to the pattern of lower life earnings that characterize many women's lives. This means that women will generally take longer to pay back their student loans. Their payment may be lower but because of the accumulated interest they will pay more for their education. The ICR loan, in effect, rewards high income earners who will be paying less on accumulated interest and penalizes the lower income earners, namely women.

The opportunity for students to use a type of RSP to finance education also works against women because of their lower earning powers. Generally, cutbacks in educational funding that jeopardize post-secondary institutions, threaten particular programs such as women's studies. Hiring opportunities as well as career advancements within post-secondary institutions will also decline for women as funding falls (Remus 1994: 3-4).

## E. THE CANADA ASSISTANCE PLAN (CAP)/
## THE CANADA HEALTH AND SOCIAL TRANSFER (CHST)

The Canada Assistance Plan (CAP) is a cost sharing arrangement between the federal and provincial governments for the provision of social assistance and social services to people in need. Under CAP, 50 percent of the costs incurred by provincial governments for a range of social services and social assistance was paid by the federal government. In an effort to cut costs, the federal government in 1990 limited the annual growth in CAP transfers to the three wealthiest provinces (Ontario, Alberta and British Columbia) to 5 percent.

The federal government's position, as articulated in both the discussion paper and the supplementary paper (HRDC 1994i) is that the social welfare provisions under CAP have lost their original function of providing short-term assistance to people in need. Instead, people have become dependent on a system which does not actively foster self-sufficiency and independence. According to these documents, this dependency, combined with the fact that child poverty persists, are indications that the welfare system is "misfiring" and in desperate need of reform.

The federal government was also concerned over the restrictiveness of federal transfer arrangements under CAP. It argued that the provinces are inhibited from using federal funds in innovative and flexible ways (HRDC 1994e: 72). Providing more latitude to the provinces should be one of the guiding principles in CAP reform (HRDC 1994e: 74).

The discussion paper provided three approaches for reforming CAP. The first option was a Guaranteed Annual Income (GAI). Debated previously in Canada, the GAI proposed that all families be guaranteed a basic level of income, whether they work or not. This option however, was not seen as a viable alternative in the documents because it is too expensive. Targeted programs, the government argued, are most practical at this point in time.

A second option, that seemed to be favoured, was the transformation of CAP to a block funded system similar to the Established Program Financing (EPF) currently used to transfer federal funds to the provinces for health and post-secondary education. Under this arrangement, the federal government would provide the provinces with a block of money with which they could design welfare systems to meet their own needs and priorities and help the federal government "limit its fiscal exposure" (HRDC 1994e: 68) Block funding could be conditional on national standards or it could be provided unconditionally as in the case of post-secondary education funding.

A third option involved redirecting funding to new programs. In this scenario, the current CAP funding would be targeted to particular programs, namely employment creation and poverty reduction. Within this, the potential priority areas included: (1) low income families with children; (2) working income supplements for low income families; (3) child care or child development initiatives; (4) child support initiatives; (5) employment development services for social assistance recipients; (6) greater independence for persons with disabilities; and (7) continuing support for social services (HRDC 1994e: 76-79).

The federal government took a definitive stand on the future of CAP in the 1995 budget when Finance Minister Martin announced that beginning on April 1, 1996 CAP and EPF would become a single consolidated block called the Canada Health and Social Transfer (CHST) (Department of Finance 1995b). The consolidated block fund will provide the provinces with less money (the CAP and EPF will be reduced by $4.5 billion over the next three years) (National Anti-Poverty Organization 1995: 1) but offer flexibility on how the funds are spent. The only condition that was mentioned in the budget speech and Bill C-76 (the legislation to implement the CHST) was that the provinces be required to provide social assistance to applicants without minimum residency requirements (Department of Finance 1995a). The bill does nothing to ensure "that provinces have a last-resort safety net in place" (Council of Canadians 1995: 8).

*Potential effects on women*
Many Canadians will undoubtedly feel the negative effects of the changes that are brought about through the CHST but it will be impoverished and low income Canadians who will suffer the most. As mentioned before, more Canadian women than men are poor in absolute terms. Women who are doubly or multiply disadvantaged (e.g., sole support mothers, Aboriginal women and women with disabilities) are among the poorest of the Canadian population. A reduction in federal funding will almost surely mean that funding for provincial programs will be cut. This will have a disproportionately negative impact on women because CAP-funded

programs affect more women than men (Woolley 1995: 34). Not only do low-income women rely on social assistance more than men, but many women rely on day care subsidies, home care, women's shelters, rape crisis centres and legal aid. In the social service fields most workers are women, so cut backs to spending means that a disproportionate number of women will be affected by job loss. Traditionally when social services are cut, women pick up the "caring" responsibilities cast off by the state (Woolley 1995: 34).

Since there are few national standards attached to the new block funding, the provinces will have free reign over the services and programs they provide. In fact, the provinces are not compelled to provide social assistance and social services. Since no cash transfers from the federal government will be involved, it is unlikely that the federal government would be able to enforce standards even if they were included. This means that social assistance and social services will vary across the country. Under CAP, participation in employment-related programs cannot be required. This can change with CHST and programs such as workfare could become the norm. This raises the concern that women will continue to be slotted into low paying, low status jobs with little or no opportunities for advancement.

The CHST will undoubtedly have a negative impact on women. Not only will social assistance and social services be cut, but also there will also be less funding available for health and post-secondary education. A block funding arrangement could also set up a competition among these services and it is difficult to imagine that this would work in the best interests of Canadian women. Given that the federal government is abdicating its role in the provision of social assistance and services, we are compelled to ask what this means for a federal role in a comprehensive child care program. With the CHST the federal government no longer has the financial authority or power to legislate a national program of child care.

## C. Summary

From the preceding discussion it is clear that many of the social policy options and recommendations presented in the SSR, the budget and Bill C-76 will not advance women's equality. Not only did the SSR fail to include the advancement of women's equality in its basic principles, it did not *add* gender sensitivity to its discussion documents. Though this issue was raised repeatedly, none of the supplementary papers were devoted to women. It was only in the final report of the Standing Committee on Human Resources Development that the importance of gender sensitivity in policy discussions became apparent and even here it is simply noted; it is not incorporated into any analysis. The pre-budget process, including the pre-budget consultations by the Finance Committee, occurred at the same time as the second set of hearings of the SSR in the fall of 1994. This process had even less gender input and, in the end, served to undermine the SSR.

The SSR also excluded a number of crucial social policy issues including housing, immigration, health care and pension policies. These exclusions seriously limited the debate over social security, particularly the linking of issues such as health and welfare.

It is disturbing that the SSR did not incorporate a gender analysis given the federal government's explicit, formal policies of promoting women's equality. What is perhaps most disturbing is the fact that women's organizations, anti-poverty groups and some labour unions not only repeatedly raised it as a central concern, but developed thoughtful, articulate positions that could have been easily incorporated into government policy, given the political will.

A major, "last ditch" attempt by women's groups to reach government was made in December 1994 when the National Action Committee on the Status of Women (NAC) organized a three day women's consultation which brought together over eighty women's groups.[17] The women analyzed the impact that the proposals in the discussion paper would have on women. The consultation session called for a feminist framework:

> It is our view that Canada's economic and social policies must be designed to advance Canada's commitment to women's human rights. Our reference points are equality guarantees, both international and domestic, and, in particular, women's economic, social and human rights. Given the breadth and seriousness of the continuing disadvantages that women experience, advancing women's equality should be a central goal of the reform of social programs and services in Canada (National Women's Consultation on the Social Security Review December 3-5, 1994: 2).

The absence of gender sensitivity, or conversely, the existence of gender insensitivity is problematic at a number of different levels. The most important issue, as this paper has shown, is that when gender differences generally, and the differential impact of economic and social policy on women specifically, is not acknowledged, the needs of women cannot be adequately addressed in policy. As a result the advancement of women's equality is seriously compromised. Moreover, the work of analyzing social policy from a gender-sensitive framework is left to women and women's organizations—a mammoth task given the fact that women's groups have had serious funding cuts and the Canadian Advisory Council on the Status of Women, which traditionally performed major research functions on women's issues, has been eliminated. Finally, social policy commentators tend to respond to the limited framework and terms outlined in the SSR and therefore gender-sensitive debates, analyses and critiques are seriously lacking.[18]

## TOWARD A GENDER-SENSITIVE FRAMEWORK FOR SOCIAL POLICY DEVELOPMENT AND ANALYSIS: LESSONS FOR THE FUTURE

Over the past three decades the federal government has made commitments to advance the status of women in Canada and a number of measures were put in place in an attempt to achieve that objective. However, inequality between the sexes persists as was pointed out in a United Nations report on human development. Based on 1990 data, Canada ranked first out of thirty-three industrialized countries in terms of its composite measure of human development and progress, but it ranked eighth on the gender-sensitive index (United Nations 1992: 21). The current backlash against the women's movement, the climate of fiscal constraints, cutbacks to social programs and the absence of gender sensitivity in the federal government's framework for the social security review have added new dimensions to the struggle for equality.

The absence of a gender-sensitive analysis of social policy issues means that women's needs generally, and the needs of specific categories of women (e.g., impoverished women, women of colour, Black women, Aboriginal women, women with disabilities and senior women) are unlikely to be met. This paper argues that making policies responsive to the needs of women requires a framework for analysis which includes the differential impact that various policy options can have on all categories of women relative to men. It also requires the active participation of women in the process of policy-making.

The creation of gender-sensitive methodologies is important not only because they can be used as standards against which to measure the impact of social policies on women but also they can assist in developing new policies which can advance the status of women. A number of countries (e.g., New Zealand, the United Kingdom and more recently Canada) and the International Labour Organization (ILO) are creating standard, gender-sensitive methodologies for policy analysis and development (International Labour Organization 1994). The ILO plans to integrate across the board "gender issues and equality concerns" in its program and project objectives and activities. This strategy is based on ". . . the recognition that women's equal participation is essential to the achievement of all major development objectives— sustainable development, eradication of poverty, human rights and democracy" (International Labour Organization 1994: 3). In Canada, some agencies and departments of the federal government,[19] and some provincial government ministries have incorporated a gender-sensitive analysis into their policy processes but this has not become a standard across governments in Canada.

In principle, the notion of incorporating gender-sensitive analyses into the mainstream policy-making process and policy analysis is a desirable objective. However, we must be cautious that this does not lead to rigid policies and programs that become unresponsive to the needs of women; that are inflexible, unenforceable and/or difficult or impossible to monitor.

A fundamental task in developing a gender-sensitive framework is to reach a common understanding of the meaning of gender equality and to establish a gender equality standard against which policies can be assessed. The term "gender equality" has evolved over time. Historically, in Canada it meant treating men and women the same (Code 1993: 48-52). This perspective is premised on the idea that all people are equal and therefore should be treated the same. It emphasizes the importance of legal rights and procedures for ensuring equal treatment. In fact, this approach results in gender neutrality which fails to recognize that there are fundamental differences in the life patterns of men and women. Women's needs are often not met when women are given identical treatment (in terms of social policy) with men. Substantive equality is a more complex concept that recognizes that the inferior status of most women in society is systemic and that advancing the status of women may mean that they have to be given preferential treatment. The focus of this approach is not on identical treatment, but on equal outcome. A guiding principle of gender equality must include a woman's right to autonomy, dignity and self-determination. Social policies must work toward respecting these rights and enabling women to make choices.

In addition to establishing a standard definition of gender equality toward which social policies will work, a number of factors must be considered in developing a framework for analysis. For example, the different patterns of involvement of women and men in economic, social and legal structures in society, and the effects that they have on their educational and career choices and family and economic statuses must be considered. The work that women do in both the paid and unpaid workforce must be recognized as a valuable contribution to Canadian society. A gender-sensitive framework must also appreciate the changing needs of women in different stages of life, the particular health needs of women and the persistence of violence against women.

Finally, it is imperative that a gender-sensitive framework for developing and analyzing social policy recognizes that women have a critical role to play in determining future policies that enhance their status. Although the social security review has been devoid of a gender-sensitive analysis, women's voices must be included in the process of negotiating the CHST with the provinces.

## NOTES

1. Bill C-76, *An Act to implement certain provisions of the budget tabled in Parliament on February 27, 1995,* was passed in the House of Commons on June 6, 1995 and in the Senate on June 21, 1995.

2. While this paper focuses on gender, it recognizes that class and race are also central areas of division in our society which, along with gender, overlap to create varying degrees of oppression. For further discussion of this see Linda Gordon (1990); Fiona Williams (1989); Gillian Pascall (1986); and Anne Showstack Sassoon (1992).

3. Virtually all of the data collected by Statistics Canada, for example, are divided along sex lines.

4. Statistics on social assistance recipients reported in the Canada Assistance Plan Report do not appear to be disaggregated by gender. See Frances Woolley (1995), 3-4.

5. This paper acknowledges and gives credit to the work of the numerous women's organizations that made presentations to the social security review process. Among others these include the Canadian Advisory Council on the Status of Women, the National Action Committee on the Status of Women, the National Association of Women and the Law, Fédération du femmes du Québec, Native Women's Association of Canada, DisAbled Women's Network, Manitoba Women's Advisory Council, Windsor Women's Incentive Centre, St. John's Status of Women Council Women's Centre, Atlantic Provinces Joint Advisory Councils on the Status of Women, Congress of Black Women of Canada, NAC-Nova Scotia, Nova Scotia Women's Fish Net, Nova Scotia Women's Ad Hoc Committee on Social Security Reform.

6. See, for example, *Agenda: Jobs and Growth, A New Framework for Economic Policy; Creating a Healthy Fiscal Climate: the Economic and Fiscal Update;* and "Creating a Healthy Fiscal Climate," A Presentation by the Honourable Paul Martin to the House of Commons Standing Committee on Finance, October 18, 1994. For a review of this process, see Canadian Centre for Policy Alternatives (1994).

7. For example, in November 1994, the Minister of Industry released a document entitled *Building a More Innovative Economy.* The Minister of Justice and the Secretary of State for the Status of Women have also been reviewing various aspects of social security. In December 1994, the *Report of the Advisory Group on Working Time and the Distribution of Work* was released (HRDC 1994k). Currently seasonal work, health care and pensions are among a series of social welfare-related areas that are, or soon will be, reviewed.

8. Women's organizations appearing as witnesses before the committee include the National Action Committee on the Status of Women, Fédération des femmes du Québec and the National Association of Women and the Law. For a complete list of organizations and individuals who appeared as witnesses and/or who submitted briefs to the Committee, see Standing Committee on Human Resources Development, *Concerns and Priorities Regarding the Modernization and Restructuring of Canada's Social Security System,* Appendix A and B, 45-66 (House of Commons 1994c); and *Security, Opportunities and Fairness: Canadians renewing their social programs,* Appendix A and B, 107-229 (House of Commons 1995b).

9. The options are outlined most clearly in the discussion paper, *Improving Social Security in Canada.* Between October 1994 and January 1995, the government released eight supplementary papers that provided more analytic details on a range of subjects including persons with disabilities, unemployment/employment insurance, income security for children, child care and child development, CAP, employment development services, post-secondary education and the context of

reform.

10. Recommendations to the SSR are proposed in the final report of the Standing Committee on Human Resources Development, *Security, Opportunities and Fairness: Canadians renewing their social programs*, February 1995.

11. While the federal government has not articulated a final position on all of the issues discussed in the SSR, some important policy directives were announced in the 1995 federal budget speech, and subsequently in Bill C-76.

12. The HRDC document entitled *Improving Social Security in Canada: A Discussion Paper*, October 1994, has been referred to (by both government and people outside of government) in a number of ways: the Action Plan, the Green Paper, and the discussion paper/discussion document. I have used the term discussion paper to be consistent with the title of the document (although in the interim report it is regularly referred to as the Action Plan).

13. The government is usually given a period of 150 days to respond to a Standing Committee report. In the case of the Committee report the members of the committee did not ask the chair to request a government response, so none is anticipated.

14. See for example, Lero and Johnson (1994); Sandra Harder (1992); and Isabella Bakker (1994).

15. For further discussion of this see David Leadbeater (1995).

16. For a detailed discussion of this see Frances Woolley (1994).

17. The National Consultation Group met with Ministers Axworthy, Martin, Finestone, Blondin-Andrew and Maria Minna, Vice-Chair of the Standing Committee on Human Resources Development. See *Verbatim Report of National Consultations with Women's Groups on Social Security Reform*, December, 1994; Verbatim Report of National Consultation with Women's Groups on Social Security Reform, "Meeting with Task Team Representative of HRDC and Women's Groups," December 3, 1994; and *Final Report of Recommendations*, National Women's Consultation on the Social Security Review, Ottawa, December 3-5, 1994.

18. See, for example, *Critical Commentaries on the Social Security Review*, published by the Caledon Institute in January 1995. This book is filled with valuable commentary on the discussion paper but not one of the thirty-eight articles is explicitly about women or adopts a gender-sensitive perspective. Similarly, *A New Social Policy Reform* (1995), edited by Keith Banting and Ken Battle, contains no articles that deal with gender.

19. For example, the Canadian International Development Agency (CIDA) and the Department of Justice.

## REFERENCES

Bakker, Isabella (ed.). 1994. *The Strategic Silence:Gender and Economic Policy*. London: Zed Books.

Baines, Carol, Patricia Evans and Sheila Neysmith (eds.). 1991. *Women's Caring: Feminist Perspectives on Social Welfare*. Toronto: McClelland and Stewart.

Banting, Keith and Ken Battle (eds.). 1994. *A New Social Vision for Canada? Perspectives on the Federal Discussion Paper on Social Security Reform*. Ottawa and Kingston: The Caledon Institute of Social Policy and the School of Policy Studies, Queen's University.

Burt, Sandra, Lorraine Code and Lindsay Dorney (eds.). 1993. *Changing Patterns: Women in Canada*. Second edition. Toronto: McClelland and Stewart.

Caledon Institute of Social Policy. 1995. *Critical Commentaries on the Social Security Review*. Ottawa: The Caledon Institute.

Canadian Advisory Council on the Status of Women. 1994. "Submission to the Ministerial Task Force on Social Security Reform." March. Ottawa: The Canadian Advisory Council on the Status of Women.

Canadian Centre for Policy Alternatives. 1994. "Liberals New Blueprint for Future Focuses on Cutbacks, not Job Creation." *CCPA Monitor*. October. Special Issue.

Canadian Federation of Students. 1995. "Social Program Cuts—Impact on Women." January. Ottawa: Canadian Federation of Students.

Code, Lorraine. 1993. "Feminist Theory." In Sandra Burt, Lorraine Code and Lindsay Dorney (eds.), *Changing Patterns: Women in Canada*. Second edition. Toronto: McClelland and Stewart.

Council of Canadians. 1995. "Danger Ahead: Assessing the Implications of the Canada Health and Social Transfer" by David Robinson. *Standing on Guard for Canada's Social Programs*. March. Ottawa: Council of Canadians.

Department of Finance. 1995a. *Budget Plan: Including Supplementary Information and Notices of Ways and Means Motions*. February 27. Ottawa: Minister of Supply and Services.

———. 1995b. *Budget Speech*. February 27. Ottawa: Minister of Supply and Services.

———. 1994a. *Agenda: Jobs and Growth. A New Framework for Economic Policy*. October. Ottawa: Department of Finance.

———. 1994b. *Creating a Healthy Fiscal Climate: A Presentation by the Honourable Paul Martin to the House of Commons Standing Committee on Finance*. October. Ottawa: Department of Finance.

———. 1994c. *Agenda: Jobs and Growth. Creating a Healthy Fiscal Climate: The Economic and Fiscal Update*. October. Ottawa: Department of Finance.

Eichler, Margrit. 1991. *Nonsexist Research Methods: A Practical Guide*. New York: Routledge.

Gordon, Linda (ed.). 1990. *Women, the State and Welfare*. Madison: University of Wisconsin Press.

Greenspon, Edward. 1995a. "Major UI reform coming, Axworthy says." *Globe and Mail* May 19: A1.

———. 1995b. "New UI plan would cut benefits." *Globe and Mail* June 10: A1.

———. 1995c. "Proposals would make UI tougher to get, paper says." *Ottawa Citizen* June 11.

Harder, Sandra. 1992. *Economic Restructuring in Canada: Developing a Gender-Sensitive Analytic Framework*. Ottawa: Status of Women Canada.

House of Commons. 1995a. *Bill C-76, An Act to Implement Certain Provisions of the Budget Tabled in Parliament on February 27*. Ottawa. (Short title is the *Budget Implementation Act, 1995*).

———. 1995b. *Minutes of Proceedings Relating to Bill C-76, An Act to Implement Certain Provisions of the Budget Tabled in Parliament on February 27*. April-May. Issues Nos. 104-109. Ottawa.

———. Standing Committee on Finance. 1994. *Confronting Canada's Deficit Crisis: Building Our Next Budget through Consultation*. Tenth Report of the Standing Committee on Finance. December. Issue No. 97. Ottawa.

———. Standing Committee on Finance. 1995. *Fifteenth Report of the Standing Committee on Finance* considering Bill C-76. May 19. Issue No. 109. Ottawa.

———. Standing Committee on Human Resources Development. 1995. Final Report. *Security, Opportunities and Fairness: Canadians Renewing Their Social Programs*. February. Ottawa: Queen's Printer.

———. 1994a. *Debates*. "Speech from the Throne." January 18. Ottawa.

———. 1994b. *Debates*. "Government Orders." January 31. Ottawa.

———. 1994c. Standing Committee on Human Resources Development. 1994. Interim Report. *Concerns and Priorities Regarding the Modernization and Restructuring of Canada's Social Security System*. March. Ottawa: Queen's Printer.

———. 1994c. *Minutes of Proceedings and Evidence of the Standing Committee on Finance*. October-December. Issues Nos. 59-94, 96. Ottawa.

———. 1994d. *Minutes of Proceedings and Evidence of the Standing Committee on Human Resources Development*. February-March. Issues Nos. 1-9. Ottawa.

———. 1994e/95. *Minutes of Proceedings and Evidence of the Standing Committee on Human Resources Development*. May-January. Issues Nos. 14, 15, 18, 26-67. Ottawa.

Human Resources Development Canada (HRDC). 1995. *Federal Support to Post-Secondary Education: A Supplementary Paper*. January. Ottawa: Minister of Supply and Services.

———. 1994a. *A Study on the Modernization and Restructuring of Canada's Social Security System: A Focus Paper*. February. Ottawa: Minister of Supply and Services.

———. 1994b. *Child Care and Development: A Supplementary Paper*. October. Ottawa: Minister of Supply and Services.

———. 1994c. *From Unemployment Insurance to Employment Insurance: A Supplementary Paper*.

October. Ottawa: Minister of Supply and Services.

———. 1994d. *Have Your Say...in changing Canada's social programs.* October. Ottawa: Minister of Supply and Services.

———. 1994e. *Improving Social Security in Canada: A Discussion Paper.* October. Ottawa: Minister of Supply and Services.

———. 1994f. *Income Security for Children: A Supplementary Paper.* October. Ottawa: Minister of Supply and Services.

———. 1994g. *Persons with Disabilities: A Supplementary Paper.* October. Ottawa: Minister of Supply and Services.

———. 1994h. *Employment Development Services: A Supplementary Paper.* December. Ottawa: Minister of Supply and Services.

———. 1994i. *Reforming the Canada Assistance Plan: A Supplementary Paper.* December. Ottawa: Minister of Supply and Services.

———. 1994j. *The Context of Reform: A Supplementary Paper.* December. Ottawa: Minister of Supply and Services Canada.

———. 1994k. *Advisory Group on Working Time and the Distribution of Work: Report.* December. Ottawa: Minister of Supply and Services.

International Labour Organization. 1994. *Information Bulletin,* No. 3. Geneva: ILO.

Leadbeater, David. 1995. "Is a Leaner and Meaner Social Policy Really Better for a Polarizing, High-Unemployment Economy?" In *Critical Commentaries on the Social Security Review.* Ottawa: The Caledon Institute, 95-104.

Lero, Donna and Karen Johnson. 1994. *110 Canadian Statistics on Work and Family.* Ottawa: The Canadian Advisory Council on the Status of Women.

Lindgren, April. 1994. "New Evidence Suggests Women Suffer Most in New Economy." Special Report. *Ottawa Citizen* July 23: A1.

National Anti-Poverty Association. 1995. *NAPO News.* Spring (45).

National Association of Women and the Law (NAWL). 1994. "The Federal Social Security Reform: Taking Gender into Account." Submission to the Standing Committee on Human Resources Development and to the Federal Department of Human Resources Development. December 22. Ottawa: National Association of Women and the Law.

National Women's Consultation on the Social Security Review. 1994. *Final Report and Recommendations.* December 3-5. Toronto: National Action Committee on the Status of Women.

Pascall, Gillian. 1986. *Social Policy: A Feminist Analysis.* London and New York: Routledge.

Remus, Cathy. 1994. "Post-Secondary Education: Notes on the Federal Government's Proposals for Post-Secondary Education as Outlined in *Improving Social Security in Canada.*" Ottawa: The Canadian Advisory Council on the Status of Women.

Sassoon, Anne Showstack. 1992. *Women and the State.* London: Routledge. (First published in 1987).

Toulin, Alan. 1995. "UI Reform Proposals Get Cabinet Scrutiny." *Financial Post* May 23: 1.

Townson, Monica. 1994. "Unemployment Insurance: Notes on the Federal Government's Supplementary Paper *From Unemployment Insurance to Employment Insurance*; Research Notes: The Social Security Review and its Implications for Women." November. Ottawa: The Canadian Advisory Council on the Status of Women.

United Nations. United Nations Development Programme. 1992. *Human Development Report 1992.* New York and Oxford: Oxford University Press.

Williams, Fiona. 1989. *Social Policy: A Critical Introduction.* Cambridge: Polity Press.

Woolley, Frances. 1995. "Women and the Canada Assistance Plan: Visions and Alternatives." February. Ottawa: Prepared for Status of Women Canada.

———. 1994. "Intra-Family Inequality: Implications for the Design of Income Support;" Research Notes: The Social Security Review and its Implications for Women. November. Ottawa: The Canadian Advisory Council on the Status of Women.

# CHAPTER 16

# IRREGULAR WORKERS, NEW INVOLUNTARY SOCIAL EXILES: WOMEN AND U.I. REFORM

*Leah F. Vosko*

## INTRODUCTION

In the post-Second World War period, the Canadian welfare state came to be characterized by an income insurance system that operated on two levels. One level administered benefits based on labour force participation. The other consisted of social assistance programs for individuals lacking standard employment. Since the waged work that many women performed, ranging from activities such as part-time, part-year and casual work to temporary work, was often unstable, state policies began to construct women as *irregular* workers in this period. Hence, with the growth of the welfare state, many women were effectively excluded from social insurance programs oriented towards *regular* workers. To this day, despite important changes in women's official labour force participation rates, many Canadian women continue to be ineligible or only marginally eligible for social insurance schemes such as unemployment insurance (U.I.). Indeed, as non-standard forms of work become more prevalent, few women fit the norms first ascribed to regular workers in the post-war era.

This chapter examines the degree to which recent and pending changes to the Canadian U.I. system reflect post-war norms attributed to the regular worker. Focusing on how emerging proposals for U.I. reform may affect the informalization of work, it argues that women non-standard workers are becoming *new* involuntary social exiles in the Canadian welfare state (Moon 1988; Pateman 1988, 1992). To substantiate this argument, the ensuing analysis is divided into two parts. Part I describes the history of the concept of involuntary social exiles and introduces a contemporary reconceptualization of this notion. Characterizing Canada as a liberal welfare state prone to adopting social policies that privilege regular workers, it then introduces images typically associated with regular and irregular workers and examines the extent to which women's labour force profile reflects dominant images of irregular workers. Taking U.I. as a case study, Part II surveys recent U.I. restructuring. It then discusses how pending changes to this system, partly emerging from two federal discussion papers, will influence women's opportunities to become regular workers with comprehensive U.I. coverage.

## PART I

*NEW INVOLUNTARY SOCIAL EXILES*

Contemporary welfare state theorists Carole Pateman and Donald Moon invoke terms such as "involuntary social exiles" and "moral exiles from society" to label citizens lacking resources for full social participation (Moon 1988; Pateman 1988, 1992). These authors generally agree that citizens belonging in this category include poor individuals who can find

Special thanks to Barbara Cameron, Patricia Evans, Geral Kernerman and Katherine Scott for their insightful comments on an earlier draft of this paper.

no one to buy their labour power and individuals who are exiles because they are supposedly *incapable* of being incorporated into society as full social citizens (Moon 1988: 41; Pateman 1992: 225). This develops Hegel's (1991) conception of women as natural social exiles (Pateman 1988: 235), presumably belonging in the *incapable* category, yet he believed that women should still be granted certain rights by the state. He argued that women must be *indirectly* incorporated into the state as family members. Thus, Hegel's solution was to create a sphere separate from society (i.e., the family) that "had its own ascriptive principles of association" (Pateman 1988: 236).

According to Pateman and Moon, Hegel's beliefs about incorporating women into the state via the family influenced early social policies adopted by liberal welfare states. Initially, these policies were designed to serve women indirectly through their attachment to male breadwinners. Eventually, however, women became full social citizens in modern liberal welfare states in an official, legal sense. Nancy Fraser (1989) even goes as far as arguing that women are now the principal subjects of the liberal welfare state. Referring to the U.S. case, Fraser (1989: 147) notes:

> On the one hand, they [women] make up the overwhelming majority both of program recipients and of paid social service workers. On the other hand they are the wives, mothers, and daughters whose unpaid activities and obligations are redefined as the welfare state increasingly oversees forms of caregiving. Since this beneficiary/ social worker/caregiver nexus of roles is constitutive of the social-welfare arena, one might even call this arena a feminized terrain.

While women may now be the principal subjects of many liberal welfare states, their social citizenship status continues to be rigidly confined to a "nexus of roles" (e.g., public sector workers, caregivers, welfare recipients) that reflect traditional "feminine" qualities which, ironically, were once used to label them as involuntary social exiles. Liberal welfare states no longer officially exclude women from social insurance schemes geared towards workers because of their *innate* nature. However, due to the dominance of outmoded social policy models oriented towards the regular post-war worker, many women workers *defacto* continue to be excluded from various social insurance schemes.

By referring to *new* involuntary social exiles, this analysis extends more stereotypical notions of social exiles to cover an emerging underclass of under employed workers in liberal welfare states who are ineligible or only marginally eligible for social insurance catered to the regular worker. In the Canadian case, many of these new precarious workers are women engaged in non-standard forms of employment such as temporary, part-time, part-year or contingent work.[1]

## CHARACTERISTIC FEATURES OF THE CANADIAN LIBERAL WELFARE REGIME

Although many authors are critical of grouping welfare states under a single regime type since each state has its own unique attributes, liberal welfare states tend to be characterized by several common features (Esping Andersen 1990; Leira 1993: 50; Lewis 1993; Orloff 1994: 3-4). Liberal welfare states generally make greater use of means-tested, targeted social assistance than other regimes. They tend to devote little policy emphasis to the decommodification of labour and broad-based social citizenship rights. Instead, liberal welfare states allow the market to erect an order of economic stratification (Esping-Andersen 1990: 27). Referring to the evolution of social assistance in liberal welfare states, Gosta Esping-Andersen (1990: 62) notes: "While the market was left unfettered to stratify its participants along the cash nexus, the liberal welfare state established an extraordinarily punitive and stigmatizing poor relief for market failures."

Canada's status as a liberal welfare state is marked by its unique mix of limited universal social programs (e.g., health care and education), a weak commitment to full employment, and neoliberal fiscal and monetary policies resulting from its vulnerability to the international market. There is also an apparent social policy commitment to maintain women's and men's separate spheres (Bakker and Scott 1995: 23). While a mixture of non-contributory and contributory social programs exist in Canada, federal and provincial governments are beginning to place greater emphasis on means-testing, under the rubric of "targeting." In combining income based and insurance based social policy models, Canada is clearly moving in the direction of residualism—social benefits are increasingly selective or contributory and state intervention into the market is diminishing (Hobson 1990: 243; Lewis 1993: 13-14; Orloff 1994: 5).

Although the belief that public provision should be residual is weaker in Canada than in the United States due to its strong universal health care, education systems and a history of universal programs such as Family Allowance, the government relies on disincentives to ensure that anyone reliant on social assistance is no better off than the poorest worker (O'Connor 1989: 132-33; Orloff 1994: 3). Specifically, the direction of social security reform denotes a shift towards linking a wider variety of social programs to labour force participation and job seeking. In the case of U.I., which always tied entitlements to labour force attachment, the federal government recently began to link eligibility for U.I. more rigidly to specific forms of labour force participation, tailoring criteria to reflect narrow post-war images of the regular worker. As a result of social security reform, new images of the "worker citizen" are arising in Canada: all citizens are expected to work and be "self-supporting" and the "good citizen" must now understand the appropriate boundaries and limitations of state support (Brodie 1994: 56-57; Fraser and Gordon 1994: 324). As this chapter shall illustrate, many women non-standard workers do not conform to these images.

## THE REGULAR WORKER

With the growth of the liberal welfare state in the 1930s, various industrializing countries initiated social insurance schemes to protect social groups that historically experienced poverty. Slowly recovering from the depression and concerned about the growing possibility of social unrest, state officials created social policies that aimed to both protect the unskilled, semi-skilled and skilled labour force and provide income support for individuals unfit for employment (Pearce 1990: 269-70).

Embedded in the policies evolving over this period, particularly those related to employment, was a relatively fixed image of the *regular* worker. In most liberal welfare states after the Second World War, the term "worker" generally evoked an image of the male breadwinner who engaged in waged activities in the primary sector of the economy. Ideally, this male worker participated in full-time, full-year employment, could perform a skilled trade of some sort and had a history of continuous employment (Callender 1993: 131; Hobson 1990: 247). However, post-war social policies marked a significant turn in state policy-making since they also provided unprecedented security to semi-skilled and unskilled male workers, cushioning them from poverty. Conversely, the image associated with the *irregular* worker strikingly resembled that of a "pauper" or that of a casual worker who largely engaged in low wage, precarious employment in the secondary sector (Pearce 1990: 270). The image of the typical irregular worker did not even apply to unwaged workers, such as women providing care to their families in the home. Rather, it represented waged workers who did not fit the norms attributed to regular workers in the age of mass production.

Although many waged workers did not to conform to the socially constructed image of the regular worker, social policies created by post-war liberal welfare states were grounded on the norms ascribed to these workers. The development of U.I. policy in liberal welfare states, such as Britain, Canada and the United States, substantiates this claim. U.I. policy models stemmed from the belief that regular workers suffering from unemployment required different social supports than irregular workers. Regular workers received assistance in job searches, training and education and substantial income supports when unemployed. They were encouraged to search for the appropriate job as opposed to seeking and accepting re-employment at any cost. According to Diane Pearce (1985: 441-42), "the emphasis focused on not allowing the unemployed to become 'unemployables.'" In contrast, upon the inception of U.I. programs, irregular workers were frequently treated as "unemployables." Due to the tenuous nature of their labour force participation, they were routinely excluded from training, job placement programs and income payments. Claire Callender (1993: 141) reinforces the way in which social divisions first emerged between regular and irregular workers in the U.K. calling attention to the "queuing principle." Applicable to other liberal welfare states as well, this principle suggested that certain groups of workers were perceived to have greater entitlements to paid employment, particularly during difficult economic times. Irregular workers were defined out of the labour force during economic slumps since they had lesser entitlements to available employment.

With restrictive definitions of the regular worker, a vast majority of women workers were excluded from U.I. in the post-war period. For example, in Canada, married women were automatically excluded from U.I. from 1950 until 1957 and, in Britain, they only began to qualify for redundancy benefits in 1975 (Callender 1993: 133). Ultimately, early U.I. policies in these liberal welfare states conveyed a strong moral message:

> In regard to women's, particularly mothers', eligibility for U.I., policies reflect the paradoxical logic that since women should not be working, those who do are at best casual workers and therefore do not deserve the help through U.I. given the serious regular worker. (Pearce 1985: 444)

To a large extent, this "moral" message continues to resonate in liberal welfare states today. However, there was a span of approximately thirty years when U.I. coverage improved incrementally for women in Canada. After U.I. was extended to include married women in 1957, the system was transformed into a social insurance scheme that officially catered to individual workers rather than providing insurance to families composed of primary bread-winners and their dependents. Canadian women finally obtained maternity benefits in 1971 and the dependency allowance, which solely recognized men's family responsibilities, was eliminated in 1975. That said, with the 1985 report of the Royal Commission on the Economic

Union and Development Prospects for Canada (the "Macdonald Commission"), which argued that U.I. provides *too* generous a subsidy to Canadians whose labour force behaviour is characterized by unstable employment, the U.I. system came under renewed scrutiny by policy-makers.

## IRREGULAR *WORKERS, WOMEN EXILES*

By invoking the concept *new* involuntary social exiles, this chapter attempts synthesis between traditional views of involuntary social exiles and the notion of the irregular worker arising from feminist literature on the welfare state (Leira 1993; Moon 1988; Orloff 1994; Pateman 1988, 1992). This reconceptualization updates traditional definitions of involuntary social exiles to include the growing underclass of irregular workers in most liberal welfare states, many of whom are female non-standard workers ineligible or only marginally eligible for U.I.

As previously noted, traditional conceptions of involuntary social exiles include two categories of individuals—poor workers who are unable to earn a living wage and individuals *incapable* of being fully incorporated into social citizenship because of their reputed *innate* nature. Feminist scholars often assert that women initially were perceived to fall into the second category of individuals and, with the growth of the welfare state, they were formally incorporated into the society as family members or "dependents" of male breadwinners (Fraser 1989: 147-48; Pateman 1992: 226; Pearce 1990: 275). Similarly, in reference to irregular workers who were not entitled to various social benefits in the post-war era, many of whom were women, it is suggested that women's initial integration into the welfare state as family members effectively confined them to certain types of work (Callender 1993: 131-32; Pearce 1990: 269-70). For example, until the late '50s, married women were ineligible for U.I. in Canada simply because they were regarded as "dependents" of male breadwinners who were entitled to redundancy benefits that covered their families. Since this assumption initially contributed to women's over-representation in casual work, an investigation of labour force trends for women is an appropriate point of departure in applying the preceding reconceptualization to the Canadian case (Callender 1993 : 131-32; Pearce 1990: 269-70; Pearce 1985: 443).

### *Labour force trends for women*

A growing number of Canadian women are becoming irregular workers. While women's overall labour force participation rates rose rapidly until 1991, increasingly they are engaged in non-standard employment, ranging from self-employment to temporary work to part-time and part-year work.[2] For example, in 1993, 60 percent of all the new jobs created were non-standard, the majority of which went to women (Human Resources and Development Canada [HRDC] 1994: 49). This trend is not surprising given that, in 1993, there was an increase of 69,000 part-time jobs for women in all sectors yet 125,000 fewer full-time jobs were available to women during the same year (Armstrong 1993: 1). Women consistently comprise approximately 70 percent of all part-time workers in Canada (Status of Women Canada 1994: 12).

In the manufacturing sector, where steady full-time jobs remain somewhat common,[3] women are under-represented with the exception of the textiles, furs, leather, clothing and food industries.[4] Altogether, they only account for 19 percent of all employees in Canadian manufacturing (Status of Women Canada 1994: 11). In the case of self-employment, between 1970 and 1990, the number of women in this category grew by 265 percent while the equivalent figure for men was 74 percent (Crompton 1993: 29). The staggering growth of self-employment for women over the last twenty years reflects the prevalence of this form of employment in service producing industries and recent government initiatives to promote small business. Women are starting small businesses at three times the rate of men and 70 percent of small businesses run by women are in the home (Status of Women Canada 1994: 14). Similarly, with regard to temporary work, married women are the mainstay of the temporary help industry where part-time work is the norm (Akyeampong 1989: 44). Married women's disproportionate participation in the temporary help industry may reflect the prevalence of part-time work in this field and the rising hourly eligibility requirements for U.I.

Labour force trends indicate that a growing number of women workers, particularly those performing non-standard forms of work, do not benefit from a reconstituted worker citizen model that privileges specialized, full-time, full-year workers and erodes social protections extended to unskilled and semi-skilled workers in the post-war period. With the pending changes to the U.I. system, comprehensive U.I. coverage for these workers is under threat. The ensuing sections probe this issue further by investigating the extent to which U.I. policy privileges the regular worker and the degree to which the federal government is recognizing the changing conditions of women's work.

## Part II

### *Restructuring Unemployment Insurance*

The restructuring of the U.I. system in the 1990s began with the elimination of the requirement for federal contributions to the U.I. fund in times of high unemployment through Bill C-21. In 1993, benefit rates were reduced to 57 percent of employment income and more stringent reporting requirements were introduced for all U.I. claimants. Simultaneously, cuts to the system also involved disqualifying workers who "voluntarily" quit their jobs or were fired for "misconduct"; these amendments to the U.I. Act were enacted through Bill C-113.

After changing the U.I. regulations in 1993, the government optimistically predicted that the U.I. account would have a $0.5 billion deficit for 1994, leaving it in relatively stable condition for workers eligible for U.I. coverage.[5] However, by the most recent count (November 1994), the U.I. account will have a $2.7 billion surplus from 1994 due to the legislative changes recently adopted. According to Employment and Immigration Canada (1994: 4): "This turnabout is due to a reduction of nearly $3.4 billion in program costs (to $17.2 billion instead of a forecast of $20.5 billion), accompanied by a small reduction in revenues." The government attributes cost reductions to several measures including "the increased effectiveness of control measures," such as tougher eligibility requirements for workers, which resulted from Bill C-113 and the most recent reforms contained in Bill C-17 (Employment and Immigration Canada 1994: 4).

Bill C-17 (June 15, 1994) raised U.I. entrance requirements, cutback the duration of claims and reduced benefits to 55 percent of employment income for the majority[6] of U.I. recipients. The rate of U.I. beneficiaries as a percentage of unemployed persons dropped dramatically as a result of this bill.

> In 1990, before the government began slashing benefits, 87 percent of the unem-
> ployed [in Canada] were U.I. beneficiaries and at the end of 1994, only 58 percent
> were receiving U.I.. In Ontario the percent of unemployed protected by U.I. has
> plunged to 42 percent. Unemployment Insurance protection in Manitoba and
> Alberta is below 50 percent. In British Columbia and Saskatchewan U.I. now
> protects slightly more than half. And in Quebec protection has fallen from 97 percent
> to 68 percent. (Canadian Labour Congress 1995: 2)[7]

Most notably, Employment and Immigration Canada assumes that, due to savings from Bill
C-17, the ratio of beneficiaries to unemployed persons will be allowed to fall to merely 56
percent nationally by the end of 1995 (Employment and Immigration Canada 1994: 13).[8]

Along with the 1994 federal budget, the government indicated that it would proceed with
further U.I. cutbacks in its next budget.[9] It also announced a national social security review,
a primary objective of which involved making proposals for U.I. reform. A discussion paper
produced by the Human Resources and Development Canada (1994), *Agenda: Jobs and
Growth. Improving Social Security In Canada (ISSC)*, and a report of the Standing Committee
on Human Resources Development (1995), entitled *Security, Opportunities and Fairness:
Canadians Renewing Their Social Programs (SOF)*, represent two recent government inter-
ventions into U.I. restructuring. While these reports make recommendations for U.I. reform
that are not yet implemented, the federal government prepared *ISSC* and commissioned *SOF*
with the explicit purpose of developing guidelines for revamping social insurance programs
such as U.I.

The complementary and conflicting recommendations arising from these reports reflect
the different mandates of those responsible for preparing the documents. In writing *SOF*, the
Standing Committee had a dual purpose. This federally appointed body, which consisted of
representatives from the Liberal Party, the Reform Party and the Bloc Québécois, consulted
with six hundred organizations and individual citizens in twenty-two cities regarding their
views on social security and independently reviewed recommendations presented in *ISSC*.
Quite distinctly, *ISSC* was initiated and prepared by elected officials and bureaucrats in the
Ministry of Human Resources Development Canada. As a consequence, *SOF* documents a
greater degree of debate than *ISSC* due to the presence of representatives from political parties
forming the opposition and the numerous submissions from organizations and individuals
opposing the direction of social security reform.[10]

The ensuing analysis provides an overview of the direction of U.I. reform by outlining
key proposals contained in these reports since, together, they create a blueprint for change that
will be instrumental to the federal Cabinet in drafting future legislation. If implemented, many
recommendations common to both reports will have devastating effects for women non-
standard workers.

## IMPROVING SOCIAL SECURITY IN CANADA (ISSC)

In presenting strategies for U.I. reform, *ISSC* presents two alternative models. One model
involves radically altering the structure of U.I. and the other involves making significant cuts
to the existing system. The first model takes a two-tiered approach to U.I.[11] Under this model,
frequent claimants[12] receive minimal financial assistance and are obligated to participate in
employment development services (EDS) such as counseling and retraining. This benefit

scheme is termed adjustment insurance. Conversely, occasional claimants, including workers claiming parental, maternity, adoption and sick benefits, receive basic insurance benefits virtually identical to those currently in place.

The proposed framework for adjustment insurance involves altering the duration of claims as well as benefit levels based on several premises derived from a recent job study produced by the Organization for Economic Cooperation and Development (OECD).[13] Concerning the duration of claims, ISSC recommends that frequent claimants receive lower levels of financial assistance for longer periods to encourage them to obtain adequate training, employment counseling and job placement that, presumably, shall enable them to become regular workers (HRDC 1994: 46). The equation for benefit levels, however, is less simple. Under this approach, benefits for frequent claimants are based on need with the following proviso: "Since frequent claimants could expect a larger investment in employment development, lower income support may be sensible" (HRDC 1994: 46). This model also recommends family income-testing as a possible mechanism for determining need. Income-testing for frequent claimants could prevent individuals with adequate family incomes from using income supports simply because they are available (HRDC 1994: 47).

As well as altering benefit levels and the duration of U.I. claims, this model involves strengthening adjustment programs such as retraining and other skills development initiatives. It also indicates that access to insurance benefits could "be conditional on a willingness to participate in such adjustment programs or other community service," implying that frequent claimants should be obliged to participate in some form of retraining or community work while receiving U.I. (HRDC 1994: 47). The proposal to make participation in these EDS mandatory is reminiscent of workfare (HRDC 1994: 38).

The second model for U.I. reform is not two-tiered. Instead of clearly distinguishing between frequent and occasional claimants, it involves making entrance requirements for U.I. claimants stricter and reducing present benefit levels. Through this model, the government proposes to alter entrance requirements through one of two measures. It would either increase entrance requirements to between fourteen and twenty weeks on a yearly basis, reducing U.I. expenditures by $350 million and affecting an estimated 42,000 people, or base U.I. eligibility on an individual claimant's work history over the past two years.

Several options for reducing benefit levels are also introduced in the second model. Although they are quite distinct, these options are not mutually exclusive. The first alternative is to reduce current replacement earnings by 5 percent across the board, from 55 percent-60 percent to 50 percent-55 percent of the recipient's previous earnings. This harmonizes benefit levels with those in the United States. The second alternative is to introduce a graduated benefit rate which decreases with subsequent claims. This option represents a less rigid, multi-tiered version of the frequent claimant versus occasional claimant option presented in the first model. It privileges regular workers with stable employment over irregular workers with part-year or intermittent employment. The third option is to shorten the duration of benefits in regions with high rates of unemployment.[14]

Embedded in these two models for U.I. reform are specific recommendations regarding how to implement family income-testing, experience ratings,[15] improved EDS and, most notably, how to distinguish frequent claimants (i.e., irregular workers) from occasional U.I. claimants (i.e. regular workers). If implemented, many of these recommendations would induce *gendered* effects: women workers are most likely to lose U.I. eligibility under family income-testing; women represent a growing percentage of frequent claimants; and EDS explicitly targets frequent claimants and "employable" social assistance recipients (Vosko 1995). However, proposals contained in *issc* are by no means fixed. There is dissension among Liberal Cabinet members and within the Standing Committee on Human Resources Development (Ecumenical Coalition for Economic Justice 1993); as well, various social movement groups are contesting the government proposals. Consequently, for the purposes of this chapter, a comparison between *issc* and *sof* is invaluable in tracking the direction and scope of U.I. reform.

## SECURITY, OPPORTUNITIES AND FAIRNESS (SOF)

The February 1995 Report of the Standing Committee on Human Resources Development endorses many proposals contained in *issc,* including recommendations for improved EDS and a so-called "electronic hiring hall" which would use information technology to link employers to available workers across the country. As well, it builds on a discussion, regarding extending U.I. coverage to part-time and contract workers initiated in *issc.* Notably, however, the report explicitly rejects *issc* proposals for family income-testing and lowering U.I. premiums and, instead, makes new proposals of its own such as the proposal to extend coverage to part-time and contract workers.

Echoing *issc,* the Standing Committee supports the consolidation of employment training, counseling and income supports for "employable" social assistance recipients and U.I. claimants through "the establishment of a network of single-window offices to serve Canadians" who are seeking assistance from federal and provincial programs (1995: 77).[16] The Standing Committee also supports giving provinces greater responsibility for the training and design of these services as well as involving the private sector in their delivery; it views the role of the federal government as purely regulatory. Interestingly, *sof* suggests that the specific needs of women be considered in the design and delivery of EDS (HRDC 1995: 80). This recommendation is quite predictable given that EDS, as envisioned in *issc,* appear to target specific groups of women, such as "employable" social assistance recipients and frequent U.I. claimants, rather than catering to all workers universally (Vosko 1995: 16-17).

If a multi-tiered U.I. system is adopted whereby EDS attend to individuals receiving lower U.I. benefits or individuals ineligible for U.I. due to a lack of continuous employment, repeat U.I. claimants and "employable" social assistance recipients will be *more* obligated to participate in these services than regular workers experiencing unemployment. Referring to what these groups have in common, *issc* notes that "some may have work-related problems that are symptoms of deeply-rooted social problems—often arising in childhood, and then passed on through failures in school and early job experiences" (HRDC 1994: 31). Elsewhere I have noted that *issc* attributes unemployment among frequent claimants and employable social assistance recipients to individual, primarily psychological, problems that may be dealt with through EDS (Vosko 1995). While it refers to the problems shared by these groups of unemployed people, *issc* neglects to acknowledge another commonality between both groups; a majority of "employable" social assistance recipients and a growing number of repeat claimants are women (O'Connor 1989: 504; Employment and Immigration Canada 1993). Although *sof* does not go to the same lengths as *issc* in promoting EDS, the agenda of *issc* is implicit in the Standing Committee's recommendation to strengthen EDS and devote specific attention to needs of unemployed women.

The Standing Committee also supports investing U.I. funds in an electronic hiring hall. Its report notes that information networks, which could be accessible in Canada Employment Centres, libraries and in the private sector, must be created using "data bases on vacancies, occupations and skill requirements as well as on workers seeking employment, profiling their skills and requirements" (HRDC 1995: 78, 79). According to *sof*, this method of matching suitable employees to employers would benefit all interested parties. The private sector, the provinces, the federal government and local volunteer sectors should cooperate to make the electronic hiring hall a reality (HRDC 1995: 80).

Although *sof* neglects to discuss how this system could serve to monitor unemployed workers to ensure that they are truly "available for work" and "actively seeking work," an electronic hiring hall has the potential to eliminate many unemployed workers from the U.I. system, particularly if they are unwilling to accept certain types of employment or to relocate. If the definition of "availability" is expanded to require unemployed workers to relocate to where a "suitable" job is available, this device could aid in enforcing modified eligibility requirements. Given this scenario, many women workers would not qualify for U.I. since women's mobility is frequently constrained by family obligations. An analogy with the situation of women in southern Europe under a common European market substantiates such concerns. After the European Economic Community (EEC) officially took shape, due to the provision permitting the free flow of labour, many Southern European women were forced into the informal economy simply because they could not afford to relocate where suitable employment was available. In other words, women's everyday lives, more than men's, were tied to particular places. As a result, the informal economies in France, Italy, Portugal and Spain are swelling and women represent a disproportionate percentage of *new* informal workers. In addition, governments now "advocate a tolerance of informal activities as a medium-term policy goal" for lagging Southern European countries (Stratigaki and Vaiou 1994: 1224).

While *sof* reinforces many of the arguments made in *issc*, it also recommends that U.I. benefits be extended to part-time and contract workers (HRDC 1995: 89). Coming from a federally appointed Standing Committee, this proposal represents an unprecedented move. It may reflect the desire to redesign the U.I. system to embrace changing labour force trends or the desire to facilitate the growth of non-standard employment and give greater symbolic legitimacy to irregular forms of work. To accommodate part-time and contract workers, the Standing Committee suggests that U.I. benefits be counted from the first dollar a claimant earns and recommends that workers be allowed to bundle hours and/or count their best-paying weeks in setting benefit levels (HRDC 1995: 89).

This recommendation is the basis of a key proposal made by Lloyd Axworthy to the federal Cabinet. In addressing Cabinet's Economic Development Committee in June 1995, based on the *issc* and *sof*, Axworthy proposed that the formula used to calculate U.I. be changed to reflect the total number of hours a claimant works over a given period rather than the total number of weeks. He further recommended that the minimum qualifying requirement for U.I. be raised from twelve weeks at fifteen hours per week (180 hours total) to 445 hours total (Greenspon 1995: A10). This type of proposal indicates that the move to extend U.I. coverage to part-time workers may primarily be symbolic. Extending coverage to part-time workers, while simultaneously changing the formula to calculate benefits and tightening entrance requirements (i.e., demanding a greater number of hours of work to qualify for U.I.), would disproportionately favour full-time, full-year workers and encourage part-time work-ers to become multiple job holders. Thus, although this appears to be a relatively progressive recommendation, its positive effects will be minimal if proposals for continuous employment requirements for new workers and "lifelong" employment insurance accompany it.

In reality, if the government lowers benefits, U.I. will not provide part-time workers with much supplementary income. In the case of multiple job holders, the system will discourage workers from making claims if they lose one of their jobs since claimants can only earn 25 percent of their U.I. benefits on top of U.I. payments before facing deductions. Mirroring the objectives of ISSC, both these proposals could contribute to creating a unique type of tiered U.I. system, one in which many workers would either experience delayed eligibility for U.I. or be excluded from a range of U.I. benefits. Regarding the continuous employment requirement for "new workers," SOF (HRDC 1995: 89) states:

> The committee also believes that steps need to be taken to discourage young people from short-circuiting their education and beginning an annual pattern of short-term jobs combined with long periods on U.I. *We believe that full U.I. entitlements for new workers should take more than the usual minimum qualifying period.* (emphasis added)

This recommendation would require new workers, presumably young people and people who have engaged in waged work on an intermittent basis in the past, to build up eligibility over a longer period than the current minimum qualifying period (HRDC 1995: 91). If imple-mented,[17] it could have devastating implications for women for two reasons. First, due to their reproductive roles, women typically take breaks from the labour force early in their careers. Thus, depending on the extended length of eligibility requirements imposed, they may be less likely than men to initially fulfill the continuous employment requirement. They are also highly concentrated in irregular forms of work. Second, women aged fifteen to twenty-four are more likely to be unemployed than any other age group of men or women (Status of Women Canada 1994: 14). If this proposal is implemented, U.I. eligibility for the next generation of young women workers could become significantly more delayed than for their male counterparts and, perhaps, even more delayed that the Standing Committee recom-mends.

Similarly, SOF recommends that U.I. has a "lifelong" application. Instead of determining a claimant's eligibility by measuring his or her labour force participation over the preceding year, an eligible worker could choose to accumulate benefits and entitlements over the course of his or her working life. The report (HRDC 1995: 90) states:

> To borrow an analogy from the life insurance industry, the current U.I. program in Canada can be thought of as a "term" insurance program. The kind of transformed U.I. program that this envisages is one modeled along "whole life" lives [sic].

Ultimately, this proposal would reward occasional U.I. claimants since they could "bank" the most benefits, and workers engaging in continuous employment (i.e. regular workers).[18] A multi-tiered U.I. system would inevitably emerge.

Recommendations for an electronic hiring hall, improved EDS, continuous employment requirements for new workers and "lifelong" U.I., clearly reflect the spirit of *issc*. Both the federal government and the standing committee favour implementing a multi-tiered U.I. system, they merely approach the issue differently—*issc* clearly distinguishes between frequent and occasional U.I. claimants and *sof* proposes specific measures that would privilege occasional claimants and prevent frequent claimants from drawing comprehensive U.I. benefits. The primary area where debate remains relates to U.I. coverage for part-time, contract and self-employed workers. *sof* indicates that there is potential for extending U.I. to these workers. However, if implemented, this measure may not provide the degree of protection for irregular workers that it promises. Proposals to lower benefit levels, privilege "lifelong" employees and promote continuous employment may counter the potentially positive effects that would arise from extending U.I. coverage to part-time and contract workers. Therefore, the Standing Committee proposal may primarily be symbolic; while *sof* officially recognizes the changing conditions of work in Canada, which are particularly drastic for women non-standard workers, it clearly supports moving towards a multi-tiered U.I. system that penalizes irregular workers.

*sof* and *issc* identify common directions for U.I. reform. Both documents make complementary proposals to alter the U.I. system, many of which are premised upon norms first attributed to regular workers in the post-war era. For example, in the case of EDS, the proposal to create single-window services suggests that irregular workers neglect to conform to regular work patterns due to a lack of initiative and training. Rather than acknowledging changing economic conditions that make irregular forms of work increasingly prevalent, the government advocates psychological and employment counseling for displaced workers and takes a passive approach to long-term job creation to induce workers to alter their employment patterns to conform to post-war norms. If implemented, the proposal to create an electronic hiring hall will also impose outmoded post-war standards on U.I. claimants by monitoring unemployment workers using EDS.

While proposals to create an electronic hiring hall and to consolidate EDS reflect traditional assumptions about regular workers, lifelong employment proposals and continuous work requirements for new workers reflect these assumptions to an even greater degree. In effect, U.I. policies that encourage lifelong employment will disproportionately serve regular workers since the worker engaging in full-time, full-year employment until retirement will accrue the greatest benefits. Ironically, however, the image of a regular worker presented in this policy is increasingly elusive—particularly with the accelerated growth of non-standard forms of work. Lifelong employment measures create the image of an "ideal" worker that, in reality, is unattainable for most women workers. Correspondingly, recommending continuous employment requirements for new workers also suggests that steady work is readily available. This proposal implies that young people, particularly young women, engage in irregular work by choice rather than out of necessity. The collapse of the opportunity structure for full-time work indicates that irregular work increasingly is the only choice. Given that the government is considering extending coverage to part-time and contract workers, pending changes to U.I. are highly contradictory. Modifications to the U.I. system may accommodate more workers yet illusory post-war norms about the regular worker clearly inform these changes.

## WOMEN NON-STANDARD WORKERS: NEW INVOLUNTARY SOCIAL EXILES?

This chapter attempted to synthesize traditional, as well as feminist, conceptions of involuntary social exiles with the notion of the irregular worker arising in the post-war period. It merged these two concepts to create a discrete analytic category—*new* involuntary social exiles—that encompasses a growing underclass of precariously employed women workers in liberal welfare states. In Canada, non-standard women workers represent an emerging group of new involuntary social exiles. Although they sell their labour power in the market, be it in the formal or the informal economy, they are either marginally eligible or ineligible for social insurance and are often unable to earn a living wage. Recent and pending changes to the U.I. system exacerbate deteriorating social conditions for this group of workers.

Together, Parts I and II of this chapter illustrated that the direction of U.I. reform is contributing to the emergence of this new category of involuntary social exiles in Canada. Part I first described the worker citizen model common to liberal welfare states such as Canada. It exhibited that non-standard workers do not conform to dominant images of the "ideal" worker embedded in this model. By valorizing the worker citizen, liberal welfare states have historically excluded irregular workers from full social citizenship. At present, they effectively cast non-standard workers as social exiles. Second, it traced the historical construction of the *regular* worker in the post-war period. Remarkably, as feminist scholarship reveals, governments initially barred women from social insurance due to their *innate* nature. Subsequently, they catered social insurance programs to regular workers. Even with their large scale entry into wage work, many women remain excluded from social insurance programs due to the nature of their labour force participation. Although women are now full social citizens of the liberal welfare state, women non-standard workers are becoming new involuntary social exiles due to the reconstitution of a worker citizen model with roots in the post-war period. The direction of U.I. reform in Canada is a case in point. Third, and finally, Part I provided statistical evidence exhibiting Canadian women's increasingly disproportionate representation in part-time, temporary and part-year work as well as self-employment. While women's labour force participation rates rose in the post-war period, and the law now guarantees women full social citizenship, synthesizing the concept of irregular workers and involuntary social exiles allows us to locate an emerging group of social exiles in Canada— women non-standard workers.

Building on the compelling evidence of women's rising participation in non-standard forms of work, Part II detailed how pending changes to U.I. may affect women non-standard workers. It compared proposals for U.I. reform contained in two important government reports to assess recent policy developments. Investigating the direction of U.I. reform, this section illustrated that a multi-tiered U.I. system which privileges an elite group of workers is emerging in Canada. Within this system, the citizen who most resembles the regular post-war worker, especially the ideal skilled worker engaged in full-time continuous employment, benefits significantly while the most irregular worker is highly disadvantaged.

In the future, the federal government may extend U.I. coverage to part-time and self-employed workers. However, if proposed changes to the U.I. system in the form of variable benefit levels, continuous employment requirements for "new workers" and the introduction of an electronic hiring hall are implemented, they could offset this potentially progressive move. Herein lies an inherent contradiction in the direction of U.I. reform. While many non-standard workers may become eligible for U.I., qualifying requirements and benefit levels increasingly hinge on post-war assumptions about the regular worker. Women non-standard workers are among the new involuntary social exiles in the Canadian welfare state and, most important, the direction of U.I. reform is entrenching their tenuous social and economic status.

## Notes

1.  In part, this group of *new* involuntary social exiles is expanding due to the intensification of the feminized character of occupations, such as clerical and service work, which have always been important for women (Cohen 1994: 108).

2.  Women of colour, particularly immigrant women, are over-represented in jobs prone to informalization, such as semi-skilled and unskilled jobs in labour intensive manufacturing sectors and clerical jobs, and under-represented in middle and upper level management positions despite high education levels (Gabriel and Macdonald 1994: 5; Ng 1990: 101-02). For example, according to the Ontario Women's Directorate, over 14 percent of women of colour who are clerical workers have university degrees as opposed to 4 percent of women in the rest of Ontario's population (Ontario Women's Directorate 1993). As a consequence of these labour force trends and with the direction of U.I. reform, women of colour may be over-represented among the new involuntary social exiles in the Canadian liberal welfare state.

3.  De-industrialization is also taking place in the manufacturing sector. This has devastating consequences for men, as well as women, since they represent the bulk of workers filling unionized jobs in manufacturing. Recent findings illustrate that when men's jobs disappear in manufacturing, they disappear altogether; they are not replaced with more contingent forms of work. Thus, the decline of manufacturing employment contributes to eroding the post-war assumptions about the primary role of the male breadwinner (Cohen 1994: 108; Brodie 1994: 50-51).

4.  Employment in these industries severely declined after the introduction of the Canada-U.S. Free Trade Agreement (Vosko 1994: 104-06). The decline of these major manufacturing employers of women is particularly devastating for women of colour, immigrant women, who are disproportionately represented these sectors (Ochran et al. 1993: 8; Vosko 1994: 7-8).

5.  This prediction was based on a 10 percent unemployment rate. Given that the economy is recovering from a recession, continuing to use a 10 percent national unemployment rate as a baseline for U.I. budgetary proposals is both unrealistic and overly cautionary. Predicted savings in the U.I. account may be conservatively low since the government admits that a 1 percent variation in the unemployment rate could have about a $1.1 billion impact on the U.I. account (Employment and Immigration Canada 1994: 11).

6.  Claimants, or claimants' spouses who support one or more persons may receive higher benefit rates (60 percent) if their average weekly earnings during their qualifying period are less than 50 percent of the maximum weekly insurable earnings (Employment and Immigration Canada 1994, Appendix VI: 7).

7.  A media commentator recently demonstrated that U.I. coverage rates have not been this low since the extension of U.I. to seasonal workers in 1957 (Monserbraaten 1994: B1).

8.  Already, by the end of January 1995, the ratio of beneficiaries to unemployed persons dipped to 52 percent (Kevin Hayes, 1995, Canadian Labour Congress (CLC), citing unpublished Statistics Canada figures, Personal Communication).

9.  In the current budget, the federal government announced $700 million worth of cuts to U.I. indicating that it aims to reduce the size of the program by no less than 10 percent by July 1996 (Department of Finance 1995). Several other regulatory changes also accompany these expenditure reductions. For instance, the U.I. fund will now be allowed to accumulate a $5 billion surplus to "mitigate unemployment insurance premium rate increases during periods of slowing economic growth" (Department of Finance 1995: 12).

10. While the dissenting opinions of representatives from the Reform Party and the Bloc Québécois

are documented in *SOF*, they are rarely discussed in the body of the text. Since their arguments appear in the appendices, the core recommendations of this report largely reflect the official position of the federal Liberal Party.

11. In its report, the government explicitly favours Model 1 (HRDC 1994: 42).
12. According to one definition of "frequent claimants" (three or more claims in five years) 38 percent of existing U.I. claims are made by frequent claimants (HRDC 1994: 46).
13. The OECD recently produced a job study that served as a blueprint for *ISSC*. I discuss the similarities between these two documents in "Recreating Dependency: Women, Unemployment and the Federal Proposals for U.I. Reform." In Daniel Drache and Andrew Ranikin (eds.), 1995. *Warm Heart, Cold Country: Fiscal and Social Policy Reform in Canada*. Toronto: Caledon Press.
14. The maximum duration of U.I. in regions with exceptionally high unemployment rates is fifty weeks.
15. Experience ratings are a method of calculating premiums where the contribution a worker makes depends upon how often he or she has used U.I. in the past and the contribution made by the employer is based on its lay-off record.
16. Extra moneys from the U.I. fund would be available for improving these services if the government lowers U.I. benefits (HRDC 1995: 89).
17. In its report, the Standing Committee does not make concrete recommendations for a revised minimum qualifying period for "new workers." However, based on *SOF*, federal Cabinet is considering raising the qualifying bar for new entrants to 910 hours (i.e., twenty-six weeks at thirty-five hours per week) (Greenspon 1995: A10). If this proposal is accepted, new entrants would effectively be required to work full-time, either by obtaining full-time jobs or working at multiple part-time jobs, in order to gain access to U.I.
18. *SOF* is shortsighted in neglecting to clearly define "lifelong" or continuous employment. For instance, it does not address the implications of instituting U.I. policies based on "lifelong" employment for workers taking maternity, parental or sick leave.

# REFERENCES

Akyeampong, Ernest B. 1989. "The Changing Face of Temporary Help."*Perspectives*. Summer: 43-49. Ottawa: Statistics Canada.

Armstrong, Pat and Hugh. 1994. *The Double Ghetto*. Third edition. Toronto: McClelland and Stewart.

Armstrong, Pat. 1993. "The Feminization of the Labour Force: Harmonizing Down in a Global Economy." Paper presented to the North-South Conference on Gender-Relations in the Era of Globalization. Toronto: York University.

Bakker, Isa and Katherine Scott. Forthcoming. "From The Post-War to Post-Liberal Keynesian Welfare State." In Wallace Clement and Glen Williams (eds.), *Building on the New Canadian Political Economy*.

Brodie, Janine. 1994. "Shifting the Boundaries: Gender and the Politics of Restructuring." In Isabella Bakker (ed.), *The Strategic Silence: Gender and Economic Policy*. London: Zed Books.

Callender, Claire. 1993. "Redundancy, Unemployment and Poverty." In Caroline Glendinning and Jane Millar (eds.), *Women and Poverty in Britain*. London: Harvester Wheatsheaf.

Canadian Labour Congress. 1995. "Federal Budget 1995: Canadian Labour Congress Analysis." Unpublished Brief. February 27.

———. 1995. "Brief to Working Group on Seasonal Work and U.I." Unpublished. January 24.

Cohen, Marjorie. 1994. "The Implications of Economic Restructuring For Women: The Canadian Situation." In Isabella Bakker (ed.), *The Strategic Silence: Gender and Economic Policy*. London: Zed Books.

Crompton, Susan. 1993. "The Renaissance of Self-employment." *Perspectives*. Summer: 22-32. Ottawa: Statistics Canada.

Department of Finance. 1995. *Budget in Brief*. Ottawa: Minister of Supply and Services.

Ecumenical Coalition for Economic Justice. 1993. *Reweaving Canada's Social Safety Net*. Toronto: ECAGE.

Employment and Immigration Canada. 1994. *Unemployment Insurance Account: Forecasts from 1994 to 1998*. Ottawa: Employment and Immigration Canada.

———. 1993. "The Unemployment Insurance Program and the Canadian Labour Market (Additional Information)." Unpublished Brief.

Esping-Andersen, Gosta. 1990. *The Three Worlds of Welfare Capitalism*. Oxford: Polity Press.

Fraser, Nancy and Linda Gordon. 1994. "A Genealogy of *Dependency*: Tracing a Keyword of the U.S. Welfare State." *Signs* 19 (21): 309-36.

———. 1989. *Unruly Practices: Power, Discourse and Gender in Contemporary Social Theory*. Minneapolis: University of Minnesota Press.

Gabriel, Christina and Laura Macdonald. 1995. "Women Organizing Around NAFTA: Prospects For A Feminist Internationality." Paper Prepared for the "Structural Change and Gender Relations in the Era of Globalization Workshop", Sponsored by the North-South Institute.

Greenspon, Edward. 1995. "New UI Plan Would Cut Benefits." *Globe and Mail* June 10: A1, A10.

Hegel, G.W.F. 1991. *Elements of the Philosophy of Right*. Edited by Allen W. Wood. Cambridge: Cambridge University Press.

Hobson, Barbara. 1990. "No Exit, No Voice: Women's Economic Dependency and the Welfare State." *Acta Sociologica* 33 (3): 235-50.

Human Resources Development Canada (HRDC) 1995. *Security, Opportunities and Fairness: Canadian's Renewing Their Social Programs*. Report of the Standing Committee on Human Resources Development. Ottawa: Minister of Supply and Services.

———. 1994. *Improving Social Security in Canada: A Discussion Paper*. Ottawa: Minister of Supply and Services.

Leira, Arnlaug. 1993. "The 'Woman-Friendly' Welfare State?: The Case of Norway and Sweden." in Jane Lewis (ed.), *Women and Social Policies in Europe*. London: Edward Elgar Publishing.

Lewis, Jane. 1993. "Women, Work, Family and Social Policies in Europe." In Jane Lewis (ed.), *Women and Social Policies in Europe*. London: Edward Elgar Publishing, 1-24.

Moon, Donald. 1988. "The Moral Basis of the Democratic Welfare State." In Amy Gutmann (ed.), *Democracy and the Welfare State*. New Jersey: Princeton University Press.

Monserbraaten, Laurie. 1994. "Born Reluctantly, UI Turned into Ottawa's Main Social Policy Tool." *Toronto Star* B1, B6.

Ng, Roxanna. 1990. "Immigrant Women: The Construction of a Labour Market Category." *Canadian Journal of Women and the Law* 4: 96-112.

Ochran, A. et al. 1993. "Industrial Homeworking and Employment Standards: A Community Approach to Visibility and Understanding." Unpublished Brief. Women Research and Education Society. Vancouver: ILGWO.

O'Connor, Julia. 1993. "Gender, Class and Citizenship in the Comparative Analysis of Welfare State Regimes: Theoretical and Methodological Issues." *British Journal of Sociology* 44 (3): 501-08.

———. 1989. "Welfare Expenditure and Policy Orientation in Canada in Comparative Perspective." *Canadian Review of Sociology and Anthropology* 26 (1): 127-50.

Ontario Women's Directorate. 1993. "Labour Force Trends For Racial Minority Women." Unpublished Paper.

Organization for Economic Co-Operation and Development. 1994. *The OECD Job Strategy: Facts, Analysis and Strategies*. Paris: OECD Publications.

Orloff, Ann Shola. 1994. "Restructuring Welfare: Gender, Work and Inequality in Australia, Canada, the United Kingdom and the United States." Paper Prepared for the "Crossing Borders: An International Dialogue on Gender, Social Politics and Citizenship" conference. May 27-29.

Pateman, Carole. 1992. "The Patriarchal Welfare State" In Linda McDowell and Rosemary Pringle (eds.), *Defining Women: Social Institutions*. London: Polity Press.

———. 1988. "The Patriarchal Welfare State." In Amy Gutmann (ed.), *Democracy and the Welfare State*. New Jersey: Princeton University Press.

Pearce, Diane. 1990. "Welfare Is Not *for* Women: Why the War on Poverty Cannot Conquer the Feminization of Poverty." In Linda Gordon (ed.), *Women, the State, and Welfare*. Wisconsin: University of Wisconsin Press.

———. 1985. "Toil and Trouble: Women Workers and Unemployment Compensation." *Signs* 10 (3): 439-59.

Status of Women Canada. 1994. "Women In Canada: A Statistical Profile." Ottawa: Minister of Supply Services.

Stratigaki, M. and D. Vaiou. 1994. "Women's Work and Informal Activities in Southern Europe." *Environment and Planning* 26 (8): 1221-34.

Vosko, Leah F. Forthcoming 1995. "Recreating Dependency: Women, Unemployment and the Federal Proposals for U.I. Reform." In Daniel Drache and Andrew Ranikin (eds.), *Warm Heart, Cold Country: Fiscal and Social Policy Reform in Canada*. Toronto: Caledon Press.

———. 1994. "Shrink, Cut, Dye? NAFTA and Women's Work in the Canadian Clothing Industry." Master's Thesis. Vancouver: Simon Fraser University.

# CHAPTER 17

# CHILD CARE AT THE CENTRE:
# CHILD CARE ON THE SOCIAL, ECONOMIC AND
# POLITICAL AGENDA IN THE 1990S

*Martha Friendly and Mab Oloman*

## INTRODUCTION

Since the Royal Commission on the Status of Women first recommended federal leadership through a national day care Act in 1970 (Royal Commission on the Status of Women 1970), child care has been part of Canada's unfinished social policy agenda. The ensuing twenty years provided a succession of federal and provincial task forces and reports, many of which recognized the legitimacy of child care as part of the social policy spectrum (see, for example, Ministry of Community and Social Services, Ontario 1992; Manitoba Child Care Task Force 1989; Canadian Paediatric Society 1987; Metropolitan Toronto Daycare Planning Task Force 1986; Cooke, Edwards, London and Rose-Lisée 1986). Despite promises and false starts—interspersed with victories and small improvements—now, in 1995, the majority of Canadian children are unable to access regulated child care of adequate quality. Indeed, in the first half of the 1990s, the child care situation has deteriorated. As the recession and the conservative agenda have influenced Canadian governments, the modest gains made in child care programs and policy through the 1980s have been eroded, and even reversed, in most regions of Canada.

## THE CONTEXT OF CHILD CARE IN 1995

Although Canada is a prosperous nation, a coherent system of child care and early childhood education has never been developed. In comparison with almost all the countries of western Europe, Canada has no rational strategy to ensure that child care and early childhood education services are available to meet contemporary child, family and societal needs. During the 1980s and 1990s, the absence of a national child care program has repeatedly been identified as a major gap in Canada's network of social programs.

Several key factors have pushed child care into the spotlight over the past two decades. First, mothers of young children are in the paid labour force in large numbers due, in part, to declining family income, a high incidence of single parent families, and changes in public attitudes about appropriate roles for women. For those with children under the age of three, the labour force participation rate is over 60 percent. Almost 70 percent of mothers whose youngest child is between three and five years old are in the labour force, as are more than 70 percent of those with school age children (Statistics Canada 1993).

A second significant factor has been the intensified awareness of the positive impact of high quality child care and early childhood education on children's development. Analysts suggest that "failure to invest in families with children has potential costs to society in the form of less healthy and more poorly functioning adults" (Keating and Mustard 1994: 99).

The current economic reality for families is the third factor. Young Canadian families with children, especially those headed by single mothers, have over the past two decades experienced a decline in income (Child Poverty Action Group 1994). Changes to the tax system, high unemployment, reduced federal funding for health, housing and welfare, and other factors have meant that real family incomes have declined significantly (Statistics Canada 1993). At the same time, the gap between richer and poorer families has grown at an accelerating rate, especially since 1990 (Canadian Centre for Policy Alternatives 1995).

## DIVERSITY OR DISPARITY?

Like other health, education and social services, child care is under provincial/territorial jurisdiction. Each of Canada's twelve jurisdictions has a child care program that includes legislated requirements for operation of services, a scheme of funding arrangements and child care policy that is more or less developed, depending on the jurisdiction.

Provincial/territorial child care programs across Canada exhibit numerous variations in the degree of public funding; legislated requirements for the provision of care; methods and schedules of monitoring and enforcement; and the range of services available. With respect to the key indicators of quality, some jurisdictions have very minimal training requirements for child care staff; several require no early childhood training. Some do not specify maximum group sizes. Several allow as many as seven or eight two-year-olds per staff person. Several permit certain services to operate (like nursery schools or family resource or drop-in-centres) but have no provision for regulating them (Childcare Resource and Research Unit 1994). Province-wide average wages for child care staff range from minimum wage to five or six dollars an hour higher than minimum (Canadian Day Care Advocacy Association/Canadian Child Care Federation 1993). Benefit packages, over and above those that are mandatory, are not the norm. Almost none of the provinces have clear policy about the inclusion of children with special needs and practices in this area vary considerably.

The supply of regulated child care varies as well. For example, in 1992 in Newfoundland and Saskatchewan, there were regulated spaces for only 3 percent of the children twelve years of age and under whereas in Prince Edward Island and the Yukon, just over 16 percent of the child population aged twelve years and under could be accommodated in regulated services; the Canadian average is child care accommodation for 7.5 percent of child population (Childcare Resource and Research Unit 1994). The regional variation in virtually every aspect of child care has been one of the factors that has prompted the observation that there is no Canadian system of child care.[1]

It is sometimes suggested that provincial diversity in child care is an appropriate response to regional variation in the needs of families and children. If child care had been tailored to meet local needs, diversity might have been a virtue, rather than a shortcoming, of Canada's child care situation. However, Canada's regional child care diversity has not developed in response to the local and unique needs of families and communities. Instead, due to differing regional economic realities and political will, and in the absence of a national policy framework, what has developed is disparity and inequity.

Few communities or families in any part of Canada have access to the services they need. This paucity is exaggerated for families in farming and other rural communities (Coalition for National Rural Child Care 1994), Francophone communities outside Quebec and for aboriginal communities both on and off reserve (Whiteduck 1993; Jetté and Dumont-Smith 1994). As a senate committee studying child care observed:

> Provincial child care systems resemble each other . . . in what they lack . . . our intention is . . . to suggest how rudimentary the system really is. (Subcommittee of the Standing Senate Committee on Social Affairs, Science and Technology 1988: 1)

The disparity and the frailty of provincial/territorial child care programs are two key elements of the Canadian context that are especially important when considering current developments in social policy. In 1995, these developments are likely not only to entrench child care as a purely regional program but, at the same time, to erode even the fragile networks of services that evolved throughout the 1980s and 1990s.

## THE LEGACY OF THE MULRONEY ERA

The period of Conservative government from 1984-93 left a lasting mark on child care as it did on other social programs. The effects were both immediate and deferred. The first national committee to undertake a thorough study of child care was the Liberal appointed Task Force on Child Care, established in 1984 (Cooke, Edwards, London and Rose-Lisée 1986). Shortly after the task force was appointed, a federal election brought the Conservatives to power. Child care was an issue in the election campaign (for the first time) as each party leader promised improvements. The Cooke Task Force was permitted to continue its work following the election but a special (Parliamentary) committee on child care (on which the majority were Conservative MPS) was also established.

The 1987 recommendations of the report of the Conservative majority on the Special Committee on Child Care were very controversial. The report recommended a market approach to child care, proposing enhanced tax breaks to parents, support of for-profit child care and continuation of a limited subsidy system. The Conservative Child Care Strategy, developed in response to the report of the Special Committee, was characterized as decentralizing and market-oriented (Teghtsoonian 1993). Part of the strategy was a national Child Care Act, tabled in the summer of 1988. The Act was widely criticized as lacking federal leadership, failing to set national standards or principles, and expanding the role of the finance minister in social programs (Phillips 1989). The Child Care Act died on the order paper when the 1988 federal election was called.

In hindsight, one of the most noteworthy aspects of the 1987 child care policy is how clearly it presaged the Conservative's constitutional and social policy directions that came into full play following their second success in the 1988 election. According to Phillips (1989: 168):

> It [the child care policy] clearly emphasizes the Conservative vision of a market system. . . . It both anticipates and reflects the Meech Lake Constitutional Accord . . . by deliberately and carefully avoiding interfering with provincial jurisdiction to shape the nature of the child care system . . . and represents a self-imposed restraint on the use of the federal spending power. . . . Finally, the child care legislation shows the importance of expenditure restraint that will be-ever central to the Conservatives in their second term.

Today, what is perhaps even more pertinent is to observe how this Conservative vision is also reflected in the direction of the Chrétien Liberals, elected to follow them in 1993. The

Conservatives never reintroduced national child care legislation as they had promised in the 1988 election campaign. Their commitment to a market-oriented, demand side, unsystematic approach to child care, however, is illustrated by the three non-legislative changes they made. The Child Care Expense Deduction, a tax measure that benefits affluent families, was enriched twice. The Dependent Care Allowance, a daily allowance provided to parents in federal training programs for the purchase of child care, grew almost six-fold during the Conservative years (Blain 1985; HRDC 1994b). These two market-oriented uses of public funds today constitute the largest part of the federal government's contribution to child care.

Finally, the 1990 federal budget placed a 5 percent "cap" on the cost sharing potential of the Canada Assistance Plan (CAP) for the three wealthiest provinces, Ontario, British Columbia and Alberta. It is through CAP that eligible low income families may be assisted with their child care costs.

The Conservative government's changes to child care funding shifted the balance even further toward a market-oriented strategy by emphasizing the user-pay approach. It did nothing to improve the supply, quality or financial stability of the regulated child care services in Canada. It appeared to support the premise that it is acceptable for the majority of children in Canada who require care by someone other than their parents to be in unlicensed, unregulated child care.

For child care, the Mulroney years began with promises:

> The Government of Canada, even in difficult circumstances, will find the resources necessary to do our share in making a child care program a national reality . . . . (Mulroney, cited in Hansard 1987).

And ended with Benoit Bouchard's (the Minister of Health and Welfare) final pronouncement on child care:

> I have the privilege . . . to be the killer (of a national child care program). It is not seen any more by Canadians as the first priority. It is now considered the last priority. (York 1992: A1)

## The Impact of Federal Policy Decisions on the Status of Child Care in the Provinces/Territories

While it has already been noted that the provincial/territorial response to child care varies considerably from one part of Canada to the other, through the 1980s, it seemed that these governments recognized their role in ensuring at least basic health and safety in child care. They had an emerging appreciation of high quality child care as an essential service for families across the social and economic spectrum, a service requiring some public funding. Modest improvements were made in child care policy and program development. Direct funding support to regulated services was introduced in most provinces and territories. This provided some fiscal stability and encouraged the growth of services. In fact, annual increases in the supply of regulated child care in Canada were as high as 23 percent in 1984, 15 percent in 1986, and 17 percent in 1988 (Health and Welfare Canada 1985, 1987, 1989).

However, following the 1988 federal election, optimism about a national child care policy dwindled. The impact of the failure of the Conservatives' child care strategy to provide new cost-sharing options, the "cap" on CAP (coupled with the erosion of federal funding for health care) and the 1990 recession, meant that child care began to lose ground in most of the country. The provision of direct funding decreased or was abolished in six provinces (see Table 1) and frozen in several others. Fee subsidies for low income parents were reduced, frozen or capped in some jurisdictions. Monitoring/licensing/support positions were lost, and even the position of Provincial Director of Child Care was eliminated in several provinces (Doherty et al. 1995). Several provinces moved from income-testing for fee subsidies back to the more intrusive, social assistance-oriented needs test (Childcare Resource and Research Unit 1990, 1994).

By 1993, the child care situation was desperate in much of Canada. In the years between 1984 and 1990, the annual rate of growth in regulated child care spaces ranged between 10

Table 1

**Reductions and Eliminations of Provincial/Territorial Recurring Funding to Child Care Programs since 1990**

| Jurisdiction | Year | Action |
|---|---|---|
| Newfoundland | 1993 | Start–up grants (new services) and operating grants (existing services) eliminated |
| Prince Edward Island | 1993 | Operating grants to centres and family day care homes cut by 9% |
| New Brunswick | 1994 | Operating grants to centres reduced by 50% |
| | 1995 | Operating grants eliminated |
| Manitoba | 1993 | Operating grants to child care centres reduced by 4%; grants to nursery schools reduced by 50% |
| Alberta | 1990 | Announcement that operating grants are to decrease to a flat $50/child by 1994 from previous $257/child 0–18 months, $78/child 3–4.5 years, $65/child 4.5 years+ |
| | 1994 | Additional $5 million cut from provincial child care budget |
| | 1996 | Additional $2 million cut, with a projected additional $4 million to be cut in 1996/1997 |
| Ontario | 1995 | Proxy portion of salary enhancement capped/reduced. Salary enhancement grant under review. |

Source: G. Doherty, R. Rose, M. Friendly, S. Irwin and D. Lero, (1995). Child Care: Canada Can't Work Without It. Occasional Paper No. 5. Toronto: Childcare Resource and Research Unit, Centre for Urban and Community Studies, University of Toronto.

Figure 1
**Annual Percentage Increase in Regulated Centre Based Child Care 1984–1993**

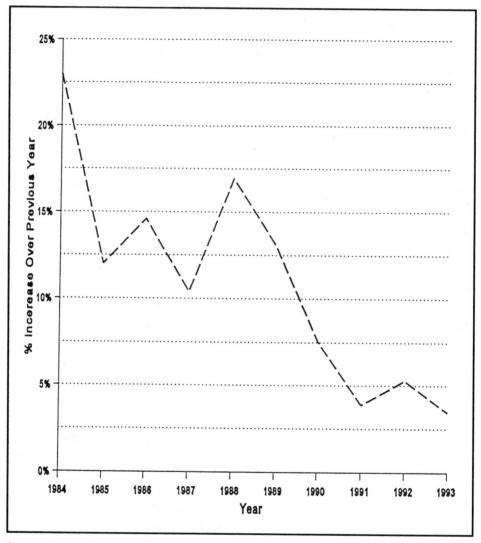

Source: Human Resources Development Canada. 1994. Status of Day Care in Canada, 1993. Ottawa: Human Resources Development Canada.
Health and Welfare Canada. 1990. Status of Day Care in Canada, 1989. Ottawa: Health and Welfare Canada.
Health and Welfare Canada. 1989. Status of Day Care in Canada, 1988. Ottawa: Health and Welfare Canada.

percent and 23 percent. Through the beginning of the 1990s, when demand has been higher than ever, expansion has slowed dramatically—to 3.46 percent in 1993 (see Figure 1). In Newfoundland, referrals by child welfare authorities no longer guaranteed a subsidized space in a child care facility. Ontario's first-ever NDP government, long an ardent champion of child care, failed to enact the significant child care funding reforms promised in their first year. Subsidy waiting lists in Metropolitan Toronto reached new heights, almost 20,000 in 1995 (Metropolitan Toronto Children's Services 1995). In Québec, child care staff demonstrated for improved wages and working conditions. In Alberta, there were cutbacks in child care, and partial user fees were imposed for kindergarten programs as budget slashing occurred in every area of public spending. The few advances that were made in the 1980s did not move the delivery of child care in Canada beyond a fragmented set of services and programs. These were mostly developed in response to adult's rather than children's needs, and inconsistent in their quality, availability and affordability. In much of Canada in the 1990s, child care has been characterized by cutbacks, changes in policy reflecting provincial government's adoption of fiscally-driven social agendas, and shifts away from the concept of child care as an essential public service. Even in provinces that have maintained the status quo or furthered child care (British Columbia, Saskatchewan, Nova Scotia, Québec and Ontario[2]), advancements have not been assertive enough to keep pace with the demands of the times.

## The Liberal's Red Book

The 1993 federal election campaign was the first to place child care within an economic context, with the Liberals and the New Democrats identifying its potential in supporting both parental employment and job creation. The Liberal's election document, the Red Book, declared that "quality, accessible child care is an economic advantage for Canada" and promised new, cumulative expenditures through to 1997. The Red Book contained two statements that seemed meaningful for child care policy. First, it stated an objective to "create genuine choices for parents . . . through the development of regulated child care alternatives." Second, it declared that "Liberals support the principal of basing fees on parents' ability to pay" (Liberal Party of Canada 1993: 38). At the time, it seemed that these commitments had implications for the future design of child care funding arrangements. When the Liberals won the federal election promising to meet the Red Book's commitments, child care advocates anticipated meaningful improvements in child care policy.

## Child Care and the Social Security Review

A major review of social programs announced by the Liberal government soon after the 1993 election was not unwelcome to some social policy and social action groups. During the election campaign, the Caledon Institute of Social Policy argued that it was time for a public debate about Canada's social security system (Caledon Institute of Social Policy 1995). It quickly became clear, however, that for the government, a primary motivation for reforming social programs was cost saving; even before an examination of the best ways to reform social programs took place, the 1994 budget established savings goals for the social security review.

The discussion paper, *Agenda: Jobs and Growth. Improving Social Security in Canada* (HRDC 1994a) was released in October 1994 as a focus for the social security review. It was a federal "first" in its identification of child care as central to three important themes: working/

employment, learning and security. Child care is characterized as "lying at the heart" of the working/employment, learning and security agendas. It is also presented as a "critical support for employment" and as a way to "provide children with a good environment in which to grow and learn" (HRDC 1994a: 53).

*Child Care and Development: A Supplementary Paper* (HRDC 1994b) was subsequently released, providing more details about federal directions and intentions. It stated that "the federal government suggests that a vision for child care and development across Canada should address the common themes of quality, availability, affordability, and comprehensiveness" and proposed "incorporation of a [national] framework of principles to guide and consolidate investments in child care and development" (HRDC 1994b: 2). This move toward a coherent national child care program shaped by a set of principles reflected the recommendations proposed by child care advocates, social policy experts and the federal Liberal Party (in Opposition) since the mid-1980s (Pépin 1987; Walker 1991; Campaign Child Care 1993; Friendly 1994).

The supplementary paper identified accountability for expenditures, quality, public funding of for-profit services, provincial/ territorial participation and expansion of services as key issues. It also reaffirmed the Red Book's "commitment to improving Canada's child care system, and to developing, with governments, parents, and the public, a national framework for child care and development" (HRDC 1994b: 25) as well as its commitment to invest new funds in child care expansion over three years, beginning in 1995/96.

For the child care community, the social security review seemed to be a good opportunity to reinforce the need for a national child care program. With new assurance, groups with an interest in child care presented briefs to the cross-country hearings of the Standing Committee on Human Resources Development. They applauded the approach being identified for their sector but cautioned that the development of child care should not occur at the expense of other family support programs.

Other sectors also identified child care as key. These included groups as diverse as the National Crime Prevention Council, the Canadian Federation of Agriculture, the National Transportation Workers Union of Canada, Canadian Labour Force Development Board, Canadian Housing Renewal Association, Canadian Federation of Municipalities, Canadian Institute of Child Health, National Youth in Care Network and many more. In addition, child care's traditional partners in the labour and women's movements, Aboriginal organizations and anti-poverty groups all spoke about the importance of treating child care as an integral component of social security reform.

The committee's report on social security reform was released in January 1995. As the report (House of Commons 1995a: 69) notes:

> Many witnesses . . . expressed concern that the discussion paper fell short of advocating and endorsing the implementation of a national child care program. They highlighted the need for upcoming federal/provincial/territorial negotiations to agree on a set of principles that would form the heart of a national child care program. [They] stressed the need to revamp the way the federal government finances child care. In their view, moving toward a more dedicated funding approach was necessary for the future.

## FEDERAL BUDGET 1995: SO YOU SAY YOU WANT A DEVOLUTION . . .?

The 1995 budget quickly followed the release of the report of the social security review (HRDC 1994a), introducing the most profound changes to social policy in Canada since the 1960s. It went far beyond anything discussed within the context of the review. Starting in 1996/97, the provinces are to receive their federal transfers for health and post-secondary education (currently paid under Established Programs Financing (EPF)) and for welfare and social services (currently cost shared through the Canada Assistance Plan) in one block fund—a single new program—the Canada Health and Social Transfer (CHST). The provinces and territories will be much freer to spend the money as they wish. However, their choices will be constrained by the fact that the federal government will also be reducing transfer payments by a substantial amount ($7 billion in the first two years alone) (Department of Finance 1995).

Health and welfare—the established programs—are also under provincial jurisdiction. They have, in many ways, been shaped by the conditions of their cost sharing mechanisms. The Canada Health Act (CHA) (1984) is based on conditional funding. It sets five broad criteria for provincial health programs that must be met prior to receipt of federal funds. The conditions set under CAP (residency prohibitions, appeals mechanism, evidence of need and reporting requirements) are more limited than those of the CHA. On the other hand, CAP is also favourable to publicly operated or non-profit services, and compels the provinces to contribute to their social programs prior to federal reimbursement. Together, the CHA and CAP have provided at least a basic level of social assistance and social services, and more than a basic measure of health care, across Canada.

The CHST has a potentially devastating message for child care. The reduced role for the federal government, "devolution" of power to the provinces, carries a number of perils. Child care is an area of social policy that has no established "home" but is dealt with through a fragmented set of provincial and federal programs. In a *de facto* manner, child care has always been devolved to the provinces. There is no national child care program; its funding and service development are left almost entirely to provincial discretion. Consequently, it has not been supported consistently or adequately enough to become a stable system. Child care has always been even more vulnerable than health care or social welfare, especially in "have not" provinces and in jurisdictions whose governments were not committed to its improvement.

With the advent of the CHST, deep cuts by the provinces to welfare, post-secondary education and health are inescapable. As these more established programs are compromised by reductions, it seems unlikely that child care will be high on the list of provincial priorities. Indeed, provinces may be tempted to pay for the short falls in other areas with funds now used for child care.

## DEVOLUTION VERSUS EVOLUTION...

Currently, provincial/territorial governments spend about $850 million per year for child care services (almost three times the amount spent by the federal government through CAP). The federal government provides other monies through the tax deduction, the Dependent Care Allowance and other programs. Local government also contributes in some parts of the country. It is estimated that in 1993/94 approximately $4 billion was spent by all levels of government on child care related activities (Child Care Advocacy Association of Canada 1995). This public contribution is, of course, minor compared to the personal contributions made by parents through their child care fees. In some parts of the country, parental contribution is estimated at more than 80 percent of the total cost of child care. It should be of concern to policy-makers and the guardians of the public purse that these expenditures are arranged in a manner that results in a fragmented, often unresponsive, set of services that are not meeting the needs of children, parents or society at large.

Accessible, high quality child care is an enabler, a conduit for positive outcomes. The absence of an effective child care system is a major deficit in Canada's infrastructure, adversely affecting our economic performance and human resources, now and in the future. Child care's place at the centre of an array of social policy objectives—healthy child development, parental job training, learning and employment, women's equality and healthy communities—suggests that a policy framework that legitimizes child care would be an astute public investment.

Public funding for child care has traditionally been considered within a narrow frame- work, entirely as a cost, not an investment. Canada still treats child care as a commodity, rather than a public good, providing it on a user-pay basis. Parents able to pay for the best possible product for their children are most likely to be able to access quality while others, with less purchasing power, have to settle for an inferior product or no product at all. This inequity is mirrored in the provincial and territorial public policy on child care. The "have" provinces are able to put more public dollars per capita into child care than the "have not" regions of Canada; whether or not they choose to is, of course, another matter.

There is an important question to consider about child care's most appropriate "home." Within the context of a new Canadian social policy framework, where should child care reside? To date, we have treated child care variously within a welfare orientation, as a women's issue, as a business expenditure and as a tool to support parental employability. Although child care has usually been placed within adult-oriented areas of concern, it has not managed to maintain a secure place on the social policy agenda. Perhaps real legitimacy will only come when children's well-being and development are the raisons d'etre of child care policy.

As devolution of federal responsibility and reduction of federal resources for social programs unfolds, a national child care program seems to have limited prospects for success. However, the following modifications to current directions could protect an incipient child care program.

Child care *per se* is not currently part of an existing shared cost program. From this point of view, it would appear legitimate to treat child care outside the CHST. In order to make this work, existing CAP cost sharing, together with other federal child care expenditures (Child Care Expense Deduction, Dependent Care Allowances, Aboriginal Head Start, etc.) would be brought together to create a separate, coherent program. This route would also incorporate the new child care funds committed in the Red Book to the expansion of regulated services, now identified as an "employability tool."

Canada's established social programs, though far from perfect, would not have achieved even the limited cross-Canada consistency without a federal role in establishing policy. An embryonic child care program, established outside the proposed CHST, would need the support of a federal policy framework for development and delivery of child care services. Recogni- tion of provincial/territorial/First Nations' jurisdiction and appropriate local planning and service delivery could be ensured through a well-designed federal framework.

An alternative to establishing a child care program outside the CHST would be to use the block funded structure of the CHST with two caveats relevant to child care. First, a Canada Child Care Act would be established, to be maintained just as the Canada Health Act will be maintained. Second, as the Standing Committee on Finance recommended, a future federal cash component sufficient to enforce compliance with federal conditions and criteria for child care would be developed (House of Commons 1995b).

A final alternative has application not only to child care but to the gamut of social/health/education programs encompassed in the CHST. The truncated democratic process to reform Canada's health, education and social programs, which began with the social security review and the national forum on health, could be completed. The CHST would be subject to public scrutiny and debate appropriate to the profound changes proposed.

Most social advocates agree that the programs in Canada's social safety net need strengthening and modernizing. The addition of a national child care program has been envisioned as a key component of modernized social policy that facilitates economic growth and reinforces the traditional Canadian commitment to social justice.

It is not too late for the government of Canada to examine alternatives that would allow its election commitment to child care to be met. Before Bill C-76 is fully established, it is critical that child care be addressed adequately. Otherwise, it would appear that a national child care program "killed" by Brian Mulroney's Ministry of Health and Welfare, may be "buried" by Jean Chrétien's Minister of Finance.

## Notes

1.  For a more detailed review and comparison of provincial/ territorial child care programs, see Childcare Resource and Research Unit. 1994. *Child Care in Canada: Provinces and Territories 1993.*

2.  The June 1995 election that brought the Harris Conservatives to power in Ontario reversed the direction of the Rae government's modest improvements to child care.

## References

Battle, K. and S. Torjman. 1995. *How Finance Re-Formed Social Policy.* Ottawa: Caledon Institute of Social Policy.

Blain, C. 1985. "Government Spending on Child Care in Canada." In Series 1: *Financing Child Care: Current Arrangements.* Background Papers for the Task Force on Child Care. Ottawa: Status of Women Canada.

Caledon Institute of Social Policy. 1995. *Critical Commentaries on the Social Security Review.* Ottawa: Author.

Campaign Child Care. 1993. *Information Package.* Ottawa: Child Care Advocacy Association of Canada.

Canadian Centre for Policy Alternatives. 1995. "Gap Widens Between Haves and Have-nots." *Monitor* 1 (9): 1. Ottawa: Canadian Centre for Policy Alternatives.

Canadian Day Care Advocacy Association/Canadian Child Care Federation. 1993. *Caring for a Living: A Study of Wages and Working Conditions in Canadian Child Care* Ottawa: Canadian Day Care Advocacy Association/Canadian Child Care Federation.

Canadian Paediatric Society. 1987. *Report of the Task Force on Quality "Out of Home" Care.* Ottawa: Canadian Paediatric Society.

Child Care Advocacy Association of Canada. 1995. *Child Care: An Investment in Canada's Future.* A

Brief to the Standing Committee on Human Resources Development. Ottawa: Child Care Advocacy Association of Canada.

Child Poverty Action Group, Family Services Association of Metropolitan Toronto, and Social Planning Council of Metropolitan Toronto. 1994. *Voices of Young Families*. Toronto: Child Poverty Action Group, Family Services Association of Metropolitan Toronto, and Social Planning Council of Metropolitan Toronto.

Childcare Resource and Research Unit. 1994. *Child Care: Provinces and Territories 1993*. Toronto: Centre for Urban and Community Studies, University of Toronto.

———. 1990. *Childcare Information Sheets: The Provinces and Territories*. Toronto: Childcare Resource and Research Unit, Centre for Urban and Community Studies, University of Toronto.

Cooke, K., R. Edwards, J. London and R. Rose-Lisée. 1986. *Report of the Task Force on Child Care*. Ottawa: Status of Women Canada.

Department of Finance. 1995. Federal Budget. Ottawa: Department of Finance.

Doherty, G., R. Rose, M. Friendly, S.H. Irwin and D.S. Lero. 1995. *Child Care: Canada Can't Work Without It*. Paper commissioned by the Canadian Advisory Council on the Status of Women. Published as Occasional Paper No. 5 Childcare Resource and Research Unit, Centre for Urban and Community Studies, University of Toronto.

Friendly, M. 1994. *Child Care Policy in Canada: Putting the Pieces Together*. Don Mills: Addison-Wesley.

Health and Welfare Canada. 1985, 1987, 1989. *Status of Day Care in Canada*. Ottawa: Health and Welfare Canada.

House of Commons. 1995b. *Final Report on Bill C-76*. Report of the Standing Committee on Finance. Ottawa: House of Commons.

———. 1995a. *Security, Opportunities, and Fairness: Canadians Renewing Their Social Programs*. Report of the Standing Committee on Human Resources Development. Ottawa: House of Commons.

Human Resources Development Canada. 1994c. *Status of Day Care in Canada*. Ottawa:

Human Resources Development Canada. 1994a. *Agenda: Jobs and Growth. Improving Social Security in Canada: A Discussion Paper*. Ottawa: Human Resources Development Canada.

———. 1994b. *Child Care and Development: A Supplementary Paper*. Ottawa: Human Resources Development Canada.

Jette, D. and C. Dumont-Smith. 1994. *National Commission on Aboriginal Child Care: Our Children—Our Responsibility. Blueprint for Action*. Ottawa: Native Council of Canada.

Keating, D.P. and J.F. Mustard. 1994. "Social Economic Factors and Human Development." In National Forum on Family Security, *Family Security in Insecure Times*. Ottawa: Canadian Council on Social Development.

Liberal Party of Canada. 1993. *Creating Opportunity*. Ottawa: Liberal Party of Canada.

Manitoba Child Care Task Force. 1989. *Report of the Manitoba Child Care Task Force*. Winnipeg: Manitoba Child Care Task Force.

Metropolitan Toronto Children's Services. 1995. Personal Communication.

Metropolitan Toronto Daycare Planning Task Force. 1986. *Metropolitan Toronto Daycare Planning Task Force*. Toronto: Metropolitan Toronto Daycare Planning Task Force.

Ministry of Community and Social Services, Ontario. 1992. *Child Care Reform in Ontario: Setting the Stage*. Toronto: Ministry of Community and Social Services.

Mulroney, B. 1987. Hansard, March 9, 1987: 3770.

National Coalition for Rural Child Care. 1995. *Presentation to the Standing Committee on Human Resources Development*. Langruth: National Coalition for Rural Child Care.

Pépin, L. 1987. *Choices for Childcare: Now and the Future*. Minority Report of the Special Committee on Child Care. Ottawa: Liberal Party of Canada.

Phillips, S. 1989. "Rock-a-bye Brian: The National Strategy on Child Care." In K.A. Graham (ed.), *How*

*Ottawa Spends. 1989-1990.* Ottawa: Carlton University Press.

Royal Commission on the Status of Women. 1970. *The Status of Women in Canada.* Ottawa: Royal Commission on the Status of Women.

Statistics Canada. 1993. *Labour Force Activity of Women by Presence of Children: The Nation.* Ottawa: Statistics Canada.

Subcommitte of the Standing Senate Committee on Social Affairs, Science and Technology. 1988. *Report of the Subcommittee on Day Care.* Ottawa: Subcommitte of the Standing Senate Committee on Social Affairs, Science and Technology.

Teghtsoonian, K. 1993. "Neo-conservative Ideology and Opposition to Federal Regulation of Child Care Services in the United States and Canada." *Canadian Journal of Political Science* 27 (1): 97-121.

Walker, D. 1991. *Discussion Paper on Child Care.* Liberal Party of Canada, Caucus Committee on Health and Social Development. Ottawa: Liberal Party of Canada.

Whiteduck, G. 1993. " Child Care and First Nations Communities." *Interaction* 7 (3): 25-26.

York, G. 1992. "Government Scraps Day-care Commitment." *Globe and Mail* February 27: A1.

## PART 6

# CITIZENSHIP, ADVOCACY AND SOCIAL SECURITY REFORM

# CHAPTER 18

# HOW TO BEAT THE CORPORATE AGENDA: STRATEGIES FOR SOCIAL JUSTICE

*Diana Ralph*

## INTRODUCTION

In the chess game of Canadian people versus capital, we are close to being checkmated. With the North American Free Trade Agreement (NAFTA) we have lost our queen, national sovereignty. Our rooks, the welfare state programs which protect basic rights, are being wiped off the board. Our knights, unions and popular sector groups, are splintered, starved for funds and directionless. Our bishops, democratic, socialist values, lie trampled under fundamentalism and neoconservative ideology (Barlow and Robertson 1994). We have lost many of our people, the crucial pawns of the chess game. Without a strong people's movement, many working class Canadians have jumped ship and joined the Reform/Conservative/neoliberal bandwagon.

Like chess, class warfare is a matter of strategy. Both depend on a clear assessment of the changing battlefield, and on thinking several moves ahead so that we can position our sources of strength and set up attacks on the weak points of the opponent. As in chess, we can learn from errors in past games to plan future victories. Even when the power of the two sides is unequal, strategy is the key factor. Our future rests on the outcome of this struggle.

For many Canadian popular sector groups, the "new" global crisis has come as a huge surprise (Finn 1995: 7-8). But we should not have been surprised. For those who looked, the signs have been visible for a long time. In 1972, for example, Finance Minister John Turner's first budget speech presaged Paul Martin's policy of accommodation to multinational priorities:

> Multinational corporate giants have come to assume an increasingly dominant role on the world economic stage and in the Canadian economy. I fear that the world is in the process of being transformed into massive trading blocs, which in itself is of immense significance to Canada as a major trading nation.... What I shall strive to do tonight is to set the stage for Canadian industry to be competitive in world markets. Our ability to gain access to world markets is a prerequisite to the success of any industrial policy that focuses on growth and jobs. (Turner, cited in Wolfe 1977: 271)

Twenty years ago, Samir Amin (1975: 44) had predicted "a structural crisis of world capitalism" in countries like Canada; no longer would "problems of transition" be restricted to the periphery but "immense problems of transition await the centre as well."

Even as early as 1907, Jack London (1907: 5) had predicted the rise of "the Iron Heel," a global oligarchy, remarkably like the current transnational corporate machine. He saw it as an inevitable outcome of the logic of capitalist accumulation based on exploitation of an ever widening sphere of people:

> Too late did the socialist movement of the early twentieth century divine the coming of the Oligarchy. Even as it was divined, the Oligarchy was there—a fact established in blood, a stupendous and awful reality. Nor even then . . . was any permanence attributed to the Iron Heel. Its overthrow was a matter of a few short years, was the judgment of the revolutionists.

We now face the reality of that Iron Heel. With the collapse of the communist bloc, transnational corporations (TNCS) rule supreme. Of the top one hundred world economies, fifty are TNCS. They exercise the power to overwhelm any nation's currency and to impose whatever policies they demand (Tester 1992a). They have crushed or co-opted most successful communist and socialist societies worldwide and, through structural adjustment, imposed a more vicious form of colonialism on the Southern Hemisphere nations (Swift 1994). The TNCS have divided the world into three competing mega-trading blocs; the European Common Market, the Asian market, and U.S.-dominated control of the Americas (Collier 1995). The majority of the world's people have been staggering under the Iron Heel of structural adjustment for decades, as poverty, environmental degradation and corruption flourish.

London predicted that the Iron Heel would rule, crushing local resistance and revolutions, for 700 years until the people of the world could finally mobilize strategically to break the Oligarchy and free themselves. In the 88 years since London made that prediction, the Oligarchy has spread around the globe and become more ruthlessly destructive. Unless we want to keep spinning our wheels for another 612 years, we need to think and organize more strategically.

My purpose in this paper is to assess the popular sector struggles in the past 20 years, and to propose some key strategic elements which might help us become more effective now and for the long haul.

## Corporate Strategy: How the Business Council on National Issues Gained Hegemony

> [G]ood strategy . . . depends on a knowledge of the opposition. We want to anticipate the moves the other side is likely to make. Before we can decide on our strategy we need to know what their counterstrategy is likely to be, what possibilities are open to them, what things they might be able to do. (Kahn 1982: 170)

The TNCS and Canadian banks have captured the strategic initiative on social policy. For us to develop an effective counter-strategy, we need to know their goals, anticipate their tactics, and assess their areas of strength and vulnerability.

Although the Canadian state has always favoured business interests, the Canadian working class was in a relatively strong position from the post-war years until the mid-1970s. We had much more influence on the state then than we do today. These were years of rapid union growth, many strikes, and "a significant shift in the share of national income going to wages and salaries" (Wolfe 1977: 260-61). They were also the years when Canada adopted many of its major social programs; unemployment insurance (1956), the National Housing Act (1964), Canada Pension Plan (1965), medicare (1966), the Canada Assistance Plan (1966), the Guaranteed Income Supplement (1967) for low income people 65 and older, and improved Family Allowances and Unemployment Insurance (1971) (Moscovitch and Drover 1987: 29-31). The proportion of Gross Domestic Product (GDP) spent on social programs has never approached those of European social democratic countries, and the form in which they were implemented served business interests at least as much as people's needs (Corrigan and Leonard 1978; Galper 1975; Gough 1979; Lightman 1990; Piven and Cloward 1971; Tudiver 1987). Nonetheless, these were real victories for the mass of Canadian people.

By contrast the Canadian business class was relatively disorganized. It had no coherent strategic offensive in place. The Canadian Chamber of Commerce and the Canadian Manufacturers Association "tended to be spokespeople for narrow sectoral interests [and] . . . appeared capable only of reacting negatively and after the fact to government policies and programs" (Langille 1987: 47-48).

But that all changed in 1976. The Chief Executive Officers (CEOs) of the top 150 Canadian corporations—many of them representing transnational corporations—joined together to form the Business Council on National Issues (BCNI). The BCNI sees itself as "the chosen vehicle through which Canadian chief executives contribute to the shaping of national priorities" (BCNI 1995). One of its key goals is to reduce Canadian workers to the level of pay and submission of workers in countries like Mexico and Uruguay (Ternowetsky and Riches 1990). According to Tester (1992a: 143) the BCNI's strategic goal is to bring structural adjustment to Canada. This includes destroying the whole notion of social insurance and social rights, and replacing these with a corporate model that forces workers to "adjust" to Third World labour conditions.

In contrast to the rather loose and reactive responses of the 1960s, the BCNI was now able to strategize in a coherent way and thereby undercut the working class's sources of power. As suggested by Langille's (1987) study of the BCNI, it focused on altering fundamental Canadian economic, social and political institutions and policies. Witness his description of these changes:

> Rather than merely reacting to government initiatives, the Business Council often takes pre-emptive or pro-active positions on upcoming issues. . . . They gain an edge if they can define the issues in their own terms and upstage the government by presenting it with a comprehensive package of analysis and recommendations. With adequate foreknowledge, the Council is able not only to arrive at a suitable consensus within its own constituency, but to anticipate the positions of other groups and suggest a "satisfactory" compromise. (Langille 1987: 55)

The BCNI's "global strategy initiative" reports directly to the executive committee of this organization. This is supported by six working groups which pro-actively develop strategic initiatives around the national economy, the environment, political reform, international economy/foreign affairs, social policy and corporate governance (BCNI 1995).

At the same time, BCNI member corporations directly influence the government by direct and indirect donations to the Conservative and Liberal parties, by placing their people at the Bank of Canada, and by serving as advisors to Conservative and Socred provincial governments in B.C., Saskatchewan, Alberta and New Brunswick (CCPA/CHO!CES 1995: 7; McQuaig 1995: 81).

Four years ago, the BCNI and the Canadian government coproduced a blueprint for adjusting Canada to the global market called *Canada at the Crossroads* (Porter 1991). It recommended restructuring social programs to force people to work and upgrade their training; a plan which is remarkably similar to the Axworthy social security review (Human Resources Development Canada, HRDC 1994).

> Aggregate social spending in Canada is not out of line compared to most other industrialized countries. However, to create an attractive environment for competitive advantage, it is crucial that social goals be pursued in a way that does not sacrifice incentives, upgrading and productivity growth. Consideration must be given to re-designing social programs that do not meet this test. (Porter 1991: 7)

## THE BCNI IN THE 1990S

The BCNI's strategy rests on three interlocking fronts: creating a massive deficit; slashing government expenditures especially in social programs; and bringing in free trade. First, consider the deficit. While the BCNI has been vocal in its attack on social spending and its impact on the deficit, it also promotes policies to produce an artificially inflated Canadian deficit. For example, it urged the government to: (1) shift the tax burden from corporations and the rich to workers; (2) privatize income-generating crown corporations, such as Via Rail, Canada Post and Petro-Canada; and (3) raise Bank of Canada interest rates and give far more lending power to the private chartered banks (Newall 1995: 3; Brooks 1994: 6-9; Chorney, Hotson and Seccareccia 1992).

High interest rates simultaneously boosted the annual deficit and enriched the banks and bond holders to whom the government owed the debt (McQuaig 1995). By strangling the economy, the high interest rates also generated near depression level unemployment, costing $109 billion in lost taxes in 1992-93 alone, thereby contributing significantly to producing the desired deficit (McQuaig 1995: 64). Double digit unemployment rates also undercut the strength of unions. As Armine Yalnizyan (1993: 11) points out, the government deficit did not emerge until 1976 and it was:

> ... fueled by deliberate government policies, a simple case of revenues not keeping up with expenditures ... by choice ... [it] began as a result of changes in tax policy, changes that led to the decline in total tax revenues relative to the size of the economy, thus raising the requirement for borrowing.

Second, the manufactured deficit allows the bond holders to use the deficit as an excuse to demand extensive budget cuts to both social programs and to the public service workers who staff them. Long before the deficit had taken centre stage as an issue, the BCNI, the C.D. Howe and the Fraser Institutes advocated for the restructuring of medicare, unemployment insurance, affirmative action, labour rights, women's rights, immigrants' rights and welfare for the employable.[1]

But until they managed to panic people about the deficit, the public stubbornly resisted the attacks on their rights and social programs. As recently as March 1994, polls were showing that "Canadians still like their social safety net" (Cobb and Kennedy 1994). Therefore the major corporations and their media stepped up the debt hysteria campaign (McQuaig 1995: 12-38). Newsprint media emphasized the "debt wall" and the necessity of "short-term pain" through slashing budgets. In this scenario, the deficit is "our" number one problem, such that social programs are too expensive, making it impossible to afford help for anyone but the "truly needy."

The deficit also was used to pit groups of working class people against one another: people with jobs versus those using U.I. "occasionally," versus "frequent" users, versus "welfare cheats"; poor children versus poor adults (including the parents of the children); working aged people versus seniors; Canadian citizens versus immigrants (and all visible minority people) (Axworthy 1994).

The propaganda worked. Between March 5, 1994 and February 4, 1995, public opinion polls showed people flipped from distrustful opposition to the cuts to seeing the debt as "the country's No. 1 concern" and supporting workfare, user fees for medicare, and restricting immigration (Cobb and Kennedy 1994; Whittington 1995). Mike Harris' election in Ontario reflects this success.

Why was it so important to the BCNI to slash and restructure social programs, transforming them from an entitlement to a form of social control? Social programs form the dike that protects us from Third World labour conditions. Social programs protect us all, not just those who happen to be poor now. They are the safety net on which all but the richest of us depend. U.I., Medicare, Old Age Security, Canada and Quebec Pension plans and many other programs "help maintain living standards for Canadians from all walks of life and all income levels who have their normal income interrupted by unemployment, illness, disability, or retirement" (Battle 1994: 25).

But even more importantly, social programs are the key to protecting the rights of the entire Canadian working and potential working class. Dismantling them leaves the Canadian labour force desperate and insecure, willing to work under any condition and pitted against each other. This is an ideal situation from the perspective of BCNI members. The BCNI's real goal had far less to do with saving money than with forcing able-bodied people to take jobs at lower wages and under worse working conditions (Moscovitch 1993: 12).

The third strategy, bringing in free trade between provinces and between Canada and its North and South American trading partners, was necessary to make the gains the BCNI had won permanent. Out-going BCNI chairman, J. Edward Newall (1995: 4), congratulated the BCNI for its pro-active planning around free trade:

> Our work started away back in 1981. We saw the beginnings of a growing American protectionism that has since manifested itself. We saw the vital requirement for better and much more secure access to our most important market.

As Tony Clarke (1994: 9) points out: "With the passage of NAFTA, the struggle for national sovereignty has been lost—at least for the time being." The Free Trade Agreement (FTA) and NAFTA basically set in place a bill of rights for corporations which supersedes any present or future laws which might benefit individuals. It forces Canada to gut its national standards and harmonize its social programs with the much lower levels of rights and services of other partners. Ken Collier's (1995: 51) analysis of the impact of world trading blocs on national standards underscores these points.

> NAFTA has the effect of steering service activities into commercially offered chan-

nels. Social Work and counseling services, for instance, may be offered in any part of NAFTA territory by private individuals or companies for fees, which may be covered by either direct payment or by insurance. They may not be covered by governments if they are not included already in services offered by government before NAFTA was signed. If any government-operated social services like these are discontinued, they may not be reinstated at a later date.

If governments try to set up a service . . . that service will be deemed a monopoly, and any firm in the USA which would or could make a profit from offering that service will have a right to sue for lost profits.

A strategic goal is to eliminate all barriers to Canadian and transnational companies' freedom to exploit the Canadian labour force for maximum profit (Mullaly 1994; Tester 1992b).

The BCNI's quiet, behind-the-scenes initiatives have been immensely successful. Largely as a result of these corporate initiatives, the Canadian government has:

- lowered inflation rates more than any other country;
- ushered in close to depression level unemployment rates;
- established free trade deals between provinces and with the U.S., Mexico and soon with the rest of the Americas;
- slashed government expenditures and public service jobs more than at any time in Canadian history;
- dismantled national standards for social assistance and unemployment insurance;
- eliminated universal social programs and funding for social housing;
- lowered corporate taxes and taxes on the rich; and
- eliminated barriers to currency speculation.

These fundamental shifts in federal policy have been accomplished even though the vast majority of Canadians did not favour them.[2] The voices of labour, women, the poor, the disabled, Aboriginal people and immigrants have all been dismissed as greedy, self-interested "special interest groups."

After twenty years of strategic maneuvers, capital has moved from a relatively disorganized lobby to dictating federal, provincial and local policy. As Gonick (1992: 209) argues, revolutions are no longer driven by workers but by capitalists. They are:

. . . revolutionising technology, revolutionising occupational structures and the international division of labour, revolutionising the workplace; weakening the trade unions; attacking the welfare state; deregulating the private sector and privatising the public sector; executing a policy of tax exploitation. We are reeling from neo-conservatism.

Under the combined threats of NAFTA reprisals, TNC speculative currency manipulations and corporate pull-outs, politicians no longer have the power to represent the will of the people, even if they wanted to. We have become as trapped as any of the Third World countries, and unless we can come up with an effective people's strategy soon, we can expect to share their living standards within the next twenty years.

## A People's Strategy

The past ten years have been frustrating for those involved in many of the popular sector struggles. We have put years of work into these struggles, and yet we have precious few victories to show for it. Things look bleaker for Canadian people now than ever before. Many of us feel hopeless. After all, the BCNI members now control over $1.2 trillion in assets (BCNI 1995), and influence media coverage and politicians. How can our cash-starved unions and groups compete with this?

Successful revolutions do not depend on the things that wealth can purchase: technology, terror, armies and control of the media and state institutions. Mobilized people's movements have turned around situations far more one-sided than is ours now. Since the Second World War, virtually all colonies have waged successful wars of national liberation. In Russia, China, Vietnam, Cuba, Nicaragua and most recently in South Africa, organized people's parties have won state power in spite of overwhelming imperialist forces massed against them.[3]

### What We're Doing Wrong

Any serious examination of our work needs to start with the question: 'Why aren't we winning?' (Penner 1994: 21)

In 1975, we lived within the rules of the post-war game of Keynesian social democracy. As Cy Gonick (1992: 202) explains:

> Working-class politics, based on unions and social-democratic (and socialist-communist) parties, united this [organized] constituency on the platform of workplace rights, social services, and decent living standards. They got elected on this platform. It was largely economistic—based on incremental reforms to the tax system and to the welfare state. Social-democratic governments could deliver these promises without having to challenge capitalism or the corporations—and, on the contrary, by supplying to the capitalists a satisfied and cooperative labour force in exchange for these improvements. . . . It is no wonder that social democracy, as it emerged in the 1950s, 60s, and 70s gave up any notion of eventually replacing capitalism.

In the 1960s and 1970s, labour and popular sector groups gave away most of their tools of militant opposition as well as their accountability to constituencies in exchange for secure wages and funding.

> Whatever its limited ambitions, social-democratic capitalism did deliver, more or less, what it promised; not the end of poverty but steadily improved wages, expanded social services, and a degree of job security—at least for the majority of working people. It seemed that capitalism could indeed be partly humanized and regulated, and that the business cycle had at least been tamed and perhaps even totally conquered. As we know today, all this proved to be an illusion (Gonick 1992: 203).

Now that these ground rules have changed, the velvet glove is off the iron fist once again. But most of us are still operating under the old rules. Here is a short list of some of the strategic mistakes we have been making:

*1. We keep expecting the government to fix it.*
Most popular sector groups seem to presume that the government is poorly informed, but well intentioned, rather than the reverse. Consequently, isolated groups compile brief after brief to explain politely to the government that poverty is growing and that people need their social programs and rights. It worked until the early 1970s. It does not any more. Under the Iron Heel, the time we waste writing briefs and grant proposals could be much better spent mobilizing and serving our grassroots bases.

*2. We are still buying into formal party politics.*
A lot of our energy goes into electoral politics, replacing one unsatisfactory party with another. Since NAFTA, none of them can fulfill progressive campaign promises, even if they want to. For example, Bob Rae's promised public auto insurance was ruled out by the Free Trade Agreement. While it is still worth voting, we should not put all our eggs in the electoral basket. Electing a well-intentioned individual cannot substitute for organizing people to act. Canadian history shows that a mobilized populace can force even Conservative governments to make concessions. Most Canadian social programs were instituted by Conservative and Liberal governments as a result of mass mobilization, strikes and riots (Finkel 1977; Moscovitch and Drover 1987).

*3. We have not developed our own independent sources of funding.*
Popular sector groups—including the Canadian Labour Congress (CLC)—all have grown dependent on government funding. This has limited their willingness to take strong stands, to mobilize their members or to work cooperatively with other groups. We need to re-develop self-reliance on the dues of our members and the funds we can raise from principled allies. In Canada, Greenpeace and the Council of Canadians have been relatively militant and successful because they do not depend on government money.

*4. We have not defined our own issues and visions.*
We have not yet forged a collective, alternate vision of what we want. National labour and popular sector groups have developed some excellent attempts. Examples are represented in the statement, "A time to stand together, a time for social solidarity" (Working Committee 1987); the Council of Canadians' 1994 "Setting the Citizens Agenda" conference and papers; and the CCPA/CHO!CES "Alternative Budget" (1995). But these have not received wide distribution or media attention. Also, at times, these documents are somewhat abstract and still need to be fleshed out through grassroots visioning and strategic planning.

In the absence of a clear platform of our own, many progressive groups are stuck in the rut of lobbying the government for "more" (or even for "not much less"). Aside from being weak and unimaginative, this kind of lobbying leaves the power and initiative entirely in the hands of the government.

It is also hard to mobilize enthusiastic popular support for welfare state programs that never satisfied anyone. Even "the good old days" of the welfare state never gave us what we needed and wanted. We wanted a just and equal society. We received inadequate, demeaning welfare. We wanted an end to violence against women, and we received underfunded shelters and rape crisis lines. We wanted an end to racism, and we received small grants to competing ethnic minorities to fight among themselves in isolation. We wanted universal child care, and we received child tax credits which benefit mainly the rich. We wanted community controlled health services and prevention from causes of illness. Instead, we received doctors insurance.

*5. In the absence of our own vision, we have relied on reactive, defensive campaigns that almost always fail.*
The issues we organize around have been defined and controlled by the corporations and the politicians they control. We react defensively, and on an ad hoc basis, to their initiatives. If we want to win, we have to re-seize the initiative, as Mao Tse-Tung (1968: 159) pointed out in 1938:

> ... the initiative means freedom of action for an army. Any army which losing the initiative, is forced into a passive position and ceases to have freedom of action, faces the danger of defeat or extermination.

BCNI strategists have figured out how to turn against us our tendency to respond reactively. They get the government to schedule endless consultations, inquiries, environmental assessments and policy reviews, for which they define the issues, the pace and how the "public" gets input. In the end, they ignore our recommendations.

The recent social security review process illustrates this tactic well. The government set the terms of the inquiry without consulting the provinces or popular sector groups. Instead Axworthy issued a report on improving social security (the Green Paper) (HRDC 1994) which proposed to slash and restructure U.I., CAP and post-secondary education. The "review" process forced people to react to those proposals only, rather than to their own priorities. The Standing Committee on Human Resources Development (HRDC 1995: 185-229) received over 1300 briefs, the vast majority opposing the proposals. Nevertheless, the recommendations of the final report supported the Axworthy proposals (Moore 1995). The final report was irrelevant anyway, since the finance committee overrode the process through cuts in the 1995 federal budget. These were imposed without any pretense of consultation.

Cascading cuts is another, even more brutal method that the neoconservative think tanks have developed to keep us defensively reacting, off balance and never able to focus on defining our own independent agenda. In the early 1980s, this technique was developed into an art by right wing governments in Britain, British Columbia, Saskatchewan, New Zealand, Alberta and New Brunswick. For example, the British Columbia Socred government consulted the British Heritage Institute about ways to slash social programs, labour and other rights. It recommended that the Socreds bring in all the cuts simultaneously. This generated popular unity resulting in an almost successful general strike (Palmer 1987). It therefore adapted the method when advising the Saskatchewan government. Before imposing the big cuts, the consultant suggested that the first step would be to quietly slash funding for advocacy groups in order to break the unity of the remaining NGOs by forcing them to compete for shrinking dollars (Stobbe 1995). This worked better. The Axworthy/Martin two-step illustrates how well the federal Liberals are learning from these provincial experiments. As Tony Clarke (1994), former chair of the Action Canada Network, points out, in order to win victories, we need to stop reacting to each cut and pro-actively plan a coordinated strategy to win back popular sovereignty.

*6. We have not targeted corporations; the real causes of our problems.*

> Challenging the government will become less relevant. Increasingly important targets for action will be transnational corporations which are flagrantly exploiting workers and communities under the new continental free trade regime. (Clarke 1995)

We have failed to identify the correct targets of our protests. Our knee-jerk reaction to every change has been to lobby the government. But the government no longer has the power (or the inclination) in the NAFTA era to give us what we want.

We need to shift our sights to those that do; the chartered banks, the Bank of Canada and the transnational corporations. The Clayoquot Sound battle against MacMillan Bloedel is a good example of the effectiveness of this strategy. The protest electrified action across Canada and internationally, bringing together environmental, Aboriginal, women's and labour groups. It won the clearcutting issue, exposed the corporate practices of MacMillan Bloedel and forged an ongoing alliance across popular sectors.

One of the advantages of targeting TNCs and banks is that, unlike the government, they are vulnerable to creative consumer and labour actions. Also they are ubiquitous—encroaching into almost every community in Canada. This makes them easy targets for local actions. Setting the locus of our struggles at the level of community is where we need to start given that we have lost most of our national sovereignty as a result of NAFTA. As Tony Clarke (1994: 9) suggests:

> The only strategic option is to shift the locus from national to community based struggles. This is not simply a pragmatic shift. In many ways, popular sovereignty is the heart and soul of national sovereignty. Unless people are prepared to fight for democratic control in their communities and workplaces, there can be little or no substance to the notion of national sovereignty.

So far, successful actions against corporations (e.g., the Nestles boycott, the grape boycott, and sit-ins to prevent construction of uranium mines and nuclear reactors) have been organized to protest the specific policies of each corporation. But we also can coordinate campaigns against corporations for broader goals, such as abrogating NAFTA, reducing interest rates, price controls, tax reform and establishing universal services.

Once we target corporations, we can re-define our relationships to municipal and provincial governments and to large community institutions (e.g., boards of education and boards of hospitals). In addition to lobbying them for improved services or policies, we can develop cooperative linkages with them for our mutual benefit. For example, we could press provincial and municipal governments to fund organizers to mobilize the public and to commit other resources to the broader fight against the TNCs for social justice (e.g., zoning to exclude Walmart). Several years ago, that strategy succeeded in England with the Greater London Council (GLC). To do this successfully we will need to run slates of progressive candidates to win power locally.

*7. We have neglected the membership base of our organizations.*
We need to put priority on re-building our membership and ally base. Over the next ten years, we will lose most of what remains of our welfare state, and we can expect a sharp rise in repressive law and order infrastructure to suppress the resulting protests and desperation-based crime. We need to start planning now to build mutual support networks. We will need them to prevent evictions and farm foreclosures, and to share food and culture during hard times.

We also need to invest in organizing and supporting workers and grassroots groups locally. At this juncture, it is far more important for unions to invest in community organizers, than in grievance staff. As jobs leak south, the unemployed will represent the most powerful pool of resistance workers. During the Devine years in Saskatchewan, the CLC assigned Dave Durning to help organize and support the Saskatchewan Coalition for Social Justice. His respectful, creative facilitation helped immeasurably in forming an effective and diverse social justice coalition which had a major role in ousting Devine.

*8. Our solidarity linkages with resistance movements in Central and South America, as well as in other trading blocs are under developed.*
Solidarity with Third World movements has been heavily dependent on government funding. As a result, groups like Oxfam, CUSO, and the Development Education Learner Centres have functioned in semi-isolation from other popular sector groups. When we have connected to Third World struggles, it is often in the form of aid, rather than mutual solidarity. Many members of popular sector groups have internalized the racist media message that "we" are different from and superior to "underdeveloped" countries because of our higher standard of living and relatively high level of social rights and services.

In the NAFTA era, however, international solidarity is no longer a moral luxury but a practical necessity. We need to build strong, working relationships with resistance movements across the Americas and around the world to prevent TNCs from playing us off against each other in competition for the most exploitative work and lowest human rights and environmental standards. We have a lot to learn from the support structures and cultural vitality of people's resistance groups in Third World countries; the water- and electricity-taking parties, the demands for return of the "disappeared," the training for resisting torture, as well as the songs, the popular theatre and rich culture of resistance.

*9. We have not linked our tactics to a coordinated strategy.*
Our leaders have shown stunningly little creativity in designing tactics. On the whole, we are asked to send postcards to MPs, write briefs, or walk up and down with placards until the press stops filming. Aside from failing to influence the politicians to whom they are addressed, these tactics fail to excite, involve or train the people we ask to participate. Even more creative tactics, such as popular theatre skits, boil down to media events to publicize our protests (which the media mostly ignores) rather than strategies to win real victories.

So where do we go from here? Here are three initial suggestions.

*1. Priorize building the popular base of our movements and connections among them, as well as with people's movements elsewhere in the world.*
We are not strong enough now to have much impact on policies or even electoral outcomes. Therefore, we need to retrench and rebuild our bases. As our main tactical strength is people,

we need to focus first on building and rebuilding grassroots groups and training participatory leaders. Our emphasis at this point needs to be on building the movement, not on expecting to influence the TNC giants.

This has to start with self-critical assessment: Who have we excluded or treated insensitively? What do we need to do to actively challenge inequalities (by race, gender, etc.) inside our organizations? How can we make our organizations welcoming, supportive and fun? How can we attract youth and train the next generation? What lessons do we need to learn from the short-comings and defeats of socialist and national liberation governments?

To have strong grassroots organizations, we need to invest in training leaders. We need to set up a training school for organizers. We need to provide good popular education of groups, not just individuals. We need to recruit and welcome new members across diversities, especially emphasizing youth. Our organizations need to be self-financing (Davis 1994).

### 2. Research the opposition better.
At this point, little is known about the BCNI members, the shadow government behind federal and provincial government decisions. If we want to take back the initiative, we need to anticipate their next moves and their likely responses to our tactics. We need to investigate their vulnerabilities (e.g., internal conflicts, scandalous behaviour, dependency on computer linkages). Also, we can develop linkages with their employees and consumers elsewhere in the world. Recent solidarity linkages between Canadian, U.S. and Mexican workers threatened by NAFTA are a good start.

### 3. Plan strategically for the long haul, rather than reactively protesting each new injustice.
Our tactics need to be linked along a timeline of short to long range goals. Too often, we have put all our energy into building toward one big event (often linked to an election or budget day). When that single action fails to influence the government, we fuel further despair among our members. It will take a long time for us to turn around the twenty years of losses we have endured. Therefore, we need to plan for the long haul.

To win, it is important to identify focused targets. We need to develop creative consumer and worker tactics that are safe, fun, and educational and which influence the corporation. For example, TNCs depend much more heavily on computer linkages than do we. We might examine ways to disrupt telecommunications networks. Another example is when the Devine government, in the 1980s, weakened collective bargaining legislation, workers at the Safeway grocery chain went on strike in Saskatchewan. Negotiations were going nowhere until groups of "consumers" began a campaign of filling dozens of shopping carts full of perishable food and leaving them in the aisles. The workers won within a few days. Public sector workers have invented a range of delightful "positive strike" models, which hurt the employer but support other working class people; bus drivers refusing to collect fares, group home workers locking out the administration and working around the clock with patients, teachers setting up freedom schools, and posties processing 10 cent postage Christmas mail (Bernard 1986).

As overwhelming as the odds are between us and the TNCs now, they are relatively small compared to the odds faced by others who have waged successful revolutionary wars. The TNCs have won the initiative—temporarily. Once we develop and apply an appropriate strategic response to this latest chess move, we hold the power to regain the terrain of struggle and win.

## NOTES

1.  See Bird 1976; Blomqvist and Brown 1994; Brown 1994; d'Aquino 1993; Green, Lazar, Corak and Gross 1994; Grubel and Walker 1978; Harris, Richards, Brown and McCallum 1994; BCNI 1987; Riggs and Velt 1993; Walker 1977, 1982; Watson, Richards and Brown 1994; Wilkinson 1980.
2.  Voters in 1994 turfed out the Tories who had advocated these same policies (and voted for the Liberals whose platform did not). The vast majority of the approximately 1300 who testified during the social security review process spoke against the type of restructuring to social programs that eventuated with the Canadian Health and Social Transfer (CHST) (Browne 1994; Moore 1995; HRDC 1995).
3.  Most of these revolutions have been defeated or co-opted in the years since they took state power. This is a serious problem, both for the people of the countries involved and also for the credibility of socialist movements elsewhere. Finding ways to prevent and solve these problems is an important task. But those failures do not wipe out the victories of strategic planning which allowed the revolutionary parties of those countries to win state power in the first place.

## REFERENCES

Amin, S. 1975. "Toward a Structural Crisis of World Capitalism." *Socialist Revolution* 5 (1): 9-44.

Axworthy, L. 1994. *Improving Social Security in Canada: A Discussion Paper*. Hull, Quebec: Human Resources Development Canada.

Barlow, M. and H.J. Robertson. 1994. *Class Warfare: The Assault on Canada's Schools*. Toronto: Key Porter.

Battle, K. 1994. "Poverty and the Welfare State." In L. Samuelson (ed.), *Power and Resistance: Critical Thinking about Canadian Social Issues*. Halifax: Fernwood.

BCNI. 1995. *Business Leadership in Canada and Abroad*. Toronto: Business Council on National Issues.

———. 1987. *Taxation Reform 1987: A Response to the Federal Government White Paper*. Toronto: Business Council on National Issues.

Bernard, E. 1986. "Labour Tactics Today." In W. Magnusson, R.B.J. Walker, C. Doyle and J. Demarco (eds.), *After Bennett: A New Politics for British Columbia*. Vancouver: New Star.

Bird, R. M. 1976. *Charging for Public Services: A New Look At an Old Idea*. Toronto: Canadian Tax Foundation.

Blomqvist, Ake and D.M. Brown (eds.). 1994. *Limits to Care: Reforming Canada's Health System in an Age of Restraint*. Toronto: C.D. Howe Institute.

Brooks, N. 1994. "Tax Breaks for the Rich." *Canadian Dimension* 28 (1): 6-9.

Brown, D.M. 1994. "Economic Change and New Social Policies." In W. G. Watson, J. Richards and D.M. Brown (eds.), *The Case for Change: Reinventing the Welfare State*. Toronto: C. D. Howe Institute.

Browne, P. 1994. *Backgrounder to the Interim Report of the House of Commons Standing Committee on Human Resources Development*. Ottawa: Canadian Centre for Policy Alternatives.

CCPS/CHO!CES. 1995. *Alternative Budget*. Ottawa: Canadian Centre For Policy Alternatives.

Chorney, H., J. Hotson and M. Seccareccia. 1992. *The Deficit Made Me Do It!* Ottawa: Canadian Centre for Policy Alternatives.

Clarke, T. 1994. *Setting the People's Agenda*. Keynote Speech. Council of Canadians Annual General Meeting. Ottawa: October 14.

———. 1995. "Community-based Resistance: The New Battle Front." *Canadian Perspectives* (Winter) 9.

Cobb, C. and M. Kennedy. 1994. "Public Wary of Liberals' Social Reform." *Ottawa Citizen* March 5: A1.

Collier, K. 1995. "Social Policy Versus Regional Trading Blocs in the Global System: NAFTA, the EEC and 'Asia.'" *Canadian Review of Social Policy* 35: 50-59.

Corrigan, P. and P. Leonard. (1978) *Social Work Practice Under Capitalism: A Marxist Approach*. London: Macmillan.

Council of Canadians. 1994. *Setting the Citizens Agenda for Canada*. Annual General Meeting. Ottawa, October 14-16.

d'Aquino Thomas. 1993. "The Economics of NAFTA: A Canadian Business Perspective." In A.R. Riggs and T. Velk (eds.), *Beyond NAFTA: An Economic, Political and Sociological Perspective*. Vancouver: Fraser Institute.

Davis, W. 1994. Personal Communication. September 16.

Finkel, A. 1977. "Origins of the Welfare State in Canada." In L. Panitch (ed.), *The Canadian State: Political Economy and Political Power*. Toronto: University of Toronto Press.

Finn, E. 1995. "Surprised and Shocked: Blind Faith in the Corporate Agenda." *Canadian Forum* June: 7-8.

Galper, J.H. 1975. *The Politics of Social Services*. Englewood Cliffs, New Jersey: Prentice-Hall.

Gonick, C. 1992. "Socialism: Past and Future." In J. Roberts and J. Vorst (eds.), *Socialism in Crisis? Canadian Perspectives*. Halifax: Fernwood.

Gough, I. 1979. *The Political Economy of the Welfare State*. London: Macmillan.

Green, C., F. Lazar, M. Corak and D.M. Gross. 1994. *Unemployment Insurance: How to Make It Work*. Toronto: C.D. Howe Institute.

Grubel, H. G. and M.A. Walker. 1978. *Unemployment Insurance: Global Evidence of Its Effects on Unemployment*. Vancouver: Fraser Institute.

Harris, R. G., J. Richards, D.M. Brown and J. McCallum. 1994. *Paying Our Way: The Welfare State in Hard Times*. Toronto: C.D. Howe Institute.

Human Resources Development Canada (HRDC). 1995. *Security, Opportunities and Fairness: Canadians Renewing their Social Programs*. Ottawa: Minister of Supply and Services.

―――. 1994. *Agenda: Jobs and Growth. Improving Social Security in Canada*. Ottawa: Minister of Supply and Services.

Kahn, S. 1982. *Organizing: A Guide for Grassroots Leaders*. New York: McGraw Hill.

Langille, D. 1987. "The Business Council on National Issues and the Canadian State." *Studies in Political Economy* 24: 41-85.

Lightman, E. 1990. "Conditionality and Social Assistance: Market Values and the Work Ethic." In G. Riches and G. Ternowetsky (eds.), *Unemployment and Welfare: Social Policy and the Work of Social Work*. Toronto: Garamond.

London, J. 1907. *The Iron Heel*. Toronto: Macmillan.

Mao, Tse-Tung. 1968. *Selected Military Writings of Mao Tse-Tung*. Bejing: Foreign Languages Press.

McQuaig, L. 1995. *Shooting the Hippo: Death By Deficit and Other Myths*. Toronto: Penguin.

―――. 1993. *The Wealthy Banker's Wife*. Toronto: Penguin.

Moore, J. 1995. *"Reforming Canada's Social Programs in an Era of Welfare Erosion: A Critical Analysis of the Political, Economic, and Ideological Underpinnings of Security, Opportunities and Fairness: Canadians Renewing Their Social Programs."* Unpublished Independent Enquiry Project. Ottawa: School of Social Work, Carleton University.

Moscovitch, A. 1993. "From the Conservative Ill-fare State to a Renewed Welfare State." *Canadian Review of Social Policy* 32 (12).

――― and G. Drover. 1987. "Social Expenditures and the Welfare State: The Canadian Experience in Historical Perspective." In A. Moscovitch and J. Albert (eds.), *The Benevolent State: The Growth of Welfare in Canada*. Toronto: Garamond.

Mullaly, R. 1994. "Social Welfare and the New Right: A Class Mobilization Perspective." In A.F. Johnson, S. McBride and P.J. Smith (eds.), *Continuities and Discontinuities: The Political Economy of Social Welfare and Labour Market Policy in Canada*. Toronto: University of Toronto Press.

Newall, J.E. 1995. *BCNI Past and Future: A Reflection*. Paper Presented at the Members' Dinner.

Toronto, April 24.

Palmer, B.D. 1987. *Solidarity: The Rise and Fall of An Opposition in British Columbia.* Vancouver: New Star.

Penner, B. 1994. "Playing to Win: Where Our Public Interest Groups Might Go." *Canadian Perspectives* (Winter) 21.

Piven, F.F. and R.A. Cloward. 1971. *Regulating the Poor: The Functions of Public Welfare.* New York: Random House.

Porter, M. E. 1991. *Canada at the Crossroads: The Reality of a New Competitive Environment.* Ottawa: Business Council on National Issues and the Government of Canada.

Riggs, A. R. and T. Velk. 1993. *Beyond NAFTA: An Economic, Political, and Sociological Perspective.* Vancouver: Fraser Institute.

Stobbe, M. 1995. Personal Communication. July 27.

Swift, R. 1994. "Squeezing the South: 50 Years is Enough." *New Internationalist* 257 July: 4-7.

Ternowetsky, G. and G. Riches. 1990. "Economic Polarization and Restructuring of Labour Markets in Canada: The Way of the Future." In G. Riches and G. Ternowetsky (eds.), *Unemployment and Welfare: Social Policy and the Work of Social Work.* Toronto: Garamond.

Tester, F. 1992a. "The Disenchanted Democracy: Canada in the Global Economy of the 1990s." *Canadian Review of Social Policy* 29 and 30: 132-57.

————. 1992b. "Local Power Versus Global Profits: The Odds Against." In J. Plant and C. Plant (eds.), *Putting Power In Its Place: Create Community Control!* Gabriola Island, B.C.: New Society Publishers.

Tudiver, N. 1987. "Forestalling the Welfare State: The Establishment of Programmes of Corporate Welfare." In A. Moscovitch and J. Albert (eds.), *The Benevolent State: The Growth of Welfare in Canada.* Toronto: Garamond.

Walker, M.A. 1982. *On Balancing the Budget.* Vancouver: Fraser Institute.

————. 1977. *Which Way Ahead: Canada After Wage and Price Control.* Vancouver: Fraser Institute.

Watson, W. G., J. Richards and D.M. Brown. 1994. *The Case for Change: Reinventing the Welfare State.* Toronto: C.D. Howe Institute.

Wilkinson, B.W. 1980. *Canada in the Changing World Economy.* Toronto: C.D. Howe Institute.

Whittington, L. 1994. "Poll Shows Debt Top Worry." *Ottawa Citizen* February 4: A1.

Wolfe, D. 1977. "The State and Economic Policy in Canada, 1968-75." In L. Panitch (ed.), *The Canadian State: Political Economy and Political Power.* Toronto: University of Toronto.

Working Committee for Social Solidarity. 1987. *A Time To Stand Together, A Time For Social Solidarity: A Declaration on Social and Economic Policy Directions for Canada by Members of Popular Sector Groups.* Toronto: CLC

Yalnizyan, A. 1993. *Defining Social Security, Defining Ourselves: Why We Need to Change Our Thinking Before It's Too Late.* Ottawa: Canadian Centre for Policy Alternatives, Social Planning Council of Metropolitan Toronto, Canadian Labour Congress.

# CHAPTER 19

# STRUGGLING FOR CITIZENSHIP IN THE GLOBAL ECONOMY: BOND RATERS VERSUS WOMEN AND CHILDREN

*Gloria Geller and Jan Joel*

This paper argues that "globalization," with all this concept implies in terms of the imperatives of competitiveness and efficiency, combined with the national requirement to wage war on the debt, have created both the conditions and a "discourse" which have laid the ideological foundations for the attack on the welfare state. We further maintain that this attack is nothing short of a war on equality. But the attack is indirect rather than head on. It is being accomplished, in part, by making Canadians see themselves, not so much as *citizens* with rights to receive social supports in times of need, but as *individuals* who can meet their needs by becoming competitive and efficient. In other words, we are asked to see ourselves, not as citizens, but as "economic man."[1]

> The broad consensus that grounded the Keynesian Welfare State (kws) and structured the pattern of federal politics for almost half a century has gradually, but certainly, given way to a very different set of assumptions about the role of government and the rights of citizens. These new assumptions and understandings both structure new forms of domination and, at the same time, reshape more familiar ones rooted in gender, race and class. (Brodie 1995: 14)

Many "popular sector" groups, women's groups being among the most prominent, have recognized that the gains they have made in terms of increased social and economic equality are either in jeopardy or have been eroded. To date, however, the women's movement and other equality seeking groups and coalitions (the "popular sector" in a collective sense) are struggling to be heard. They are attempting to effectively state their cases or stake their claims as citizens endowed with rights to a certain social minimum, at the very least, and genuine social and economic equality at best. In this struggle certain questions emerge. To whom or to what entity do equality seeking groups direct their focus? How do they ensure their voices are heard? And how can they get beyond *pro forma* consultations with governments about working in partnership that tend to lead nowhere? In short, how can these groups and coalitions truly influence and change the neoliberal policy agenda?

Feminist scholars such as Janine Brodie (1995) and Jane Ursel (1992) question whether the nation state will continue to be the critical site of women's struggle for equality given that the current global organization of production outstrips the boundaries of its control. In her study of strategies Brodie (cited in Bakker 1994: 56) presents a similar argument:

> The boundary shifting associated with this round of restructuring has eroded the political spaces from which the contemporary women's movement found much of

its cohesion and empowerment. Social welfarism in its familiar patriarchal form is being rapidly taken off the political agenda.

Today we are inundated with the message that we can no longer afford the kind of social services we enjoyed in the past because they impose a crushing burden on the economy and create huge deficits that will ultimately bankrupt our children's generation. In his first budget speech as Liberal Finance Minister, Paul Martin (Department of Finance 1994: 2) told Canadians that for too long governments have been "promising more than they can deliver and delivering more than they can afford. That has to end. We are ending it." In his 1995 budget speech, Martin (Department of Finance 1995: 3) announced that his reductions in government expenditure were "unprecedented in modern Canadian history." At a news conference later in the day Martin (Freeman 1995: A1) gave the following message to reporters.

> The best you can do for Canadians of low and middle income is to clean up the nation's finances. . . . It doesn't take a stroke of genius to understand that we have broken the back of the deficit and, in fact, that the rating agencies should have no concern . . . .

And so the never-ending, seemingly futile battle to fight the deficit through fiscal restraint that began with the Mulroney regime continues apace under the Liberal government of Jean Chrétien. But what difference does it make? Roughly two weeks later, in spite of the admittedly drastic spending cuts outlined in the federal budget, Moody's Investors Service downgraded Canadian bonds.

Many Canadians believed they defeated the Tories and elected the Liberals precisely because job creation was more important than deficit reduction. The Liberals, however, have taken up the cause of deficit reduction with as much fervor as the Mulroney Conservatives and, like the Tories before them, continue to dismantle the social safety net. The virtual sameness of political parties in terms of their obsession with deficit reduction has led to an interesting commentary on the power of international finance capital to set the political agenda. As an American observer (Friedman 1995: A20) noted, "Moody's and the bond market are now imposing on democracies economic and political decisions that the democracies, left to their own devices, simply cannot take." Whether they "cannot" make decisions that would please a majority of citizens as opposed to the interests of the money lenders is contentious. What is clear is that governments fear risking a bad rating from the lending and rating agencies. There is evidence, however, that they might secretly welcome the threat of the Moody's downgrade hanging over their head.

As Linda McQuaig (1995: 43, 44, 51) points out, Vincent Truglia, Moody's Investors Services' senior analyst specializing in Canada, surprised her in a personal interview when he confessed that Canada was the only country he handled "where, usually, nationals from that country want the country downgraded even more—on a regular basis." In an attempt to clarify the confusion surrounding the seriousness of Canada's debt, Truglia issued a Moody's "special commentary" on the topic, only to receive an angry phone call from a Canadian at "a very large financial institution" who berated him for stating in his commentary that "Ottawa's fiscal situation was not 'out of control'" (1995: 44). Although McQuaig (1995: 51) does not argue that the deficit is no problem at all, she makes a convincing case that the numbers have been "manipulated and exaggerated, leaving us the false impression that we are staring at a 'debt wall,' which we are not."

Putting aside the question of the severity of Canada's debt, it is undoubtedly the case that nation states have witnessed the erosion of their sovereignty through the globalization of capital markets. International financial institutions have become more active and powerful in this process and in many respects have come to play a key role as enforcers of the global logic of the market. At first in the developing world, but now increasingly in developed nations, the state has become an institution whose task it is to enforce the logic of the self-regulating market on the grounds that this serves the national interest by maximizing efficiency and welfare. From this perspective, the national interest ceases to be defined through a domestic political process. Instead, "states are actively encouraged to demonstrate their 'political will' by resisting the demands of those who do not share this definition of the national interest" (Bienefeld 1991: 17). The demands of those opposing these market-driven definitions of national interests are treated as "illegitimate and counterproductive attempts" that serve "narrow, selfish interests at the expense of the general interest" (Bienefeld 1991: 18).

In spite of the fact that the human costs of allowing the "self-regulating market" to run its course are tragically high (as has proven to be the case in many African countries and currently in Mexico) there is no backing down on the part of either the World Bank or the private money lenders. We are witnessing the virtual "stripping away society's defenses against unrestrained international and national market forces" (Bienefeld 1991: 26) and international lending agencies continue to call for radical spending cuts and more deregulation.

In Canada, trade agreements such as the Canada-U.S. Free Trade Agreement (CUFTA) and the North American Free Trade Agreement (NAFTA) have institutionalized certain rights and arrangements that benefit corporations and financial institutions to an extent that seems to preclude governments from making policy decisions that contravene their interests. Now federal and provincial governments appeal to and satisfy, not the Canadian electorate, but the international money lenders and the bond raters.

This is not to say, however, that all of this is inevitable or that there is no alternative. On the contrary, as economist Manfred Bienefeld (cited in Joel 1994: 22) argued at a conference on social and economic policy alternatives, globalization is "a matter of political will and political organization" and we must challenge it precisely because it has robbed us of the ability to "make socially and politically defined choices about the trade-offs between efficiency, leisure, social stability, environmental protection or the maintenance of moral or ethical limits to competition."

While the elite of the Canadian investment community ensures the promulgation of its consensus that Canada faces a "debt wall," those who challenge this view and/or believe other issues such as equality, increasing poverty and joblessness deserve more attention, consistently face a "brick wall" when attempting to bring these issues to the top of government's public policy agenda.

The reasons for this are many. In the first place, groups making such claims do not have the same access to the media as the business elite. Their voices are not as loud as those of their opponents. Typically the voice of business interests echoes in the public conscience. Second, if their voices are heard, they are usually portrayed as those of "special interest groups."

Additionally, governments confuse the matter by claiming to share the concerns of women's groups and anti-poverty groups, especially in the area of children's poverty. Indeed, many of those in government likely do care about poor children, but the solution governments now pose is based on "market logic." According to Finance Minister Paul Martin (Freeman 1994: A6), "the laws of compound interest and the laws of capital markets" dictate the boundaries surrounding what we can and cannot do in the areas of social and economic policies. Good fiscal health is a prerequisite for social well-being and good fiscal health is predicated on eliminating the deficit. As we head toward the new millennium the "laws" of the market have become as natural and inevitable as the law of gravity! Market religion is firmly entrenched.

Women have always had a different relationship to both the market and the welfare state than men; women's relation to the welfare state in particular is more complex and contradictory. On one hand, even a minimal and inadequate safety net increases the leverage of women who are economically dependent on individual men. On the other hand, welfare programs that are inadequate reinforce and institutionalize the feminization of poverty. Reducing or eliminating welfare programs enhances private or familial patriarchy while defending these programs consolidates public or social patriarchy, in part because the Keynesian welfare state (KWS) always assumed that families do or should contain one primary breadwinner—a man and an unpaid domestic worker—a woman (Fraser 1989: 104, 107). The Canadian welfare state has thus always rested on the unpaid domestic work of women.

Immigrant women, women of colour and First Nations women have always had a different relation to the welfare state than white middle class women. Many women of colour and immigrant women were in the labour force all along, some working in sweat shops, others working as "domestic help." First Nations women on reserves were not full citizens at the time of the founding of the welfare state in that neither they nor their male counterparts could even vote until 1960.

The welfare state is "the culmination of a protracted crisis and political struggle conducted by, among others, women and workers." At one and the same time "it introduced the concept of social citizenship, but the social safety net was constructed as a gendered and hierarchical system" (Bakker 1994: 53). The KWS was built with a particular family at its core: the white, patriarchal family. Its preservation was paramount—important enough that social security measures were instituted, albeit gradually and in a piecemeal fashion, to ensure that these families, who were perceived to be the backbone of society, were stable and functioning. The welfare state is thus premised on the sexual division of labour with women at home, in the private sphere, taking care of society's reproductive work both in the sense of giving birth to and raising children (the future labour force) and providing the male breadwinner with the domestic supports he requires to enter the public sphere and participate in society's production.

At the foundation of the welfare state lay the fear of a "crisis in the family." In its unmediated, unregulated form, the wage labour system came to be seen as destructive of the patriarchal family. A consensus that something had to be done to stabilize it was shared by women's groups, labour, church groups, farmers organizations and even some businessmen. The broad-based nature of the consensus attested to how fundamental patriarchy was to the organization of the social system. Social reforms consciously fought for and justified the "indispensability of the patriarchal family" in terms of its role in social reproduction (Ursel 1992: 37). The family wage concept became the key to solving that crisis.

In order to ensure adequate family income and security, two essential types of social welfare programs were developed on a gendered basis. Masculine social welfare programs such as unemployment insurance were developed as contributory programs, with payments being made by employers and workers. Recipients were viewed as "rights-bearers" and were not stigmatized. Feminine social relief programs were financed through general revenues. Recipients were perceived as clients of public charity (Fraser 1989). Mothers allowance was first adopted in Manitoba in 1919 and in Ontario in 1920, largely in response to women's organizations' criticism of the destitution of families without income, particularly fatherless families (Moscovitch and Drover 1987: 24). It was clearly a response to the failure of the patriarchal family or the absence of the male breadwinner. Family allowance, which was instituted much later in 1944, was an attempt to deflect trade union pressure to lift wartime wage controls that would lead to wage increases for low paid workers.

Leonard Marsh, in his *Report on Social Security in Canada* which appeared in 1943, attempted to lay out the plans for a comprehensive social welfare system in Canada and situated family allowance as its centerpiece. According to Linda McQuaig (1995: 222), "[t]he allowance, paid each month for each child, was large enough to contribute significantly to the family's income, particularly in families with a lot of children." McQuaig points out that even the Bank of Canada provided "important support" for the proposal. Graham Towers, the Bank's Governor personally supported the idea "partly because he saw it as a way to stem upward pressure on wages" (McQuaig 1995: 222).

If programs such as family allowance were about socializing the costs of reproduction, the current dismantling of the welfare state that has the Bank of Canada's support today is very much about the attempt to reprivatize the costs of reproduction. Having the costs of reproduction socialized through the welfare state in an era of globally organized production is problematic in relation to the competitiveness imperative. Since there are now few barriers to capital's flight from the costs of reproducing labour, if labour is too costly to reproduce in one nation, capital can move to a country where the costs of reproducing it are lower. Workers of the world today truly are united in the sense that there is a global labour market and global competition. This is turning out to be disastrous for a number of the world's people. To start with the relatively privileged among the losers, workers in the developed world, particularly industrial workers who are mostly men, have been experiencing downward pressure on their wages, benefit packages and standard of living.

Sir James Goldsmith (1994: 20), a corporate raider in the 1980s, now a member of the European Parliament, describes the logic behind global free trade as well as its implications using the following example:

> Take two enterprises, one in the developed world and one in Vietnam. Both make the identical product destined to be sold in the same market . . . both can use identical technology; both have access to the same pool of international capital. The only difference between the two is that the Vietnamese enterprise can employ 47 people for the cost of only one French [worker]. You do not have to be a genius to understand who will be the winner in such a contest. . . . [The winners under global free trade] . . . will be those who can benefit from an almost inexhaustible supply of very cheap labour.

Unleashing capital from any responsibility for social reproduction, an outcome of global free trade, is clearly one of the most serious threats to the well-being of the vast majority around the globe, particularly women and children. Not only will workers in the developed world suffer setbacks, women, especially in the "Third World," will have even greater burdens added to their already overburdened lives. While capital can flee from the costs of reproducing labour, women cannot.

In terms of the global division of labour, women in North America and Western Europe who operate within a social patriarchal mode of reproduction produce low quantity, high cost, highly skilled and educated labour. Third World women, operating within a familial, patriarchal mode of reproduction, produce high quantity, low cost, "unskilled," uneducated labour (Ursel 1992: 50). Women in the developed world are being asked to carry a heavier load as the state increasingly pulls out of its responsibilities—"the shrinking of the public sphere" as Brodie (cited in Bakker 1994: 48) refers to it—for social reproduction in the name of global competitiveness. In other words, by failing to provide universal, affordable childcare and by implementing cuts to social and health services, the state is asking the "family" and the "community" to play a more significant role. This, of course, means that caring for the sick, for the elderly and children will mainly fall to women in the "private" sphere.

Women in the Third World have already experienced the socially devastating consequences of structural adjustment policies that were implemented by the International Monetary Fund (IMF) starting nearly two decades ago. Third World women were on the front line, so to speak, in terms of bearing the brunt of the implementation of market principles. In the developing world, these principles were enforced by the IMF and the World Bank in conjunction with the nation state.

In Canada, these principles are being promoted and "enforced" by private investors, bond holders and bond raters, in conjunction with the state. Federal and provincial governments have not been *forced* to implement structural adjustment programs, but they have chosen to bow to the imperatives of the market upheld by the investment community. In attempting to justify their political decision to do this, they put forward the economic argument in a manner that implies that they have no alternative. "There is no alternative!" is one of the rallying cries of the "restructuring discourse."

In much of the developing world and certainly in Canada, global free trade and the agreements that enforce the free trade agenda such NAFTA and CUFTA have been protested. "Visit India and you will find that there have been demonstrations of up to one million people. ... In the Philippines, several hundred thousand farmers protested against GATT [the General Agreement on Trade and Tariffs] because it would destroy their agriculture" (Goldsmith 1994: 22). In Canada, there were demonstrations organized against both the CUFTA and NAFTA.

A key question emerges at the present time when family insecurity is once again identified as a major social problem by mainstream analysts: why is this crisis not perceived, at least by those who hold power, as the same kind of threat to social stability as it was in the earlier decades of this century? Is it simply that those who have power, including the power to define the present consensus, simply believe that they can insulate themselves from the kind of social problems that a genuine crisis in social reproduction is bound to create? Or is it because the crisis is perceived to be a crisis, not of the white patriarchal family, but of some "other" family type?

In Canada the families most prone to poverty are women-led. According to the report of the National Council of Welfare, *Poverty Profile 1993* (1995a), over the period 1980-1993 some six out of ten families headed by single parent mothers under the age of sixty-five were poor. "The highest rate was 62.8 percent in 1984, and the lowest was 52.9 percent in 1989" (1995a: 14). The presence of children causes a family's chances of poverty to soar (Child Poverty Action Group 1994: 6-7). This is especially true for families with children headed by someone under twenty-five years of age, but also true even for families with children headed by a person between twenty-five to thirty-four years of age (CPAG 1994: 6-7). Although there is recognition that single parent women, elderly women and young families in general face the greatest risk of poverty, and that economic insecurity particularly for young families is on the rise, the current answer to many of their problems is assumed to rest with individual initiative.

The social security review process made clear that the federal government chooses not to see the problems of single parents and young families as structural ones. Rather, they are generally seen to have skills deficits (Human Resource Development Canada 1994: 34-38). They are presented as needing social programs that will act as a "springboard" for them to enter the job market. There is little recognition that the labour market has given youth few opportunities as of late or that single mothers have an important role to play in raising their children. In a very real sense, these basic facts tended to remain invisible in social policy calculations. Again it is "market logic" that provides many of the answers to the perceived (misconstrued) problems.

Perhaps the most important difference between now and when the foundations of the welfare state were being laid is the growing participation of women in the labour force. This has been accompanied by increasing demands that women and other equality seeking groups have placed on the state. For more than two decades, feminists in Canada have developed strong national organizations to defend their interests at the level of the nation state. Groups such as the National Action Committee on the Status of Women (NAC) and the Legal Education and Action Fund (LEAF) aimed their lobbying efforts at the federal government for the most part, largely because the operation of the welfare state was premised on the centralization of power at the federal level (Ursel 1992: 300). Since the election of the Tories at the federal level in 1984, women's organizations have been forced to expend enormous amounts of time and energy fighting the "Tory agenda," otherwise known as the "corporate agenda," "neoconservative agenda" or the "neoliberal agenda." This has meant "defending the rights that women achieved in the Charter of Rights and Freedoms and defending the welfare state" (Brodie 1995: 65).

Much to the horror of some people, "opinion makers" and "consensus manufacturers" among them, equality seeking groups are not just asking for equality of opportunity; rather they are insisting upon equality of outcome as well. *Globe and Mail* editorialist William Thorsell (1995: A18) decries this phenomenon, concluding that Section 15 (2) of the Canadian Charter of Rights and Freedoms, which speaks to the issue of equality of outcome, is simply "wrong, a blight on the Charter." In an argument clothed in the language of classical liberalism, Thorsell challenges one of the few mechanisms for achieving equality in Canadian society that is entrenched in the Charter. "'Outcome measured' affirmative action," he argues, "suspends the individual's right to equal protection and benefit of the law, described in [Section] 15 (1)," which makes an "open-ended commitment to equality of opportunity."

Thorsell prefaces his arguments with the comment that, "[s]ome people understand equality as a *process*, others as an *outcome*." The "process people" are happy no matter what results emerge, as long as people have *equality of opportunity*—freedom is the key. The "outcomes people" actually want results; quotas, for example, are important so that goals can be set and the move toward greater equality (or movement away from it) can be measured. Although Thorsell never explicitly refers to market freedom or the market, it is clear that the equality of opportunity clause of the Charter does not interfere with market freedom. A different clause, that which talks about outcomes, requires state intervention. It acknowledges that the market might not "deliver the goods" to all citizens equally.

Zillah Eisenstein (1984) argued that neoliberals were hostile to the welfare state because it tried to create equality of conditions rather than equality of opportunity, unleashing what were perceived to be expectations that were endless. In this sense then, the backlash against feminism and the attack on the welfare state are fundamentally linked. But rather than seeing the attack on the welfare state as an attack on women and children, it is more politically accurate and astute to comprehend the attack on the welfare state as an essential by-product of the attack on equality of condition which is the core of the neoliberal agenda: "equality for women cannot be achieved without a substantial modification of the gender order—a transformation of the state" (Franzway et al. 1989: 54).

In light of this analysis, bowing to market principles, either under the auspices of adhering to the "law of compound interest" and "the laws of capital markets" or as acceptance of the imperatives of flexibility, competitiveness and efficiency, is not first and foremost an economic decision; rather, it is a political decision. It is profoundly political because it is a decision about "who wins and who loses," although it is never presented as such. Above all else, it is a political decision that takes aim at equality, particularly women's equality.

It is not inevitable that Canada, or societies in general, must be restructured according to market criteria:

> Canadians have been too quick to accept the determinism and unrestrained economism of restructuring discourse. We have not sufficiently challenged its impositional claims as 'impositional'—as invested interpretations of reality which favour certain groups over others. . . . Our silence has implicitly endorsed neoliberalism's capacity to delegitimize political, cultural and moral claims. (Brodie 1995: 80)

It is true that the bond raters' and investors' claims, which governments have largely accepted, about what must be done in the face of globalization are consistently heard in the media; alternative responses to restructuring are not. But it is not strictly true that we have remained silent, although it would certainly *seem* that way. This observation leads to the necessity of considering another significant difference between the late twentieth century and the early to mid- 1900s: according to French social theorist Guy Debord (cited in Raboy 1992: 4), the most significant social fact of the twenty some years between 1968-90 was

> the unbroken continuity of the spectacle. . . . All discussion of what the world's rulers do is organized through the spectacle, through the unilateral and uni-directional communication via the mass media of the results of decisions that have already been made. Only that which is recognized by the spectacle has historical validity; only

those consecrated by the spectacle are entitled to speak with authority.[2]

These theories bear consideration if we are to come to grips with the need to reclaim or "recover the political" (Brodie 1995: 81). To date, it is the international investors who have been able "to dominate the political"; their claims continually ring in our ears. They have seized a valuable opportunity: they have successfully labelled the crisis and imposed the claim that we face a "debt crisis," we may even be facing "the debt wall." They have been able to convince a number of people that if we are to come to terms with globalization in a positive way by remaining competitive we must come to terms with our debt and deficit crisis; this means coming to terms with our social spending.

We have seen above how the manufacturing of this crisis has been consciensciously attended to by the Canadian investment community in conjunction with foreign investors and bond raters. Women's groups and other popular sector organizations do not have the same access to capital as the financial elite, nor are they "consecrated by the spectacle" (Debord cited in Raboy 1992: 4). They are relegated to the status of "special interest groups." Such groups have not been successful in labelling the crisis, in part because they have not been able to gain legitimacy. But perhaps, in a collective sense, the popular sector (and to some extent the women's movement itself) has not been relentless enough in articulating the message that we are facing a crisis of equality—social, economic and political equality. This crisis is so obvious, yet submerged in the endless important discussion about the collapse of the welfare state, the attack on our social safety net, the jobless recovery, child poverty and so forth. A key question then is: how does the popular sector effectively and continuously bring this simple and *fundamental* issue to the forefront of all discussion about the meaning of globalization?

Another more fundamental question, however, might be: "Is there anything at all to be gained by focusing tremendous amounts of energy on influencing the public debate and the policy-makers by mounting campaigns to raise the profile of certain issues? Such a question is of utmost importance since we are clearly in the midst of

> . . . a prolonged and conflict-ridden political process during which old assumptions and shared understandings are challenged and are eventually either rejected or transformed while social forces struggle to achieve a new consensus—a new vision of the future to fill the vacuum created by the erosion of the old." (Brodie 1995: 15)

While the neoliberals have a "vision" of sorts based on market principles, theirs is not a vision of *society*: ultimately, for them, the world is populated by individual taxpayers or consumers—in short, by "economic man." Thus there is an opportunity for the popular sector in general (and the women's movement in particular) to fill the vacuum created by the utter bankruptcy of this ideology. The former is without a vision of collective action and/or a collective vision of how people might share the world's resources for the benefit of all and in a manner that reverses the present path of environmental degradation. New concepts of citizenship need to be created since, with restructuring, we are simultaneously involved in a process of "falling apart and building up again of an entire political-cultural order." We are moving towards a new "configuration of social, economic and political life" (Brodie 1995: 15). And perhaps these concepts of citizenship need to be developed and understood through direct participation or experience, which, if we agree with Debord (cited in Raboy 1992), is the only "reliable knowledge" in the age of the spectacle.

This is a conclusion that many people are reaching as they struggle to build alternatives, including an alternative vision. At a national conference held in 1993 focused on building a research agenda on social and economic policy alternatives, a diverse group of people who participated in defining the agenda concluded: "We need to start implementing alternatives, not just by talking but by doing. We must learn by doing" (cited in Joel 1994: 7).

At this conference an example of the attempt to build an alternative economic framework and vision was presented by Melanie Conn, a member of WomenFutures Community Economic Development Society, and a long-time activist in the women's movement, cooperatives and community economic development (CED). Conn presented "progressive CED" as starting with a "framework that challenges conventional structures and traditional economic objectives." In CED the focus is placed upon a "community-directed process . . . that attempts to integrate social, economic, ecological and spiritual elements." Women's CED shares these principles and, in addition, "starts with women and the work we do. Women working in CED consistently acknowledge unpaid work and support women's numerous roles" (cited in Joel 1994: 111-13). This starting point leads to very different conclusions about how to measure and evaluate all manner of things. In the course of conducting research on women's CED initiatives, WomenFutures found four common features: the need to redefine productivity (i.e., establish a new productivity equation that counts unpaid work, such as domestic work, for example); the need to establish a "multiple bottom-line" as opposed to the traditional bottom line that simply measures monetary profit or loss; the need to develop collective resources; and the need to ensure inclusivity. People at the conference tended to see women's CED as a model for developing public policy on a larger scale. Thus the question was raised: "How do we relate the thinking that is at the community level (women in CED and issues from the blockade [to protest clearcutting on First Nations land]) to the broader policy arena?"

The answer to the question of whether women's CED initiatives and the knowledge gained through this type of practice can expand or "translate" to a broader level and eventually affect policy change on a wider scale is significant. What is its social and political impact? Since CED experientially helps define new ways of participating in social and economic life, albeit on a small scale, it has some potential, in the long term, to help define new forms of citizenship.

It is also significant that women's CED, because it acknowledges the contribution of women's unpaid work, presents a challenge to traditional economic thought and the division between the private and public spheres in a very concrete and practical way. Women's CED initiatives, on a micro scale, model a type of feminist economic practice that feminist economists such as Marilyn Waring, Marianne Ferber, Julie Nelson and others have been theorizing. Both the small scale women's CED initiatives and emerging feminist economic thought provide key tools on both a practical and a theoretical level to challenge current claims about the restructuring of our economies and societies.

The point of this discussion is not to say, however, that the women's movement or the popular sector as a whole should build a political strategy by focusing only on the micro or grassroots level, although working at this level is absolutely essential. The Martin budget, however, has prefigured a new relation between the social movements and the federal government in terms of the claims these movements have traditionally attempted to make *vis a vis* the state's provision of a national program of social and other essential human services.

Bill C-76 (the Budget Implementation Act 1995) which lays out the new framework for federal funding to the provinces for post-secondary education, health and social services, has "three key features," according to the National Council of Welfare (1995b: 8): "repeal of the Canada Assistance Plan, creation of a Canada Health and Social Transfer (CHST) to help provinces pay for welfare and social services as well as medicare and post-secondary education, and cuts in federal financial support for all of these programs." The cash transfer portion of the CHST paid by the federal government would not be earmarked specifically for medicare, post-secondary education or welfare; rather the money would simply go into the consolidated revenue fund at the provincial level. The block funding arrangement comes with few principles or guidelines attached. In the budget speech it was noted that Minister Axworthy would invite his provincial counterparts "to work together on developing, through mutual consent, a set of shared principles and objectives that could underlie the new Canada Social Transfer" (cited in National Council of Welfare 1995b: 9). Therefore analysts reasonably argue that once the legislation is implemented the money from this fund could be used by the provinces to pay for other things, e.g., interest charges on their debts. This would further entrench the erosion of national standards which began under the Conservatives in the 1980s.

Given the devolution of responsibility for welfare to the provinces, it is questionable whether the nation state will continue to be the critical site of resistance for the women's and popular sector movements. During the consultations and all the activities leading up to SSR, including a conference where women were discussing their social policy agenda,[3] women's groups made very clear statements about the need to maintain the articles of CAP so as to ensure national standards for social programs. In a pamphlet describing its position on *Strengthening Social Programs: Fighting For Women's Equality,* NAC (no date, np) laid out its approach to the federal role in relation to social programs in terms of what it called a "Three Nations Framework." Within this framework,

> the right of aboriginal peoples to self-government must be respected. So must the desire of the majority of the people of Québec to have the Québec government manage and deliver their social programs. In the rest of Canada, the desire of most residents to have the federal government play a strong role and maintain standards for social programs must be respected.

A national consultation with women's groups on social security reform was also held in Ottawa in December 1994. Members of the Human Resources Development Task Force, including senior officials in the ministry, were present and discussions were held on a number of issues. The verbatim discussion of the consultation (National Consultation with Women's Groups on Social Security Reform 1994) reads in a disjointed fashion, as one might expect. Yet the account of the event is worth reflecting upon insofar as it illustrates what consultation with the federal government has come to mean for a number of popular sector groups. For example, at one point in the meeting, a few of the participants at the meeting, unidentified by name on the transcript, were attempting to determine if CAP would be cut. Eventually, it was stated that CAP would indeed be cut, by an HRDC assistant deputy minister (1994: np).

"So what's the point of the consultation then?" asked an unidentified speaker. "The decision is already made." To this the official replied, "That's right, yeah. Those are the fiscal parameters in which social security reform is happening. . . . " The consultation continued nevertheless.

The "fiscal parameters" constitute the only legitimate claim now perceived by governments. If the women's movement and other popular sector groups are to change this, they will need to work simultaneously on a number of levels: locally, provincially and internationally. Regarding the international level, women's groups and anti-poverty groups in particular are starting to build their case that Canada's restructuring of its social safety net contravenes certain agreements Canada has signed, such as the International Convention on Economic, Social and Cultural Rights.

The demise of the nation state and the current tendency of mainstream political parties to satisfy one interest alone (international finance capital) have caused increasing numbers of people, particularly women, to simply given up on the electoral process and mainstream parties. Today in Saskatchewan, for example, there are visible signs of women's disaffection with all political parties. Women are beginning to discuss the formation of a "Women's Party."[4] As well, during the provincial election, which the NDP was always assured of winning, the Pay Equity Coalition of Saskatchewan built a successful and visible "protest vote" campaign[5] around the issue of pay equity and the fact Saskatchewan is one of the few provinces without Pay Equity Legislation. In a campaign marked by a lack of political debate, the work of this coalition stood out as a reminder that a social justice issue such as pay equity is one that many citizens consider important. Attempts such as these implicitly, if not explicitly, speak to the notion of the need to start "reclaiming political space." In this case, a claim is made with women and women's issues at the centre of the "space" traditionally occupied by Canada's "mainstream" parties: the Conservatives, Liberals, New Democrats and now, on the federal scene, the Reform Party and Bloc Québécois.

Regardless of the level on which claims are made, change will be forged only if those claims effectively challenge the sovereignty of the "free market" and the (re)emergence of "economic man" as the model citizen of the late twentieth century. Cultivating new forms of citizenship, in an inclusive manner and respecting diversity, is the task the women's movement and the other equality seeking movements of the popular sector must creatively and holistically pursue. This will entail a strong commitment to equity (on the level of gender, race and class) within and between nations, a genuine commitment to future generations and the long-term survival of the planet.

## NOTES

1.  For a thorough and illuminating discussion of *Homo economicus* see Ferber and Nelson's (1993) edited collection *Beyond Economic Man*.
2.  Debord characterizes the spectacle as "the autocratic reign of the market economy."
3.  For example, the Social Administration Research Unit, the National Action Committee on the Status of Women and the Fédération des femmes du Québec co-sponsored a national conference on women and social policy September 30-October 2, 1994. The goals of the conference were threefold: to discuss a women's social policy agenda for the 21st century that responds to the needs of women and families; to share and develop responses to the federal review of social policy and make a submission to the Parliamentary standing committee as well as to assist groups in preparing submissions to the committee; and to assist in mobilizing for a feminist social policy.
4.  For, example, discussions of this are taking place in Regina, Saskatchewan. Whether or not this is a widespread phenomenon is difficult to determine as initiatives such as this are new.

5.  The Pay Equity Coalition called on the people of Saskatchewan to register a vote for pay equity at the ballot box. The coalition produced 500 lawn signs that stated: *Pay Equity has my vote.* Residents, therefore, could visibly signal their support for an issue such as pay equity and, at the same time, signal their disenchantment with the mainstream parties. The odd household had pay equity signs in combination with a lawn sign from a political party, usually the NDP. But roughly 90 percent of houses with Pay Equity lawn signs had no other election sign. The lawn signs were distributed primarily in urban areas. The coalition also developed ten billboards reminding the government that it promised to implement pay equity four years ago and that people were still waiting.

## REFERENCES

Bacchi, C.L. 1983. *Liberation Deferred: The Ideas of the English-Canadian Suffragists, 1877-1918.* Toronto: University of Toronto Press.

Bakker, I. (ed.). 1994. *The Strategic Silence: Gender and Economic Policy.* London: Zed Books.

Bienefeld, Manfred. 1991. "Karl Polanyi and the Contradictions of the 1980s." In M. Mendell and D. Salée (eds.), *The Legacy of Karl Polanyi.* New York: St. Martins Press.

Brodie, J. 1995. *Politics on the Margins: Restructuring and the Canadian Women's Movement.* Halifax: Fernwood.

———. 1994. "Shifting the Boundaries: Gender and the Politics of Restructuring." In I. Bakker (ed.), *The Strategic Silence: Gender and Economic Policy.* London: Zed Books.

Child Poverty Action Group, Family Services Association of Metropolitan Toronto, and Social Planning Council of Metropolitan Toronto. 1994. *The Outsiders: A Report on the Prospects for Young Families in Metro Toronto.* Toronto: Family Service Association of Metropolitan Toronto.

Dale, J. and P. Foster. 1986. *Feminists and State Welfare.* London: Routledge and Kegan Paul.

Department of Finance. 1995. *The Budget Speech.* Ottawa: Department of Finance.

. 1994. *The Budget Speech.* Ottawa: Department of Finance.

Eisenstein, Z.R. 1984. *Feminism and Sexual Equality: Crisis in Liberal America.* New York: Monthly Review Press.

Ferber, M.A. and J.A. Nelson (eds.). 1993. *Beyond Economic Man: Feminist Theory and Economics.* Chicago: University of Chicago Press.

Franzway, S., D. Court and R.W. Connell. 1989. *Staking a Claim: Feminism, Bureaucracy and the State.* Cambridge: Polity Press.

Fraser, N. 1989. "Women, Welfare and the Politics of Need Interpretation." In P. Lassman (ed.), *Politics and Social Theory.* London and New York: Routledge.

Freeman, A. 1995. "Ottawa Aims to Shrink Deficit." *Globe and Mail* February 18: A1, A4.

———. 1994. "Martin Vows to Slash Deficit." *Globe and Mail* October 18: A6.

Friedman, T. 1995. "Don't Mess with Moody's." *Globe and Mail* February 27: A20.

Goldsmith, J. 1994. "The Case Against GATT: An Interview with James Goldsmith." In *Multinational Monitor* 15 ( 20): 20-23.

Human Resources Development Canada. 1994. *Agenda: Jobs and Growth. Improving Social Security in Canada.* Ottawa: Minister of Supply and Services.

Joel, J. (ed.). 1994. *Building a Vision: Proceedings from a National Conference on Social and Economic Policy Alternatives.* Regina: Social Administration Research Unit.

Marsh, L.C. 1943. *Report on Social Security for Canada.* Ottawa: Edmond Cloutier Printer to the King's Most Excellent Majesty.

McQuaig, L. 1995. *Shooting the Hippo: Death by Deficit and Other Canadian Myths.* Toronto: Penguin Books.

Moscovitch, A. and G. Drover. 1987. "Social Expenditures and the Welfare State: The Canadian Experience in Historical Perspective." In A. Moscovitch and J. Albert (eds.), *The Benevolent State: The Growth of Welfare in Canada.* Toronto: Garamond Press.

National Action Committee on the Status of Women. Undated. *Stop. There is Another Way! Strengthening Canada's Social Programs: Fighting for Women's Equality.* Toronto: National Action Committee on the Status of Women.

National Consultation with Women's Groups on Social Security Reform. 1994. *Meeting with Task Team Representatives of Human Resources Development Canada and Women's Groups.* Verbatim Report. December 3.

National Council of Welfare. 1995a. *Poverty Profile 1993.* Ottawa: Minister of Supply and Services.

———. 1995b. *The 1995 Budget and Block Funding.* Ottawa: Minister of Supply and Services.

O'Brien, M. 1995. "Group Takes Complaint to UN." *The Leader-Post* April 28: A6.

Raboy, M. and B. Dagenais (eds.). 1992. *Media, Crisis and Democracy: Mass Communication and the Disruption of Social Order.* London: Sage Publications.

Ross, David et al. 1993. *Family Security in Insecure Times.* Ottawa: Canadian Council on Social Development Publications.

Thorsell, W. 1995. "There are Not Two Kinds of Equality in the World." *Globe and Mail* March 18.

Ursel, J. 1992. *Private Lives, Public Policy: 100 Years of State Intervention in the Family.* Toronto: Women's Press.

Waring, M. 1988. *If Women Counted: A New Feminist Economics.* New York: Harper Collins.

# CHAPTER 20

# SOCIAL POLICY, DEVOLUTION AND DISABILITY: BACK TO NOTIONS OF THE WORTHY POOR?

*Michael Bach and Marcia H. Rioux*

## INTRODUCTION

Much has been made by social policy historians and analysts of an assumption that the Canadian welfare state has not got much beyond its Poor Law roots and its "residual" function, even in the period of massive expansion since the Second World War (Guest 1980). Given our analysis of public policy on the basis of this generally well-founded assumption, we find ourselves in a curious position in the wake of the federal government's budget brought down in February 1995. In one fell swoop it reduced the level of funding for social assistance and, with the introduction of the Canada Health and Social Transfer (CHST), ended the conditionality for federal transfers to the provinces for social spending, a set of conditions that have evolved, at least in relation to the Canada Assistance Plan (CAP), over the past thirty years. If anyone thought we did not have a residual welfare state before this budget, they must surely be convinced of this fact now. But does the end of conditionality make any difference? If we have always been rooted in a residual model, is not this just more of the same?

This paper explores these questions and the implication of the CHST from the perspective of people with disabilities. It argues that, while the welfare state in Canada has retained its residual roots to a large extent, a new framework of human rights has evolved which brings these roots into question. This framework has provided some foundation for undermining the worthy/unworthy poor distinction which has been a cornerstone of the welfare state in Canada and served to justify the exclusion of people with disabilities from the mainstream of society. We examine how the CHST does little to advance the human rights foundation of the welfare state and may in fact serve to undermine it.

We can gain some insight into the nature of the Canadian welfare state by viewing it from the perspective of people with disabilities. The roots of the welfare state in Canada can be found in the English Poor Laws, which established a distinction between the worthy and the unworthy poor. Through the evolution of this distinction in the succeeding years, the state established some obligation to care for those considered to be worthy poor. These include the aged, infirm and disabled. The implications of this distinction have most often been analyzed from the perspective of those considered "unworthy," "able bodied" and "able minded" men and women, those who were considered able but unwilling to work. For those who fall into this category, the welfare state has been minimalist and residual and has reflected the "less eligibility" principle.[1] Without recognition of the structural factors which have led to unemployment, poverty, ill health and illiteracy, welfare state provision has entangled people and families in a web of meagre provision, disentitlement, discretionary benefits, contradictory eligibility rules, surveillance and targeted programs (National Council of Welfare 1987; The Roeher Institute 1988). These have had the effect of entrenching rather than ameliorating inequality. As many of the poor are seen as "unworthy" through the lens of welfare state institutions, provision for this group has remained minimalist and residual. The recent budget is likely to exacerbate this situation.

From the perspective of the "worthy" poor, a category which has tended to include a large proportion of people with disabilities, the welfare state has in some respects been minimalist but not "residual." Often the problem has been one of "overfunding" and "overserving" rather than underfunding. A different set of obligations were established for the "worthy poor" than for those considered "unworthy." These obligations could only be exercised by constructing legal and social differences that have served to legitimate different treatment and obligations between the worthy and unworthy poor (Rioux 1994). The category of "worthy poor," however, has become a double- and triple-edged sword for people with disabilities. Under the legal and social regime of the "worthy poor," people with disabilities became the object of charity, but at the cost of basic citizenship rights (Rioux 1993). Considered incompetent to function in society, this being the ticket to becoming "worthy," the welfare state established systems of segregation for people with disabilities. These systems segregated them from their families, educational institutions, labour markets, political participation, from the exercise of rights of self-determination and from their communities. The monuments to the "disabled but worthy" poor are the institutions, special schools, vocational workshops and segregated classrooms. The costs of being "worthy poor" have been high for people with disabilities (extremely high rates of unemployment, violence and abuse, illiteracy, poverty, illness, social isolation and discrimination).

In the immediate post-war period the framework of obligations for the welfare state in Canada, emphasizing security, citizenship and democracy, entrenched the worthy/unworthy distinction. These became the pillars of the Canadian state, the framework for well-being, and provided the basis for massive investment in building the institutional infrastructure for welfare provision (The Roeher Institute 1993). While the notion of citizenship as a broad set of social, economic and political entitlements was being formulated in this period (Marshall 1963), the figure of the "citizen" that remained entrenched was that of the self-made, rational and independent individual exercising basic democratic and legal rights. A democratic state and society was to be constituted by such individuals securing for themselves, and largely on their own, "the good life." Because many people with disabilities did not meet the tests imposed by such a concept of citizen, they were to be taken care of through the "security" pillar of the welfare state. Investment in institutional facilities, special education, segregated vocational training and employment and community services exclusively for persons with disabilities grew substantially in the post-war period. In this way the post-war framework for securing the welfare and well-being of Canadians ironically institutionalized exclusion for people with disabilities.

Cracks in this post-war framework for well-being began to emerge in the 1960s. Claims for its restructuring gained momentum through the 1960s to the 1980s, first from the civil rights movement and later from the growing disability rights movement. In response to these challenges, a new foundation of rights was established in Canada and internationally for people with disabilities. The entrenchment of the rights for people with disabilities within human rights legislation, and the entrenchment of constitutional equality rights for people with disabilities within the Charter of Rights and Freedoms (1982)[2] have had important consequences in Canada. These are now legally entrenched on an equal basis with the rights accorded to women, people of minority races, cultures and religions and older Canadians. The prohibition against discrimination under provincial human rights statutes has been extended in the past fifteen years from issues of employment for those with physical handicaps to include services, facilities and accommodation for people with both mental and physical handicaps. Therefore these statutes are a much more expansive instrument of rights protections. Canada is also signatory to a number of international agreements which guarantee political, social and economic rights for people with disabilities, such as the United Nations Universal Declaration of Human Rights (1948); the United Nations Convention on the Rights of the Child (1989); the United Nations World Program of Action Concerning Disabled Persons (1983); the UN Declaration on the Rights of Disabled Persons (1975); and the United Nations Standard Rules on the Equalization of Opportunities for Persons with Disabilities (1993).

## A New Framework for Social Well-Being

The obligations found in the human rights protections have established a new framework for social well-being, one that builds upon the post-war framework but which also brings some of its underlying assumptions into question, in particular that of the worthy/unworthy poor distinction. The key elements of the new framework for social well-being are self-determination, democratization and equality. The basis for the social commitment to self-determination is articulated in the international human rights instruments to which Canada is a signatory, and in the rights entrenched in the Charter of Rights and Freedoms to life, liberty and security of the person. Commitments to collective rights of self-determination are also embedded in the Constitution and the Charter.

People, communities and societies hold the principle of self-determination as one of their most cherished values. In a society increasingly defined by cultural, linguistic, ethnic and other differences, the promotion of self-determination is essential if there is a commitment to respecting these differences. Without mutual respect for self-determination these differences become the basis for conflict rather than dialogue and cooperation. The exercise of self-determination is not simply a good idea from a sociological perspective. The importance of this concept to definitions of what it means to be a person and a society has been recognized for centuries in ethics and in law. However, it cannot be the only element of a framework for social well-being because people and groups cannot be self-determining all on their own. People with disabilities and many other groups experience frustration because they continually encounter institutional barriers to exercising self-determination. The traditional categorical and targeted programs established for people with disabilities under the welfare state in Canada have for the most part removed their rights to self-determination and vested decision-making authority in social assistance officers, service providers, public and private guardians.

Democratization is a second element of the framework which began to emerge for social well-being. The struggles through which diverse people and groups in Canada have sought to obtain recognition for themselves and for their aims have been defined as "the politics of recognition" (Taylor 1992). Democratization makes a constructive politics of recognition possible. It goes beyond the conventional meaning of the term "democracy" and refers to the process of enabling the democratic participation of individuals and diverse groups in a wide scope of decision-making processes that directly affect their lives and their well-being. Seeking and granting recognition to diverse groups and regions in public policy decisions are very much a part of our history and continue to be at the heart of the dilemmas of public policy and politics in Canada (Drover and Kerans 1993). The underlying principle of this conceptualization of a democratized government, society and economy is participation in decision-making. The economy would not rest on "global forces" or "market pressures." It would rest on the idea that economies should serve people and communities. It would assume that social and economic equality is the norm by which economic arrangements are to be judged in order to challenge the inequalities fostered by current arrangements (Heilbroner 1992).

In a society where democratization is an integrating force, the prospects for social well-being improve. There are existing obligations and commitments in Canadian society that provide the foundation for democratization. The right to vote, collective bargaining arrangements and individual and collective rights entrenched in the Charter are all important aspects of this foundation. Canada's first Constitution in 1867 provided a foundation for democratization and mutual recognition by granting status in institutions and decision-making processes to both French and English communities. The process of democratizing institutions to give greater representation to the communities that make up Canada has continued. Québécois and Aboriginal nationalist movements have sought recognition for their cultural and linguistic differences and have sought forms of collective representation in order to improve their status. Their claims have challenged conventional interpretations of equality rights, the federal state and the collective rights the state should recognize (Jenson 1993).

Equality is another element of social well-being when it is defined as the absence of barriers to mutual respect and recognition between people "who are equally free from political control, social pressure and economic deprivation and insecurity to engage in valued pursuits, and who have equal access to the means of self-development" (Lukes 1980: 218). However, to a large extent, our institutions are not designed to enable the practice of this kind of equality. This is because the "formal" interpretation of equality predominant in public policy and court rulings requires treating similar cases in similar ways. Yet, this formal interpretation no longer responds to the demands for equality made by diverse groups in Canadian society. It is difficult, if not impossible, to claim that people with disabilities are "situated" in society in the same way as people without disabilities. Challenges to this formal understanding of equality have been advanced in recent years (Smith 1986).

Subsequent to the introduction of the equality provisions of the Canadian Charter of Right and Freedoms, courts in Canada have begun to rewrite the standards of equality. In particular, significant judgments have been handed down by the Supreme Court of Canada, such as that of *Andrews v. Law Society of British Columbia* (1989). In that judgment, the Supreme Court determined that the principle of equality does not necessarily imply similar treatment; it may require treating people differently. In this view, the differences arising from nationality, gender, race and ethnicity, religious belief, disability, etc., are not a reason to deny people the supports they need to exercise their self-determination. If people are to exercise self-determination, institutions in society should be structured to recognize, respect and support the presence of diverse languages, identities and cultures (Kymlicka 1989; Young 1990).

This evolving framework for social well-being has provided the basis for overturning four hundred years of law and policy which resulted in the social, economic and political exclusion of people with disabilities. The impact of the legal entrenchment of this framework has been both direct and indirect. Successful legal challenges have been important; so too have been the indirect ways in which the legal entrenchment of rights has influenced policy and attitudes. There has been a shift from the traditional way of viewing people with disabilities to the introduction of a more systemic analysis of the discrimination faced by people with disabilities. The notion that disability is a result of individual pathology has given way to at the least a nominal recognition of the roots of inequality in the state organization of environmental and social relationships.

There are many examples of this shift. For instance, in June 1989, the federal Commons Committee on Human Rights and Disability was mandated with the investigation of human rights and disability in contrast to earlier committees that linked disability to health rather than human rights. Legal and policy questions have been raised about the fairness of keeping people in segregated workshops. Governments have developed polices that plan for the closure of large institutions. Governments are beginning to establish legislative and policy provisions for "assisted" and "supported" decision-making as an alternative to the removal of rights through guardianship.[3] Hospitals are being challenged, legally and ethically, on their policies of refusing treatment to newborns and other persons with severe disabilities (Endicott 1988, 1990). Protocols have been introduced by some provincial Attorneys General to ensure that people with intellectual and other disabilities can give evidence in court and therefore receive the same access to justice as others.[4] Income assistance programs have been established that provide direct funding to people with disabilities to contract for their own choice of services. This is an alternative to traditional funding through service agencies (The Roeher Institute 1993).

There have been successful legal challenges to the denial of rights in the past fifteen years. In 1986, the Supreme Court of Canada ruled in the Eve[5] case that people who have an intellectual disability cannot be required to undergo a non-therapeutic sterilization authorized by any third party including parents, next of kin, the Public Trustee or the administrator of a facility. The basis of its decision is that such an intrusion into the rights of a person could never be in his/her best interests.

In 1983, the Supreme Court of British Columbia ruled that Stephen Dawson,[6] a six-year-old boy, had the right to life-sustaining medical treatment to which his parents had refused their consent. In 1982, an Ontario District Court judge denied a guardianship application by Justin Clark's[7] parents to have him declared mentally incompetent to prevent Justin from exercising his choice to leave the institution, where he had been for all his life (eighteen years), to live with friends in Ottawa.

In 1987 a basic democratic right of citizenship was restored to those with an intellectual disability when the Federal Court of Canada struck down a clause in Section 14(4) of the Canada Elections Act. This clause disqualified those "restrained of . . . liberty of movement or deprived of the management of . . . property by reason of mental disease" from the right to vote. The recent decision in the Eaton[8] case found that denying a choice for a child with an intellectual disability to go to the neighbourhood school was not an issue of pedagogical theory, or even the right to education, but was in substance a denial of the equality right found in the Charter of Rights and Freedoms.

In January 1991, the Québec Human Rights Commission found the administration of Pavillon Saint-Theophile of Laval, an institution for people with an intellectual disability, guilty of exploiting the institution's residents. The eighty-eight people who lived in the centre were awarded $1 million to be split between them: $700,000 in compensation for moral damages for enduring humiliation and attacks on their dignity; and $300,000 in compensation for the intentional exploitation to which they had been submitted. The administration of the centre was found to have misused government funds and to have treated residents in a manner described as "punishment, deprivation and infantilization."[9] The case established that justice for people with disabilities includes treating them with respect and protecting their fundamental rights. All these changes reflect a shift towards ensuring the social well-being of people with disabilities; their self-determination; participation in decisions that affect their person and their life; and equality with others regardless of their differences.

## IMPLEMENTING THE CANADA HEALTH AND SOCIAL TRANSFER AND RETURNING TO THE "WORTHY/UNWORTHY POOR"

The new Canada Health and Social Transfer (CHST) establishes a new block funding arrangement with the provinces. Under the CHST, the federal government will roll together its cash contributions for income assistance and social services, health care and post-secondary education into a single block fund for each province. The CHST will also represent a reduction in the amount of federal cash transferred. The trade-off for the provinces is that the federal government will remove any conditions on how its cash contribution for income assistance and social services is spent, save the one condition that the provinces cannot impose residency requirements for those seeking such assistance. Gone are the conditions under the CAP, now repealed with the passage of Bill C-76 (the Budget Implementation Act 1995), that required provincial governments to provide income and social supports for those deemed to be in need. The CAP guidelines did not insure adequacy of income and support but they did establish a national minimum for social security.

What do implementation of the CHST and ending conditionality mean for people with disabilities? While new foundations for the welfare state and policy directions have been accomplished with respect to disability, they have not been fully realized. Given the economic and ideological context of the mid-1990s, it is our view that implementing the CHST will create serious hardships for people with disabilities. Without attached conditions, reduced funding will put pressure on the provincial governments to re-introduce the worthy/unworthy distinction, either implicitly or explicitly, bringing to a halt and reversing the momentum that has been generated in deinstitutionalization, income reform, service system reform and in recognizing disability as a rights issue.

We suggest three main reasons why the CHST will lead to these outcomes. First, with fewer dollars for social spending and with even fewer conditions on how it will be spent, there is less likelihood of governments investing in transition from the legacy of an institutional and segregated system established to serve the "worthy poor." In the long run it may be less costly, from a fiscal perspective alone, to include people with disabilities in the labour market, education, the housing market, generic health and social support services. The federal government has played a key role in levering social and economic inclusion of people with disabilities by providing transition dollars for this purpose. However, with fewer dollars and fewer conditions to meet the requirements of a framework of self-determination, democratization and equality, provincial governments will have to establish some justification for spending the few dollars they do have.

Second, in an ideological environment of "tax revolt," the demand for an end to provincial budgetary deficits and the political backlash against people on social assistance, governments will be pressured to establish highly targeted and categorical programs that are politically saleable. There is no better target for such a purpose than the "worthy poor," no better group to fill the bill than people with disabilities. There is already evidence of this trend in Ontario with the decision by the recently elected Conservative government to roll back welfare rates by 22 percent except for people with disabilities and the elderly. Once again a legal and social mechanism will be needed to distinguish the worthiness of those whose poverty imposes some greater obligation on the state. To do so, restrictive eligibility requirements will be needed to ensure that people with disabilities are seen to be different and are treated differently as the condition for obtaining welfare provision. It will be a matter of showing that the state maintains some obligation to those in need, while the burden on the state is minimized. People with disabilities will once again have to be constructed as objects of charity, pity and incapacity.

In the past, being construed as a member of the "worthy poor" has been a means by which people with disabilities were defined as a social burden. In the post-war period, the advance of a human rights framework and the attempts from Marsh (1975) on to develop comprehensive social policy were the context in which categorical and targeted programs were established for people with disabilities. Since the 1970s, within a statutory framework of human rights and a discourse of comprehensive social policy, targeted income and service programs could be challenged on the basis that they undermined people's rights.

Third, the CHST signals the end of a role for the federal government in managing and encouraging a national discussion on comprehensive social policy in which public policy and welfare state provision would be critically examined from the perspective of universal rights. The CHST represents the withdrawal of the federal government from the social policy field and its retreat to the role of a clearing house for tax dollars. This retreat has been pursued in the name of decentralization and respect for constitutional division of power, as though these were goods in and of themselves. However, decentralization is not to be equated with democratization. True democratization means giving people with disabilities and others a real voice in the shaping of social policy. This was the hope for the 1994 social security review (SSR) launched by the federal Minister for Human Resources Development Canada. Instead, with the CHST and Bill C-76, the federal government has simply closed this option and walked away from the debate on social policy.

Is there any hope that provincial governments will take on the job of establishing a comprehensive social policy framework and creating a new national discourse on social policy in Canada? It is only within such a discourse that questions of disability, public policy and human rights can be considered, and through which claims for self-determination, democratization and equality can be articulated. Recent trends in the structures for allocating dollars and services in the areas of health, income support and social development suggest that provincial governments are moving in quite a different direction. We are currently witnessing a massive reorientation by provincial governments in social policy and health and social services. This shift is reflected in the regionalization of health services through community and regional health boards; similar regionalization in the areas of social services; and the wish by some governments to allocate funds to community boards to make decisions about "who gets what." In such a context, debate on social policy moves from legislatures and bureaucracies to the far more dispersed locales of community board meetings vested with the responsibility of deciding how to allocate in the community their block grants from provincial governments.

Legislatures and bureaucracies have not been paragons of accountability to people with disabilities, but at least there have been policy debates. The media has been an important tool in ensuring these take place, and justifications for spending decisions have had to be proffered. Holding accountable hundreds of health and social service boards to the concerns and rights of people with disabilities in Canada hardly seems a viable model for securing democratization. In this new age of privatization, defining who counts as "worthy poor" and what they will get will be left to community boards. Communities have not secured inclusion and equality for people with disabilities in the past. Can we expect them to do so now, when they are left more on their own in the midst of fiscal straightjackets, structural unemployment and a growing number of groups making demands?

This dispersal of the social policy debate in Canada, first to the provincial levels of government and then to numerous boards, commissions and agencies mandated with the responsibility for allocating shrinking resources, is evidenced also in international trends. Laurell and Wences (1994: 382), writing in the Mexican context, set in perspective this shift from social policy debate to community resource allocation:

> The promotion of selective poverty programs, as opposed to integral, comprehensive and universal social policies, results from their being compatible with the permanence of basic neoliberal economic policies and state withdrawal from its responsibilities as the main financier and organizer of social services. . . . Given the scarcity of public resources, the argument continues, the way to achieve this objective is through carefully targeted poverty programs that complement the satisfying of social needs through market and family mechanisms. . . . [T]he end result is the same as that stated by the neoliberal doctrine: social welfare belongs primarily to the private domain—to markets, family and community—and only when it cannot be resolved in this way should the state intervene and guarantee a social minimum using public resources.

Arguably, the CHST and the end of CAP mark that we are in the full throes of the neoliberal era of social policy in Canada. However, the neoliberal era is something other than a return to the residual welfare state, and it is certainly more than rolling back welfare state benefits by "stealth" (Gray 1990). With the neoliberal era comes the replacement of a discourse on comprehensive social policy with a discourse of "civil society," a belief in "community," and building the "capacity of communities" to take care of their own. We are not simply to go back to the self-reliant individual, the family and the market. The vagaries of the market and its consequences for children and families are too obvious for even the more hardened neoliberals to ignore. Rather, this time refuge will be sought in the "community." "Communities" will protect children and families and buffer them from the demands of globalized trade and markets.

Communities do have an integral role in ensuring social well-being. But they can only play this role when they are supported within a social and economic policy framework that does not undermine their economic base on the one hand, as neoliberal economic strategies have done in the case of many communities, and on the other hand turn over to communities huge responsibilities for social development and support. Seen in a broader international context, the CHST, combined with the restructuring of provincial health and social service funding and delivery, is the kind of social policy rationalization consistent with a neoliberal economic agenda.

The framework for social well-being, and the belief in the need for comprehensive and universal social policies, evolved in Canada in a *federal-provincial* environment in which each level of government has checked the other, one being able to take the high ground when the other has submitted to expediency. Conditionality has been an expression of this dynamic. The particular conditions in shared cost agreements like the CAP undoubtedly need reform to make them more consistent with a framework of social well-being. However, to give up on conditionality altogether in favour of an abstract view of the division of powers is to deny the history of the relationship that spawned the welfare state in Canada in the post-war period which led to establishing a framework for social well-being. To give up on conditionality is to give up on the belief that governance has to do with social policy debate and formulation, and with considering the requirements for justice and equality in our society. The obligations for enabling social well-being cannot be the responsibility of one or the other level of government. The framework was conceived in a federal-provincial context; the specific obligations for self-determination, democratization and equality rest at both levels and between them; it is only in such an interrelated context that a social policy framework to secure social well-being can be established.

If we view the establishment of the CHST and the jettisoning of conditionality in Canada as a reassertion of residualism then, while we can criticize it on that basis, we can only conclude that it is simply a continuation (albeit exacerbation) of past practices. However, if the struggles over the welfare state in Canada have resulted in a new framework for social well-being as we have argued, then the critique of the CHST becomes more fundamental. In the current political and ideological context the CHST becomes a tool for entrenching the worthy/unworthy distinction putting pressure for continued segregation and thus limiting the social obligation to people with disabilities.

## Notes

1. This principle was explicitly stated in the 1834 revisions of the Elizabethan Poor Laws. The principle of less eligibility required that public support for an individual guarantee a lower standard of living than that of the poorest paid labourer. BPP 127
2. Section 15 of the Charter of Rights and Freedoms ("Equality Rights") provides that all persons are equal before and under the law without discrimination on grounds including physical and mental disability.
3. The governments of Manitoba and the Northwest Territories have recently passed legislation enabling persons to use assistance in decision-making as an alternative to meeting the strict and exclusionary standards of competence. How far such provisions go in enabling people with intellectual disabilities to maintain their rights to self-determination remains to be seen.
4. See, for example, Department of the Attorney General and Department of the Solicitor General, *Protocol for Investigation and Prosecution of Cases Involving Persons with Special Communication Needs*, Nova Scotia, April 12, 1991.
5. *Re Eve*, [1986] 2 S.C.R. 388
6. *Re Stephen Dawson*, [1983] 3 W.W.R. 618 (BC Supreme Court)
7. *Clark v. Clark* (1982), 40 O.R. (2d) 383 (Co. Ct)
8. *Re Eaton and Brant County Board of Education* (1995), 22 O.R. (3d) (Court of Appeal)
9. *Commission des droits des personnes du Québec c. Centre d'accueil Pavillon St-Théophile* (1991), 16 C.H.R.R. D/124

# REFERENCES

Andrews v. Law Society of British Columbia. 1989. 1 S.C.R. 143; 56 D.L.R. (4th) 1.

Canada. 1982. *Charter of Rights and Freedoms*. Part I of the Constitution Act, 1982, Being Schedule B to the Canada Act 1982 (U.K.), Ch. 11.

Department of the Attorney General and Department of the Solicitor General. April 12, 1991. *Protocol for Investigation and Prosecution of Cases Involving Persons with Special Communication Needs*. Nova Scotia.

Drover, G. and P. Kerans (eds). 1993. *New Approaches to Welfare Theory*. Aldershot, U.K.: Edward Elgar Publishing.

Endicott, O. January 1990. *The Right of Persons with Intellectual Handicaps to Receive Medical Treatment*. Toronto: Canadian Association for Community Living.

————. 1988. "It is Still a Capital Offence to Have Down Syndrome." *Entourage* 3 (3): 17-22.

Gray, G. 1990. "Social Policy by Stealth." *Policy Options* 11 (2): 17-29 (March).

Guest, D. 1980. *The Emergence of Social Security in Canada*. Vancouver: University of British Columbia Press.

Heilbroner, R. 1992. *Twenty-First Century Capitalism*. Concord, ON: Anansi Press.

Jenson, J. 1993. "Deconstructing Dualities: Making Rights Claims in Political Institutions." In G. Drover and P. Kerans (eds.), *New Approaches to Welfare Theory*. Aldershot, U.K.: Edward Elgar Publishing.

Kymlicka, W. 1989. *Liberalism, Community, and Culture*. Oxford: Clarendon Press.

Laurell, A.C. and M.I. Wences. 1994. "Do Poverty Programs Alleviate Poverty? The Case of the Mexican National Solidarity Program." *International Journal of Health Services* 24 (3): 381-401.

Lukes, S. 1980. "Socialism and Equality." In J. Sterba (ed.) *Justice: Alternative Political Perspectives*. Belmont, Calif: Wadsworth Publishing.

Marsh, L. 1975. *Social Security in Canada*. Reprint. Toronto: University of Toronto Press.

Marshall, T.H. 1963. "Citizenship and Social Class." *Sociology at the Crossroads and Other Essays*. London: Heinemann.

National Council of Welfare. 1987. *Welfare in Canada, The Tangled Safety Net: A Report by the National Council of Welfare*. Ottawa: National Council of Welfare.

Rioux, M. 1994. "Towards a Concept of Equality of Well-Being: Overcoming the Social and Legal Construction of Inequality." *Canadian Journal of Law and Jurisprudence* 7 (1): 127-47.

————. 1993. "Exchanging Charity for Rights: The Challenge for the Next Decade." *British Institute of Learning Disabilities* 89 (June): 1-8.

The Roeher Institute. 1988. *Income Insecurity: The Disability Income System in Canada*. North York: The Roeher Institute.

————. 1990. *Poor Places: Disability-related Residential and Support Services*. North York: The Roeher Institute.

————. 1993. *Social Well-Being: A Paradigm for Reform*. North York: The Roeher Institute.

Smith, L. 1986. "A New Paradigm for Equality Rights." In L. Smith, G. Côté-Harper, R. Elliot and M. Seydegart (eds), *Righting the Balance: Canada's New Equality Rights*. Saskatoon: Canadian Human Rights Reporter.

Taylor, C. 1992. *Multiculturalism and "The Politics of Recognition": An Essay*. Princeton: Princeton University Press.

Young, I.M. 1990. *Justice and the Politics of Difference*. Princeton: Princeton University Press.

## PART 7

# CONCLUSIONS

# CHAPTER 21

# SOCIAL POLICY CHOICES
# AND THE AGENDA FOR CHANGE

*Jane Pulkingham and Gordon Ternowetsky*

## INTRODUCTION

Social policy is about making choices that involve the allocation of resources and decisions concerning "who gets what." Social policy is also about winners and losers as some benefit and others lose as a result of particular policy decisions. This is illustrated in the new CHST where Ottawa may be considered a winner. It has reduced the size of its overall financial obligation for social programs and has freed itself of the unpredictability of these expenses by eliminating the cost shared arrangements of the CAP.

It also seems clear that the provinces and territories have lost. They may have gained more power to shape social programs, but their financial resources will decline while the demand for government intervention will likely continue to rise. The real losers are, however, the people who live across this country. With less resources the provinces and territories will be re-allocating and making new decisions concerning what services will and will not be paid for through the public purse. This rationing process has already begun.

As this is being written Canada's premiers are meeting in St. John's, Newfoundland. They have set up a council of ministers to deal with the implications of the CHST for national standards and to clarify what health services are "essential" and which are "non essential," with only the former being publicly funded (O'Neil 1995: A1). There is the unraveling of universality, and the shifting of more of the burden of health care costs to individuals, and for those who can afford it, private health insurance. A health care system which is formally two-tiered appears to be in the making. In terms of this process and outcome, three points are of note. First, health care was not even on the social security reform agenda, yet the reduced CHST is forcing provinces to develop a new and more limited configuration of fundable health services. Second, the social security review invited Canadians to consult and give direction to the government concerning the future of social programs. What evidence is there to suggest that Canadians favour the type of health care restructuring that we are beginning to see unfold? This question leads to a third concern about the social security review. Did the views of participants really matter? Or was the agenda for reform predetermined and always under the control of the Department of Finance?

It would seem that public participation has made little difference in the social security review. Such a conclusion seems appropriate because what we are witnessing is a devolution of social program responsibility. This devolution is being driven by deficits, debts and fiscal issues but is resulting in a welfare state where public provisions are being replaced by a system in which responsibilities are shifting back to "communities," families and individuals. This is happening at a time when unemployment, underemployment, poverty and social assistance caseloads are high and/or growing and where the structure of opportunity seems to be collapsing. It seems unlikely that this is the type of welfare state people envisioned in the comments made to the Standing Committee on Human Resources (House of Commons 1995: 21).

> ... Canada's social security system is a valued national institution, a distinguishing feature of the country. Existing social programs, however inadequate and incomplete they may be, represent for many Canadians a heritage of achievements fought for and built by previous generations. . . . [O]ur system of social programs is more than a 'safety net'; it is based on compassion, on providing basic support for people who are in need and who cannot work. It is a system that rests on considerations of protection, investment, and citizenship.

So where do we go from here? What is to be done? Do we accept what seems to be emerging as inevitable, or do we continue to struggle in an effort to shape social programs that are more responsive to the context, needs and wishes of people? The arguments put forward in this book and raised during the Seventh Conference on Social Welfare Policy, point to a number of key themes that need to inform policy decisions. Some of these have been dealt with in past discussions of Canadian social policy. Others appear to be emerging as new solutions and avenues to be considered. This chapter looks at the following issues: the revenue side of the deficit; the financial transaction tax; full employment and U.I.; non-standard employment and U.I. reform; labour market changes and retirement income; and a rethinking of some of the problem areas of Keynesian policies. In examining these, it is suggested that these areas need to be placed firmly on the public agenda for current and future social policy rounds. Otherwise the debate on "Where do we go from here?" and "What social policy choices can be made?" will remain restricted and one-sided, with the result that the users and consumers of social services will continue to lose ground in the social policy changes that occur.

## REVENUE, DEFICITS AND DEBTS

Deficits, Canada's rising debt and interest payments, are driving forces behind the current social security review. This is not a new phenomenon. Former Canadian governments of different political persuasion have also chosen to deal with the deficit by squeezing social program expenditures. This emphasis on the spending side of the deficit offers, however, only a partial and very limited view of how the Canadian debt was created. In the discussion that follows the revenue side of debt creation is considered.

The first point to note is the conclusion in Statistics Canada's recent study *On the Growth of the Federal Debt* and the factors contributing to the current "level of indebtedness" (Mimoto and Cross 1991). The major finding of this research is that the debt is a problem of declining revenue and not social program spending. This shortfall in federal revenue is an outcome of tax changes and the transfer of tax points to the provinces (Mimoto and Cross 1991: 1). The tax changes referred to are "tax expenditures" where, rather than collecting taxes that are owed, governments create tax deferrals, credits, deductions and thereby forego collecting these revenues. Tax expenditures are designed for individuals, businesses and corporations. While the policy purposes of different tax expenditures vary, they have "financial implications similar to those of direct spending"—they lower government revenue (Department of Finance 1993: 3).

It is also important to note that a dollar of tax expenditures is "often worth substantially more . . . than a dollar of direct spending" (Department of Finance 1993: 13). Direct spending on U.I., for example, is usually taxable while tax preferences are not. As a result and as noted by the Department of Finance (1985: 6; 1993: 13), the "value of a dollar of tax reduction" is around "one and one-half to two times the value of a dollar of direct spending." This is a very important acknowledgment by Finance that tax expenditures are expensive and constitute a more important drain on revenue than direct spending. In addition, as tax expenditures benefit higher income earners and corporations, it is easy to see "who wins" when they are excluded or not completely accounted for in the debate on government spending and deficits.

A third point is that the Standing Committee on Human Resources (House of Commons 1995: 6), after its hearings and consultations, argued that "social tax expenditures" be included in the SSR. This is an important inclusion. However the terms "social tax expenditures" and "tax expenditures" seem to be used interchangeably by the Standing Committee and require clarification. Some tax incentives in the personal tax system are designed with social policy outcomes in mind. These include RRSP and RRP deductions, the Disability Credit, the Equivalent to Married Credit, tuition fees and education credits. There are also a range of tax breaks in the personal tax system that have no explicit social policy outcome. Some examples include the numerous provisions for capital gains exemptions and deferrals, investment tax credits, allowable business investment losses and capital loss carry overs. All "tax expenditures," however not simply those with designed social policy outcomes, need to be included in the equation on lost revenue.

Fourth, from an international, comparative perspective, the only area that Canada's tax rate as a percentage of GDP exceeds the OECD average is in the level of personal taxes (CCSD 1995). Corporate, payroll and goods and services taxes fall below the OECD average. The first two are also less than their respective tax levels in the United States, the country with which there is the greatest pressure to harmonize. There appears to be room to harmonize upward, and in the process gain more revenue.

Fifth, since the 1960s the share of revenue coming from corporate taxes has steadily declined while that from personal income tax has increased. Between 1967 and 1991 the percentage of total revenue from personal tax rose from 33.7 percent to 51.7 percent. The share of corporate taxes, in contrast, fell from 19.2 percent to 10.2 percent in this same period (Mimoto and Cross 1991). There are two major reasons for this. One is that many profitable, larger corporations pay little or no tax. For example in 1990, 63,577 firms with total profits of more than $13 billion dollars paid no corporate income tax (Ternowetsky 1994:108). A minimum tax of 20 percent would have raised an additional $2.6 billion. Another reason is that corporations can defer taxes, often indefinitely, and without incurring interest charges. In 1993, Canadian corporate firms owed $36 billion in deferred taxes. As noted by the Ontario Federation of Labour (1994: 2) "if the Government of Canada simply charged these corporations a reasonable interest on their deferred taxes [say prime plus 2 percent], it would result in almost $3 billion in additional revenue each year."

A sixth and related point is whether tax breaks geared to help business profits and investment are warranted. What is the total cost of these tax incentives? How do they benefit the people in this country? It is difficult to answer either of these questions. Unlike the cost of social programs that are published annually and available for public scrutiny, there is no regular and complete method for estimating the revenue cost (or loss) of selective tax measures. The main public source is the periodic government publication *The Cost of Personal and Corporate Income Tax Expenditures*. These estimates are, however, always dated, incomplete and are punctuated with "n.a." not available and "S," indicating the cost is less that $2.5 million (Department of Finance 1993: 13, 27-37 (see Table 2)). That these types of expenditure estimates of corporate tax breaks are debatable is underscored by the Finance Department's decision not to total these costs in its last account of the cost of corporate tax expenditures (Department of Finance 1993: 22-36). Given the magnitude of revenue foregone each year, this is a dubious and questionable accounting method. It needs to be tightened and figures released annually so the cost of corporate tax expenditures can be accurately assessed when spending choices are made.

Other data suggest there are few public benefits from these corporate tax breaks. Clearly the loss of revenue has exacerbated the fiscal crisis that has led to the squeeze on social program spending. There is also evidence that profitable firms, in receipt of public assistance through tax breaks and direct grants, are downsizing their work force (Ternowetsky 1994; Ternowetsky and Thorn 1991). This elimination of jobs by profitable firms in receipt of government assistance, reduces government revenue, increases demand for assistance and further complicates Canada's fiscal crisis. Fewer jobs means a smaller number of workers, a smaller number of pay cheques, less personal tax, less spending and a drop in consumption taxes. At the same time fewer jobs puts pressure on U.I. and welfare. In periods of economic restructuring and fiscal restraint there needs to be more accountability. Is it unreasonable to ensure that when public instruments and public funds are used to boost private sector profits, that some direct job creation is a result? In view of the persistent and high levels of unemployment in Canada and the cost of unemployment both in financial and personal terms, this would seem to be an appropriate measure of accountability.

## THE FINANCIAL TRANSACTION TAX

The Financial Transaction Tax (FTT) links the area of government revenue to that of national sovereignty. First proposed by James Tobin in 1978, it was designed as a means to both slow down currency speculation and raise revenue. Today currency traders, speculating on values of national currencies, move more than $1 trillion a day around the world in their search for speculative, short-term profits (McMurdy 1995: 20). In 1994 and 1995 these activities forced currency devaluations and interest rate increases in numerous countries including Spain, Portugal, Mexico, Britain, France, Italy, U.S. and Canada. Currency speculations are, however, untaxed. It is estimated that a small FTT on world money market speculation would raise $1.5 trillion (U.S.) a year (Corcoran 1995: B2). It would also act as a disincentive to short-term money speculation and give governments greater control over their domestic monetary and fiscal circumstances.

The following points concerning the FTT have been made in relation to Canada. In 1993 Canada's GDP was $700 billion, compared to short-term money market trading of $1.9 trillion. An FTT on these latter transactions would slow down speculation, "stabilize the daily fluctuations in interests rates and exchange rates, and encourage long term more stable investing" (Grant and Biddell 1994: 2; Grant 1994). Such a tax would give Canada greater control over its monetary policy and offer some protection to "the feeding frenzy when global markets turn against a country" (McMurdy 1995: 29). It would help us protect against increased interest rates which further contribute to budgetary deficits, slow down the economy, push up demand and force governments to cut back on social spending. The FTT also has considerable revenue potential. According to Grant and Biddell (1994: 1) the value of financial transactions from Canadian stock exchanges, bond markets and money markets reached $3.6 trillion in 1993. The imposition of a FTT of one tenth of one percent on these activities would yield approximately $3.5 billion. The FTT seems to have the potential for increasing revenue and national sovereignty. It warrants further attention in discussions concerning Canadian social policy.

## FULL EMPLOYMENT AND UNEMPLOYMENT INSURANCE

Unlike the reforms of the early post-Second World War years, or those pursued in the early 1970s, reform 1990s-style rests on an explicit rejection of the notion that increased market insecurity should be met with greater social security (Pulkingham 1995). Despite the widespread recognition of the increasing precariousness of stable, full-time employment, the current strategy is intended to severely curtail entitlement and coverage in a range of social programs.

In its backward gaze, the government has set its sight on the earlier part of this century, squarely rejecting policy mechanisms of the Keynesian welfare state (KWS). These policies include full male employment, economic growth produced by stimulating effective demand and the two-track system of contributory and non-contributory benefits. While full male employment was presumed to provide a living wage for those who worked, the two-track system of benefits was intended to provide income supports for those who could not do so.

Part of the rejection of the KWS is reflected in the successive redefinition, over the past two decades, of "full employment." In the early post-Second World War period, full male employment typically implied a level of official unemployment around 1 percent to 2 percent. Arguably, Canada has never officially pursued a full employment policy, and certainly never achieved levels of unemployment approaching 1 percent to 2 percent. However, since these early post-war years, unemployment has been rising in Canada. Indeed, the "natural" rate of unemployment (Non-Accelerating Inflation Rate of Unemployment or NAIRU) has been revised upward on a regular basis so that it now rests at (at least) 8 percent. (Currently this amounts to more than 1.2 million unemployed.) Policies resting on this assumption need to be challenged and placed on the public agenda so people are aware of the underlying premise informing government policies and definitions of full employment.

With levels of unemployment considerably above this (already inflated) "core" rate, it is not surprising that one of the central preoccupation's of the SSR is reform of U.I. In fact, the decade of the 1980s represented a lengthy period of inquiry and debate culminating in 1989-90 in a number of changes to U.I. (through Bill C-21) that reinforced the trend toward reduced generosity begun in the mid-1970s (Green and Riddell 1993: S108). Arguably, the changes introduced at this time heralded a new phase of U.I. reform. Unlike previous reforms, this phase is aggressively pursuing the goal of producing "savings" and "active" rather than "passive" income support measures. Proposals to reform U.I. articulated through the SSR represent an intensification of efforts already begun in this phase. There is an unwarranted assumption that at the end of the day jobs will be available for the retrained, reskilled and retooled unemployed. As Kerans (1994: 119) notes, a major problem with this emphasis on active measures "focused as they are on employability rather than on employment," is that they can quickly become "yet another exercise in victim blaming." To help avoid this "punitive" result, job creation must be a major focus of reform and "jobs for all" the principle goal of economic and social policy.

## Non-standard Employment and U.I. Reform

High levels of unemployment are but one symptom of the employment restructuring that is a central component of the attack on the welfare state today. Others include the proliferation of non-standard or contingent work arrangements (i.e., part-time, part-year, multiple job holding and self-employment), underemployment and labour force exit (e.g., voluntary early retirement or forced joblessness among older workers and "discouraged workers"). As suggested above, there appears to be a contradictory trajectory between these employment trends and government's response. The SSR, in its handling of the issue of employment, unemployment and U.I. reform, demonstrates this clearly.

For example, the document *From Unemployment Insurance to Employment Insurance* (HRDC 1994) devotes a full chapter to the issue of the coverage of non-standard work. On the one hand, it discusses the inequities inherent in the current system regarding the differential treatment of various categories of non-standard workers, and raises the possibility of changing this to provide greater coverage for some (e.g., part-timers versus part-year workers, multiple job holders, etc.). On the other hand, ultimately its response to the high representation of non-standard workers, especially part-timers (the majority of whom are women and youth) excluded from U.I., is not encouraging. The document summarily dismisses the problem of the exclusion of a significant portion of part-time workers, reinforcing the stereotypical view of women part-time workers as "marginal" and inconsequential.

But the proposed U.I. reforms have serious implications for men too. A significant portion of the document (Chapters 2-4) is devoted to defining and describing the problem of "frequent" users, and suggesting reform options that would reduce and/or eliminate their recourse to U.I. The majority of frequent claimants are seasonal workers and men: two-thirds of frequent ("3 in 5 years" definition) claimants are seasonal workers, of these almost two-thirds (64 percent) are male (HRDC 1994: 25, 39); 60 percent of frequent claimants are male (HRDC 1994: compiled from data in Table 4.1, p. 33); and male frequent claimants represent 44 percent of *all* U.I. claimants (this compares to a figure of 31 percent for females). Given the government's clear preference to target frequent claimants as the main mechanism for reforming U.I., almost one-half of male, compared to one-third of female, U.I. claimants stand to lose through benefit changes.

The fact still remains, however, that the majority of workers presently excluded from U.I. coverage are women and the current phase of U.I. reform quashes the possibility of extending protection to these workers. Moreover, gains that have been made will be eroded quickly as many women presently covered by U.I. lose some or all of their benefits and entitlements. The impact of the proposed U.I. benefit and entitlement changes for men and women needs to be made clear. People need to recognize that under the rhetoric of reform and retraining they will lose benefit entitlements and rights that they held in the past. In response to the question "Who wins from these proposed reforms?" it is clear that Canadian workers will lose. The reforms to U.I., as measured by their outcome, fit nicely into a corporate agenda. They increase the insecurity of workers on the one hand, and on the other, lower the costs and security of labour.

## Labour Market Changes and Retirement Income

Another area of concern, and one that is beginning to dominate the social policy agenda, is reform of public pensions. In 1993, after a lengthy period of improvement associated with changes in public pensions, poverty rates among Canadians over the age of sixty-five began rising. The incidence of poverty among unattached seniors rose from 48.4 percent in 1992 to 51.1 percent in 1993 (Statistics Canada 1994). Statistics Canada (1994) has suggested that one of the reasons may be lower investment incomes due to lower interest rates prevailing at the time. This trend exposes the vulnerability of seniors as a group to market forces in retirement and highlights the importance of ensuring adequate income security in an aging society. Proportionately more elderly people are poor, and large inequalities in income exist within the elderly population. Income inequalities in later life are largely a function of income inequalities and financial preparedness at younger ages. Inequalities in income in later life tend to widen due to the long-term impact of income-and-education and gender related differences in the ability to generate investment income (Gee and McDaniel 1991).

Prospective pension changes are also likely to widen income differentials in later life. The most recent announcement (1995 federal budget) regarding the future administration of the Old Age Security (OAS) claw back (determining OAS eligibility based on household income, and deducting the claw back from monthly payments based on the previous year's tax return) will likely increase income disparities. The ramifications for seniors living with spouses (59.6 percent of men and 38.5 percent of women aged sixty-five years plus) and those in multi-generational living arrangements (14.8 percent of men and 13.5 percent of women aged sixty-five years plus) (1991 Census, special tabulation) are of particular concern. It remains to be seen what other changes to the OAS, GIS and C/QPP will ensue. However, given what appears to be contradictory labour market and income security policy trajectories, careful examination of the impact of labour market restructuring and increasing financial insecurity on people's ability to prepare for the future is needed. These trends and their implications for financial security in later life need to be made available for public debate and inspection so that the people most affected can lobby for changes based on informed choices. Given the aging of Canada's population and the growing numbers exiting the labour market at an early age, this scrutiny is warranted as more people prepare for or are forced into retirement.

## RETHINKING KEYNESIAN POLICIES?

Despite the obvious limitations to the government's reform agenda embodied in the SSR and the last two budgets (1994 and 1995), the government is not alone in reaching back. Many in the social policy community would have us return to the Keynesian policies upon which the post-Second World War welfare state was based. However, there are a number of problems with the uncritical application of Keynesian policies. The boundaries of the Keynesian welfare state were constructed on the basis of exclusion and inclusion (Squires 1990). In our scramble to preserve existing levels of protection and programs, we often lose sight of this fact. For example, the principle of full employment itself is not without problems. To begin with, the post-war welfare state was constructed around a *particular notion* of full employment—*white male full-time paid* employment (Keane and Owens 1986; Armstrong and Armstrong 1988). Furthermore, the counterpart of full employment is the wage labour imperative (Keane and Owens 1986).[1] Full employment, pursued in conjunction with a supporting array of contributory benefits, is a component of a fordist industrial stratagem that entrenched the dishonorable and illegitimate status of non-wage labour. The fordist-industrial deception was to provide workers (primarily "white working men") the appearance of economic independence (Fraser and Gordon 1994). Importantly, the deception of wage labour's independence was in part consolidated through the two-track system of contributory and non-contributory means-tested programs.

The reforms the Liberals are pursuing today reinforce, rather than undermine, this deceit. This is achieved through the marshaling of new, and the entrenchment of old, categories of claimants based on their level of non-wage labour "dependence" (Pulkingham 1995). While women, First Nations peoples and people of colour were the principle victims of earlier attempts to exclude, restructuring today has a broader reach. The new rhetoric of "dependency," the central concern of the current round of social security reform, has ensured that many more will lose benefits or entitlement altogether.

The current agenda is transforming a defining feature of the post-war welfare state in Canada: it is decoupling and reassembling the relatively privileged status of "first-track" compared to "second-track" benefits (Pulkingham 1995). Until relatively recently, contributory benefits, provided through programs like U.I. and c/QPP, have escaped the stigmatization associated with means-tested benefits. But the honorable status of "first-track" programs is now under threat. It is tempting, then, to try to defend the integrity of the privileged status of contributory benefits. What else is there to hold on to? But should we not take the opportunity to challenge the taken-for-granted equation of wage labour with "independence" and its corollary, that independence is an unqualified good? Is it possible to recognize unpaid labour, promote interdependence and reject the consumption-oriented economic paradigm informing Keynesian policies? Can this be done while retaining the principle of full employment? If not, how can we articulate and pursue an alternative agenda for change without losing more ground?

Unfortunately, the circumstances in which the present decoupling is taking place work against this kind of questioning. The transformation of a significant proportion of U.I. claimants into "U.I. dependents" is intended to fortify rather than unseat assumptions about the independence of wage labour. The new distinctions drawn between "frequent" and "occasional" claimants actually sharpen the "dependence/independence" dichotomy, intensifying the wage-labour obligation. In the struggle to preserve existing levels of protection, it is difficult to remind ourselves, let alone challenge the fact, that the status quo was achieved in part by entrenching the deliberately constructed distinction between the "deserving" and "undeserving."

The degradation of "first track" employment based benefits has serious implications in the context of the ongoing restructuring of employment. Reflecting the general pattern of income polarization and declining middle, the creation of new social divisions is shrinking the pool of "deserving" and expanding the class of "undeserving." This is hardly the outcome anticipated by Canadians as they responded to the Axworthy challenge to participate in the review of social programs. There are no easy policy prescriptions for these difficult times. But we cannot merely strive to reincarnate Keynesian policies. It is important to recognize that many of these policies were flawed to begin with. In pursuing policies for the late 1990s, it is important to devise concrete mechanisms that redress the ways in which past policies have excluded and marginalized particular groups.

## CONCLUDING COMMENTS

We started this chapter noting that social policy is about choices and that these choices determine "who gets what" and "who wins and who loses." We also noted that the agenda for the SSR had been captured by concerns with deficits and debts. This has resulted in a downsizing and reduction of state protection during periods of increased insecurity. Given what we can surmise as outcomes of the social security review, this appears to be the way of the future. Unlike the reforms characteristic of the early post-war period, state intervention is now being withdrawn while the demand for help and assistance is on the rise. At stake are the rights of citizenship that we have come to accept as defining characteristics of our nationhood. Whereas our social policies were once based on the importance of protecting people, they are now being reshaped to fit fiscal and market imperatives.

The economic circumstances of more and more Canadians are declining as unemployment persists and secure, well paid, middle income jobs are harder to find. It is in this context that the social security provisions we once took for granted are increasingly under jeopardy as the federal government, tied to its agenda of fiscal restraint, has attempted to legitimate a further dismantling of social programs through public consultation in the social security review. Given the type of changes so far announced and anticipated, it is clear that the voices of the people most affected have not been heard and responded to in this review process. Why is this the case? The analysis provided by the Canadian Conference on Catholic Bishops (1985: 209-10) in its critical rejection of the recommendations of the Macdonald Report (Minister of Supply and Services 1985) ten years earlier, is just as appropriate today as it was then. According to the Bishops the "basic contradiction of our times" rests in the "structural domination of capital . . . over people, over labour, over communities."

This contradiction is reinforced by both the agenda and outcome of the social security review. We have been told that there are no alternatives other than to restructure social programs to fit the realities of our fiscal situation and the market requirements of increased global competition. While our social programs are not perfect and need improvement, it is our view that they be designed to reflect the needs of people and communities. This has not been the outcome of the SSR and ground has been lost in this round of the review. Considerable regrouping of popular and progressive groups is required so that the voices of communities and people can once again be heard.

To influence the agenda for social programs means that that the issues of equality, opportunity, joblessness and poverty are given more weight than fiscal and market imperatives. To this end we need to offer credible and well publicized critiques of agendas that are quick to locate the causes of our social and economic problems in deficits, debts and excessive social program spending. As noted in this chapter and other places in this book, there are alternatives. One major task is to get these onto the table. Another is to ensure that these details are publicized and openly debated so there is greater public awareness of the policy and spending choices that are available to governments and people as they shape Canadian social programs for the future.

## NOTE

1.  Kean and Owens (1986: 14) refer to this as the "fetish of employment."

## REFERENCES

Armstrong, Pat and Hugh Armstrong. 1988. "Taking Women into Account: Redefining and Intensifying Employment in Canada." In Jane Jensen et al. (eds.), *Feminization of the Labour Force: Paradoxes and Promises*. Oxford: Polity Press and Basil Blackwell.

Canadian Conference of Catholic Bishops. 1985. "Moral Vision and Political Will." In D. Drache and C. Cameron (eds.), *The Other Macdonald Report*. Toronto: James Lorimer.

Canadian Council on Social Development (CCSD). 1994. *Submission to the Parliamentary Standing Committee on Finance* November 15: 1-13.

Corcoran, Terrence. 1995. "Outbreak! Ottawa catches Tobin Tax Virus." *Globe and Mail* March 22: B2.

Department of Finance. 1993. *Personal and Corporate Income Tax Expenditures*. Ottawa: Minister of Supply and Services.

———. 1985. *Account of the Cost of Selective Tax Measures*. Ottawa: Minister of Supply and Services.

Fraser, Nancy and Linda Gordon. 1994. "A Genealogy of Dependency: Tracing a Keyword of the U.S. Welfare State." *Signs* 19 (21): 309-36.

Gee, Ellen and Susan McDaniel. 1991. "Pension Politics and Challenges: Retirement Policy Implications." *Canadian Public Policy/Analyses de Politiques* 17 (4): 456-72.

Green, David A. and W. Craig Riddell. 1993. "The Economic Effects of Unemployment Insurance in Canada: An Empirical Analysis of UI Disentitlement." *Journal of Labour Economics* 11 (1): S96-S147.

Grant, Jordan. 1994. "Submission to the Commons Finance Committee On Alternatives To The GST." (unpublished mimeo).

——— and J. I. Biddell. 1994. "Revised Proposal For a Financial Transaction Tax." January (30): 1-3.

House of Commons. 1995. *Security, Opportunities and Fairness: Canadians Renewing Their Social Programs*. Ottawa: Queen's Printer.

Human Resources Development Canada. 1994. *From Unemployment Insurance to Employment Insurance: A Supplementary Paper*. Ottawa: Minister of Supply and Services.

Keane, John and John Owens. 1986. *After Full Employment*. London: Hutchinson and Co.

Kerans, Patrick. 1994. "Universality, Full Employment and Well-Being: The Future of the Canadian Welfare State." *Canadian Review of Social Policy* 34 (Winter): 119-35.

McMurdy, Deirdre. 1995. "Shifting Ground." *Maclean's* March 20: 28-30.

Minister of Supply and Services. 1985. *Macdonald Royal Commission on Economic Union and Development Prospects for Canada*. Ottawa: Minister of Supply and Services.

Mimoto, H. and P. Cross. 1991. "The Growth of the Federal Debt." *Canadian Economic Observer* June (3): 1-17.

O'Neil, Peter. 1995. "Premiers to Unite Over Social-program Losses." *The Weekend Sun* August 26: A1.

Ontario Federation of Labour. 1994. "Unfair Shares: Corporations and Taxation in Canada." Don Mills, Ontario: The Ontario Federation of Labour and the Ontario Coalition for Social Justice.

Pulkingham, Jane. 1995. "Remaking the Social Divisions of Welfare: Gender, 'Dependency,' and Social Security Reform in Canada." Unpublished Paper, under review.

Squires, Phil 1990. *Anti-Social Policy: Welfare, Ideology and the Disciplinary State*. New York: Harvester/Wheatsheaf.

Statistics Canada. 1994. *Income Distributions by Size in Canada, 1993*. Ottawa: Ministry of Industry, Science and Technology.

Ternowetsky, Gordon. 1994. "Hunger in Regina: Where Do We Go From Here?" *Canadian Review of Social Policy* 34 (Winter): 100-10.

——— and Jill Thorn. 1991. *The Decline in Middle Incomes: Unemployment, Underemployment and Falling Living Standards in Saskatchewan*. Regina: SARU, Faculty of Social Work, University of Regina.

Valpy, Michael. 1995. "The Better Bet Just Gets Downgraded." *Globe and Mail* March 1: A2.

# *New related titles*
## *from Fernwood Publishing*

## Rethinking Child and Family Policies
### Struggles and Options
*Jane Pulkingham (Simon Fraser University)*
*and Gordon Ternowetsky (University of Northern BC)*

The papers in this collection address the changing context of Child andFamily Policies which have been ushered in by the Liberal govern ment's Social Security Review (SSR). The contributions analyze the implications of government policy shifts showing how they are particularly devastating for children of low income, welfare, First Nations and single parent families. They suggest policy options and some directions that advocacy groups might take in developing a politics of influence.

288pp  Paper   ISBN 1 895686 60 1      $24.95   July 1996

## Politics of Community Services
### Immigrant Women, Class and the State Second edition
*Roxana Ng (OISE)*

This study deals with the issue of state funding in relation to community groups.

"Students like it a lot. It is readable, although it offers a complex argument. It is practical and speaks to experiences that many (students) have had. It offers a model of what an empirical study using social organization of knowledge looks like." — *Marie Campbell, Social Work, Univ. of Victoria*

"The relevance of the book continues to lie in its clearly presented methodology which can be read by students and understood. Also, of no mean importance is the fact that the study is focused on services to immigrant women which continues to be an area of policy concern. If anything, the issues highlighted have more visibility today than when the research was being conducted in the early eighties."
— *Sheila M. Neysmith, Social Work, Univ. of Toronto*

110pp   Paper   ISBN 1 895686 64 4     $12.95     March 1996

# Banking on Deception
## The Discourse of Fiscal Crisis
*Thom Workman  (New Brunswick)*

Through the discourse of the fiscal crisis the proponents of the neo-liberal agenda—emphasizing market determination and minimal government interference—deceive Canadians by presenting this agenda as the only reasonable and rational alternative. This deception is successful because the discourse resonates positively within the broader cultural canvas by a) appealing to and emphasizing notions of individual responsibility (including the analogy to household finance), b) absorbing gender themes (including notions of rationality and a take control machismo), c) drawing on an ethic of moderation (including liberal/socialist characters) and d) (re)representing history (such as the idea of past government excesses or triumphalist post-Cold War sensibilities). The appeal to "common sense" has become the central theme in selling the debt.

110pp    Paper    ISBN 1 895686 62 8    $12.95    April 1996


# Women in Trouble
## Connecting Women's Law Violations to their Histories of Abuse
*Elizabeth Comack (Manitoba)*

This book addresses two areas of feminist scholarship—the recognition of violence against women and the endeavour to make visible the lives of women in prison. Beginning with women's own accounts of their troubles with the law, Elizabeth Comack uses a combination of socialist and standpoint feminism to piece together the stories of twenty-four women incarcerated for a range of offences. In the process, the women's experiences of abuse since childhood, the nature of their law violations, and the (inter)connections between the two are revealed. The book also examines whether the experience of prison enables the women to resolve their troubles and concludes by raising several questions that pertain to our efforts to respond to violence against women.

Contents: Introduction • Situating Women's Law Violations • Women's Histories of Abuse • Making Connections • The Prisoning of Women • Concluding Remarks

170pp    Paper    ISBN 1 895686 61 X    $14.95    April 1996

# Jutsider Blues
## A Voice from the Shadows
*Clifton Ruggles with Olivia Robinescu*

"The articles that appear in this book originate in the shadows—those marginal spaces that Black people have been forced to inhabit ever since the first slaves reached the shores of North America ..."

"I experienced what I call the 'shadowlands' while working in the back rooms of restaurants and hotels and on the trains, when people looked through me but didn't see me."

"The Black male in North America is forever treated as suspect. Border guards suspect us, police suspect us, store owners suspect us, school officials suspect us. In this society Black males become visible only when we become suspects. The rest of the time, we are 'invisible.' "

Ruggles tells us that "Black is more than just a racial category, it's a way of viewing the world." It is out of this set of eyes that Clifton Ruggles writes a column in the Montreal Gazette. This book is a collection of those columns and of Ruggles' photographs, which visually illustrate the "Black" experience. He tells stories of Black people everyday lives, provides non-stereotypical role models, details their contributions to culture, politics and so on—stories which are often either ignored or underplayed. Among the photographs are two photo essays, one autobiographical and one entitled *Shadowlands*. The book also includes an article by Olivia Robinescu entitled "Deconstructing Racism."

256pages Photos Paper ISBN 1 895686 65 2 $19.95 April 1996

# Anti-Racism Education
## Theory and Practice
*George Dei (OISE)*
Anti-racism education is a proactive, process-oriented approach to addressing the racial and ethnocultural differences which students bring to schools. Dei engages "integrative anti-racism" to capture the relational aspects of social difference. He argues that analyzing the intersections of race, class, gender and sexual oppression is essential if we are to fully address educational equity, social justice and change. Dei examines how we can value our differences while equitably sharing power and discusses ways to counter the reproduction of societal inequalities in our schools.

134 pages Paper ISBN 1 895686 63 6 $15.95 May 1996